SHERMAN

Soldier · Realist · American

GENERAL WILLIAM T. SHERMAN

SHERMAN

Soldier · Realist · American

By B. H. LIDDELL HART

New introduction by Jay Luvaas

DA CAPO PRESS

Library of Congress Cataloging in Publication Data

Liddell Hart, Basil Henry, Sir, 1895-1970.
  Sherman: soldier, realist, American / by B. H. Liddell Hart; new
introduction by Jay Luvaas.–1st Da Capo Press ed.
    p.   cm.
  Originally published: Boston : Dodd, Mead & Co., 1929.
  Includes bibliographical references and index.
  ISBN 0-306-80507-3
  1. Sherman, William T. (William Tecumseh), 1820-1891. 2. Generals–
United States – Biography. 3. United States. Army – Biography. 4. United
States – History – Civil War, 1861-1865 – Campaigns. I. Title.
E467.1.S55L713   1993
973.7'092 – dc20   92-43695
[B]   CIP

First Da Capo Press edition 1993

This Da Capo Press paperback edition of *Sherman* is an unabridged republication
of the edition published in New York in 1929, with the addition of a new introduction
by Jay Luvaas. It is reprinted by arrangement with Lady Liddell Hart.

4 5 6 7 8 9 10   03 02 01 00
Published by Da Capo Press, Inc.
A member of the Perseus Books Group

To

MY FATHER——AND FRIEND

INTRODUCTION
Sherman and the "Indirect Approach"

In 1928 Captain B. H. Liddell Hart, an English military journalist, theorist, and reformer already well known for his provocative writings on military tactics, training, and mechanization, was asked by an American publisher to write on one of the great figures of the American Civil War, "preferably Lee." Two years previously he had published his first book of an historical nature, *A Greater than Napoleon — Scipio Africanus,* soon after followed by *Great Captains Unveiled,* a compilation of articles about Jenghiz Khan, Saxe, Gustavus Adolphus, Wallenstein, and Wolfe. Both books reveal a careful reading of the primary sources and an acquired skill in making the past speak to the present on questions of tactics, strategy, and organization.

He chose instead to focus on William Tecumseh Sherman, in his judgment "the most original and versatile" of the Civil War commanders and an ideal vehicle for conveying his own emerging theories of mobile warfare and the strategy of "Indirect Approach." Determined to avoid repetition of the trench deadlock of 1914-18, where massive assaults had resulted only in massive casualties, Liddell Hart had already turned to mechanization as the way to restore mobility to warfare. Now he hoped that Sherman, whose campaigns in 1864 had overcome "a somewhat similar deadlock," might provide clues that could be applied to the present. For his purposes Lee's campaigns were less relevant — and Lee himself, however skilled in the operational art, was no innovator.

By 1927 Liddell Hart had begun to realize that a direct approach to the objective along the line of natural expectation usually yielded negative results, and when he began research for the Sherman biography the following year all the ingredients for his "Strategy of Indirect Approach" fell into place —

the concept of "deep strategic penetration," the importance of simultaneously threatening "alternative objectives," and the "baited gambit," which combined offensive strategy with defensive tactics. Had Liddell Hart already formulated his "Strategy of Indirect Approach," *Sherman* could have provided convincing examples, but in fact it was the other way around. Only by entering Sherman's thought process could Liddell Hart develop his theory in detail, and in his *Memoirs* he acknowledged that reading the message traffic in the *Official Records of the Union and Confederate Armies* gave access to "the-day-to-day, and even hour-by-hour impressions and decisions" of commanders on both sides. A glance at Sherman's official letters and orders throughout the Atlanta Campaign and during the subsequent march to the sea offers convincing evidence that Sherman had indeed pondered the thoughts and alternatives attributed to him.

In 1929, the same year that *Sherman* was published in the United States, Liddell Hart produced another book that elevated Sherman's operational techniques into a doctrine adaptable to mechanized war, using examples from the more distant past to substantiate his theories and give them universal validity. In only six of more than 280 campaigns, he asserted, had decisive results followed a strategy of direct approach.

> History shows that rather than resign himself to a direct approach, a Great Captain will take even the most hazardous indirect approach – if necessary, over mountains, deserts, or swamps, with only a fraction of his force, even cutting himself loose from his communications. Facing, in fact, every unfavourable condition rather than accept the risk of stalemate.[1]

The Decisive Wars of History was followed a decade later by a second edition entitled *The Strategy of Indirect Approach,* which included the most recent campaigns in World War II. Subsequent editions dealt with the "Indirect Approach" as it had been applied in the Arab-Israeli War of 1948, and had Liddell Hart been alive at the time of the recent Gulf War he most assuredly would have compared the so-called "Hail Mary" maneuver in Desert Storm to Sherman's plan to pry the Confederates out of their mountain fortifications around Dalton in May, 1864 – pointing out of course that General Schwarzkopf was reputed to have had a copy of Sherman's *Memoirs* on his night stand. Certainly he would have made much of the fact that *FM 100-5,* the current U.S. doctrinal manual supporting AirLand Battle, asserts that "successful tactical maneuver depends on skillful movement along indirect approaches supported by direct and indirect fires," that the ideal campaign plan "embodies an indirect approach that preserves the strength of the force for decisive battles," that "the ideal attack should resemble what Liddell Hart called the 'expanding torrent,' " and that

> surprise and indirect approach are desirable characteristics of any scheme of maneuver. When a geographically indirect approach is not available, the commander can achieve a similar effect by doing the unexpected – striking earlier, in greater force, with unexpected weapons, or at an unlikely place.[2]

On this point, Sherman and Liddell Hart would have agreed.

There is evidence that Liddell Hart's *Sherman* had an immediate if perhaps a somewhat superficial impact on the British army. The principal exercises in 1931, stressing significant reduction in the scale of transport and the weight of the soldier's load, were known as "a Sherman march," and in 1934 the first complete armored force in the British army conducted exercises in making deep thrusts into the "enemy's rear areas." In 1932 a future German War Minister and Commander-in-Chief conveyed to Liddell Hart that he had been "greatly impressed" by his exposition of Sherman's technique and was applying it in his own training methods. As later events would show, he was not the only German General to accept the idea of deep strategic penetration by armored forces.[3]

Several months before the Allied landings in Normandy in

1944, Liddell Hart had an opportunity to talk with General George Patton, who claimed

> that before the war he had spent a long vacation studying Sherman's campaigns on the ground in Georgia and the Carolinas, with the aid of my book. So I talked of the possibilities of applying "Sherman methods" in modern warfare – moving stripped of *impedimenta* to quicken the pace, cutting loose from communications if necessary, and swerving past opposition, instead of getting hung up in trying to overcome it by direct attack. It seemed to me that by the development and exploitation of such Sherman methods, on a greater scale, it would be possible to reach the enemy's rear and unhinge his position – as the Germans had ready done in 1940. I think the indirect argument made some impression. . . . The way that, after the breakthrough, he actually carried out his plans, in super-Sherman style, is a matter that all the world knows.[4]

The reader might also bear in mind another of Liddell Hart's observations, written as he was finishing the book.

> The profoundest truth of war is that the issue of battles is usually decided in the minds of the opposing commanders, not in the bodies of their men. The best history would be register of their thoughts and emotions, with a background of events to throw them into relief.[5]

This, in essence, is what *Sherman* attempts to achieve, and the reader should remember that this is as much a work of military theory – a very influential work – as a campaign history or military biography. It is in fact the best example of how the three can be combined.

> – JAY LUVAAS
> Carlisle Barracks, Pennsylvania
> November 1992

1. Liddell Hart, *Thoughts on War* (London, Faber and Faber Ltd., 1944), p. 64. This is from a note dated October 1928.
2. Headquarters, Department of the Army, *FM 100-5: Operations* (Washington: Department of the Army, 1986), pp. 12, 30, 109, 122.
3. B. H. Liddell Hart, ed. William T. Sherman, *From Atlanta to the Sea* (London: The Folio Socity, 1961), pp. 14-15.
4. "Note on Two discussions with Patton, 1944." 20 February 1948. Liddell Hart Papers, States House, Medmenham.
5. *Thoughts on War*, p. 150.

PREFACE

THIS study of Sherman is an attempt to portray the working of a man's mind, not merely of a man's limbs and muscles encased in uniform clothing. The man is William Tecumseh Sherman who, by the general recognition of all who met him, was the most original genius of the American Civil War. And who, in the same breath, is often described as "the typical American." To reconcile the apparent contradiction, of the exceptional and the general, is a problem which in itself invites study and excites the creative imagination. It is curious that the attempt at a solution has been neglected so long. For if this man was both so original in mind and so characteristically American, that combination—which many in Europe would say was paradoxical, if not improbable—may help to illumine our understanding not only of the last seventy years but of the tendencies still in the womb of fate.

Thus the book, further, seeks to project the film of Sherman onto the screen of contemporary history. For there are vital lessons to be learnt from this man, his character and his career, his struggle with his environment and his ascendancy over it—keys to the modern world and to modern war. And, if those keys had not lain so long neglected in the dusty lumber-room of history, the problem of the world war might have been better understood, and a worn world have suffered less from a peace which passeth understanding.

For it was the "War in the West," neglected by European military thought in the half century which followed, that revealed not only the essential nature of a modern war of nations but also the essential influence of economic and psychological factors upon the course of such a war. And it was the conscious exploitation of these factors by Sherman in his famous "March through Georgia" and the Carolinas which finally decided the issue, long and expensively postponed, even mortally endangered, by the direct battle-lusting strategy which had governed the campaign in Virginia. Yet so far as any impression of the American Civil War penetrated the consciousness of the General Staffs of Europe it was that of the battledore and shuttlecock tournament in Virginia—which they faithfully imitated with even greater lavishness and ineffectiveness on the battlefields of France from 1914 to 1918.

This book, however, leaves the parallel to emerge by reflection from the portrayal of Sherman's mind, of the influence which moulded it and the influence it exercised on the course of the Civil War.

Those accustomed to the conventional military history and biography may complain that the account of battles is uncomfortably bare and scantily furnished with details. I shall welcome the complaint. This book is a study of life, not of still life. An exercise in human psychology, not in upholstery. To place the position and trace the action of battalions and batteries is only of value to the collector of antiques, and still more to the dealer in faked antiques. Those who believe that exactness is possible can never have known war, or must have forgotten it. And even if by supernatural means we could recreate the action in such detail, it would be historically valueless. For the issue of any operation of war is decided not by what the situation actually is, but by what the rival commanders think it is. Historically and practically, it is far more important to discover what information they had, and the times at which it reached them, than to know the actual situation of the "pieces." A battlefield is not a chessboard.

Finally, passing from the sphere of war to that of sociology, this study of Sherman may serve to give the European reader a clue to the better understanding of the American character as it has evolved from its "prototype," and to give the American reader an opportunity of testing, by the acid of Sherman, the purity of the present product and how far the reality corresponds with the ideal set up by that most realistic of idealists.

CONTENTS

MAPS

CHAPTER I

THE MOULD

How far do heredity and environment, respectively, mould character and foreshadow a career? From three generations of judges, and earlier forebears who would not compromise with their principles, was begotten a man who judged the case of the Southern Confederacy more acutely and dispassionately than almost any of his contemporaries. The man who finally executed the sentence of destiny and industry upon secession.

The first significant link in the chain of heredity is a sturdy Puritan of Dedham in Essex, named Edmond Sherman. Two of his sons sailed from England, probably in 1634, with several of their cousins to seek not only freedom of conscience but fortune in a virgin country. More mobile than their fellows they soon forsook the first settlements in Massachusetts to strike out afresh, and migrated into Connecticut. From one of the cousins was descended the Roger Sherman who signed the Declaration of Independence. From one of the sons, Samuel, was descended the William Tecumseh Sherman who, almost a century later, was the decisive military agent in annulling the declaration of independence made by the Southern States. That he thereby made possible the national and economic greatness of the permanently United States is his claim to immortality. That his attitude to separation and his action were governed by calculation of the economic effects is his claim to foresight. That he was far from satisfied with the immediate moral consequences is his final claim to realism.

In the formation of his mind, environment first intervened to supplement heredity when his ancestor left the aptly named hamlet of Dedham behind. It stepped in again when his grandfather, Judge Taylor Sherman, was appointed by the State of Connecticut as one of the commissioners to settle the title and boundaries of the "Fire-Lands" in the Western Reserve. In reward for his services there the judge was granted the title to two "lots" in the territory

1

which subsequently became northern Ohio. The next factor of destiny appeared when his twenty year old son, Charles Robert, just admitted to the bar, fell in love with and married Mary Hoyt. The improvident youth, unable to support a family in "civilization," promptly migrated to seek briefs and his fortune in the new settlement of Lancaster, Ohio.

A year later, prospects were sufficiently hopeful for him to fetch his wife and first-born, carrying them both on horse-back through the wilds, a long and venturesome ride. The second year of their new life at Lancaster was temporarily interrupted by the outbreak of war with England, and the Ohio militia was called on to share in General Hull's abortive invasion of Canada—launched, curiously, into Essex county. Hull was forced to retire—as a prelude to his surrender on his own soil—through the cutting of his communications by the Shawnee chief Tecumseh who, driven out of his lands by the Americans, now paid his debt to those who had given him refuge. Of rare skill even among his kind as scout and guerrilla general "he was admired by the red men, because he taught them to combine and to sink their old feuds, but still more by the white, because he possessed the virtues, unusual in an Indian chief, of strict adherence to his pledged word, and of a humanity that was absolutely unknown to his fellows."

Is there magic in a name? The superstition would gain credit, and almost credence, from the historical coincidence which had its origin in the campaign, and the beginning of its fulfilment a few years later.

For Charles Robert Sherman, like many men of peace, was acutely susceptible to the romance of war, all the more perhaps because his single brief taste of it had been in the non-combatant rôle of a temporary commissary. Apparently he found no adequate object for his martial hero-worship among the American leaders of the war of 1812—if the onlooker proverbially sees most of the game, he often sees too much to maintain his illusions—and so transferred his admiration to the more remote if more reputable figure of the Indian chief.

Thus when, on February 8, 1820, the third son, and sixth child, came to bless his "union" he gratified a wish hitherto deferred to his wife's desire to honour and perpetuate her brothers in the naming of her sons. The baptismal shower of fraternal names being now at last exhausted, this son received the paternally cherished name of Tecumseh.

The addition to Charles Sherman's family was soon followed by a welcome addition to his income, although the latter was single, the former annual. The year after his third son's birth a vacancy arose in the Supreme Court of Ohio, and in a petition to the Governor from a number of influential citizens he was recommended in glowing terms—"From a long acquaintance with Mr. Sherman, we are happy to be able to state to your Excellency that our minds are led to the conclusion that that gentleman possesses a disposition noble and generous, a mind discriminating, comprehensive, and combining a heart pure, benevolent and humane. Manners dignified, mild and complaisant, and a firmness not to be shaken and of unquestioned integrity. But Mr. Sherman's character cannot be unknown to your Excellency, and on that acquaintance without further comment we might safely rest his pretensions."

It is at least a practical proof of the sincerity of this archaically worded tribute that on his early death friends and neighbours hastened so readily to take charge of and adopt his children. For he had but a short time to enjoy the dignity of emoluments of a judge of the Supreme Court; too short to make adequate provision for a family. On a June day in 1829 the children were suddenly called out of school, to return to a home distraught by the news that their father, distant a hundred miles on the circuit, had been suddenly ill and was mortally sick. The mother left at once by coach, but while still on her harrowing and toilsome journey was stopped by word of his death.

To William Tecumseh, aged nine, it fell to be taken into the home of Thomas Ewing, a fellow citizen of Lancaster, who had worked his way up from manual labour to be a member of the United States Senate. Helped by the elder Sherman, he was now glad to repay his debt to the son, and by so doing make the country his own debtor. And rich as his political achievements, his memory is more enduringly, even more worthily preserved in Sherman's simple tribute that he "ever after treated me as his own son."

For several years the change of home made little difference to young Sherman's education, as he merely continued to attend the academy at Lancaster, where the teaching was good and the curriculum had a sound classical bias. At fourteen, however, he "was notified to prepare for West Point"—a euphemistic way of saying that he was not consulted in regard to a decision and a destination which sounded ominous to the ears of a boy brought up in the freedom and "naturalness" of Ohio in the thirties. For little as the boys of Ohio knew of West Point they knew it as a synonym for strictness of discipline and straightness of outlook. Sherman had still a couple of years before he would reach the age of entry and to develop his mathematics and French to the required standard.

But the time of grace drew to an end. And on a May morning in 1836 the stage-coach left Lancaster for Zanesville with a "tall, slim, loose-jointed lad, with red hair, fair, burned skin, and piercing black eyes."

At Zanesville he transferred to one of the coaches of the Great National Road, the main service which connected the East with the Middle West. After three days', and nights', continuous journey they reached Frederick, in Maryland, where others among his fellow-passengers took the new railroad to Baltimore, and thence to Washington. But the boy, capable enough of looking after himself, recoiled distrustfully from the hazardous experiment of trying this new means of transport, and completed his journey by coach. The incident, amusing in itself, is a fresh proof that "Pauline" converts are the strongest advocates. Within thirty years this rail-scared boy was to be first among great commanders to realize and demonstrate the decisive influence of railways upon modern strategy. But the light did not come on the journey to Washington.

After a stay with his foster-father in Washington he passed on to stay with uncles in New York, there to be an object of polite amusement to his cousins, who viewed him "as an untamed animal just caught in the far West." When he entered the gates of West Point the "animal" must have felt that, in truth, he was entering a cage, and its bars of custom and discipline were to be a sore restraint on body and spirit alike, overflowing with nervous energy.

In his memoirs Sherman's brief comment on his four years at West Point is the more vivid because of its brevity. "At the Academy I was not considered a good soldier, for at no time was I selected for any office, but remained a private throughout the whole four years. Then, as now, neatness in dress and form, with a strict conformity to the rules, were the qualifications for office, and I suppose I was found not to excel in any of these." Could any indictment of the orthodox system and standards of military education be more quietly damning? "In studies I always held a respectable reputation with the professors, and generally ranked among the best, especially in drawing, chemistry, mathematics, and natural philosophy. My average demerits, per annum, were about one hundred and fifty, which reduced my final class standing from number four to six."

Nevertheless, it is a proof of his character, better even than his high "passing-out" place, that he had endured to the end while fifty-seven of the hundred who had entered with him had fallen out.

On that isolated cliff amid the Highlands of the Hudson, they were as cut off from the outside world as if they had been in a prison. And the course seemed peculiarly designed to suggest the prison atmosphere. There were no organized games to relieve the monotony of the long hours in class and the still more trying confinement of their scanty leisure hours. Not even a riding-school existed during Sherman's first years. Awakened by the reveille at dawn they hurriedly dressed themselves in the uncomfortable uniform, relic of Georgian fashion, with its short-tailed grey coatee, tight trousers of white drill, clumping shoes and that "little-ease," the high black stock. Then out onto the bleak parade-ground to answer roll-call and back to sweep out their bare and chilly rooms before settling down to long grinding hours of study, in and out of class. Hours broken only by the brief release from quarters between 4 P.M. and the sunset gun, and by the grotesque practice, which soldiers share with convict gangs, of being marched to meals—meals here dreary almost as prison fare. Frequent and harassing inspections of quarters, person, and presence heightened the similitude. The cadets were swaddled in regulations every infraction of which meant a black mark—a "demerit" in West Point language.

Save for the long-dreamt-of furlough once in two years, the only escape was to the annual ten weeks camp in the summer. A change of scene but not a change of spirit. Merely from drilling facts to drilling muscles. And while the mechanical educational process of the times was, at West Point, enlivened by certain gifted teachers, the cadets' training in camp aimed at little more than the production of automata in the style and tradition of Frederick the Great, ably maintained, in a far less suitable medium, by the régime of "Old Fuss and Feathers"—that redoubtable soldier General Winfield Scott.

You think, perchance, rugged reader, that the picture is too blackly shaded? You would argue that this Spartan training makes men and that the system of an institution which produced so many great leaders is above criticism? But much depends upon where one puts the emphasis. Makes *men*, only in so far as it instils manly virtues, but every check to initiative, self-reliance, and the growth of personal judgment detracts proportionately from their manhood. *Makes* men, unhappily too often, by giving to the conventional what is euphemistically called "a useful start" in their profession, all the more useful in a profession whose real test, war, comes so rarely. By its aid, provided that their individuality remains dormant, they may hope to keep the lead from their fellows who are handicapped by an uncomfortably progressive mind—which "makes trouble"—or by an excess of moral courage—which betokens a "lack of discipline." For smooth answers smooth the path to promotion.

As for the argument that this system of "education" has produced many great leaders, its validity depends on the complementary question whether they have become great because or in spite of the system. The criterion "by their fruits ye shall know them" is fallacious if there is only one tree which grows fruit, one way by which a profession can be entered. The real question, then, is why a blight was felt by so many blossoms, and whether even the best fruits would not have been better if they had escaped the blight as blossoms.

On this question the comment of Sherman on his own experience is significant. More significant because it was uttered by one who was the commanding general of the national army. And still more significant because it was confirmed by U. S. Grant, a fellow-statesman from Ohio, and a "plebe"—or first year man when Sherman was in his fourth year.

For so trying did Grant find life at West Point, so uselessly vexatious its routine and regulations, that he confesses in his memoirs that the years "seemed about five times as long as Ohio years," and he fervently longed for the success of a bill which was brought forward in Congress to abolish the institution of which he was an unwilling member.

If there are flaws even in their splendid later records, how far are these to be traced to the early blight? And in assessing the final product we should remember, too, that both Sherman and Grant broke off their army career at an early date and found in a civil career of the most contrasting type a powerful counter-active to the limitations of outlook imposed on them during their cadet experience.

To discern unnatural effects of these years we need not wait until maturity, and the years of achievement, are reached. For the atmosphere, if not the direct influence, of the system reveals itself in Sherman's early letters, which for a time become marked by a stilted, artificial style, as unnatural as if a kitchen table had been covered incongruously with a coat of polish. Making an allowance for the extreme formality then fashionable in letter-writing, this aping of fashion by a boy reared in homely simplicity and sturdy independence cannot be adjudged a healthy sign. But the style is less disquieting than the artificiality of the sentiments often expressed—as if a record had been put on a gramophone. We can almost hear the grating of the needle—"my whole attention should be paid to my studies"—"we all endeavour to be well prepared in our studies both for our own good and that the persons (always influential) may carry off a good opinion of the Institution."

The boy's most frequent letters were addressed to little Ellen Ewing, five years his junior, and if this difference of age made him the object of her child-like admiration, the years of companionship in her home, which was also his, had forged ties of affectionate comradeship. But now for her comfortless consumption his language was artificially chilled, in such remarks as "you certainly misunderstood me with regard to your mother. Although I should feel highly honored did she condescend to notice me, still, I am fully aware how slight are my claims to her regard." The effect was due, of course, to imitation as well as to the imposition of his environment. But that seems to exert a slightly unnatural restraint even on the spirit of revolt which, burning within him, occasionally finds utterance.

"We often feel disposed to break over our imposed limits, and 'go forth' but the consequences would be of too serious a nature to admit of such an idea for a moment."

Happily, the boy's nature is at bedrock too solid to be spoilt by the surface incrustation. Even as one sentence makes us fear that he is on his way to graduate as a prig, the next redresses the balance or by its underlying good sense retrieves the priggish form in which it is couched.

In an early letter to his younger brother, John, just launched into an engineering job at the early age of fourteen, there is implicit pride in the process of mastering a profession by hard apprenticeship, and a certain wistfulness, as well as a profound truth early appreciated.

"I hope that you still have as favourable opinions as ever with respect to your employment, for in my opinion a man's success in his profession depends on the impressions he receives at the beginning; for if these are favourable most undoubtedly he will endeavour to succeed, and success will be the necessary consequence."

There is still sound sense underlying a letter of a year later, but it is overlaid with a trite and rather self-righteous spirit, often the product of an institutional code.

"I hear that you are engaged in speculating in salt, and are waiting for the river to rise to take a load down to Cincinnati. Are you doing this on borrowed capital or not? Or does it interfere in the least with your duties as engineer? If it does, I would advise you not to engage in it at any rate, even if you can make a fortune by it; for a reputation for a strict and rigid compliance to one's duties, whatever they may be, is far more valuable than a dozen loads of salt."

This spirit also pervades the next letter:

"I judge that your speculations did not turn out as well as expected. You must not be astonished if I say that if such be the case I am glad of it, because, had you succeeded, your attention would have been turned from your present business. . . ."

Early in 1839 the Maine boundary dispute caused a grave tension in the relations with Canada and Great Britain. "It is an ill wind that blows nobody any good," and this at least did the cadets at West Point a service by loosening the tension upon them. The prospect of war leads Sherman to remark, rather sententiously, to his brother, "For my part, there is no nation that I would prefer being at variance with than the British, in this case more especially as our cause is plainly right and just."

A more boylike attitude and reaction, however, is disclosed in a letter wherein he says: "Sometimes it appears that war with England is inevitable; books are thrown in the corner, and broadswords and foils supply their place. Such lunging, cutting and slashing— enough to dispose of at least a thousand British a day." It is a welcome change from soda-water sentiments, and has in it a pleasant dash of sceptical humour. The last quality is still more refreshingly marked in a letter to Ellen: "All the talk in this part of the world now is about war with England. Every person seems anxious for it and none more so than the very persons who would most suffer by it, the officers of the army and the corps of cadets. But ours, I fear, arises more from selfishness than true patriotism, for should war break out we would be commissioned and sent into the 'field'— at all times preferable to studying mathematics and philosophy, and it would undoubtedly prove a better school for the soldier than this."

Sherman at last reaches the fourth year of the course which embraced civil and military engineering, fortification and siegecraft, artillery and infantry tactics, as well as "Mineralogy and Geology, Rhetoric, Moral Philosophy, International and Common Law . . . which the scientific officer requires." In camp he has now a plebe allotted to him "whom I made, of course, tend to a plebe's duty, such as bringing water, policing the tent, cleaning my gun and accoutrements, and the like, and repaid in the usual and cheap coin— advice . . . he is a good one and a fine fellow; but should he not carry himself straight, I should have him fined in January and sent off, that being the usual way in such cases, and then take his bed, table and chair to pay for the Christmas spree. . . ."

The commissioned prospect was brightening as the end of cadetship approached. "Already have we given directions . . . for swords, epaulettes, hats, chapeaux and feathers. . . . Thus you see that by adding things of this nature, which will constantly keep the future before our minds, we break in upon and enliven our otherwise monotonous life."

His high place in the class entitled him to make his choice of corps. "This choice," he tells his mother, "will be, unless war breaks out with England, the Fifth Regiment of Infantry, because it is stationed on the north-west frontier, a country which I have always felt a strong inclination to see. . . . Also it is probable that the Indians will break out again, in which case I should have an opportunity of seeing some active service. Should war, however, be the consequence of this Maine difficulty, I should prefer the artillery, for the reason that it is stationed east of the mountains, which would be the seat of war, and it is an arm of the service which I would prefer in a war against a civilized people. . . . Whether I remain in the army for life or not is doubtful; but one thing is certain— that I will never study another profession. Should I resign, it would be to turn farmer. . . ."

Here the pent-up feelings find an outlet—"I will never study an-· other profession." These four years have sickened him, even though he has successfully endured them. But his distaste is for the meaningless customs and not for the profession itself. The germ of soldiering is now in his blood, and never will it loose its hold. All that is spiritual in the West Point tradition has been absorbed into his soul, as into his mind all that is profitable in the West Point education. So, too, he approaches the time of taking his commission with a sense of self-dedication, "confirmed in the wish of spending my life in the *service of my country*," and forcefully saying of a friend's decision to quit the army for the law that "I would rather be a blacksmith."

But his Grail is real soldiering, stripped of the shams and conventions which mask its face, and enable connoisseurs of buttons to pass as soldiers. For military mannequins and mannikins alike his contempt is deep. And he ascribes these products, not without truth, to the influence of social custom and the mentality it breeds. Indeed to Ellen he had revealed the inner motive of his inclination to choose service in the infantry—in order to "be stationed in the Far West, out of the reach of what is termed *civilization*. . . ." That his choice finally turned to the artillery, despite the absence of a war with England, is, by inference, due to the fact that the Third Artillery, his first regiment, was stationed in Florida, a district almost as remote and as militarily active as the Far West.

Home for three months' furlough, after receiving his commission as second-lieutenant, the abrupt relapse to simplicity in his phrases reveals more vividly than any explanation the release of his spirit. With his return to duty he dons the conventional garb again, until Ellen breaks out in revolt. And then in a letter of contrite apology for this "adherence to ceremony" he discloses the cause—if he still cannot throw off the form. "No one regrets more than I the disposition of this world, to surround the sweetest and best pleasures of this life with the cold garb of formality, and if at any time I should bow to its dictates it is because I fear that a departure from them would give offence."

In October, 1841, he had sailed from New York to Savannah, and then transferred to a small steamship for Florida. His regiment occupied a chain of posts along the Atlantic coast, and he was posted to A Company at Fort Pierce, whose log-stockades crowned a steep sand bluff beside a mangrove-bordered lagoon. Sherman revelled in the open-air life. Duty was light and leisure ample. Leisure to be spent, not cooped up in quarters or in stuffy ballrooms, but in acquiring the arts of shark-spearing, of trolling for red-fish, and netting green turtles. Best of all was the joy of possessing a horse and being able to ride far afield, with the additional thrill imparted by the possibility of lurking Indians. His letters to Ellen Ewing pulsate with a new life and leave no doubt of his preference, as a means of education, for Seminoles over seminaries.

Regarding her now, moreover, as a "playmate" in a deeper sense, he is eager to fill the delicate girl with his zest for physical self-expression—"I hope that you have opportunities and avail yourself of them to take a gallop across the country, and if ever I have the pleasure to come home again the first thing I will expect of you will be to mount the wildest horse and charge over the hills and plains. Next to drawing it is the most ladylike accomplishment in my mind." The comparison is amusingly incongruous.

Yet, despite his surplus of youth's hot blood and his adventurous delight in hunting Indians—destined for forcible transplantation to the Indian territory in the West—his sense of realism was too deep-rooted to allow him to blind himself to the "other fellow's point of view," and to find hypocritical excuses for his enjoyment of this blood-sport. "You doubtless little sympathize with me in hunting and harassing a poor set of people who have had the heroism to defend their homes against such odds for such a period of time."

Still more exceptional is the mature insight of another letter: "As to the history of the war—the same as all our Indian wars. A treaty for the removal is formed by a few who represent themselves as the whole; the time comes and none present themselves. The Government orders force to be used; the troops in the territory commence, but are so few that they all get massacred. The cowardly inhabitants, instead of rallying, desert their homes and sound the alarm-call for assistance. An army supposed to be strong enough is sent, seeks, and encounters the enemy at a place selected by the latter, gets a few hundred killed. The Indians retreat, scatter, and are safe. This may be repeated *ad infinitum*. The best officer is selected to direct the affairs of the army—comes to Florida, exposes himself, does all he can, gets abused by all, more than likely breaks down his constitution, and is glad enough to get out of the scrape. Treaties, terms, and armistices have been and are still being tried, with what success is notorious. The present mode of conducting things is to dispose the troops at fixed points, and require them to scout and scour the country in their vicinity—about as good a plan as could be adopted, and one which would terminate the war if small columns . . . were to make excursions into the interior."

How true to the experience of all colonial history and campaigns! And in the methods which Sherman advocates there is a peculiar parallel with those ultimately adopted, on a greater scale, by the British to solve the perplexing problem of the later stages of the war against the Boers in South Africa.

No clearer picture of the geographical conditions and handicaps, under which this chase of the Seminole Indians was conducted, could be painted than in Sherman's own words, when he describes the peninsula of Florida as "one mass of sand, with few rocks of the softest consistency, and, were it not for its delightful climate, would be as barren as the deserts of Africa. It is cut up by innumerable rivers, streams, and rivulets, which, watering the soil, nourish a rank growth of weeds and grass, which, continually decomposing, gives a rich soil, and gives rise in time to a heavy growth of live oak, palmetto, and scrub of every kind. These are the dreaded hummocks, the stronghold of the Indian, where he builds his hut, and has pumpkin and cornfields. The stream furnishes him with abundance of fish and alligators, the palmetto its cabbage. The thick growth conceals his little fire and hut, secures his escape, enables him to creep within a few yards of the deer or turkey feeding on the border, and drive his copper-headed, barbed arrow through the vital part. In a word, the deep streams, bordered by the dense hummock, have enabled the Indians thus far to elude the pursuit of our army."

Sherman bore his full share in the risks of this pursuit, which often involved perilous excursions alone or with a handful of companions, and although he says little, either in his letters or memoirs, of his own achievements, his promotion to first lieutenant after only seventeen months' service was not merely fortunate. Many officers had to wait six or eight years for this step. It meant his transfer from Company A to Company G, and a move from Fort Pierce to the independent command of a little isolated detachment at Picolata, where there was only one other house besides the men's quarters. He had already had the opportunity to observe that a Florida summer was less "beautiful" than a winter. But his health did not suffer—perhaps because he found in his love of animals a counterattraction to the customary ways of passing the enervating hours in this tropical climate. "I've got more pets now than any bachelor in the country—innumerable chickens, tame pigeons, white rabbits and a full-blood Indian pony—rather small matters for a man to deal with, you doubtless think, but it is far better to spend time in trifles such as these than drinking and gambling." His bedroom presented an amusing spectacle—a hen sitting in one corner, crows roosting on bushes in another, and a third filled with a bed of rushes for a fawn.

Thus when in June, 1842, he was ordered to Fort Moultrie, South Carolina, the headquarters of the regiment, he did not relish the change as much as did officers more dependent on human society.

"Every morning at daylight all get up at reveille, attend a drill . . . at sunrise, breakfast at seven, have a dress parade at eight, and half an hour after the new guard takes the place of the old one. . . . After that each one kills time to suit himself till reveille of next morning commences the new routine. Thus it is every fair day except Sunday, when we have an extra quantity of music, parade and inspection in honor of the day and to keep our men in superfine order at church."

The ceaseless round of parties and picnics in the hospitable and pleasure-loving South began to weary him more and more, and led him to reflect in a letter to his brother, that "A life of this kind does well enough for a while, but soon surfeits with its flippancy— mingling with people in whom you feel no permanent interest, smirks and smiles when you feel savage, tight boots when your fancy would prefer slippers. I want relief, and unless they can invent a new Florida war I'll come back and spend a few months with you in Ohio."

Perhaps his boredom and his slight reaction to the charms of Charleston society, and its pretty girls, was due also to the counter-action of having a permanent interest elsewhere. For when in the autumn his Ohio leave matured, so also did his boy and girl comrade-ship with Ellen Ewing mature into a definite engagement. Yet it is equally characteristic of him that he curtailed his stay in Ohio in order to explore new ground, travelling back to Fort Moultrie by the longest way round.

For succinct impressionism it would be difficult to surpass his description of his journey down the Mississippi: "Imagine yourself, as I was, at the mouth of the Ohio in a heavy snowstorm, the shores clothed in ghostlike garb; the following day the snow is no longer seen, and before another day passes by the shores are clothed here and there in green corn and grass. Soon the oak appears with its green leaves, then the magnolia, orange, etc., and soon you find yourself down between the rich sugar fields of Louisiana, the stalks ungathered and waving beautifully and luxuriantly in the breeze. . . ."

From New Orleans, he went on to Mobile, then up the Alabama River and through Georgia to Savannah, whence he took the steam-ship to Charleston. Twenty years later the knowledge then gained was to bear fruit a hundred-fold. Not, however, in that trip alone, for he had hardly returned to duty before he was appointed, per-haps partly in consequence, as a member of a board which travelled for three months through Georgia and Alabama, investigating the excessive claims made by the State militias for the loss of horses in the Florida war of 1837-38. Their report and its exposures of fraudulent claims saved the United States treasury large sums, but nothing to what it ultimately gained through the study of topography, economic geography and psychology of the districts by the youngest member of that horse-board.

But these years in the South were a formative period in other ways. Here and there in Sherman's letters we get glimpses which are significant. Ellen as a devout Catholic was concerned with his spiritual welfare, and her concern produced one of Sherman's rare allusions to the subject of religion.

"Since I left home six years ago I have practised or professed no particular creed, believing firmly in the main doctrines of the Christian Religion, the purity of its morals, the almost absolute necessity for its existence and practice . . . to assure peace and good-will amongst all. Yet I cannot, with due reflection, attribute to minor points of doctrine or form the importance usually attached to them. I believe in good works rather than faith, and I believe them to constitute the basis of true religion, both as revealed in Scripture and taught by the experience of all ages and common-sense."

His religion could be epitomized in the single word "truth," and his intellectual life was a research for it, in its varied forms. The simplest was well expressed in a rebuke to a friend, "If you have any regard for my feelings, don't say the word 'insinuation' again. You may abuse me as much as you please, but I'd prefer, of the two, to be accused of telling a direct falsehood than stating anything evasively or underhand." Truth is beauty, and beauty, truth, so that it is not surprising to find, nor incongruous here to note, that at this period, too, he felt growing in him a "great love for painting and find that sometimes I am so fascinated that it amounts to pain to lay down the brush, placing me in doubt whether I had better stop it now before it swallows all attention, to the neglect of my duties."

If his future father-in-law had known of this, it would have sorely irked a mind already chagrined at Sherman's love of soldiering. For Thomas Ewing had wished him to enter the engineers as a gateway to civil engineering, and now had cause for regret that he had compelled an unwilling boy to enter the gateway of West Point. Early in 1844 Sherman tells his betrothed of receiving a letter, the first after several years' silence, "which was very kind but wound up with a hope that I was studying for 'civil life.' Now I thought he had long since relinquished that idea and his opposition to the army. . . . I would have to depend upon some one till I could establish myself. . . . Do you think I could do so? Certainly not, and should health be preserved to me, I shall never depend upon anybody, nay, not even were he a brother. I would rather earn my living by the labour of my hands."

Nevertheless, for Ellen's sake, Sherman utilized his leisure, if not to his pleasure, in fitting himself for a change of career, and is soon able to tell her "I am endeavouring so to qualify myself that should you not like to encounter the vicissitudes that I am now liable to, I may be enabled to begin life anew in a totally different sphere."

The most obvious of such different spheres was the law, in which his brother John had already graduated, from engineering. In beginning his study, Sherman, however, did not so acutely practise the principle of taking the line of least resistance as in his strategy later—whence perhaps his repulse from legal aspirations: "I have seized upon a book that young lawyers groan over—'Blackstone,' and I have with avidity swallowed its contents, and shall continue to study and read hard all summer. . . . But . . . somehow or other I do not feel as though I would make a good lawyer, although I meet with but little difficulty in mastering the necessary book knowledge." His feeling that he was not "naturally fitted for public speaking" was reinforced by the more profound cause of objection that he had acquired "a contempt for the bombast and stuff that form the chief constituents of Modern Oratory."

That reasoned contempt, so enduring a conviction, and perhaps not surprising in one who had such a hereditary experience of the law and politics, found voice in an explosive letter of October, 1844, to John, who had early followed the family tradition: "What in the devil are you doing? Stump speaking! I really thought you were too decent for that, or at least had sufficient pride not to humble and cringe to beg party or popular favour." This was the first rub of a fraternal friction, often fierce but always friendly, which was intellectually good for both—and of goodly amusement to those who read their interchanges.

Sherman's studies were interrupted by a temporary change of station more profitable to his future career, for in the late summer of 1845 he was sent on duty to Augusta arsenal, and thereby was enabled instead to pursue his study of Georgia. In his far-ranging rides he was able to relieve the disappointment of missing what then seemed a more useful chance. For the strained situation on the Mexican border had led the Government to reinforce the troops in Texas, and among these reinforcements was a company from the Third Artillery. "Everybody supposed the Colonel would send the company to which I belonged, because we, its officers, are all young and unmarried, whereas the others were all differently situated, but in army affairs age has precedence of merit." Sherman's regret was soon more poignant

For with the coming of spring in 1846 there came also the certain prospect of active service, a prospect with a proverbially springlike reaction on the spirits of any young soldier. And in this connection the term "young soldier" includes most soldiers, for such a prospect has a miraculous rejuvenating property. War with Mexico was now imminent, and in that war most of the future leaders of the Civil War were to bring themselves to notice and to establish claims which were a powerful asset when the days of greater trial arrived. Out of evil comes good, to the soldier, and however dubious its ingredients the Mexican war was a more than merely exhilarating tonic to those who quaffed it most deeply.

But for Sherman it was a season of disappointment. Assigned that year to a turn of recruiting duty, a diversion eagerly sought after in times less promising of excitement, he left Fort Moultrie late in April and was soon established at the St. Charles Hotel in Pittsburgh. It is a sidelight on contemporary conditions that even to so easterly a centre he had to travel the last part of the way by stage-coach, as the railway was not yet carried west of the Alleghany Mountains.

The menace of war, with its demand for recruits, offered in this duty at least an outlet for energy. But Sherman, as ever, had a surplus. He had already written, on arrival, to the august and distant disposer of destiny, the Adjutant-General in Washington, to plead that he might be sent on any expedition, the more hazardous the better. And in the hope of hustling destiny, Sherman personally conducted to Cincinnati the two dozen recruits he had collected: an impulse of the moment inspired by the ingenious idea that he might be allowed "to go along with them" by the river route to the theatre of war. Once there he might have stayed, for under active service conditions it is often easy to be lost, and for lost sheep to find a new fold.

But in May, 1846, the important reinforcement for the army in the field was unhappily reduced by one. For on reporting to the superintendent of the recruiting service at Cincinnati, Sherman found that his zealous initiative was not appreciated, and instead he was vehemently cursed for leaving his post unordered. The lesson appears to have made a strong impression—as a lesson in language at least. And who, surveying his vocal record in the Civil War, should dare to say it was not turned to profit?

After a leisurely journey back to Pittsburgh, he found a reply from the War Department relieving him of recruiting duty and posting him back to the Third Artillery—to Company F, which was under orders to sail for the Pacific Coast to help in despoiling the Mexicans of their Californian territory. It was a good tribute to the young man's reputation in his own unit that his posting was due less to his own entreaty to the War Department than to the application of the commander of Company F for his services.

Thus the horizon suddenly brightened. All the worse was the disappointment when he found it to be a false dawn. For, as an opportunity for martial glory, the expedition was to prove an unsatisfying satisfaction of his request, and the more so because another company had already gone to join the field army in Texas— a company commanded by Bragg, his future opponent on several battlefields, while Thomas, his future comrade and subordinate, was a subaltern in it. Time has its compensations—one might paraphrase a familiar proverb by saying "he brags best who brags last." For if Sherman missed the chance of fighting he widened his horizon and, by going to California, was to extend indirectly and eventually, his knowledge of men and affairs to still greater effect. California, indeed, set its imprint on Georgia in 1864, to Sherman's benefit and Georgia's detriment.

On finding the summons, Sherman was guiltily conscious of the double crime of having quitted his post and having dallied on the journey back. Fearful that the company might sail without him, he sat up until 2 A.M. clearing up his accounts and records for his successor. Rising again at dawn, he scribbled before departure a note to Ellen Ewing which amusingly reveals his impulsive eagerness, his concern for his own posthumous reputation—perhaps, too, a precocious sense of its value—and his feelings towards his future wife.

"I start this morning and shall be ruined if the ship has sailed. . . . I have merely thrown a few things into my valise and leave all else in confusion to be packed up and . . . sent for. . . . The bookcase is my pet and will, I trust, receive a few caresses from you. It is left with all its memorandums, etc., to tell a tale for or against me. Your letters I leave in their places as I know they are sacred. . . . I ought to take a few with me, for you have let me go forth upon a wild and long expedition and without any token, any memento, save a small lock of hair that has been guarded when all else was neglected." The closing words are shrewdly calculated to appeal to feminine sentiment; so shrewdly calculated that we are left wondering, after noting the real point of emphasis earlier, whether the expression was not more powerful than the feeling.

Sherman's anxiety lest he might miss the transport at New York was misplaced. Not until July 14 was the *Lexington* towed out of New York harbour and, with sails spread, set out on its seven months' voyage to Monterey. For the way to California was round —a long round—Cape Horn. Their first port of call was Rio de Janeiro, after sixty days of monotony unrelieved even by the painfully picturesque ceremony which attends the crossing of the equator, for the democratic principle had not yet penetrated the ramparts of U. S. naval etiquette, and officers were exempted from Neptune's baptismal shave. To any one who studies the portraits of these military heroes of the mid-nineteenth century the question suggests itself whether their immunity from the ordeal was due less to the resistance of naval etiquette than to the resistance of what is graphically termed their "face-fungus"—for Neptune might well shrink from damaging even his razor and wasting his soapsuds on such impenetrable protection.

At Rio, Sherman toured the sights with Lieutenant Halleck of the engineers—sixteen years hence to be his chief, and in three more a source of bitterness. The leisurely course of the voyage and the long pause at Rio gave him ample time for writing to Ellen Ewing. His letters reveal a passion for knowledge rather than a passionate love. And we are proportionately grateful, for the products are

more uncommon. In a young soldier his desire for action is not remarkable; his desire for information is—in a profession whose members normally mature late. Perhaps the object of his affections and
letters was less surprised than we are by the unquenchable curiosity,
the minuteness of his observation, and the brilliant descriptive
power of his letters, which were accompanied and amplified by
neatly drawn maps and marginal sketches. Whether he deals with
the topography of a district or with a native custom there is an
exactness of detail and vivid impressionism which brings the picture
into the reader's eye.   Popularly, exactness and vividness are
assumed to be contrasting qualities. Actually, is not one the com-
plement of the other, and their combination the product of an essential realism of mind? Sherman's whole career is evidence in support. Because of this realism he saw war as an instrument of policy
rather than as an impassioned drama or glorious adventure.

While waiting in New York harbour he had written—"That we
are to take possession of some point in California there is no doubt.
. . . A port, if guarded and supplied with such articles as ships
need, would soon become of vast importance. Now, apart from the
mere fact that we will be usurpers, do you not think it will be a great
thing to be the pioneers in such a move, to precede the flow of population thither, and to become one of the pillars of the land?" His
candour about the "mere fact" was characteristic. And in a letter
from Rio he remarks: "The war excites much speculation here, but
all seem to think the people of the United States are determined to
possess North Mexico, regardless of the principles involved. Such
is pretty near the truth. . . ."

From Rio, their passage round Cape Horn more than kept up the
reputation of that ill-favoured Cape, so rough a passage that "it
seemed more than once as though the ship must be swamped." The
repeated sight of broken crockery and furniture, of meals and men
rolling in the scuppers, impelled Sherman to the reflection that
"This sea is no respecter of persons and things, for not one of us
but in his turn has served as a laughing object for the rest. . . . I
can now understand why all sailors are so good-tempered—not that
nature made them so originally but because the sea kills or banishes
all who have any malice in their composition."

For the soldiers on board, the ordeal was peculiarly trying because of their enforced helplessness, but Sherman, blessed with a strong stomach, found calm of spirit in reading in his cabin, even though his thoughts occasionally wandered to the prospect of a watery grave. "I have read all of Washington Irving's works that are aboard. 'Pickwick,' 'Barnaby Rudge,' Shakespeare, everything I could get, and yesterday cast about to determine which I should attempt next—the Bible, 'History of the Reformation,' or the 'Wandering Jew,' but have postponed such a task till even a time less urgent than the present."

If the crisis did not bring him to a mood of repentance, it combined with the tedium of the changeless days to inspire an outburst of prophecy—in a letter to his sister Elizabeth—"If you hear about a subscription opening to dig a canal across the isthmus of Panama, you may put me down any amount, for really I do not fancy a voyage of twenty-four thousand miles to accomplish a distance of less than two thousand." In the same letter he sheds light on his excessively hurried departure from Pittsburgh—"I started without regard to private risk or interest lest I should be too late and lose a reputation for prompt and willing obedience of dangerous orders. I wish now I had . . . made better preparation for so long an absence."

At last, sixty-four days out from Rio, they made the harbour of Valparaiso, where they had "news from the California coast" that "all the towns" were "in the possession of our fleet, so that we'll have . . . no fighting . . . that's too bad after coming so far. . . ."

In the harbour lay an English squadron and they were visited by the Admiral, Sir George Seymour. "The English evidently dislike our following their example in making conquests, but I do not believe, however, they intend any opposition to our steps." So yet another hope of a scrap was dashed and Sherman tried to raise his flickering hopes with consoling rumours of a French fleet in the Pacific "so that it is within the range of possibility that stirring scenes are yet in the future for us."

He relieved his indefatigable exploration of Valparaiso with attendance at a steeplechase, which was won by an English midshipman, riding the Admiral's horse. Sherman remarks that watching, and, still more, riding in a horse-race, "would be deemed discreditable" in the U. S. navy. " 'Tis different with the English who by all means encourage athletic sport and, go where they will, must introduce the hurdle-race or some similar sport." Sherman, in contrast, spent the remaining forty days of the voyage in reading and re-reading the collection of books on California, its exploration and people, that he had brought from New York.

Valparaiso was the *Lexington's* second and final port of call, and at last early in the New Year they arrived in sight of the Californian coast. The officer who came off to pilot them into Monterey Bay brought thrilling news of an insurrection among the Californians and a country filled with guerillas. Spirits rose at the prospect of a fight, but the newcomers soon found that like all military prospects it was subject to the restrictive conditions of time and space, and that a fight at Los Angeles had little meaning for them in a country where a Mexican ox-cart was the most rapid, indeed, the only means of transport. And even the news of this fighting was soon overshadowed by that of its sequel—the piquant but hardly edifying dispute between the various American commanders, General Kearny, Colonel Frémont, and Commodore Stockton over the right to control California. The politically bolstered Frémont was the source of the dispute, and Sherman's brief experience here as a subordinate of Kearny at least served to prepare him for his own experience of Frémont in Missouri fourteen years later.

With the simultaneous departure of Kearny and Frémont tranquillity settled on the land, where Sherman remained as acting adjutant-general to the new and unchallenged commander, Colonel Mason. Halleck, similarly, became Mason's chief assistant on the political side, acting as secretary of state. Thus, with two such junior officers the "lieutenants" of the ruler of so great a territory, the humble army rank of lieutenant was for once reinvested with a semblance of its original significance. California in the 'forties was assuredly a land of scope as well as hope. If more exalted, this new post was perhaps less valuable experience for Sherman than when, on first landing, he had acted as quartermaster and commissary of the force and thereby acquired a grounding in emergency supply problems which was to stand him in good stead when, in later years, he had to approach problems, similar but greater, from a different angle.

CHAPTER II

SOLDIER AND CIVILIAN IN CALIFORNIA

WAR might flourish in Mexico, and laurels thicken, but near the isolated cluster of adobe-houses, log-huts, and a half-built fort on the hill, that was Monterey in 1847, the only targets on which Sherman could expend powder and shot were the ducks and geese in the plains, and the deer and bears in the mountains behind. Once only did a breath of excitement enliven this tranquillity. Kearny, before his departure, had nominated a gentleman with the euphonious name of Boggs as alcalde of the little settlement of Sonoma. But Boggs sent into Mason a complaint that the officially evicted alcalde, Nash, refused to vacate his throne, claiming that he held it by right of popular election and that this overrode military nomination.

Sherman was assigned the pleasing if potentially precarious task of making the little world of Sonoma unsafe for democracy. On reaching Sonoma and ascertaining Nash's whereabouts, Sherman waited until dark and then, posting an armed sailor on each side of the house where Nash was supping, opened the door and, covering him with a pistol, compelled him to come out. He was then bundled into a cart and driven away to a boat to be duly conveyed to Monterey, the interference of the "electorate" having been thus neatly avoided. On the way to Monterey, Sherman, as he wrote later "explained fully to him the state of things in California, and he admitted he had never looked at it in that light before, and professed a willingness to surrender his office. . . ." But however persuasive Sherman's tongue, it would seem that the light really came through the fright caused by looking at Sherman's pistol, and the still worse qualms of sea-sickness which followed.

Sherman's enjoyment of the experience was not lessened by being the executant of such summary methods of jurisdiction. As he cheerfully and pointedly remarked in a letter to his brother, "military law is supreme here and the way we ride down the few lawyers who have

23

ventured to come here is curious . . . yet a more quiet community could not exist."

The trip brought Sherman the incidental experience of a call at the unprepossessing little village of Yerba Buena on the Bay of San Francisco which boasted four hundred inhabitants, most of them Kanakas from the Sandwich Islands. The site had recently been surveyed and was being sold in lots, at sixteen dollars each. An army friend, Folsom, urged Sherman to buy some but he ridiculed the suggestion, feeling "insulted that he should think me such a fool as to pay money for property in such a horrid place as Yerba Buena." But Folsom and his friends had a sharp sense of opportunity if a poor eye for a site. For, as Sherman records at his own expense, by changing the name of this village to that of the bay on which it stood, a bay whose name was familiar to sailors everywhere, they thereby ensured that all the ships which began to come in growing volume to the new territory should naturally discharge their cargoes at the landing place of "San Francisco." If Sherman, in consequence, had forfeited a potential fortune, he learnt a lesson not unprofitable to his later career—that an eye for economic factors is useful even to a soldier.

Early in 1848 he learnt another to the same effect. For, one day, two men came to his office desiring to see Colonel Mason, the Governor, and in his presence produced half an ounce of placer-gold from a deposit which had been discovered near a saw-mill in the Sierra Nevada. From that discovery came the great gold-rush upon which the fortunes of California and its swift expansion in commerce and population were founded. So rapidly did the rush develop that before the year was out the settlers were evacuating the coast for the mines and fresh seekers of fortune were pouring into the country, while even the soldiers, stricken with the gold-fever, were deserting —all the faster because the discovery synchronized with the treaty of peace with Mexico. As a consequence all volunteers had to be discharged, the military control became annulled without a civil government to take its place, and two shrinking companies of regulars were left to guard an immense territory dotted with magazines of military stores. As the higher wages of labour tempted men away, so did glut of money and excess of mouths raise the price of goods higher and higher until, as Sherman complained, "blankets worth one or two dollars in New York sell here for $50," so that "we cannot possibly exist on our pay."

But Sherman had profited in mind at least, by earlier lessons. For he urges his brother, "If you can at once ship to San Francisco a cargo of the following articles, you will make a splendid venture." He appends a list of the most saleable articles(emphasizing that "cloth is of little value, as no one has time to make it up." So impressed is he with this idea of a commercial venture that he repeats and amplifies it a few days later.

He had himself just returned from a trip to the gold-mines, where he studied the whole process in the diggings and the conditions under which the workers lived, noting with characteristic thoroughness all that he saw. And a further trip in the autumn led him to become a partner in a newly founded store "in order to share somewhat in the riches of the land." But it was also on his initiative that, after the first visit, a special courier was sent back to Washington, with full and accurate information of the discoveries, compiled by him, and with samples of the gold—thereby spreading the authentic news to the national benefit, and inaugurating the development of California in the interests of the whole, not merely of the few.

The gold-discovery had come at a critical moment for Sherman. His restlessly active spirit, which required constant outlet in both physical and mental enterprise, was sorely irked by the humdrum round of office routine and garrison life in this isolated settlement. If he were suffering from home-sickness, he was suffering worse from that more profound soul-sickness which, in times of stagnation, so easily seizes those who set their caps at a high destiny. The previous November he had written in depression to Ellen Ewing—"I am so completely banished that I feel I am losing all hope, all elasticity of spirits. I feel ten years older. . . . To hear of war in Mexico and the brilliant deeds of the army, of my own regiment and my own old associates, every one of whom had gained honors, and I out here in California, banished from fame, from everything that is dear, and no more prospect of ever getting back than one of the old adobe houses that mark a Californian ranche!" To the student of James Wolfe's life and letters there is a ring so familiar in these phrases that it bridges the gap of a century, and draws a parallel between Wolfe and Sherman which many other letters intensify. Each, too, went west to seek his fortune, and while the one contributed, inadvertently, to the establishment of the United States, the other contributed, permanently, to its greatness, its expansion and endurance. Each too, attained his goal, but Sherman alone his full promise.

Little wonder that Sherman felt cut off from the world, for he was cut off even from his letters. When the mail-steamer *California* reached Monterey on February 23, 1849, the first steamship seen on the Pacific coast—drawing from the wondering natives the common cry "Tan Feo!" ("how ugly")—she marked the beginning of a new life for California. But to Sherman and his comrades it was momentarily more important that she marked the renewal of an old life. Sherman, who in his eagerness had rowed a mile out to meet the ship, expresses both the reaction and the past isolation in telling Ellen that it "has turned us all crazy. . . . Until this arrival I had not heard from you or any of my correspondents for a whole year."

But the thirst for news was more easily assuaged than the thirst for opportunity. Lonely he did feel, but the greater emphasis in his letters, and in his mind, is on the barrenness of his prospects. This truth is confirmed by his action. For the *California* had brought reinforcements, and among them a Major Canby to relieve him as adjutant-general of the Department. Sherman seized the chance to hand in his written resignation from the army—in order, not to leave California, but to stay there. For he "had received several splendid offers of employment and of partnership." His motive in resigning was due not only to a sense of military inopportunity, but of mortification—that he had missed his military opportunity. Indeed, he had contemplated the step when the news of peace had come, writing then, "I have felt tempted to send my resignation to Washington and I really feel ashamed to wear epaulettes after having passed through a war without smelling gun-powder."

Fate intervened, beneficially, to prevent his resignation at this moment. If it was only to be postponed, certain vital changes were to influence his career during the few years of postponement. In 1849 the instrument of fate was General P. F. Smith who had come on the *California* to assume command of the newly created Division of the Pacific, with headquarters at San Francisco. He vetoed Sherman's resignation on the ground that he himself required an acting adjutant-general who knew the country and its conditions. So Sherman once again ascended to a post more exalted than was natural to his rank of lieutenant. For the moment his chief value to his commander was in knowing not the military, or even the political, but the domestic conditions. The real military problem of 1849 was how to live, with inadequate pay and without servants. Its solution was doubtless useful experience for his "March to the Sea" and we are not surprised that he was lenient in controlling his foragers in 1864-65. It is more surprising that no one has traced the cause of this leniency to acute fellow-feeling in a man of acute memory.

Happily his own chief in the earlier struggle with Californian prices and profiteers had a sense of humour. Sherman used later to relate how often he had seen General Smith carrying to his house "a can of preserved meat" and how on meeting a negro he would take off his hat, replying to curious questions that the reason for his politeness was that "they were the only real gentlemen in California."

Eventually the struggle became so hopeless for these Uncle Sam-salaried officers that as a last expedient they sent their families home and, pooling their rations, lived together in camp. Sherman, on a lieutenant's pay, had only been able to maintain himself through the winter owing to the $1,500 he had made out of his share in the store. This first venture into commerce he now extended with his chief's sanction—in face of necessity. By carrying out sundry civil surveys he earned sufficient to buy three "lots" in Sacramento City which he sold at a profit.

In the military sphere almost the only active duty was the chase of deserters, for the enlisted men were seizing any opportunity to make a bolt for the mines, secure in the assurance that once there they would be protected from recapture. But the hopes of one party were frustrated by Sherman's unique knowledge of the country, the result of his constant exploratory rides in his leisure hours. By a night ride across country he caught the party and, using the darkness to cloak his lack of support, disarmed eighteen deserters by sheer force of personality. Soon two other officers came up, and the three sufficed to conduct the now weaponless men back to camp.

At last, in the winter of 1849-50, came the end of Sherman's long isolation from civilization. General Smith had to send despatches back to General Winfield Scott in New York, and Sherman was made the bearer. Taking also two young sons of a friend, on their way to school in the East, he embarked on January 2 for Panama, crossed the isthmus by mule and river in four days, and arrived at New York towards the end of the month. On delivery of his despatches, he was invited to dine with General Scott, but the general's effort to entertain him with stories of the campaign in Mexico increased his depression—for "I thought it the last and only chance in my day, and that my career as a soldier was at an end." And Scott's prophetic remark that "our country" was "on the eve of a terrible civil war" seemed too incredible to be true, besides being too distasteful to be a desirable substitute for the chance that had passed.

From New York, Sherman travelled on with the despatches to the War Department at Washington. There he found that his "foster-father," Thomas Ewing, had become Secretary of the Interior, and he rejoined the family. Soon, he became a member of it in a deeper sense. In those leisurely and romantic-minded times it was still true that "absence makes the heart grow fonder." The mild gaieties of Washington in the 'forties had not distracted Ellen Ewing's thoughts from the boy who, five years older, had always been the object of her admiring affection. His wide travels, his distant adventures, invested him with a halo of romance well calculated to reinforce the ties of common upbringing in counteracting the paler attractions of the city-bred youths she met at dances. Those frequent comments, too, in his letters, on the outward charms of damsels seen in course of travel were as aptly suited to excite the possessive instinct as the final assurance that none had displaced her was gratifying to feminine vanity. And as the most formidable obstacle of the age, parental approval, was removed from the path, it was natural that the old understanding between playmates, which had already ripened into a definite engagement, should now be consummated.

Thus Ellen committed herself to a destiny higher than dreams, while the time-honoured feminine chorus lamented that she was throwing herself away on a penniless lieutenant, and sacrificing a fine match on a matrimonial altar so bare. But the nave was not bare—when William Tecumseh Sherman and Ellen Ewing were united in the holy bonds of matrimony on the first of May, 1850. Labour day!—a prophetic start, for Sherman was to be neither the first nor the last young man to prove that hard work under the spur of ambition is a better dowry than dollars. And his marriage had also an auspicious start, for President Taylor and all his cabinet graced the ceremony.

There is a historical parallel between Sherman and Pershing in that they both married into a powerful political family. Yet in relation to his father-in-law it is not possible to trace even superficially in Sherman's case the influence on his career which later could be ascribed superficially, and unjustly, in Pershing's case. For while Pershing received on his own merits a due, and overdue, acceleration in promotion, Sherman early quitted the sphere where influence might have helped him—in times when it was more vigorously used.

At the outset, however, it seemed that this influence might be of service. For a bill was then in passage through Congress providing for four extra captains in the Commissary Department, and Sherman's six months' leave of absence had hardly expired before he received one of the vacancies, thereby obtaining a step in promotion, missed by inactive service in California, although amply deserved, and now only attained by transfer to a non-combatant branch.

While he was still on leave, after his return from the honeymoon, an incident occurred which Sherman records, and which is well worth recording here for its light on his character. Seeking to attend the debate in the Senate on the "Compromise" Bill, which was the occasion of Daniel Webster's last great speech, he found the galleries densely packed. Refusing to be baulked, he sought a senator with whom he was slightly acquainted and boldly asked to accompany him on the floor of the Senate. Sherman's own account cannot be improved on for the rest of the story—the Senator "asked in his quizzical way, 'Are you a foreign ambassador?' 'No.' 'Are you the Governor of a State?' 'No.' 'Are you a member of the other House?' 'No.' 'Have you ever had a vote of thanks by name?'

'No.' 'Well, these are the only privileged members.' I then told him he knew well enough who I was, and that if he chose he could take me in. He then said, 'Have you any impudence?' I told him, 'A reasonable amount if occasion called for it.' 'Do you think you could become so interested in my conversation as not to notice the doorkeeper?' (pointing to him). I told him that there was not the least doubt if he would tell me one of his funny stories." The pair thus successfully passed the senatorial Cerberus, blandly disregarding his fire of stereotyped questions. Once inside, the Senator said, "Now you can take care of yourself." And the epilogue of this story is not the least illuminating part, for Sherman took, not a back seat, but one close behind Mr. Webster, and in equally audacious proximity to General Scott.

When, in September, Sherman was promoted captain into the Commissary Department, he was posted to St. Louis, a city henceforth to be intimately connected with his career even until the end. His first stay was short, if not quite as short as he anticipated. For in a letter of January, 1851, to his brother John, he wrote: "I . . . am still expecting to be sent away in the spring, but where to is hard to tell. I ask no imprudent questions of the authorities at Washington, but leave them to act as the good of the service to them may seem fit. . . . Write me from Washington the political news, and again let me advise you to shun politics like poison except it advance you in the profession of the law." The dissuasion was vain—a failure not without benefit to William Sherman's interests—and so the jibe at politics and politicians was to be the forerunner of many more in the friendly interchanges of the brothers, for in Sherman's attitude to politics family familiarity bred contempt, perhaps all the more because he was as politically minded as he was politically antipathetic in spirit.

.   .   .   .

The 'forties had been the heyday of the professional politician, helped by the convention method of nominating candidates and by the apparently unslakable public thirst for stump oratory—or verbosity—which in turn grew with the growth of railroads that could the more easily bring the purveyor to the consumer. But in 1851 politics and parties seemed likely to be thrust into the background by economic pressure of a happy type. The great and growing current of industrial development, mercantile expansion, and westward migration was absorbing both the imagination and energies of the people.   The Mexican war had added new territories, the railroads were stretching out to link up new areas, the gold discoveries were offering new sources of wealth, the clipper ships were beginning their onslaught on the ocean trade.   Best of all, the internal political atmosphere seemed calmer and clearer than it had been for a decade.

The possession of the new territories had temporarily split the two historic parties—Whigs and Democrats—along the territorial line of North and South.   And while Congress argued whether they should be allowed slaves or not, the settlers had to remain without law and government.   Tired of waiting to be organized as a Territory, California had made herself a State, under writs of election issued by Sherman's chief, and drafted a constitution prohibiting slavery.   By settling her personal issue, she seriously unsettled the Union.   For the actual admission of California to the Union would upset the political balance between the free and slave States and, by its acceptance of the slave ban in so large a part of the new possessions, would tilt the economic balance more than ever against the slave-holding states, who now began to suffer acutely the feeling of envelopment by a growingly superior economic power.   A feeling all the less bearable because for over a generation the South had been taking a course of auto-suggestion in its own social and ethical superiority.

At this crisis the Southern Democrats, under the oratorical leadership of Calhoun, gave tongue for secession.   And were met with concession.   By the Compromise of 1850 the admission of free California was palliated by a more rigorous law for the recapture of fugitive slaves.   Peace shone on the land and political divisions receded into the shadow.   The great illusion.

Actually, politics and parties were cast into the melting pot, to be heated by the fires of sentiment and remoulded under economic pressure.   The Whigs melted first.   Fortified by endorsement of the Compromise, the Democrats gained an overwhelming victory in the presidential election of 1852, which inaugurated an eight years' reign, but in the process became stamped as the conservatives and conservers of slave-property.   The Whig party, by the anti-slavery tendencies of its northern members lost the allegiance of its southern members, and by its indecision dissatisfied their northern, whose views in the meantime were hardened by the close up view of runaways being chased in their towns.   Then, in 1854, the proposals of a transcontinental railroad led to proposals to organize the bordering country into the new Territories of Kansas and Nebraska, and these in turn to a proposal by Douglas, the Northern Democrat, to leave the question of slavery in them to the vote of the settlers—"popular sovereignty."   But this would violate the compromise of 1820 whereby slavery was definitely prohibited in any new Territories created to the westward of Missouri.   Nevertheless, the bill was carried through by an almost solid Democratic vote, the North blazed with indignation, and on the ashes of the Whigs rose a new Republican party, pledged to resist the extension of slavery.   Frémont was its first presidential candidate, in 1856, when he lost to Buchanan, the Democrat.   But it soon found a greater leader in Abraham Lincoln.

On the heels of Buchanan's election came the famous and momentous decision of the Supreme Court on the case of Dred Scott, a slave who claimed his freedom on the score that he had been taken by his master into free territory.   The Supreme Court, by a majority decision, gave a ruling which meant that no Act of Congress could deprive citizens of slave-property which they carried into a Territory before its erection into a State.   Theoretically, all the Territories were thus open to slavery and the Missouri Compromise was nullified.   Practically, the preponderance of Northern settlers ensured that on becoming States they would prohibit slavery.   And in Congress the Northern advantage was shortly increased with the admission of Oregon and Minnesota as free states.   But the immediate result in Kansas and Nebraska was to lead to a violent bickering between the more fanatical or less reputable "pros" and "antis" among the settlers, which degenerated into an internal guerrilla warfare.   In this school John Brown graduated in homicide as a preliminary to his 1859 raid into Virginia with the idea of freeing and arming the slaves.   There he was surrounded and captured by troops under Colonel Robert E. Lee and, his life ending on the scaffold, he was speedily exalted yet higher—to be the martyred hero of abolitionism.

Here, in brief outline, we have sketched the political background to the next decade of Sherman's career, a background which in spite of himself was ultimately to throw him into bold relief.

.   .   .   .

While at St. Louis Sherman rode far afield, as keen as ever in his topographical observation, and it is in a letter from here that he refers to that practice which is often the quaint badge of those who share this proclivity—"my old rule never to return by the road I had come."

Commissariat duties in civilization were palling quicker than in isolation, despite the new domestic bonds, and to his wife, temporarily absent at her old home in Lancaster, Ohio, he reveals the onset of the "wanderlust"— "If you should hear of my joining some expedition or other, you must not be surprised, for had I authority or permission I would certainly make some summer trip of this kind." If the unrest was subdued on her return, it blazed up again as soon as she had gone northwards, as usual, the next summer. In early August, 1852, he declares—"I am getting tired of this dull tame life and should a fair opportunity occur for another campaign on the frontier, I cannot promise to keep quiet. Commissaries are not fighting men, but I could effect an advantageous exchange." His restlessness was temporarily interrupted, if not assuaged, by a summons to New Orleans to relieve the local Commissary, who had become embroiled in a controversy concerning the abuse of army patronage of contractors.

When Sherman moved to New Orleans, his family, now augmented by two children, were still on their summer holiday at Lancaster. While he was seeking a home for them, his letters, most unromantically full of comments on the economic condition and future of Louisiana, show that his mind was searching for a new personal objective. "Here, Cuba is all the go, but I don't know what the northern Democrats think on the subject. If Cuba can be got fairly, it will be a beautiful state, and I would not object to a station at the Havannah as commissary. Of that in due time. Since my arrival I have not lost sight of the necessary preparations for your coming. Boarding is exorbitantly high, beyond our means, housekeeping, too, is no sinecure, but then we can endeavour to control expenses."

Marital duty might lead him to talk of house-hunting and house-keeping as an affectionate sop to his wife, but even as he wrote his thoughts were straying, and as he candidly confesses in another letter—"Nothing but activity and continued interest contents me, and when these fail an impulse moves me that reason, nor pleasure, nor any ordinary motive accounts for." It was the spur of self-fulfilment, which is the merciless goad of such men and the ache of their wives, unless these be of a temperament which can sink self in the fulfilment of the husband's destiny.

Here destiny decided the issue by the fact that Ellen Sherman's arrival at New Orleans coincided with that of a Major Turner, a friend from St. Louis, with proposals that Sherman should enter into partnership in a bank to be established in San Francisco, as a semi-independent branch of the well-known St. Louis firm of Lucas and Symonds. Turner, having planted the seed in Sherman's mind, continued on his way to California, but his departure was soon followed by the arrival of Lucas, to water a seed that had already become a shoot. In such circumstances Lucas's task of persuasion was not difficult, although Sherman was sufficiently mindful of the maxim—shared alike by sound commerce and generalship—"no advance without reconnaissance," as to take six months' leave of absence in which to explore the situation on the spot before definitely resigning from the army. His leave arranged, he sent his family to Ohio, disposed of his house and furniture, and, early in March, took ship to Nicaragua en route to California.

A letter to his brother reveals the grounds on which he had finally taken the decision. "Turner is a particular friend of mine, and is already in California; he is quite wealthy. Lucas is decidedly the richest property-holder in St. Louis, and has credit unlimited. Now I, of course, could not have better associates in business if I am ever to quit the army, and in these prosperous times salaried men suffer." To which John Sherman consolingly and discerningly replies: "The spirit of the age is progressive and commercial, and soldiers have not that opportunity for distinction which is the strongest inducement in favour of that profession. . . . Besides, officers of the army must either be in large cities, where their pay is insufficient . . . or on the borders of civilization, where their families must either be separated from them or share their banishment."

Sherman's desire for "activity and continued interest" was to be satisfied, indeed sated, in the next few years. And even the journey out was in the nature of an ominous promise that they would be far from "dull and tame." The first incident occurred when, after crossing from Nicaragua to the Pacific coast, he embarked on the ship for California. There was a rush to reserve state-rooms, and he had just booked a berth in one of the best state-rooms on deck when a feminine fellow-passenger from New Orleans, calling to him, asked that he would secure berths on deck for herself and a friend. The harassed purser put them down for the other two berths in Sherman's state-room, saying that he would make a change-over when the rush had subsided. But, then, the best berths were all filled and the two ladies being in occupation of his state-room, Sherman had to move. They not only appropriated his state-room but appropriated him, for the steward completed the unconscious conspiracy by seating them beside him at meals. And in the sequel he lost not only his reservation but nearly his reputation also, for the entry was recorded as "Captain Sherman & ladies," and some time after in San Francisco he discovered, from the customary tactful friend, that they were well-known prostitutes. As he remarked ruefully, "Society in California was then decidedly mixed," although he still stoutly maintained that "his ladies" were among the most modest in behaviour while on board.

This potentially narrow shave from domestic shipwreck was succeeded by a real, indeed a double, shipwreck. For the ship ran aground on a reef in the night a few miles north of San Francisco, having overshot the port. The passengers were lucky enough to reach the shore in the ship's boats, safely but wet, and Sherman then hired a small schooner in order to reach the city and send help. This in turn was upset close to the harbour by a violent gust. Sherman extricated himself from the tangle of rigging, swam round to the stern and clambered on to the keel. The capsized schooner, however, was drifting rapidly out to sea, when a row-boat came to the rescue and thus in a third form of sea-transport Sherman at last reached his destination—covered with sand, dripping with water, and having lost part of his baggage.

The next shipwreck was to be financial. But much troubled water was to be crossed ere that came. On arrival his first impression was of the utter change in the face of San Francisco. "This is the most astonishing place on earth. Large brick and granite houses fill the site where stood the poor, contemptible village; wharves extend a mile out, along which lie ships and steamers of the largest class, discharging freight in a day that used to consume with scows a month. Yet amid all this business and bustle there is more poverty than in New York. Not a day without distressed individuals ask for money."

The "boom" was then at its height, yet Sherman, trained to acute observation, evidently detected unhealthy symptoms. He appreciated the opportunity, but did not rush blindly into it. And, understanding the conditions of time and place, he realized the main element of danger and the essential safeguard in such unstably balanced conditions. "My business here is the best going, provided we have plenty of money. Without it, I stick to Uncle Sam, most emphatically." Having discussed the prospects and financial needs with Turner and the other partner, Nisbet, he made up his mind that if adequate capital was assured he would take the plunge.

Yet a deeper doubt must have lingered, for a curious sentence creeps into a letter to his wife—"I fear I will never enjoy a full and fair field for my natural activity of mind and body until both are crippled." Perhaps a bout of his old trouble engendered this depression, intuitive beyond any reasonable calculation. For in a letter six weeks later to his wife, when he was getting ready to leave for home, he tells her: "I have been pretty free of asthma for a long time, though this climate is peculiarly suited to produce it. . . . I had a pretty severe attack shortly after my arrival, but Dr. Hitchcock says it was not owing to lungs but a kind of fever, and, strange to say, prescribed quinine. It relieved me promptly, and upon a recurrence of any symptoms I have taken quinine. . . . If you hear by telegraph of my arrival in New Orleans write promptly to Saint Louis and hold yourself in readiness to leave home for New Orleans by September 1."

Wives still took and some of them kept the vow of obedience in those days! But leaving aside the military curtness of these marital instructions, when one reads the political discursions, topographical descriptions, and economic analyses in Sherman's letters one feels that Mrs. Sherman was born to verify that "love suffereth all things."

In July Sherman made his way back to New York and then to St. Louis. There Lucas agreed to his proposal that the new branch should start with a capital of $200,000, and a credit in New York of $50,000. He further promised to expend a further $50,000 in the building of a new banking house. With all his conditions thus met, Sherman went on to Lancaster, and after discussing the terms with his wife and father-in-law, sent his resignation to Washington. And on September 6, 1853, his first career in the army finished—at the age of thirty-three.

A fortnight later he sailed from New York with his wife, her ten-months' old baby, Lizzie, and a nurse. Travelling once more by Nicaragua, they reached San Francisco after a tiring journey, and there rented a small frame house on Stockton Street from the son of the well-known author, Captain Marryat. This modest accommodation had to suffice until Sherman had the opportunity and means to buy a small brick-house on Green Street.

Henceforth Sherman had his wife with him to comfort and sustain him in times and fits of depression throughout his Californian civil career, save for one break in 1855, when she returned to the East for the summer to see her eldest child, Minnie. He was thus left in charge of two young "handfuls," for to Lizzie had now been added a boy, named after his father. One letter to his wife during this break provides a rare glimpse of Sherman in a domestic rôle, and of his expedients—as a far-from-stern father—to console his charges for their mother's absence.

"I think you will be satisfied at least that they are in good condition. They are both very fat. Willy is as heavy a load as I want to carry and he tyrannizes over me completely, making me carry him all round the yard an hour after each meal. He cries for me, and I have to steal away as I used to from Lizzie. . . ." Then he passes on to his other activities. "In business, times are mending slowly. Lucas and Simmonds have at my request made modifications in our contract that is to my benefit some three or four thousand a year. Indeed they do anything I ask. . . . I only fear they may form too high an estimate of me, and increase my responsibility, in proportion. . . . I ought to relieve my mind from so much and yet I don't see how it can be done. In order to accomplish success there must be but one head, and that head must know everything. . . ."

If times were mending slowly, there were worse rips to mend than he conveyed in this heartening letter, and it was well that he had the children to distract his mind from business worries. Soon after his arrival in San Francisco he had discovered, when once actively engaged in the banking business, that there were flaws in his original calculations. And it is characteristic of the man that when years later he wrote his memoirs, he should candidly expose his own miscalculations, despite the fact that, then, political foes and the embittered partisans of other commanders were eager to probe any flaw in his record and to suggest unfairly that he had failed in business as a supplementary proof of the accuracy of their criticisms of him as a commander.

Sherman, quick in penetrating to the fundamentals of the business despite his inexperience, soon reached the conclusion that the three per cent. charged as premium on bills of exchange was a disappearing profit when freight, insurance and overhead costs were fully taken into account. Loans, too, were not only attended by a risk disproportionate to the rate, but were restricted by the fortnightly ebb and flow of the deposit account, low-tide—a very lowtide—synchronizing with each steamship departure. Unhappily the other bankers, and even his own partner, failed to gauge the deeper factors, and Sherman, a novice and newcomer powerless to change established rules and customs, was caught up in the professional whirlpool and "had to drift along with the rest toward that Niagara that none foresaw at the time."

"None"—surely one, for Sherman's contemporary letters justly cancel the self-reproach implied in his memoirs. Moreover, when the great lumber-dealing firm of Meiggs, Neeley, Thompson & Co. failed, and its head, Meiggs, absconded to make a fresh fortune in Chili, leaving a million dollars of debt behind, Sherman's previous inspiration, due to psychological intuition, in gripping the rock of caution—in the contraction of Meiggs' credit—kept his own firm from drifting towards the brink of insolvency as rapidly as others.

But the Meiggs crisis was followed by a worse when disquieting rumours spread, early in 1855, about the position of Page, Bacon & Co., foremost of all California's banking-houses. For several days there was a steady run on this bank, while the others waited in anxious expectation for the run to spread, taking such emergency precautions as they could.

Receiving a call for help from one of the Page, Bacon partners, Haight, Sherman went round after dark and was told with alcoholic assurance that "all the banks would break." Thus cautioned rather than encouraged, Sherman offered to buy for cash a proportion of the firm's bullion, notes and bills, but declined the risk of converting a simple into a compound fracture.

A number of fellow-citizens and friends were about to sign a statement, prepared by Haight, for publication, certifying that they had personally examined the books, that the bank was solvent, and able to pay all its debts. On this paper being handed to Sherman he pointedly asked them how far their personal examination had gone. Haight thereupon intervened and offensively asked, "Do you think the affairs of such a house as Page, Bacon & Co. can be critically examined in an hour?" Sherman retorted that they had twelve hours' grace before the bank was due to open and, fortified by his knowledge that the system here used was similar to his own, declared that there was ample time to check the ledger and the coin, bullion and bills in the vaults. When Haight demanded that his word should be taken, the others refrained from signing the statement.

The incident illustrates both human nature and Sherman's nature. Not only had he an uncommon dislike of sacrificing truth to policy, but a still more uncommon preference for the public interest over the interest of his reputation as a "good fellow." When most men, from sentiment, weakness, or short-sight are prone to hold the claims of loyal comradeship more sacred than the abstract claims of morality, and deem the world well lost if friends can be saved, Sherman had the discernment and, more rare, the moral courage to take an unpopular course. Friendship is a great force for good; so also is loyalty. Yet the bulk of the harm which history records has been wrought in the name of these twin virtues. It is a sobering reflection.

One more day passed and then Page, Bacon & Co. closed their

doors. But still the storm held off, although the streets were filled with clusters of people in ominous discussion. The next morning came the suspension of another bank and then suddenly the stream of excited depositors became a surging torrent. Bank after bank failed, but Lucas, Turner & Co. held out against it successfully, helped by Sherman's energetic measures, before and during the emergency, and also by the personal trust which he inspired in sundry big depositors. Every demand was met, and finding them met, the torrent slackened as rapidly as it had risen. The clue to the situation was aptly expressed in Sherman's anecdote—"At our counter happened that identical case, narrated of others, of the Frenchman who was nearly squeezed to death in getting to the counter, and, when he received his money, did not know what to do with it. 'If you got the money, I no want him; but if you no got him, I want it like the devil!'"

This crisis, from which Sherman's firm emerged with prestige enhanced but profits impaired by the general loss, was followed next year by another of a different kind. Again, Sherman's share is characteristic. The prologue to it synchronized with the sequel to the first crisis, when the banks were striving to restore confidence. Their efforts were hampered by a malicious attack in a paper edited by James Casey, whose alternative profession was that of politician, and the paper was printed on an upper floor office in Lucas, Turner & Co.'s building. On his attention being drawn to the paper, Sherman warned Casey that if the attack was repeated he would "cause him and his press to be thrown out of the window." Taking the hint Casey moved elsewhere in time. The prologue was complete when Sherman, in May, 1856, agreed to accept the commission of Major-General of the Second Division of the State Militia.

A few days later the curtain rose on the Vigilance Committee reign of 1856, a period as historic as it is unhistorical—for the subsequent histories, from which most later writers have taken their cue, reek of propaganda. If a great event in the life of California it is but an incident in Sherman's, and a sense of this proportion must govern its treatment here. A short time previously James King of William, an editor more reputable than Casey, had undertaken the mission of cleansing the city by fire of tongue—and, having given many others a grievance, eventually annoyed the com-

paratively insignificant Casey by revealing that he had graduated
in the Sing Sing penitentiary, whereupon Casey became a man of
action, not merely of words, and shot his "fellow" editor. He then
escaped the crowd and found shelter by delivering himself up to
the Sheriff. The jail was soon surrounded by an angry crowd
anxious, in primitive Western American fashion, to anticipate the
uncertain course of justice. While all waited to see whether King
would live or die, the resolution that Casey should die was formulated and organized by the revived Vigilance Committee of 1851,
which comprised many of Sherman's friends. Sherman's reaction
to the crisis was, in contrast, to take the oath as Major-General of
Militia and undertake to maintain order—having as yet no troops.
He then accompanied the Governor to a meeting with the President
of the Vigilance Committee where the Governor, forcefully warned
that the Sheriff's honesty was suspect, gave his personal guarantee
that Casey should be brought to trial, and to a trial presided over by
a reputable judge. And as a more convincing guarantee, the Vigilantes were allowed to place ten of their number on guard in the
jail. The so-called "Law and Order" party were indignant with the
Governor for making terms, but their distrust of these took a
less practical form than that of the better armed and prepared
Vigilantes who, when they heard that King was dying, marched
on the jail in such force that resistance was hopeless. They brought
away Casey and another murderer, to keep him company, and upon
King's death duly hung the two as a funeral accompaniment. The
Governor, with discretion, refrained from any attempt to intervene.

But, having tasted power, the Vigilance Committee was loth to
relinquish it, and, taking charge of the city, set about a vigorous
spring-cleaning. However worthy their motives, their assumption
of divine right was more than the exponent of constitutional right
could tolerate, and the Governor accordingly summoned Sherman
to meet him at the headquarters of General Wool, the local Regular
Commander, at Benicia. Sherman then agreed to call out volunteers on condition that General Wool would hand over the necessary
arms and ammunition from the United States arsenal, and that the
local naval commander, the later famous Farragut, would provide
a ship to transport them to San Francisco. Sherman then drove
with the Governor to see Farragut who, however, was reluctant to

become engaged in civil troubles without authority from Washington, and said that he had no ship immediately available. Disquieted by this initial obstruction, Sherman took the precaution to obtain General Wool's confirmation in the presence of the Governor, that he would issue the arms and ammunition on demand.

The Chief-Justice then issued a writ of *habeas corpus* for the handing over of one of the prisoners of the Vigilance Committee, and on this being evaded the Governor issued a proclamation commanding the Vigilantes to disperse. Thereupon Sherman called out the Militia, stating that "when a sufficient number of men are enrolled, arms and ammunition will be supplied." Excitement in the city rose to fever heat, and accusations of causing civil war were freely bandied. When friends came to Sherman, beseeching him to avoid a collision, he took the logical and constitutional course of replying that it was for the Vigilantes to avoid it—by evacuating their fortified headquarters and keeping their armed bodies off the streets. Furthermore, he sought to strengthen the hands of certain citizens who were seeking in "third-party" conciliation a peaceful solution by giving them an assurance that he had the power to obtain arms.

Thus the city was in suspense when an acquaintance told Sherman that he had heard General Wool declare that he did not intend to hand over the arms. Sherman promptly wrote to Wool saying that "any hesitation on your part would compromise me as a man of truth and honor," that he did not believe the arms would ever be needed but that the sure promise of them would suffice to ensure a peaceful dispersal of the Vigilantes' organization.

Wool's reply was evasive, and on being communicated to the Governor and his supporters evoked an outburst of indignation. While others exerted their vocal energy in vituperation of Wool, Sherman the realist, pointed out that the only arms outside the arsenal were in the Vigilantes' possession, and that "the part of wisdom for us was to be patient and cautious." He thus, despite opposition, secured an audience for the "conciliators," who brought a promise that the Vigilantes' power, although kept in being, should be kept out of sight. This failed to satisfy the more violent advocates of "law and order," headed by the Chief-Justice, and, seeing that they persisted in the intention to use force, without possessing it, Sherman handed the Governor his resignation. His brief comment is "I never afterward had anything to do with politics in California, perfectly satisfied with that short experience." His successor continued to prepare for trouble and was soon overtaken by it. For the Vigilantes, having arms, forcibly dispersed the militia, chased the commander out of the country and put the Chief-Justice in jail. A solution quite peaceful, if not constitutionally satisfactory.

It is perhaps symptomatic of the difference between William and John Sherman, that while the lawyer-politician sympathized with the immediate moral aims of the Vigilance Committee, the soldier-banker based his action on the ultimate moral danger of condoning the power of the mob, however moral the particular mob might be. But he was sufficiently a statesman to reject aims which were, practically, unrealizable and to seize any chance of gaining the end along the line of least resistance. Thus in California may be traced one more link in the chain of causation of his strategy.

The correspondence between the brothers during these years sheds further light on William Sherman's intellectual growth. Here is a letter earlier in this period: "I have seen by the papers that you are elected to Congress. I suppose you feel entitled to the congratulations of all the family, and I should not have been so late in giving you mine, only I expected that you would announce by letter the fact of your plans. . . . The Senate is, in my opinion, the only body which reflects an honour upon its members, and should you aspire to a seat there, I should be proud to learn of your success. As a young member I hope you will not be too forward, especially on the question of slavery, which it seems is rising more and more every year into a question of real danger, notwithstanding the compromises. Having lived a good deal in the South, I think I know practically more of slavery than you do. . . . There are certain lands in the South that cannot be inhabited in the summer by whites, and yet the negro thrives in it—this I know. Negroes free won't work tasks of course, and rice, sugar and certain kinds of cotton cannot be produced except by forced negro labour. Slavery being a fact is chargeable on the past, it cannot, by our system, be abolished except by force and consequent breaking up of our present government. As to restraining its further growth, the North have a perfect right to their full vote, and should, as a matter of course use it. . . . Let slavery extend along the shores of the Gulf of Mexico, but not in the high salubrious prairies of the West. It was a mistake to make Missouri a slave State, but it was done long ago; and now there is no remedy except in the State itself. Slavery can never exist here or north of us, so the North now has the power and can exercise it in prudence and moderation."

Then, passing on to the question of territorial expansion, he says: "My idea is to leave our present limits alone until we have more population, and then to make other adjacent territories pay for coming into the Union. The Sandwich Islands and Cuba, as long as held by Spain, or are independent, are more useful to us than if annexed as territory. If we had a colonial system like England, whereby we could govern them absolutely, it would be good property, but to admit the Kanakas of the Pacific and mixed Creoles of Cuba on a par with ourselves, would not exalt them, but would degrade us. . . ."

Again, shortly before his attention was temporarily diverted to a narrower field by the Casey crisis, he wrote, on March 20, 1856: "I see you are placed on the Committee of Foreign Relations, which is deemed a compliment. Since you are embarked in politics, I shall watch your career with deep interest, and of all things I shall expect you to avoid localism and to act as a representative of a great developing nation rather than a mere emblem of the freaks and prejudices of a small constituency. The slavery question is forced on you in spite of yourself. Time and facts are accomplishing all you aim at, viz.: the preponderance of the free over the slave States. This is so manifest that the politicians and people of the South feel it, and consequently are tetchy and morose. . . . Kansas will be a free State, so will Missouri and Kentucky in time; but the way to accomplish that is to let things go on as now, showing the eminent prosperity of the free States, whilst the slave States get along slowly. Self-interest is the great motor. . . . Therefore, to accomplish any political end, no provoking speeches are necessary, but on the contrary defeat the object in view." Here is political wisdom and prophetic vision. "I think you may do yourself credit and a public good by aiding California and the Pacific coast, which is poorly represented. There are now Indian wars going on to the north of us that will appeal to you. Don't meddle in it . . . these wars are doubtless provoked by the indiscriminate robbery of the Indians who, driven from the valleys, find no alternative but to steal and kill. All the Pacific coast is mountainous, and the valleys are limited in extent.   From these the Indians have been expelled, and of right they resist.   The settlements have pushed forward more than the extent of the white population warrants, and they cannot be re-strained, save by the danger of Indians, a proper and necessary restraint."

"The time for the great national railroad is not yet," but he urges the development of a good wagon road.   "A stage will use the wagon road as soon as the wants of the people demand.   The great object to be accomplished is to afford convenient resting places, where the emigrant can buy a mule or ox and can have his wagon repaired at a moderate cost.   This post should be fortified . . . and supplied in advance of any necessity with all the munitions of war."

Foreign affairs in turn come within the scope of a letter in April, 1856, to his father-in-law: "Of course we feel deeply interested here in everything that looks like war with a nation of such formidable naval strength as England. . . . We cannot believe that any clique of politicians would involve us in such a war, for such contemptible subjects as that of the logwood colony Belise or the enlistment of a few men, who were, doubtless, a good riddance to our country. . . . War would be fatal to California—not that any European nation could capture or occupy it, but England could blockade the coast." As a counteraction to this danger Sherman urges, in this paternal and political quarter, the importance of making the wagon-road as a link between the Pacific coast and the East, and, to add political weight to his argument, forwards a public petition in favour of such a scheme.

His views were not inspired by mere personal self-interest, how-ever foresighted, for in this same letter he foreshadows his own with-drawal from California: "Since I embarked in this scheme affairs have much changed.   Almost every bank has failed. . . . Real estate has fallen from an exaggerated rate to almost nothing.   As all this time we have had much money loaned it has been a period of deep anxiety to me, and I have thought more of acquitting my duties to my associates to making anything for myself. . . . I am de-termined if I live to stick out my full term of six years and then will be prepared to act for the future. . . . At times I do think I would like to free myself from the anxiety attending credit transactions in so desperate a country, but I am in for it, and must take the chances. . . ."

The subsequent seizure of power by the Vigilance Committee hardly tended, for the time, to enhance the sense of commercial security in San Francisco, and with the coming of the new year Sherman reported to Lucas in St. Louis that his money would be safer and could be used more profitably elsewhere than in San Francisco. Lucas, gratefully accepting the advice, instructed Sherman to draw out gradually, preparatory to removing to New York, and the San Francisco business was wound up—on the seventh anniversary of his wedding.

Leaving San Francisco early in May, 1857, and travelling by way of Panama and New York, Sherman took his family to Ohio and then, after a visit to St. Louis, went back alone to New York. Here he took rooms in the same house where Lieutenant J. B. McPherson, his future and famous subordinate, was boarding. The acute depression from which he was suffering, aggravated by his asthma, is revealed in a letter to his wife soon after arrival:

"I know no position in life so unenviable as one of fame not deserved, of position not merited, and like most people I think I occupy that most unenviable post. . . . Of course we did not break. We held high reputation among men, but who can tell the secret sorrow of the most pleased looking man who walks the highway? Of all lives on earth a banker's is the worst, and no wonder they are specially debarred all chances of heaven. . . . Several officers sent me money to invest and I did so. I fear the utter depression in California is such that I cannot get that money in at once, and they are asking me for it . . . so that I must sell my St. Louis property —all—and trust myself to the San Francisco securities. Our fate has been cast in a wrong time and I regret I ever left the Army, though at every turn flattery and magnificent future prospects are held out to me. . . ."

The hopeful early prospects in New York were soon dispersed. "I seem to fall on bad times in business, for I am not fairly installed before failures have begun. To-day the great Ohio Life and Trust Company failed." This caused a financial panic, and although

Sherman's firm was not directly affected, the indirect harm caused by the general uneasiness soon spread its ripples more widely. One ripple is seen in Sherman's next letter to his wife: "About your coming east—do not commit yourself for some weeks yet. Mr. Lucas is evidently not relishing these successive dangers which threaten his property, and I would not blame him if he would conclude as soon as this storm blows over, to draw out of this dangerous business." Then, telling her of the loss at sea of the *Central America*, laden with $1,600,000, he suggests ominously that—"this sad accident may be the last ounce that broke the camel's back."

The fracture, however, came by surprise, and in St. Louis, not in New York. For while still in bed one morning in October his cousin brought him the morning paper with the news that the parent bank in St. Louis had suspended payment.

Having spent the day in winding up the affairs of his branch Sherman sat down at night to write to his wife. One sentence revealed the man: "I am going to quit clean-handed—not a cent in my pocket. I know this is not modern banking, but better be honest."

Twenty years later, in his memoirs, he was able to write: "I may say with confidence that no man lost a cent by either of the banking firms of Lucas, Turner & Co., of San Francisco or New York; but, as usual, those who owed us were not always as just." As he was then a national figure, and his statement ensured of a nation-wide circulation, it had a ring of truth such as few of the like have possessed, and fewer still could have dared.

From New York Sherman went to see Lucas at St. Louis, and then returned to his family at Lancaster. A momentary rift in the clouds came at the end of the year from the possibility of an increase in the army establishment, and led him to write: "I think rather than be idle or to undertake any new indefinite scheme, I would return to my old business (the army), for which I am better qualified than any other. There will be great press for the higher appointments of Colonel, Lieutenant-Colonel, and Major: still, I have very many friends among the higher officers, and think by vigorous efforts I might get one of them."

But the scheme of expansion was still-born, and after a visit to San Francisco at Lucas's request, to collect outstanding debts, Sherman embarked on a new civil career in 1858. Ironically, it was in

the profession he had previously rejected—the law—and through
the aid of him who was now in a dual sense his father-in-law. Two
of Thomas Ewing's sons, both lawyers, had opened a practice at
Leavenworth, in Kansas, and he entrusted his share of the interest
to Sherman, who became the senior partner in the new firm of
Sherman and Ewing, the idea being that Sherman should look
after the financial side, for which his banking experience qualified
him. Nevertheless, he felt that he ought to take out a license to practise, and was somewhat amusingly relieved of the need to develop
his early studies to examination standard by the decision of the
United States Judge Lecompte to admit him on the ground of "general intelligence." But this qualification did not avail, on the only
occasion when he used his license, to win his case.

Much of his work, and the most valuable, was done in surveying
new areas and roads. And his flair for topography served to prevent certain further accessions to those unending disputes which
arose from lawyer-drawn "lines." A most unprofitable flair from a
lawyer's point of view. We are not surprised to hear that, although
his firm's connection grew, profits did not grow in proportion.

The question of constructing a railroad to the Pacific coast was
then being considered by the government and at his brother's request, Sherman prepared a personal report on the problem, the
route and the method, which his brother, with more than brotherly
praise, termed the "best statement of the arguments pro and con,
and the difficulties to be overcome" that he had seen.

Soon afterwards John Sherman went abroad on a holiday, which
coincided with the opening of the war in Italy, of 1859. William
was full of friendly envy, and a letter to John shows how keenly he
was waiting for news of the campaign, and is remarkable for its insight into the strategic situation. His comments are prefaced by
the fervent wish, "I should like of all things to be in your stead,"
and with accurate prophecy he continues, "I think ere this I would
be near the Lake of Maggiori, within a circuit of thirty miles of
which, I feel satisfied, will be or have been fought several great
battles."

The atmosphere of Leavenworth, indeed was not good for Sherman's peace of mind. By bringing him into contact with the army
—for it was a garrison post—it reminded him too strongly of the

life he loved but no longer shared, the career that he had sacrificed for a mess of pottage, as it seemed. Drawn as if by a magnet he had gone up to the fort on arrival, and from there had written to his wife a self-revealing note: "I got here the evening before last and am perfectly at home with drum and bugle, with officers and soldiers whom I know not of former acquaintance save of one, but because I know their feelings and prejudices. I doubt if ever I can gain the same knowledge of the secret recesses of citizens at large."

This attraction and reaction were the more intense because of the repulsion which he felt for the civil settlers. Indeed, his early impression was that "thus far Kansas has been settled by lawyers and politicians instead of farmers and mechanics." It was the winter of Sherman's discontent, and even when spring came to Kansas there was little spring in Sherman's heart. He hid it from the world, save in so far as the discerning might diagnose the cause of his more frequent eruptions of temper, but at last to his wife gave vent—"I am doomed to be a vagabond, and shall no longer struggle against my fate. . . . I look on myself as a dead cock in the pit and will take the chances as they come. . . ."

If spring came late it came at last. This was written in mid-April, 1859, and, belying his own resignation, Sherman wrote in June to an old acquaintance, Major D. C. Buell, then assistant adjutant-general in the War Department, to ask if there was any vacancy among the army paymasters or in any other semi-military employment. Buell replied that although such a vacancy might occur, "You must remember, however, that in these times everything turns on political or other influence." "In the meantime, however, I enclose you a paper which presents an opening that I have been disposed to think well of." This was the prospectus of a new "military college" about to be inaugurated by the State of Louisiana, to be called the "Louisiana Seminary of Learning"—to which were shortly added the words "and Military Academy"—and later to become the Louisiana State University. "If you could secure one of the professorships and the superintendency, as I think you could, it will give the handsome salary of $3,500." Buell added that General G. Mason Graham, the half-brother of Sherman's old commander in California, had strong influence in the appointment.

As so frequently in his career Sherman was now to benefit by the solid reputation he had made with those for whom he had worked. It is, indeed, curious to note that although he had strong family influence in political quarters this was of little service, and that he consistently mounted by steps cut, by hard work, in the hearts of hard task-masters whom he had served. His application was warmly backed by Buell and Mason Graham, who even sought to pave the way for his candidate by a skilful "puff" in the local press—it is an ironical reflection that the "Fourth Estate" so abused by Sherman should have been enlisted to improve his estate.

But there were many candidates, each with their backers, and the electoral body, meeting on a hot and sultry August day, had waded through a mass of applications backed with glowing testimonials when they came to this brief contrast:

"Sir: Having been informed that you wish a superintendent and professor of engineering. . . . I beg leave to offer myself for the position. I send no testimonials. . . . I will only say that I am a graduate of West Point and an ex-army officer; and if you care to know further about me, I refer you to the officers of the army from General Scott down, and in your own state to Col. Braxton Bragg, Major G. T. Beauregard, and Richard Taylor, Esq.

Yours respectfully,

W. T. Sherman."

Directly this letter was read, Sam Henarie, a plain, and perspiring business man, exclaimed: "By God, he's my man. He's a man of sense. I'm ready for the vote!" The President of the board protested that there were many more to read, only to meet the retort, "Well, *you* can read them, but let me out of here, while you are reading." But he duly returned in time to add his vote to those which gave Sherman the double post. Time of the year and economy of time had been sponsors hardly less useful than Mason Graham and Buell. No others were called on.

CHAPTER III

AN ANCHORAGE IN THE SOUTH

So in September Sherman, leaving his family behind, came south to take up his residence at the "Seminary," a fine building situated on the Red River near Alexandria. He had already prepared himself by a "reconnaissance of the ground"—throwing his net wide to gain information as to the methods adopted in the Virginia Military Institute and similar colleges. He visited the one in Kentucky, and also sought the advice of Captain G. B. McClellan, of the Illinois Central Railroad, both on the systems of foreign institutions and on the choice of engineering text-books.

The pleasure of his journey south was marred by the discovery, in conversation with his fellow travellers, that an ominous neap-tide of feeling was rising in the slave States. "I find southern men, even as well informed as ——, as big fools as the abolitionists. Though [John] Brown's expedition proves clearly that the northern people oppose slavery in the abstract . . . very few go so far as to act. Yet the extreme southrons pretend to think that the northern people have nothing to do but to steal niggers and to preach sedition."

But on reaching Alexandria he was cheered by the cordiality of his personal reception, and found full occupation for his mind in the labours of creating an organization on a foundation which consisted only of the bare floors and walls of the college building, without even a chair, table or blackboard—although he certainly had the advantage of a "clean slate." But he had need of diplomacy in order to use his own chalk upon this.

The board of supervisors was split into two sections of opinion as to the curriculum. Mason Graham, the vice-president, wanted it to be modelled on the strict routine and discipline of West Point, and looked to Sherman as the apostle of West Point smartness. Another of life's little ironies. The opposing party wanted the military aspect to be kept in the background, and the institution to be conducted on university lines. The cleavage of opinion placed

Sherman in a difficult position—all the more because he did not share Graham's belief in extreme "militarism," but desired greater elasticity of spirit and system. He had planned to adapt the uniform, the hours of study and drill, and the terms to the conditions of climate, and to invest the limited amount of military training with such interest as to whet the boys' appetite for soldiering, where his own had been sated. By showing Mason Graham that moderation was the way to overcome opposition on the board and among parents, he gained Graham to his own way with the boys.

In preparing the college for their reception he was sustained by faith, hope and charity, but little else. Little money was available, and he was sorely tried by the dilatory ways of the South in meeting his elementary requirements, and in delivering the furnishings he ordered. There was, however, an old rail-fence around the college and a large pile of boards. Engaging four carpenters he set them to work making school-furniture from these. A proof that, given energy and the gift of improvisation, bricks can be made without straw.

In this work he took a hand, as well as a voice, to urge on the carpenters, and himself lived and messed with them. Humorously he comments to his wife on this experience: "I had rather a lonely Christmas, nobody here but my poor drummer and myself. . . . The old cook Amy always hid away for me the last piece of butter and made my breakfast and dinner better than the carpenters', always saying she 'knowed' I wasn't used to such living. She don't know what I have passed through." He continues: "Negroes on plantations are generally allowed holiday the whole week but we can't give it here, as their work is devoted to clearing up after the dirt of plastering, painting, tobacco spitting over seventy-two rooms, halls and galleries." He had received several invitations for Christmas, including one from Sam Henarie, but had declined all rather than leave the property unprotected.

His reward came when, promptly to time, the college opened on New Year's Day, 1860, with five professors and nineteen cadets, aged between fifteen and twenty-one. Fifty-nine cadets should have come, and eventually did, drifting in a few each day in "southern fashion." His own labours, however, increased, for he had to combine the rôles of superintendent, treasurer, commissary, and even, for a time, be steward as well. Perhaps it was fortunate, in view of his limited qualifications as a professor of engineering that "few cadets were yet sufficiently advanced to take his classes," and so he was enabled instead to lecture them in a subject that he did know—geography. His listeners in after years remembered "his clear, instructive and often original presentation." For if his own range of knowledge was limited, perhaps because of it, he had an acute perception of the receptive limits of others. And, as David Boyd, one of his professors and post-war successor, relates, "He had no patience with inefficient teaching, whether from want of ability or too much ability, rendering it difficult for the learned savant to come down to the plane of comprehension of beginners."

An anecdote lends point to this comment. Anthony Vallas, the fat and prosy professor of mathematics and philosophy, asked permission to give a formal inaugural lecture, which Sherman attended. Vallas "talked as he might have talked to the faculty and seniors of Harvard. I noticed Sherman looking glum and biting his lips; and the lecture over, passing out near him . . . he whispered, 'Every damned shot went clear over their heads!'" Boyd, who tells the story, adds, "But he soon clipped the wings of our grandiloquently soaring eagle, and made him a plain barnyard fowl—a practical, useful instructor."

"He was not himself a scholar in the professional sense . . . [but] he was eminently practical; and whatever subject it was necessary or desirable for him to be informed about, his strong, quick mind soon went to the bottom of it." Boyd declared that Sherman had the intuition of genius more than any other man he, ever met. "His mind went like lightning to his conclusions, and he had the utmost faith in his inspirations and convictions." In illustration Boyd relates that Sherman once said to him, "Never give reasons for what you think or do until you must. Maybe, after a while, a better reason will pop into your head." If the *mot* is both characteristic and amusing, it does not altogether establish Sherman's neglect of reasoning in favour of intuition, for psychologically it is not an uncommon, if uncommonly confessed, tendency of the acute expository mind. All reasoning is not "slow motion."

Another aspect of Sherman's highly developed mind is revealed in the remark that "He was a natural born detective. From the least little clue he would infer what a cadet was doing." Tecumseh was certainly an inspired name for him.

But he used this power only for sympathetic understanding of his charges. "In the 'off hours' from duty or drill he encouraged the cadets to look him up and have a talk. And often have I seen his private rooms nearly full of boys listening to his stories. . . . Nor could he appear on the grounds in recreation hours without the cadets one by one gathering around him for a talk . . . the magnetism of the man riveted us all to him very closely, especially the cadets. . . . And if a cadet fell sick . . . he was at his bedside several times a day and at night, watching him closely, consoling and encouraging him."

Let us pause for a moment to see the physical impression he made at this stage of his career—"Tall, angular, with figure slightly bent, bright hazel eyes and auburn hair; with a tuft of it behind that would, when he was a little excited, stick straight out." That danger signal must have been raised often during the first few months.

For Sherman had a hard tussle, of his character against their up-bringing, before he acquired the ascendency over the boys to which Boyd, and others, bear witness. The board of supervisors had recognized and summarized the problem when in their opening announcement they had declared that "the greatest obstacle in the way of the success of southern schools is found in the inherent propensity of southern youth to resist authority and control. . . . This difficulty is admirably overcome by the military system in which the young men are themselves made an essential element in the governing power."

But the system which Sherman designed to apply, even though modified from that of West Point and more akin to the prefectorial system of the English public school, had not only a difficult subject but an unsuitable instrument in the hot-blooded and home-pampered youth of Louisiana.

At first, curiosity and novelty aided the attempt. So great was the former that one youth rode in from a place one hundred and twenty-five miles distant to discover whether it "am a fact" that such an institution had been opened. And Sherman, writing to his wife on January 27, mentions that "we have had many visitors, ladies with children, who part with them with tears and blessings, and I remark the fact that the dullest boys have the most affectionate mothers, and the most vivacious boys come recommended with all the virtues of saints. Of course I promise to be a father to them all."

For a few weeks the boys were inclined to treat as a picnic the task of making their own beds and sweeping out their own rooms, instead of being waited on by ever-ready slaves. But as the novelty wore off they became restive, and southern tempers fretted against the authority of "prefects." Especially of "prefects" who had not learnt self-discipline. A cadet sergeant provoked a junior, who brought out his knife in resentment. Sherman investigated the case and expelled both. Thereupon, in protest, several other boys left, and went home to pour their grievances into fond ears—and were promptly posted by Sherman as "deserters." Other boys had sought relief from irksome discipline by smashing crockery, ragging the servants, and smearing professorial chairs—not Sherman's—with hair-grease. When checked they complained to their parents that they were "treated like negroes," and an indignant father wrote to ask, "Will our sons submit to the arbitrary commands of dictators."

Sherman mentions to his wife: "We have just passed through a critical week, the struggle for mastery resulting in five boys being gone. It would take a volume to record it, but I am now rid of five noisy, insubordinate boys. . . . There can be but one master,"— and laughingly adds: "I must now rest satisfied with the title of the 'Old Man,' the 'cross old schoolmaster.' "

This tussle he did not mind, even enjoyed it for its demand on his personality, but the prospect of temporary unpopularity, and consequent check on the inflow of pupils, accentuated a greater difficulty. This was the delay in passing a bill for the state endowment of the institution—and such endowment Sherman held to be necessary for an adequate scheme of education and an adequate remuneration for himself. His impatience was aggravated owing to overtures which had been made to him by a banking firm—to go to London as their representative, and there open a branch. Others evidently thought more highly of his ability as a banker than he did himself. And the offer meant a much higher return than he could hope for in the scholastic world.

His uncertainty of mind is wittily disclosed to his wife: "If you hear I have concluded to stay here, just make up your mind to live and die here, because I am going to take the bit in my mouth, and resume my military character, and control my own affairs. Since I left New Orleans, I have felt myself oppressed by circumstances I could not control, but I begin to feel [a] footing and will get saucy. But if I go to England, I shall expect a universal panic, the repudiation of the great National Debt, and a blow up generally. I suppose I was the Jonah that blew up San Francisco, and it took only two months' residence in Wall Street to bust up New York, and I think my arrival in London will be the signal of the downfall of that mighty empire. Here I can't do much harm, if I can't do any good; and here we have solitude and banishment enough to hide from the misfortunes of the past.

"Therefore, if Louisiana will endow this college properly, and is fool enough to give me $5000 a year, we will drive our tent pins and pick out a magnolia under which to sleep the long sleep. But if she don't, then England must perish, for I predict financial misfortune to the land that receives me. . . ."

The possibility so alarmed Mason Graham that he wrote to the Governor of Louisiana entreating him to immediate action, because "we are in imminent danger of losing our irreplaceable superintendent, the apprehension of which has kept me awake for more than half the night." In urging the solution of the salary problem, Mason Graham declared, "I have never known a less sordid and unselfish gentleman," and pointed out that "It will not be this amount of money which will influence him so much, as the relief he will thereby experience from the apprehension which is becoming somewhat morbid with him, that occurring political events, and the position of his brother in the U. S. Congress, may or do conspire to affect his position and usefulness here."

While Mason Graham pleaded with the Governor, Bragg pleaded with Sherman—"The more you see of our society . . . the more you will be impressed with the importance of a change in our system of education if we expect the next generation to be anything

more than a mere aggregation of loafers . . . squandering their
fathers' legacies and disgracing their names. I hoped, and still
hope, your Seminary may be the entering wedge of a reformation. . . ."

For two of Sherman's staunchest supporters now were Bragg
and Beauregard—who sent, originally, one son, and then a second.
Two men who, two years hence, were to be his opponents on the field
of Shiloh, and subsequently the unavailing obstructors of his cul-
minating advance through the Carolinas. Was ever the irony of
history so exquisite! That not only the South, but these two men
in particular, should have striven, successfully, to prevent his
migration from America, and perchance his total abstention from
influence on the war. For the London post meant a two years' contract, to a man scrupulous of contracts, and with this delay his rise
to supreme command in the West would scarcely have been possible.

The "joke" was deeper far than Sherman realized when he said
to his brother-in-law: "I cannot but laugh in my sleeve at the seeming influence I possess, dining with the Governor, hobnobbing with
the leading men of Louisiana, whilst John is universally black-
guarded as an awful abolitionist." His laughter, however, was the
only thing he concealed. For even at that exalted dinner-table,
with his fortune in the balance, and heated slave-owners all round
him, he expressed his views freely and defended his brother, while
disagreeing with the extravagance of his brother's speeches. So,
too, when the unknowing asked if he was related to the "black"
John Sherman, he replied, "Only a brother and I don't care who
knows it." And by southern witness he invariably testified his
belief that "the Union was supreme and secession treason. We all
knew what he thought and what he would do if war came."

Equal honour is due to the man who spoke and to those who
heard him. None ever abused his brother when they knew he was
his brother, nor gave the least hurt to the feelings of one whose
fearless honesty cloaked an almost morbid sensitiveness. What a
testimony to the chivalry of these southern gentlemen! The consideration shown to him in Louisiana was, if unconsciously, a fit
return for the consideration which he also had shown.

On his way thither in September, 1859, he had written to beg his
brother to "take the highest ground consistent with your party

creed," and continued to urge on him moderation of view and expression. "The rampant southern feeling is not so strong in Louisiana as in Mississippi and Carolina. Still, holding many slaves, they naturally feel the intense anxiety all must whose property and existence depend on the safety of their property and labour. . . . It would be the height of folly to drive the South to desperation, and I hope, after the fact is admitted that the North has the majority and right to control national matters and interests, that they will use their power so as to reassure the South that there is no intention to disturb the actual existence of slavery." [Jan. 16, 1860.]

Next month he regretfully ruminated on various "bad signs," chief among them the growing and glib acceptance of the idea of disunion. "I was in hopes that the crisis would have been deferred till the States of the North-west became so populous as to hold both extremes in check. Disunion would be civil war, and you politicians would lose all charm."

If his concern was enhanced by his own position, his desire for a peaceful solution had been manifested long before he had thought of going South. And, as an earlier letter to his wife shows, his fear of his brother's fiery speeches was less on his own account than because it imperilled his labours.

"His extreme position on that question will prejudice me, not among the supervisors, but in the legislature where the friends of the Seminary must look for help. . . . Of course there are many here . . . that know I am not an abolitionist. Still if the simple fact that my nativity and my relationship with Republicans should prejudice the institution I would feel disposed to sacrifice myself to that fact, though the results would be very hard, for I know not what else to do.

"If the Southern States should organize for the purpose of leaving the Union I could not go with them. If that event be brought about by the insane politicians I will ally my fate with the North, for the reason that the slave question will ever be a source of discord even in the South. So long as the abolitionists and the Republicans seem to threaten the safety of slave property so long will this excitement last, and no one can foresee its result; but all here talk as if a dissolution of the Union were not only a possibility but

a probability of easy execution.   If attempted we shall have civil
war of the most horrible kind. . . ."

While his wife's influence was cast in the scales against the
Louisiana post from a motherly fear of physical epidemics, Sherman's mind tilted in its disfavour from fear of a moral epidemic.
If also from faith in the superior virtues of hard cash.   For unless
honour, truth, or duty was at stake, it is a biographer's impression
that Sherman's thought was apt to balance on his bank-balance.   In
so far at least had the new money god of the Middle West set its
seal on his brow.

Thus, although his conditions were mainly met, he still inclined
towards London rather than Louisiana, and took leave in order to
go north to investigate the former offer before giving his decision on
the latter.   Even so there are signs of relief in his decision that the
financial side of the London offer was not as clear cut and secure
as he considered necessary.   Signs, too, of pleasure in going back
to his boys who "hailed my return as though I was their grandfather."   His unreserved decision cost him $500, for with a financial
sense at least as marked as his own, the Governor had previously,
but privily, decided that "we can afford to give the Major an additional one thousand dollars salary which I trust will retain him,
but I would agree to the five thousand dollars rather than lose him."

The second term opened in May with sixty-two cadets, the addition of "Military Academy" to the name, of Colonel to Sherman's,
and recognition of the Seminary as a State arsenal.   Although there
was still opposition on the board to the military system, parents
were now seeing the virtues of, and the boys responding to, Sherman's interpretation of it.   For directly the challenge to his
authority had been abandoned he guided the boys on a light rein.
Nor did he forget the lump of sugar, peculiarly acceptable to a
southern colt.   It was the more natural for him to indulge the
Louisiana love of gaiety, because he himself had changed per-
ceptibly since those youthful days at Charleston when he scorned
the fair company and ballrooms of the South.   He had now been
married ten years.   So, "fond himself of young society and dancing he gave the cadets frequent hops, the planters and their pretty
daughters coming in swarms."   Boyd, who served the one in peace,

the other in war, declared that Sherman and Stonewall Jackson had much the same type of mind, but remarked, "how strange the contrast that Jackson, the stern, ascetic, ever-praying Puritan in religion, if not in blood, was a southern leader, while Sherman the gay, joyous, lively man of the world . . . was a northern general."

But by encouraging, even taking the lead in these parties, Sherman was able to make them a social lesson. Expenses were kept down to a level at which all could afford to share equally, so that the poorer boys felt neither a strain on their resources nor a strain on their self-respect—as would have been the result of allowing the wealthier to bear a larger burden of the hospitality.

There is another sidelight on Sherman's sense of the subtler educative values in his care for the planning of the new buildings and the lay-out of the grounds. For, as he told Mason Graham, "where a taste for beauty and fine scenery is inculcated, look for the qualities that adorn society and give stability to a state. I would then at the Seminary attach much importance to embellishment. Not costly gravelled walks and artificially trimmed trees, but a general care of the natural features with enough art to set it off."

So, save for the rumbling murmurs of the coming storm, the summer passed tranquilly, the internal calm of this secluded retreat only once seriously disturbed. As a sequel to a "rag" in which the servants suffered, Sherman expelled two more cadets— not for ragging, but for a lying explanation. His summary act caused some doubts among the supervisors, because these boys were of "good families and large connections." Sherman held his ground firmly—"The truly penitent shall never appeal to me in vain, but hypocrisy and falsehood shall, when I can, be spotted and blotted out."

At the end of July the cadets dispersed for the vacation, which lasted until November, and Sherman went north, first to Lancaster and then to Washington, to procure muskets and equipment for the cadets, as well as a library. Whether a sign of Sherman's good name or of the Government's good faith, the War Department made no difficulty about handing over the two hundred muskets for which Sherman asked. The local Alexandria paper thereupon said gleefully, and with unconscious irony, "That looks like getting the sons of Alexandria ready for an emergency of civil war or servile insurrection that may arise; the thanks of the people of the State are due to Colonel Sherman for his promptness and efficiency, not only in this important matter but in everything that pertains to the good of the Seminary."

On returning to Ohio to relax for once in the midst of his family, Sherman was the more impressed with the bounteousness of the harvest because his mail from Louisiana brought news of the exceptional poorness of the crops. A not insignificant historical fact, because it generated a current of dissatisfaction easily inflammable, a grievance with nature that could find a target in man. But to Sherman the contrast suggested a deeper lesson—"May it not be one of the facts stronger than blind prejudice to show the mutual dependence of one part of our magnificent country on the other."

The mail from Louisiana brought another disturbing piece of news. In his absence the tussle of views and wills on the board of supervisors had continued, and culminated in concessions to the opponents of the military system, among them the formation of an Academic Board to share the control. Unwilling to accept the compromise which his extreme military "line" had provoked, Mason Graham resigned the vice-presidency. Although Sherman doubted the practicability of this duality of control, it is a tribute to his personality that the board found him more rather than less indispensable.

In November the new term saw an increase to a hundred and thirty cadets, while the college now, by local verdict, was "running beautifully in all its departments." But if there was a new spirit of discipline among the boys, there was also a new restlessness. One small and yet significant symptom was that in elocution classes they chose selections from the speeches of fervent southern orators. And outside the institution excitement ran high over the presidential election. Back in June Sherman had warned his brother that "this year's presidential election will be a dangerous one; may actually result in civil war . . ." and warned him, further, that however "reasonable and moderate" Lincoln might be, his name was like a red rag to the South, and so a more dangerous Republican nomination even than Seward. "All the reasoning and truth in the world would not convince a southern man that the Republicans are not abolitionists . . . reason has very little influence in this world:

prejudice governs. You and all who derive power from the people do not look for pure, unalloyed truth, but to that kind of truth which jumps with the prejudice of the day. So southern politicians do the same." While he was on holiday, friends in Louisiana had sent him ominous accounts of the growth of feeling so strong, they said, that "whoever accepts or holds office under Lincoln will be lynched."

Now back in Louisiana, and on the eve of the election, he tells his wife "In case Lincoln is elected, they say South Carolina will secede and that the Southern States will not see her forced back." So strong did feeling run that he received a friendly hint that he would be wise to vote for the Democratic ticket, but he sturdily refused to vote, declaring: "If I am to hold my place by a political tenure, I prefer again to turn vagabond."

Immediately after Lincoln's election he notices "that many gentlemen who were heretofore moderate in their opinions now begin to fall into the popular current, and go with the mad, foolish crowd that seems bent on a dissolution of this confederacy." From the viewpoint of grand strategy he examines the consequences if South Carolina, Alabama, Georgia, Florida and Texas secede. "All these might go and still leave a strong rich confederated government, but then comes Mississippi and Louisiana. As these rest on the Mississippi and control its mouth, I know that the other States north will not submit to any molestation of navigation by foreign states. If these two states and Arkansas follow suit then there must be war, fighting and that will continue till one or the other party is subdued."

For his own part his decision is already made, and its fulfilment turns on a simpler issue. He had been waiting to welcome his wife to the house newly built for them, but on November 26, he writes to say that if South Carolina and Alabama secede "Then it would be unsafe even for you to come South. For myself, I will not go with the South in a disunion movement, and as my position at the head of a State Military College would necessarily infer fidelity and allegiance to the State as against the United States, my duty will be on the first positive act of disunion to give notice. . . ."

Then in successive letters to wife and brother, we see the fast-flowing tide sweeping Louisiana to war. On November 29 he notes a new and "ugly" tone in the Governor's proclamation, "business dead in New Orleans," and "signs of loosened discipline" in the school. On December 1: "The quiet . . . was merely the prelude to the storm of opinion that now seems irresistible. Politicians, by hearing the prejudices of the people and running with the current, have succeeded in destroying the government." On December 9, "all attempts at reconciliation will fail, Louisiana will follow where others lead." Next, following the definite secession of South Carolina, on December 20—"Governor Moore takes the plain stand that the State must not submit to a black Republican President. Men here have ceased to reason. . . ."

Sherman adds that "A rumour says that Major Anderson, my old captain, has spiked the guns of Fort Moultrie, destroyed it, and taken refuge in Sumter. This is right. Sumter is in mid-channel . . . whereas Moultrie is old, weak and easily approached under cover. If Major Anderson can hold out till relieved and supported by steam frigates, South Carolina will find herself unable to control her commerce, and will feel for the first time in her existence, that she can't do as she pleases."

His brother was urging him to quit—"The very moment you feel uncomfortable in your position in Louisiana, come away. Don't, for God's sake, subject yourself to any slur, reproach or indignity." But no one in his circle ever subjected Sherman to slur or suspicion. The explanation, apart from southern chivalry, is given by Boyd— "The threatening of war disturbed him—pained him more I really think, than any one knew. He was constantly talking about it, openly as well as privately. But his moral courage, his free, outspoken thought commanded the respect of the people of Louisiana. Besides he was so singularly efficient . . . and so universally popular, that there was no feeling against him . . . only a general regret that so good and true a man differed from us. The question of the leading men of Louisiana was to keep him there at the head of the school, his opposition to secession notwithstanding."

But on January 10, 1861, the cock crew. That day the United States arsenal at Baton Rouge was surrounded—and surrendered— by order of Governor Moore, although Louisiana had not yet seceded. By supreme irony a part of the seized arms were consigned to Sherman—as superintendent of a State arsenal—who felt not merely "a receiver of stolen goods" but an accessory to "treason."

In a letter of January 16, to his wife, he tells her: "I went to Alexandria in a hard rain yesterday. . . . I spoke my mind fully and clearly, that these were acts of unjustifiable war, and that I could no longer remain silent. I asked to be relieved." There is unconscious humour in the words "no longer remain silent." He asks her to look out for some job for him as he "would not stay in Ohio ten days without employment," living on the charity of relations.

Two days later, although begged to postpone his decision, he sent his resignation to Governor Moore, president of the board of supervisors, saying: "As I occupy a quasi-military position under the laws of the State I deem it proper to acquaint you that I accepted such position when Louisiana was a State in the Union, and when the motto of this Seminary was inserted in marble over the main door: 'By the liberality of the Government of the United States. The Union—*esto perpetua.*' Recent events foreshadow a great change, and it becomes all men to choose. If Louisiana withdraw from the Federal Union, I hope to maintain my allegiance to the Constitution as long as a fragment of it survives, and my longer stay here would be wrong in every sense of the word. . . . I beg you to take immediate steps to relieve me as superintendent, the moment the State determines to secede, for on no earthly account will I do any act or think any thought hostile to or in defiance of the old Government of the United States."

In acknowledging his letter "with the deepest regret" the Governor replied: "You cannot regret more than I do the necessity which deprives us of your services, and you will bear with you the respect, confidence, and admiration, of all who have been associated with you." The hand which actually penned this letter was that of Braxton Bragg, now the recognized leader of Louisiana's military preparations. Another who regretted Sherman's decision as deeply was Mason Graham, whose distress was not even alleviated by the martial exhilaration of the moment. "Whatever we may think and feel we must go along with our section in the contest which has been forced upon us. I did what I could to make the people sensible of this before the election, but . . . now we must all go over the cataract together." Not all in Louisiana were firebrands, but fatalistic patriots also contribute to fatality.

The step, to him irrevocable, taken, Sherman busied himself in settling up affairs and accounts, determined that the College should suffer as little interruption as possible in its smooth-running, and that his successor, when appointed, should be able to grasp the controls without fumbling. So careful of the interests entrusted him, and yet equally careful to ensure that he himself before departure received every dollar justly due to him.

But even during these weeks, members of the board were striving to change his decision, assuring him that war would not follow secession, that the Government at Washington would not take up the gauge. These assurances carried no weight with Sherman who, looking with the eyes of a grand strategist upon the economic physiology of the national body—in which war is but a symptom of a diseased peace—diagnosed the condition thus—"even if the Southern States be allowed to depart in peace, the first question will be revenue. Now, if the South have free trade, how can you collect revenues in the eastern cities. Freight from New Orleans to St. Louis, Chicago, Louisville, Cincinnati, and even Pittsburgh, would be about the same as by rail from New York, and importers at New Orleans, having no duties to pay, would undersell the East if they had to pay duties. Therefore, if the South make good their confederation and their plan, the Northern Confederacy must do likewise or blockade. Then comes the question of foreign nations. So, look on it in any view, I see no result but war and consequent change in the form of government."

If he realized that war was inevitable, it was infinitely more repugnant to him than to more superficial patriots, and even the unaffected affection shown by those who bade him farewell brought little consolation of spirit on his journey northwards—the fourth change in four years, "each time from calamity." Soon his old friends, colleagues and pupils followed him, but under a different banner and with arms in their hands. One of them, Boyd, was to share in Stonewall Jackson's brilliant campaign in the Shenandoah Valley, to cherish the memory of his great leader, and yet to leave no doubt that he regarded Sherman as the greater man as well as "the master grand strategist of our Civil War."

CHAPTER IV

STUDY OF A REALIST IN WONDERLAND

THUS it was in a mood of extreme depression that Sherman made his way north. He had gone south with high hope that at last his weather-beaten fortune had reached a fair haven. Professionally and personally, these hopes had been justified. In the South he had at last found a secure anchorage. And then a cataclysm of nature—human nature—had not merely disturbed the surface of the water but changed the whole face of the land. His career was adrift once more. Adrift, because where there had been a harbour there was now no longer one—blotted out by the earthquake. It was a crowning irony of fate, after surviving so many local storms in which his bark had nearly foundered.

His depression, too, was deepened by his feeling that the disaster had been the outcome of futility and not of fatality, that the fortunes of the nation and of himself had been wrecked by the folly of politicians against which he had so long and so helplessly pleaded. Taking the long view, the economic view, he had been sure that the political will of the North must ultimately prevail through the pressure of economic force. Now political hastiness had transferred to the uncertain arbitrament of the sword a case that, in his judgment, was already settled. And his impressions of the earnest spirit and military preparedness of the South, in comparison with the apathy and unreadiness of the North—except with its tongues—led him to despair almost of the outlook. For the worst would be that there was neither victor nor vanquished, but only a common loss. That loss would be the future of the United States.

In this mood, and with this feeling, he could not share in any military enthusiasm. Nay, not even in the prospect of renewing his old love and returning to his old profession. The politicians had created the conflict; they "might fight it out." They had dug the pit, and as he had no confidence in their power to struggle out, he had no wish to drop in too. For only if the still united states put forth all their energy could the United States be re-created, and for anything less it would be folly, and worse, to fight.

His just pessimism, based on realism, was intensified—and his personal attitude strengthened—soon after his return north. At Lancaster he had found two letters. One from John asking him to go to Washington; the other from his old partner, Turner, which held out the prospect of an appointment as "President of the Fifth Street Railroad"—a post the importance of which was more accurately gauged by its modest salary of two thousand five hundred dollars than by its imposing title. Both Turner and Lucas were working to secure Sherman's appointment, and he gratefully replied that he would accept, although he felt that he ought to go to Washington, to consult with his brother, while the election to this office was pending.

If anything could have deepened his gloom it was the atmosphere at Washington. "Even in the War Department and about the public offices there was open, unconcealed talk, amounting to high-treason." And among the loyal there seemed little grasp of the situation. Ignorance and inertia were enthroned. That the Government should postpone preparations, in order not to inflame Southern feelings while there was still a possibility of negotiating, was an attitude with which Sherman could sympathize. But that it should remain inert from an incapacity to appreciate the reality of Southern determination was a folly that made him despair. Least of all men could Sherman suffer fools gladly. And among these he was for a moment inclined to class Lincoln.

For he had been taken by his brother to see the President. The conversation was neither prolonged nor inspiring. "Mr. President, this is my brother, Colonel Sherman, who is just up from Louisiana, he may give you some information you want." "Ah, how are they getting along down there?" "They think they are getting along swimmingly—they are preparing for war." "Oh, well, I guess we'll manage to keep house." The careless tone reminds us of that more famous incident, not long after, when the seizure of four Confederate passengers from the British steamer, *Trent*, provoked an additional crisis, and Lincoln met anxious enquiries as to the issue of the case with the equally casual comment, "Oh, that'll be got along with."

If Sherman's second impression of Lincoln was to be a revised impression, perhaps it was not only the impression which had changed, and deepened. Burdened with cares as was the President, this lack of interest in a chance to obtain first-hand information from one uniquely placed to obtain it, to tap the inner feelings of the influential in Louisiana, was not suggestive of political wisdom. The casual manner and the complacent phrase froze up the outlet of the information so copiously stored in Sherman's mind, and, lacking encouragement he made no further conversational opening, beyond an offer of his services which was met with a smiling rebuff—"We shall not need many men like you, the affair will soon blow over." Deeply chagrined, Sherman was glad to quit the room. Only when he got outside did his unwonted silence break, and then he showered on John his curses on all politicians—"you have got things in a hell of a fix and you may get them out as best you can."

When John pleaded with him for patience, in the interest at least of his career, he retorted that if the country chose to sleep on a volcano, he was going to seek a safer dwelling at St. Louis. With his customary rapidity he took a train for Lancaster, collected his family and furniture, and moved thence to St. Louis in anticipation of his own election to a humbler "presidency." It is a proof of the depth of mind beneath the turbulent surface of his temperament that, in this hour of personal and patriotic disappointment, he could write—"Lincoln has an awful task, and if he succeeds in avoiding strife and allaying fears, he will be entitled to the admiration of the world; but a time has occurred in all governments, and has now occurred in this, when force must back the laws, and the longer the postponement, the more severe must be the application."

On April 1, having been duly elected, he took charge of his street tramway. The choice of April Fool's Day was apt, for if Mahomet did not wish to come to the mountain, the mountain would erupt under him, and in its eruption uproot his refuge, of spirit as well as of place. Zealously as he devoted himself to his new work, he was soon to be driven out by force of events to handle a greater piece of transportation than that of a service of horse-drawn street cars. Nor did he take much driving. For no one was ever less suited to the vocation of a hermit than William Tecumseh Sherman. And in the eventful year, 1861, a street-car office in St. Louis was as unnatural an isolation, however modern and American in its form, as the solitary pedestal of St. Simon Stylites.

His temperament, moreover, is the clue to his outwardly perplexing attitude a few days later when he had, and rejected, the opportunity to exchange his lowly refuge for another, as elevated as Simon's and much safer.   For on the evening of April 6, he received this urgent message from Washington:

"MAJOR W. T. SHERMAN:
Will you accept the chief clerkship of the War Department?   We will make you assistant Secretary of War when Congress meets.
                                M. BLAIR, *Postmaster-General*."

Laconically, Sherman answered by telegram "I cannot accept," and by letter elaborated but hardly elucidated his attitude:

"Office St. Louis Railroad Company.
                                Monday, April 8, 1861.
HON. M. BLAIR, *Washington, D. C.*
I received, about nine o'clock Saturday night, your telegraph dispatch, which I have this moment answered, "I cannot accept."
I have quite a large family, and when I resigned my place in Louisiana, on account of secession, I had no time to lose; and, therefore, after my hasty visit to Washington, where I saw no chance of employment, I came to St. Louis, have accepted a place in this Company, have rented a house, and incurred other obligations, so that I am not at liberty to change.
I thank you for the compliment contained in your offer, and assure you that I wish the Administration all success in its almost impossible task of governing this distracted and anarchical people.
                                Yours truly,
                                W. T. SHERMAN."

More truly, a sting in the tail!   Despite the tempestuousness of his speech and manner Sherman was no ardent cavalier, to be swept away in a surge of martial enthusiasm and popular excitement to a gallant but useless sacrifice.   His patriotism was essentially rational, not emotional.   Others might instinctively put the ideal of service first, heedless of the value of that service.   He was too conscious of the value of the cause either to trust or to aid any spurt of ill-founded enthusiasm.   The Kitchener of 1861, he took the long view, and saw that a long war was inevitable, and prepared to await the ripening of opinion. Had his reason for rejecting this offer been as self-centred as its words suggest, he would certainly have accepted it. For it manifestly offered a tenure at least more secure, a remuneration much higher, and a prospect infinitely wider than those of a tramway presidency in a city and a state which were already cracking under the torsional strain of divided sympathies.

The potential value of the Washington post was, indeed, amply indicated in a letter from John Sherman. For although he seemed to endorse William's decision, he mentioned that "Chase is especially desirous that you accept, saying that you would be virtually Secretary of War, and could easily step into any military position that offers." Knowing William's determined nature, and his present mood of disgust, John sought to guide him on a light rein. "By all means take advantage of the present disturbances to get into the army, where you will at once put yourself in a high position for life. . . . You are a favorite in the Army and have great strength in political circles. I urge you to avail yourself of these favorable circumstances to secure your position for life; for, after all, your present employment is of uncertain tenure in these stirring times." Then as a flick of the whip he adds: "those who look on merely as spectators in the storm will fail to discharge the highest duty of a citizen, and suffer accordingly in public estimation."

But neither oats nor whip could make Sherman budge an inch beyond his reasoned position. Outwardly more impetuous than his Senatorial younger brother, inwardly he was more solid. The opening extract from John Sherman's letter reveals indirectly the root of William's opposition to the Washington post—his desire for an active military rôle instead of an office stool, however elevated. And a still deeper layer of resistance was his distaste for a political environment. So, years later, in the heyday of his fame, was he to resist all suggestions of the Presidency.

But, keen though his desire for real military employment, he was in no hurry to seek it. First, because he had a family whose livelihood and future had been jeopardized so often in his past career as to make him wary, for their sake, of making a fifth leap in the dark. Second, because he had no confidence in the military policy of the Government and, at the same time, owing to his long sight, a complete confidence that the government policy, and not his, would have to change.

This patience of an impatient man is one of the rare phenomena of history. Reading this letter let us remember with admiration that it was written in April, 1861—"But I say volunteers and militia never were and never will be fit for invasion, and when tried . . . will be defeated, and dropt by Lincoln like a hot potato. . . . I will bide my time. . . . The first movements of the government will fail and the leaders will be cast aside A second or a third set will rise, and among them I may be, but at present I will not volunteer as a soldier or anything else. If Congress meets, and if a National Convention be called, and the regular army be put on a footing with the wants of the country, if I am offered a place that suits me, I may accept."

The last condition may seem the product of an unduly calculating spirit at a time of national emergency. Calculating, yes; but not in the ordinary sense of self-interest or self-esteem. It would, of course, be absurd to contend that Sherman entirely forgot self. That is not the way of those who rise to high position in any army, and he who cherishes romantic beliefs to the contrary will be disillusioned if he studies history and historical diaries. The best that can be said is that the best men place self second to country.

But, if self was not omitted from Sherman's calculations, their foundation was a realistic grasp of the problem—the balanced opinion that the best service could be rendered by the man who served in the place for which he was best fitted. Such an opinion itself accorded with that adjustment of the end and the means which is the underlying secret of victory.

Other men, many others, have shared Sherman's reluctance to serve in a post inferior to their self-estimated capacity. Where Sherman was exceptional was in the exactness of his estimate. And still more in his equal reluctance to occupy any post which in his judgment was higher than his capacity at any period warranted.

In the early morning of April 12, the Confederate guns had opened fire on Fort Sumter, fired on the stars and stripes. This was the tocsin of war—because it was a toxin in the blood, raising a fever of popular indignation which could not be allayed. Yet, actually, it was not the first act of war—for that had taken place on January 9, when the steamer, *Star of the West*—truly a prophetic name—had been fired on and forced to retire from Charleston harbour with its supplies undelivered to the garrison of Fort Sumter.   Then, however, President Buchanan had, with scriptural obedience, turned the other cheek, and now this also had been duly smitten.   Smitten too hard to ignore.   On Sunday, April 14, at noon, Fort Sumter surrendered, and on Monday morning Lincoln, accepting the challenge, issued a proclamation calling for 75,000 men to serve for three months.   No more apt or pungent comment could be supplied than was done by Sherman, on hearing the news—"Why you might as well attempt to put out the flames of a burning house with a squirt-gun."

But even his brother could not understand Sherman's attitude and sought to goad him into service—"Every man will have to choose his position.   You fortunately have the military education, prominence and character, that will enable you to play a high part in the tragedy.   You can't avoid taking such a part.   Neutrality and indifference are impossible.   Some of your best friends here want you in the War Department. . . . If you want that place, with a sure prospect of promotion, you can have it, but you are not compelled to take it; but it seems to me that you will be compelled to take some position and that speedily. . . . For me, I am for a war that will either establish or overthrow the government and will purify the atmosphere of political life.   We need such a war, and we have it now."

Sherman, however, did not wish to play a part, even a leading part, in any tragedy, still less in a melodrama.   His complaint was that the atmosphere was too full of the stage atmosphere, too lacking in reality.   And he formulated his position in his reply: "If, when Congress meets, a clearly defined policy be arrived at, a clear end to be accomplished, and then the force adequate to that end be provided for, then I could and would act with some degree of confidence, not now."

While he temporarily held aloof, the instinct of the strategist was strong in him, and shrewd sentences of military advice dripped from his pen.   Now in theory as later in practice his mind was irradiated with Napoleon's truth that "the whole secret of the art of war lies in being master of the communications."   Thus as an indispensable preliminary to any policy of expansion and invasion he asserts the need of fulfilling certain conditions. "I take it for granted that Washington is safe; that Pickens can beat off all assailants; that Key West and Tortugas * are strong and able to spare troops for other purposes; that, above all, Fort Monroe"—at the mouth of the James River and astride the sea gateway to Richmond—"is full of men, provisions, and war materials, and that the Chesapeake is strongly occupied. Then the first thing will be the avenues of travel. Baltimore must be made to allow the free transit of troops without question, and the route from Wheeling to the Relay House kept open."

Realizing the vital nature of the approach by Harpers Ferry and the upper Potomac to Pennsylvania he urges the importance of concentrating to guard it and the moral value of route-marching troops through western Maryland, where the scales of feeling hovered in the balance betwixt Union and secession, dipping ominously towards the latter. That he proffered further suggestions we know from his brother's reference to the Secretary of War's approval of certain of them, including the occupation of Fort Smith and an island off Mobile, the vital port in the far South. Whatever the influence of his suggestions it is a tribute to his strategic insight that the possession by the Union of these points proved not only a stepping stone to offensive operations but essential links in the blockade chain which was soon to be forged and tightened round the Confederate arteries of oversea supply.

Moreover, Sherman's vision transcended the military horizon. As a foundation for a policy he urged, to his brother, that "The question of the national integrity and slavery should be kept distinct, for otherwise it will gradually become a war of extermination—a war without end." This rose above strategy to grand strategy, for a clear definition and limitation of the object is fundamental to success and to the economic adjustment of means and end.

Grand strategy, too, permeated his comment of April 25—"I cannot but think that it was a fatal mistake in Mr. Lincoln not to

---

* Fort Pickens in Pensacola Harbour and the forts at Key West and Tortugas off the Florida coast were the only forts which the Union succeeded in holding onto in the South. As early as February 1, Sherman had written from Louisiana to warn his brother—"Fort Sumter is not material, save for the principle; but Key West and Tortugas should be held in force at once, by regulars if possible, if not, by militia. Quick! They are occupied now, but not in force."

tie to his administration by some kind of link the Border States. Now it is too late, and sooner or later Kentucky, Tennessee and Arkansas will be in arms against us. It is barely possible that Missouri may yet be neutral . . . the Governor and the legislature are strongly secession. I understand to-day the orders at the custom-house are to refuse clearances to steamboats to seceding States. All the heavy trade with groceries and provisions is with the South, and this order at once takes all life from St. Louis. Merchants, heretofore for peace and even for backing the administration, will now fall off . . . and the result will possibly be secession, and then free states against slave—the horrible array so long dreaded. I know Frank Blair desired this plain, square issue. It may be that sooner or later it is inevitable, but I cannot bring myself to think so. On the necessity of maintaining a government, and that government the old constitutional one, I have never wavered, but I do recoil from a war, when the negro is the only question."

In a similar but still more prophetic vein were two self-explanatory letters to his wife's family. The first—"I have seen enough of war not to be caught by its first glittering bait, and when I engage in this it must be with a full consciousness of its real character. I did approve of the President's call and only said it should have been three hundred thousand instead of seventy-five. . . ." The second—"The Mississippi River is the hardest and most important task of the war, and I know of no one competent [to undertake it], unless it be McClellan. But as soon as real war begins, new men, heretofore unheard of, will emerge from obscurity, equal to any occasion. Only I think it is to be a long war—very long—much longer than any politician thinks."

The mind of William Tecumseh Sherman as revealed in his letters, not only during this crisis but in the years which preceded it, illuminates not merely the course of his life but the course of history. More statesmanlike than the statesman, as some of the best soldiers have been, he was also more conscious than any soldier of the economic factors which underpin military strength, and more acutely appreciative than either of the limitations of force—physical or legal. As he had argued against any political step tending to precipitate the military settlement of a problem which would, in his view, be gradually resolved by economic laws, so he was now almost unique among statesmen and soldiers in feeling none of the relief which normally follows upon action—after a long period of tension. That vast human sigh of relief is one of the most recurrent phenomena in history, marking the outset of every great conflict, down to 1914.

But when almost all others were swept away by the surge of emotion, Sherman kept his feet on the ground, his head above water, his eyes fixed on the far bank. And equally, while Lincoln and most of his advisers, political and military, believed that a brief military demonstration would suffice to bring the seceding States back to the Union—an opinion shared even by Grant—Sherman realized how distant was the end and how great the means that would be necessary. It is in the light of this "appreciation" that we can understand the reason of his desire to limit the political issue as a means to limit the distance of the goal, and to minimize the possible obstructions which might increase the difficulty of reaching it.

This exchange of views led his brother to understand, if not to relish, his attitude. But to others, in these passionate days, it was more puzzling and popularly to be interpreted by the motive of disloyalty. An interpretation which was the more natural because so many officers had already placed loyalty to their State above loyalty to the Union. The Washington view of the Regular Army is well illustrated in one of John Sherman's letters. "The old army is a manifest discredit. The desertion of so many officers (treachery I had better say), the surrender on parole in Texas of so many officers where all the men were true to their allegiance, has so stained the whole regular course of officers that it will take good conduct on their part to retrieve their old position." This political feeling of resentment was expressed in the appointment of so many volunteer officers to high commands at the outset, and the failure of the North in comparison with the South to utilize professional experience.

In Sherman's case the suspicion of disloyalty also had a reaction, for it impelled him to make his position clear to the War Department. And the coincident action of the President cleared his path. For on May 3 Lincoln decided not only to increase the Regular Army, but to call for volunteers for three years' service. Hence on May 8, Sherman wrote to the Secretary of War: "Dear Sir: I hold myself now, as always, prepared to serve my country in the capacity for which I was trained. I did not and will not volunteer for three months, because I cannot throw my family on the cold support of charity, but for the three years' call made by the President an officer could prepare his command and do good service. I will not volunteer, because, rightfully or wrongfully, I feel myself unwilling to take a mere private's place, and having for many years lived in California and Louisiana, the men are not well enough acquainted with me to elect me to my appropriate place. Should my services be needed, the Record or the War Department will enable you to designate the station in which I can render best service."

The dignity and seemliness of the letter are enhanced when we recall that, as Sherman had recalled to his brother, "Lincoln said to you and me that he did not think he wanted military men."

The War Department was quicker this time to make use of his offer, and only hesitated whether to make him a Major-General of volunteers, or Colonel of one of the new Regular regiments of infantry. He was also considered for the post of Quartermaster-General of the Army to replace Joseph E. Johnston, his future opponent on the way to Atlanta, who had thrown in his lot with the Confederacy.

On May 14 Sherman heard from his brother of these possibilities, in a message telling him to go at once to Washington. Before starting, he penned a reply which fits perfectly into his character as here diagnosed, but fits not at all into an egoistical delineation. "You all overrate my powers and abilities and may place me in a position above my merits, a worse step than below. Really I do not conceive myself qualified for Quartermaster-General or Major-General. To attain either station I would prefer a schooling with large masses of troops in the field, one which I lost in the Mexican War by going to California. The only possible reason that would induce me to accept my position would be to prevent its falling into incompetent hands. The magnitude of interest at issue now, will admit of no experiments. . . ."

A few days after reaching Washington Sherman had definite intimation of his appointment to the Colonelcy of one of the new three-battalion regiments, the 13th, a decision which pleased him, not least because it restored him to the Regular Army. "I prefer this to a Brigadier in the Militia, for I have no political ambition, and have very naturally more confidence in Regulars than Militia. Not that they are better, braver, or more patriotic, but because *I know* the people will submit with better grace to them than to Militia of any particular locality. . . ."

This remark throws light on his earlier refusal of the offer, made by the Union leaders in Missouri, to make him brigadier-general of their militia.   For his sense of statesmanship, which is also grand strategy, told him that, "The greatest difficulty in the problem now before the country is not to conquer but so to conquer as to impress upon the real men of the South a respect for their conquerors." He argued that "if Memphis be taken, and the army move on South the vindictive feeling left behind would again close the river. . . . It is for this reason that I deem Regulars the only species of force that should be used for invasion."   This care to safeguard the rear of an offensive by conciliation, thus economizing force otherwise wasted in guarding the rear and communications, is true grand strategy.

But the natural question will be how we can reconcile it with the "March through Georgia" three years later.   By one of those violent fluctuations of temper and temperament which led superficial observers to term Sherman "mercurial"?   Not necessarily; indeed, it is the least convincing explanation.   For a more natural one stands out against the historical background.   The character of the war and the conditions of the opposition had radically changed by 1864.   Furthermore, the "March through Georgia" did not leave a hostile population athwart Sherman's lines of communication— because he had no communications, having deliberately abandoned them.

His views gained point from recent experience.   For he had just received his baptism of fire—at the hands of the "militia" whom he might have commanded.   Jackson, the Secessionist Governor of Missouri, had planned to seize the St. Louis arsenal in the name of the State, and as a preliminary had formed a camp where the Confederate volunteers, thinly disguised as the State Militia, could train for their intended coup.   They were anticipated, however, by Captain Nathaniel Lyon who, on May 10, marched out from the arsenal with his battalion of Regulars and several regiments of Union militia christened the "Home Guards," and mainly composed of Germans. They surrounded Camp Jackson and compelled the surrender of the Confederates, who were marched under escort to the arsenal.

The sudden move threw the city into a feverish turmoil. When Lyon's troops emerged from the arsenal alarmed citizens rushed to barricade their houses, while others more inquisitive, and less prudent, followed the column out to Camp Jackson.

Sherman tells a delightful story of this ferment. While waiting for news he was walking up and down the street with his seven-year-old son, Willie, when a distressed neighbour told him that her brother-in-law was in the camp and "she was dreadfully afraid he would be killed." She refused to be comforted by his assurance that Lyon had taken ample force to make resistance impossible, saying that the Camp was made up of the young men from the first and best families of St. Louis, and that they were proud, and would fight. "I explained that young men of the best families did not like to be killed better than ordinary people." Soon he heard cries of "They've surrendered" and went back to reassure her, only to have the door angrily slammed in his face. With feminine inconsistency, she and many of her kind were now equally distressed because their kinsfolk had proved too proud to fight, against such odds.

This reaction, most immediate among the large crowd which accompanied the homeward "procession," generated a dangerous temper. Dangerous, that is, to the crowd. For the raw "Home Guards," flushed with a novel sense of power were equally liable to be seized with panic when they found an abusive crowd hanging on their flanks. A sudden block, a slight clash, and the "Home Guards" began firing into the crowd. A stampede followed, but still the fire continued. "Hearing balls cutting the leaves of trees" over his head, Sherman threw himself flat, with his boy, and directly the fire slackened, picked Willie up and ran back with him to a gully which gave shelter. A good eye for cover!—the value of Sherman's topographical researches had thus their first "battlefield" illustration. Several other spectators, however, had been killed, including a woman and child, and more wounded. Sherman's dispassionate verdict, in telling his brother, was that the provocation at the point of contact did not condone what followed. "The rest was irregular

and unnecessary, for the crowd was back in the woods, a fence between them and the street."

We are told that there is a silver lining to every cloud. Here the
lining was perhaps that the Union troops were not more accurate
in their shooting, the crowd not more aggressive. For, by a coincidence which in fiction would be excessive, among the non-combatant
spectators of that ill-omened march were the two men who were
destined to lead the Union armies to victory; not only Sherman but
also Grant—then working in a small store at Galena, the last of
several humble jobs in which he had eked out a living after resigning his commission.

    .   .   .   .

Let us pause, as the curtain rises on the entry of these two men,
to review the war situation and prospects. The Regular Army
numbered only some 16,000, and although the men as a whole remained loyal to the Union, the greater part were scattered in the
frontier posts, especially in the Far West, and were held to this
duty, so that only a small proportion were available for active operations. Most of the Southern-born officers, having stronger State
ties, resigned their commissions to join the Confederate service,
where their experience was at first better utilized than those of their
comrades who remained loyal to the Union. For, instead of using
the Regulars to season the new levies, Lincoln left these to be raised
and officered by the State governments, and kept the Regular Army
separate. It was expanded by the raising of eight new regiments
of infantry, and one each of cavalry and artillery, in May, 1861,
but these only increased its strength by some fifty per cent.

Hence the issue depended on, and the war was fought out by, the
civilian manhood of North and South. In the cold abstract light of
census returns the odds seem heavily in favour of the North, for the
white population of the nineteen free states was nearly nineteen million, while the eleven seceded states had only five and a half million
whites—who possessed between them three and a half million slaves.
The four border slave states (Delaware, Maryland, Kentucky and
Missouri) which did not secede were so full of Confederate sympathizers that their actual contribution to the two armies was probably equal.

But strategical factors modify this impression of Northern advantage. To fulfil its purpose the South had merely to make the North weary of the attempt to restore the Union by force. In contrast, the North had to conquer its opponents and convince them that resistance was hopeless and that the North could not be wearied. Moreover, the Southerner was bred to arms and through his code of "honour" had acquired a readiness of self-defence and an instinct for fighting which the Northerner had lost through disuse. So also the forests which, except for interspersed clearings, covered most of the theatre of the war gave an advantage to the native woodsman. And the war, be it remembered, was fought out on Southern soil. An even greater asset was the simpler and lighter diet of the Southerner, which enhanced his strategic mobility, whereas the heavy-feeding Northerner was not only handicapped by dependence on rail-borne supplies but strained the capacity of the railroads to supply him with beef and corn. The battlefields also offered a pungent proof of the difference—in the Northerner's quicker decomposition as a corpse.

These compensating advantages were augmented by the greater promptness and thoroughness of the Confederacy to convert its raw material into armies. Jefferson Davis called for 100,000 twelve-month volunteers as early as March 6, 1861, and applied conscription only a year later—in ironical repudiation of the Confederacy's stand for States' rights. Another year passed before Lincoln introduced conscription, and even then with gaping holes in the net; temporary exemption being allowed on payment, and permanent, on provision of a substitute.

Lincoln's original call for 75,000 three-month volunteers was largely met by the enlistment of the volunteer State militias and the semi-social military companies, which, with few exceptions, had little more experience than an annual "Cornwallis," or sham-fight. Subsequent calls were met by raising entirely new regiments in the various States. The establishment, or nominal full strength, of each regiment was 1,050, and their normal strength about half. Except the new Regulars, all were single-battalion regiments and organized in ten companies—a relic of the traditional practice of forming a battalion in a close-ranked body of eight companies while two extra companies of skirmishers armed with rifles covered its

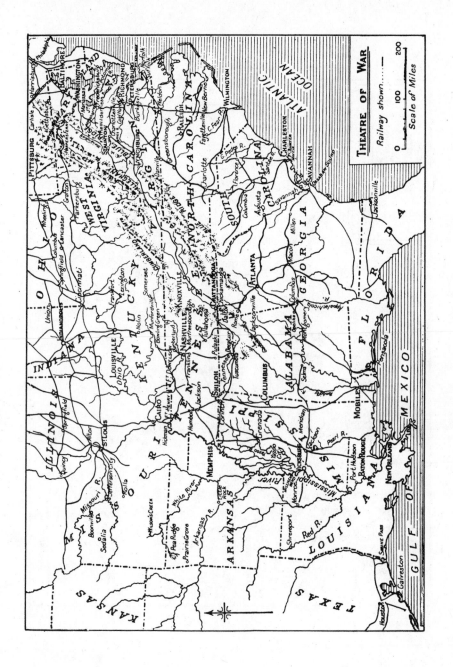

THEATRE OF WAR

Railway shown......

0   100   200

Scale of Miles

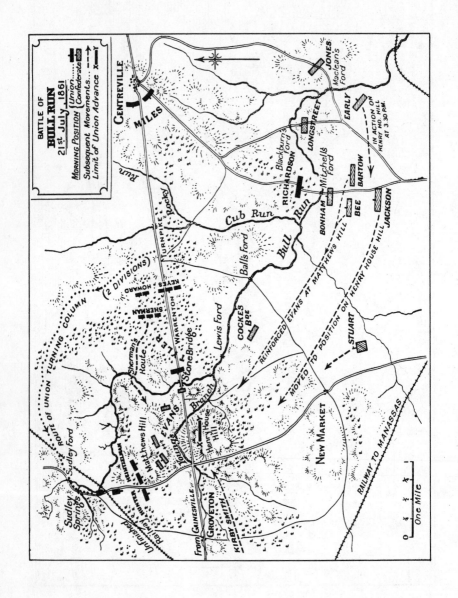

front and then fell back to the flanks. This distinction between companies disappeared in the Civil War but the organization, tactically inconvenient, survived, and was even revived in the post-war army—although Sherman strongly advocated the four-company battalion which eventually became standard in all armies.

The disappearance of the distinction was due rather to a levelling down than a levelling up. For close formations were still the rule until the hard lesson of the bullet dispersed them. And military conservatism had kept the standard issue of firearms far behind the march of technical progress. The rifle did not become general until midway through the war, and, even so, was usually a muzzle-loader. But, in this respect, the North was at least ahead of the South and the breech-loaders in use were replaced fairly soon by ones with a magazine. By 1864 the Union cavalry and a percentage of the infantry were armed with these new repeating rifles. And the more rapid rate of fire, as well as the ability to fire when lying down, gave to the brigades so armed a vital advantage in some of the later battles.

The change, however belated, from the smooth-bore musket to the rifle endowed the defence with a power of resistance that stamped its effect on the war. While the military hierarchy was as slow to realize the change as to change their weapons, the increased effect of the bullet soon taught the fighting soldier a lesson, and out of the lesson grew the trench or breastwork, until every battlefield became a network of entrenchments. In consequence, a frontal attack on an enemy in position became an almost hopeless venture. Fools continued to make such attacks, wise men enticed their enemy to make them.

At sea, similarly, the initial condition of equipment was farcically obsolete although, under pressure of emergency, change was more rapid than on land. The Union kept the Navy, but this only comprised twenty-four steamships in commission, none of them armoured, and the sailing ships did not count except on paper. The Union, however, also had the manufacturing resources, and by the end of 1861 partly armoured river gun-boats were being produced to gain command of the Mississippi. Then on March 8, 1862, the *Merrimac*, a half-burnt steam frigate which had been converted by the Confederates into an ironclad and renamed the *Vir-*

ginia, appeared in Hampton Roads and "automatically" made the whole wooden fleet of the Union obsolete. Fortunately for the Union, the civilian Ericsson had, with the customary difficulty, so far penetrated the shell of professional opinion as to induce the Navy Department to construct an ironclad from his design. This much-scorned experiment, the *Monitor*, providentially arrived on the 9th to neutralize a danger that threatened to paralyze Navy, Army, and Government alike. Henceforth the blockade of the South could be pursued tranquilly, and tightened as the Union fleet increased. So far at least as was possible round a coastline of 3,500 miles—from the Chesapeake to the Rio Grande. Indeed, the blockade never became fully effective until the actual harbours were occupied, or cut off from the interior, by the army. Until then, it might pinch, but could not strangle, the Confederacy.

CHAPTER V

BULL RUN AND KENTUCKY

THE 13th Infantry, of which Sherman had received command—
but was never to command—was as yet no more than a name. He
expected to return West to enlist the men at Jefferson Barracks,
near St. Louis, but on reporting to the aged Commander-in-Chief,
General Winfield Scott, he was told that his lieutenant-colonel could
carry out this preliminary task, and that he himself must remain at
Washington attached to General Scott's staff for inspection duty.
And in consequence he, who had thought to be "in the second or
third set," was launched into the first premature offensive, which
fulfilled his prediction by its failure—but not the complementary
forecast that the leaders would be "cast aside."

When Congress met on the 4th of July—now by the irony of history to answer, not to make, a "declaration of independence"—it
lent its ear to the President's demand for 400,000 men, but it lent its
voice to swell the public clamour for immediate action. And Scott's
contrary but somewhat vague plan of building up a grand army of
invasion was not helped by the widespread military belief in the
power of a short, sharp blow to quell the secession. Another spur
was the expiring engagement of the three months' volunteers, who
themselves echoed the popular cry of "On to Richmond!" Yet if
these hopes were ill-founded there was justification for the argument that an early battle would have a good moral and political
effect—even though its fulfilment took an inverted form! For if
the North forfeited the prestige of an early success they gained the
awakening effect of an early disaster.

Scott's enfeebled opposition was soon overcome, and a general advance ordered for the middle of July. Already a force under Patterson had regained the crossing higher up the Potomac at Harper's
Ferry, whence the 11,000 Confederates under Johnston had retired
southward without resistance. East of Johnston's position and
thirty miles south of Washington was the main Confederate force of

some 22,000 men under Beauregard, the "victor" of Fort Sumter. Lying around Manassas Junction, this force covered the direct approach towards Richmond, and to overthrow it was now the task assigned to the main Union force, moving south from Washington. Brigadier-General McDowell, just promoted from major, was in command of the raw and motley collection of troops, which had to be hurriedly sorted out and organized into brigades and divisions. For these, in turn, commanders had to be improvised, and Sherman was summoned to take over the Third Brigade of Tyler's First Division.

He had barely a fortnight's grace in which to organize his command and numerous difficulties to overcome. Out of five volunteer regiments, he picked out the four best, but, even so, one of the four was not eager for the honour. This was an Irish regiment from New York, and many of the men clamoured for their discharge on the ground that their ninety days' engagement should be reckoned from date of enrolment, and not from the date of being mustered in. It is a curious sidelight on the "war-conditions" of 1861 that the Commander-in-Chief had to be invoked to write a letter appealing that "his Irish friends would not leave him in such a crisis." Nevertheless, while "the officers generally wanted to go to the expected battle . . . a good many of the men were not so anxious."

If enthusiasm was sometimes lacking, discipline was at all times lacking, and musketry training not begun. What this army lacked in uniformity was somewhat inadequately balanced by variety of uniform. The Federal Blue had not yet been issued and the regiments wore diverse and often diverting patterns of militia uniform; the flamboyant Zouave kit, as variously interpreted by local fashion, and the Bersaglieri plumage of the "Garibaldi Guards" were among the most colourful. One of Sherman's regiments, the 79th New York, had only abandoned their kilts and sporrans on leaving Washington, and another, the 2nd Wisconsin, went to battle in Confederate grey. However, to compensate this, many of the Confederate troops were clad in civilian dress, and some of their senior officers still wore the Federal Blue!

The Southward march resembled a holiday saunter, except that the troops, cramped by their own military formations, covered no longer distance in a day than a party of anæmic ramblers would travel without fatigue in a couple of hours. Men broke away from the ranks at will to pick blackberries, to fill their water-bottles, or even to recruit their energy by repose in the sylvan tranquillity of the road-borders. They had ample time to catch up, if they wished, for all the five divisions, totalling 35,000 men, were converging on Centreville and the nearer they came to it the more they blocked each other.

There is an illuminating contrast between the early days of the American Civil War and those of the French Revolutionary wars, in which the troops were almost as raw and undisciplined, and still worse equipped and supplied. But their very lack of supplies, forcing them to live on the country, forced them to keep apart, and thereby facilitated quicker movement and more effective manœuvre. In 1861, however, half a century of military theory, worshipping at Napoleon's shrine and standing on its head in true Father William fashion, had inverted his practice and made a fetish of the "strategic concentration." It was in accord with this inversion that the Union forces, having squeezed themselves into a jamb at Centreville, had now to shake themselves out before they could manœuvre against the Confederates, who had more discreetly spread themselves out along Bull Run—which by American standards was a small stream, and by English standards a river, unpleasantly obstructive to raw and immobile troops.

On that funeral march of Northern hopes there was, however, one man at least who needed no lesson in the truth that mobility is the mainspring of war. Indeed, Sherman's belief in the importance of marching light was now carried in practice to a pitch that would seem extravagant, almost to absurdity, if he had not survived to justify it in 1864-65. For even his long-suffering and well-trained wife must have felt some irritation on being told, in acknowledgment of her letters, that "As I read them I will tear them up, for every ounce on a march tells." However, the next letter from him, penned on the eve of battle, was more soothing to her wifely pride, if not to her anxiety—"I know to-morrow and the next day we shall have hard work, and I will acquit myself as well as I can. With regulars I would have no doubt, but these volunteers are subject to stampedes. Yesterday there was an ugly stampede of 800 Massachusetts men. . . . My faith in you and the children is perfect, and let what may befall me I feel they are in a fair way to grow up in goodness and usefulness. . . ."

On July 18, McDowell, like a bather trying the heat of the water, dipped one toe in and as quickly withdrew it, blistered. The toe was a brigade of Tyler's division. To support it, Sherman was belatedly and hurriedly ordered out of camp, and, taking his brigade "at the double-quick," arrived at Blackburn's Ford in time to cover the confused retirement of the first brigade. The shock was so painful to it that one regiment and one battery insisted on their immediate discharge, and early on the 21st, as McDowell bitingly remarked "marched to the rear to the sound of the enemy's cannon."

For July 21 saw the unfolding and prompt collapse of the Union plan. The experience of the 18th had convinced McDowell—as the experience of history might have done at less expense—that a frontal attack, unless in greatly superior strength, was hopeless with raw troops. Accordingly he planned to turn the Confederate left flank. The Confederates had a similar idea in regard to his own.

McDowell's plan, already marred by his own slowness of advance, was thwarted by the slow and disjointed execution of the turning movement, and by Patterson's failure to pin down Johnston's force away to the West. But this failure helped, paradoxically, to stultify the Confederates' plan. Johnston, preceded, and accompanied by part of his force, arrived on the evening of the 20th to join Beauregard and assume supreme command. The junction of minds did not make for unity of thought and delays occurred in the initiation of the Confederate turning movement. Thus before it was ready the enemy attack forestalled it, and the Confederate commanders, more cautious than inspired, abandoned their own manœuvre without reasonable hope of transferring their full weight to the other flank. However, as so often in war, the defensive-offensive—resistance followed by a riposte—had the same dislocating effect on the opponent as an offensive manœuvre might have produced. And produced it with less strength and less exertion.

McDowell advanced in the morning with three of his four divisions against the precariously weak Confederate left, where the Stone Bridge was held by a mere demi-brigade under Evans. While the leading division (Tyler) moved directly on the bridge the next two diverged to the right to make their turning movement via Sudley

Ford, two miles further west. Evans, with keen intuition and prompt initiative, took eleven of his fifteen companies westward to Matthews Hill, overlooking Sudley, in order to ward off this greater menace. And, thanks to the slowness of this turning movement to develop, Evans was still holding the leading Union brigade in check when the Confederate brigades of Bee and Bartow arrived to reinforce him. Thus at this point the flank attack had become a frontal assault.

Meantime only one brigade had been engaged at the Stone Bridge, where its path was effectively blocked. Behind it lay Sherman's and Keyes's brigades, resting in enforced inactivity. But Sherman himself was not. His restless spirit of enquiry, so invaluable a military asset, had impelled him to ride out to reconnoitre the ground in the vicinity, and he noticed a horseman descend the far slope of Bull Run and reappear in a field on the near side. Trained mind acting upon trained eye had at once suggested that here might be a feasible ford which McDowell's reconnaissance had failed to discover. When, towards noon, he received the order to move to the assistance of the turning column, now checked, he led his brigade through the stream at this point instead of making the long detour by Sudley Ford. And thereby he arrived on the flank of the Confederates who were facing the turning column. By the time his brigade reached the actual scene of action the Confederates were giving way, and he was ordered to join in the pursuit.

The discrepancy between the Union and Confederate accounts of how the issue was decided in this first phase, on Matthews Hill, and the dispute as to the effect of Sherman's intervention—a dispute in which Sherman took no part—show a curious disregard of the psychology of battle. Some Union officers have declared that the Confederates were in retreat before Sherman arrived; Confederate officers say that his attack on their flank and rear settled the issue. Both may well be right and yet wrong, and the difference can be explained by a natural deduction. The Confederates should assuredly know best what caused their retreat. This cause, however, was not Sherman's attack but the appearance of his brigade *en route* to deliver such an attack. The psychological after-impression that a threat had actually become a fact is well known in military history, and many times has an army, fighting stubbornly, suddenly given way when a fresh body of the enemy has merely appeared on its rear flank. Armies, too, that were far more hardened to the nerve-strain of battle than those which fought at Bull Run.

The Confederates' disordered retreat down the dip to Young's Branch, across the stream, and up the further slope to the Henry House Hill, was harassed by the Union artillery and became dangerously close to a rout. But a further brigade, Jackson's, had now reached the Henry House Hill and taken up a position well behind the crest, thus sheltered from artillery fire and gaining the tactical advantage of surprise upon the pursuers when, breathless and disorganized, they came over the crest. The situation and the effect were reminiscent of Wellington's characteristic battles in the Peninsular War.

If the sight of Jackson's brigade, "standing like a stonewall," was a disagreeable shock to the pursuers, it was a moral restorative to the pursued, who began to rally behind Jackson's line. Once the resistance had hardened, it was a calculable probability, in the light of historical experience, that the 6,500 Confederates on the hill would be able to repulse superior numbers in an attack which had now become purely frontal. Probability became certainty when odds which might have been three to one became only three to two. For out of eight brigades within reach of the scene, only four came into action against Henry House Hill. And their effect was still further reduced by being thrown in piecemeal. McDowell's excuse was that an attempt to check and reform his enthusiastically undisciplined troops might have paralyzed their energy, but there is clear evidence that he ordered individual regiments to attack in turn, even when a whole brigade was available.

The wonder is not that the Union troops were repulsed, but that they kept up these spasmodic efforts so long. But after about two hours the impulse had faded and the constant trickle of wounded walking to the rear had swelled into a continuous human stream, in which the wounded in body were outnumbered by the wounded in spirit. Real battles are rarely decided in the manner made familiar by heroically minded artists, and there is little room to doubt that at Bull Run the scales turned with the turning away of the disheartened Union soldiers, and not with the counter-advance of the Confederates, which began in "Stonewall" Jackson's brigade, coinciding with the arrival of Kirby Smith's fresh brigade, and soon developed into a general advance. This was certainly no irresistible charge sweeping the enemy off the hill and across the valley of Young's Branch. If the defeated gradually became, with certain exceptions, a confused mob of stragglers, it was not under shock pressure but under the influence of mass suggestion. Men had had enough, they saw others walking away, and they followed. The battle ended like a bath—draining away through a waste-pipe.

Sherman's brigade was the last to feel the suction. As each of his regiments in turn were driven back he had exerted himself to re-form just behind the near crest of the hill, where on first arrival he had perceived that a deeply worn roadway would afford a passably sheltered assembly position. Intent in this task of reorganization, when he realized that his own men were slipping away, he found that the others had slipped, and that his brigade was almost alone, except for a battalion of regulars.

The drain away of the Union force might have become a run away, on the battlefield, if this battalion and Sherman's brigade had not, as the enemy commander testified, made "a steady and handsome withdrawal," which sufficed to quench the remaining energy of the victors.

Sherman's eye and instinct for country served him once more before the retreat was ended. For while the straggling mass poured down the main road to Centreville, converging on the bridge over Cub Run, there to become a struggling mob under the urge of one Confederate battery, Sherman made a circuit which avoided this moral danger point. At Centreville that night he received the order to continue the retreat to the Potomac, but in the course of this even the regiments of his brigade dissolved into the general torrent of begrimed and sodden soldiery who, sick of soul and weary of body, poured back towards the capital which they had quitted so gaily.

Sherman utilized the Potomac River to bring some order into the human river, for as soon as he reached the riverside he placed a strong guard over the aqueduct and ferries which led to the camp at Fort Corcoran, and sifted the men into their regiments and companies, so that a resistance could be improvised if the Confederates sought, as was feared, to reach and occupy Washington on the heels of the defeated.   Self-reliance, and uncompromising candour, marked his brief report to the Adjutant-General on arrival at Fort Corcoran—"I have this moment ridden in [with], I hope, the rear men of my brigade, which, in common with the rest of our whole Army, has sustained a terrible defeat and has degenerated into an armed mob. I know not if I command [here], but at this moment will act as such." He then crisply details his measures to strengthen the posts and to stop the fugitives.

So also in the days that followed he laboured to reorganize his brigade and restore discipline, keeping the men's minds occupied and their bodies fit by exercise. But while Congress was voting the enlistment of half of a million men, defeat had not acted as a tonic on the actual troops that had suffered it, and the moral slough into which they had fallen can be measured by the time they took to recover. Depression, indeed, spread with reflection.

With Sherman the bitterness of this experience can be measured in his letters to his wife, the first on July 24. "The battle was nothing to the shameless rout that followed and yet exists. With shameless conduct the volunteers continue to flee. Well, as I am sufficiently disgraced now, I suppose soon I can sneak into some quiet corner. I was under heavy fire for hours, touched on the knee and shoulder, my horse shot through the leg, and was in every way exposed, and cannot imagine how I escaped except to experience the mortification of retreat, rout, confusion. . . . Courage our people have, but no government. . . ." The continued demoralization of the troops draws from him ten days later the sarcastic comment: "I shall make a requisition for two nurses per soldier to nurse them in their helpless, pitiful condition. Oh but we had a few regulars."

Another aspect of this moral deterioration was a blow to Sherman's fundamental instinct for law and order. Telling his wife of the disorders on the way out to Bull Run he says:—"I always feared the result, for everywhere we found the people against us. No curse could be greater than invasion by a volunteer army. No Goths or Vandals ever had less respect for the lives and property of friends and foes, and henceforth we ought never to hope for any friends in Virginia." Even defeat seemed to him less shameful than these abuses, and military recovery secondary to the aim "that a common sense of decency will be inspired into the minds of this soldiery."

His feeling was in part due to his perception of the value in war of the ethical factor—"In all the Southern States they have succeeded in impressing the public mind that the North is governed by a mob (of which unfortunately there is too much truth) and in the South that all is chivalry and gentility."

But, in a large section, the sense of honour and duty alike were slow to recover from the shock of Bull Run. Nearly a month after the battle Sherman had to order out his Regular battery, with shotted guns, to overawe a part of his troops, three years' as well as three months' men, who were clamouring for their discharge. Nor was the trouble limited to those who had been at Bull Run, for new regiments had been posted to his brigade, and yet, as he told his brother, "Out of my seven regiments three are in a state of mutiny, and I have been compelled to put about 100 men as prisoners on board a man-of-war." The strain thus thrown on the commander is illustrated in his comment—"I have not undressed of a night since Bull Run, and the volunteers will not allow of sleep by day."

Even the officers were affected. And thereby hangs the tale of an incident which led Sherman to revise his first impression of Lincoln.

One morning after reveille, he had just given permission to a regiment to fall out, after the roll had been taken, when an officer said to him casually, "Colonel, I am going to New York to-day. What can I do for you?" Sherman cuttingly replied, "I do not remember to have signed a leave for you." Then, in the hearing of an interested congregation of men, eager for a cue, the officer declared bluntly that he had served more than his three months' engagement, that he had neglected his law business long enough and was going home.

"Sauce for the goose is sauce for the gander," and "sauce" from an officer meant worse from the men. So, in equally clear tones Sherman sharply said, "Captain, this question of your term of service has been submitted to the rightful authority, and the decision has been published in orders. You are a soldier, and must submit to orders till you are properly discharged. If you attempt to leave without orders, it will be mutiny, and I will shoot you like a dog! Go back into the fort *now*, instantly, and don't dare to leave without my consent." The officer looked at Sherman, as if to see that he meant his words, then turned back, and the men dispersed.

Later in the day Sherman saw the President driving out to see "the boys." He asked Lincoln if he intended to address them, and on being told "yes," asked him "to please discourage all cheering, noise or any sort of confusion; that we had had enough of it before Bull Run to ruin any set of men, and what we needed were cool, thoughtful, hard-fighting soldiers—no more hurrahing, no more humbug." If the intervention showed Sherman's moral courage the reception showed Lincoln's moral strength. He took the rebuke not only in good humour but with a sense of humour. For when, after a speech most apt to the conditions, the men began to cheer, he checked them with the remark, "Don't cheer, boys. I confess I rather like it myself, but Colonel Sherman here says it is not military, and I guess we had better defer to his opinion."

When they reached Fort Corcoran and Lincoln had repeated his address, the officer who had been the cause of the earlier incident forced his way through the press and said, "Mr. President, I have a cause of grievance. This morning I went to speak to Colonel Sherman and he threatened to shoot me." After he had repeated his charge, Lincoln looked at Sherman and then said in a very audible stage-whisper, "Well, if I were you, and he threatened to shoot, I would not trust him, for I believe he would do it." The reply drew a roar of laughter and, as they drove on, Sherman explaining the facts, Lincoln remarked, "Of course I didn't know anything about it, but I thought you knew your own business best."

If Lincoln had still many slips to make in his conduct of war, here can we perceive the early dawn of that attitude which has made his name a synonym for the wise conduct of war and discerning support of his military executants, and a symbol of the right relation between statesman and general.

Soon afterwards Sherman's one unfulfilled prediction was fulfilled in a contrary sense. McClellan had been called from West Virginia—now safely seceded from the Secession—to take supreme command, and a drastic reshuffle of the subordinate commands began. But, as they were expecting demotion, Sherman and several others of the leaders of Bull Run were surprised by promotion—to the rank of brigadier-general of volunteers. Their feelings were well expressed by one when the rumour came—"By ——, it's all a lie! Every mother's son of you will be cashiered." But rumour was soon confirmed, and the assurance was an encouragement to Sherman, grown rusty in technique during years of civil life, to refurbish his detailed knowledge and exercise his mind on the drill-books. For the tactical drill had changed since his early retirement, and profound as his grasp of strategy, as also of tactics—which is essentially applied common-sense—it was characteristic of him that he was unwilling to be dependent on subordinates for the drill execution of his tactical conceptions. If drill could speed up tactics, he was determined to make himself a drill-master in order to be a still better tactician.

This attitude, however, had a wider bearing. For, while he was striving to pull his men out of the mire, he himself was sunk in a slough of despond, less visible but more clinging. Although courage and resolution never flagged—"the bluer the times the more closely should one cling to his country"—hope and faith were frail plants. The combination seems curious, and many will wonder how the existence of the former qualities can be reconciled with the absence of the latter. The explanation is to be found in the difference both between the realistic and the fatalistic temperament, and between the realistic and the romantic. Sherman's depression had in it neither resignation nor dejection, but was the expression of deep-seated disgust. Disgust at the stupidity of men, including himself, to rise to the level of their opportunities and emergencies. He was disgusted at the way the war was being handled, and equally at the way he had handled his own life. Starting life with a dynamic confidence in himself, he had suffered repeated set-backs and gradually, instead of blaming them on fate, he had begun to blame them on himself. Yet conscious that he was being unfair to himself.

Thus the public outcome of Bull Run and his personal ignorance of the new drill-books induced a fresh fit of disgust which made him sensitive to his own limitations. Even after his promotion, at his next interview with Lincoln he declared emphatically that he wished "to serve in a subordinate capacity, and in no event to be left in a superior command." The request appealed afresh to Lincoln's sense of humour and drew from him the comment that his chief trouble was to find places for the too many generals who wanted to be at the head.

Sherman's doubt of his own capacity was seemingly unshared by others, for this interview itself was the outcome of a special request for his services, while the fulfilment of the request was in turn postponed for a week because McClellan was unwilling to spare Sherman until he was sure that the menace of a Confederate advance on Washington had passed.

The request came from Robert Anderson, the defender of Fort Sumter and Sherman's old company commander at Fort Moultrie. The cleavage of feeling in Kentucky was coming to a cleavage of action, and at this crisis Anderson was appointed to command the Department of the Cumberland. For assistants, Sherman was the first choice, and Thomas another. Sherman's comment to his wife on his own appointment is significant—"I think Anderson wanted me because he knows I seek not personal fame or glory, and that I will heartily second his plans and leave him the fame. . . . Not till I see daylight ahead do I want to lead. But when danger threatens and others slink away I am and will be at my post."

There was some doubt, shared by Lincoln, of Thomas's loyalty, as a Virginian, but Anderson's wish for him was strongly endorsed by Sherman. Back in June, while Sherman was on his way to Washington, he had written to his brother. "You are with Gen. Patterson. There are two A No. 1 men there, George H. Thomas, Col. Second Cavalry and Cap. Sykes 3 Infantry. Mention my name to both and say to them that I wish them all the success they aspire to, and if in the varying chances of war I should ever be so placed, I would name such as them for high places. But Thomas is a Virginian . . . and he must feel unpleasantly at leading an invading Army. But if he says he will do it, I know he will do it well. He was never brilliant but always cool, reliable and steady, maybe a little slow. Sykes has in him some dashing qualities. This early opinion and advocacy have peculiar significance in view both of later events, when the two were intimately associated in Georgia, and of still later controversy, when the partisans of Thomas sought to magnify him at Sherman's expense, by complaining of Sherman's treatment of their hero, and of the unfairness of his gentle criticism of Thomas's slowness.

As soon as Sherman could be relieved he followed Anderson to Cincinnati, Ohio, to begin a mission that was "diplomatic" as well as military. For, as he wrote to his brother before leaving, the idea was to "mingle with the people, satisfy ourselves of their purpose, to oppose the Southern Confederacy and then to assist in the organization there of a force adequate to the end in view, that when Kentucky is assured in her allegiance that we then push into East Tennessee." And in character with his contemporary outlook he concluded, "I feel well satisfied that unless Kentucky and Tennessee remain in our Union it is a doubtful question whether the Federal Government can restore the old Union. . . . There is no time to be lost and I will not share my individual efforts, though I still feel as one groping in the dark. Slowly but surely the public is realizing what I knew all the time, the strong vindictive feeling of the whole South."

CHAPTER VI

THE KEY TO THE WAR

To grasp the course and character of the war in the West—in the vast belt between the Alleghany Mountains and the Mississippi—it is essential to realize two conditions. First, that the Western theatre bore to the Virginian theatre east of the Alleghanies the relation of a large back garden to a narrow front door path. Second, that the operation was governed by the strategic "tapes" formed by the great rivers which intersected the area and, in turn, formed the main channels of move-

ment and supply.

This river system may be likened to a gigantic "K," and the resemblance heightened if the letter be written with a flourish. The left-hand stroke of the "K" is the Mississippi between St. Louis in the north and Memphis in the south. The upper right-hand stroke is the Ohio River, with Louisville at the tip. The lower right-hand stroke is the Tennessee River, with Shiloh at the tip; if this stroke be written with an exaggerated flourish, doubling its length and sweeping slightly upwards, it will reach and represent the position of Chattanooga, the "gateway to Georgia." Where the upper and lower right-hand strokes join is Paducah, and where they merge into the left-hand stroke is Cairo—midway between St. Louis and Memphis on the Mississippi.

There is still one "strategic" river to weave into the literal simile —the Cumberland. Suppose that the lower right-hand stroke, naturally made last, is written with a split nib. Then it will form representatively not only the Tennessee but the Cumberland which, at first parallel to the Tennessee, splays out more widely after Fort Donelson. But, with a far wider gap, the flourish carries both halves of this split stroke off to the right, or east. Lastly, to bring the campaigns in Tennessee into visual relation with their 1863 development southwards, let us suppose that the left-hand stroke, the Mississippi, be prolonged as far again southwards, and we have the position of Vicksburg. And if the prolongation be itself doubled we reach New Orleans and the sea.

Sherman had welcomed the opportunity to go west from the cramped area and outlook of the Virginian theatre because he was filled with the conviction that in Kentucky and Tennessee lay the key to the immediate future, and in the Mississippi the key to the ultimate victory. But he saw that they were stiff keys to turn and that a light grip was futile. From Cincinnati he wrote to his brother a letter which bears evidence of previous argument to this effect:

"I think it of vast importance and that Ohio, Indiana and Illinois must sooner or later arm every inhabitant, and the sooner the better. I hardly apprehend that Beauregard can succeed in getting Washington; . . . supposing he falls back, he will first try to overwhelm Rosecrans in Western Virginia and then look to Tennessee"—the prediction corresponded closely to the event. "We ought to have here a well appointed army of a hundred thousand men. I don't see where they are to come from, but this is the great centre. I still think that Mississippi will be the grand field of operations. . . . I think it of more importance than Richmond."

But Sherman's view of the grand strategic centre of gravity, although shared by Winfield Scott in his usual indeterminate way, was contrary to the plan which the new Commander-in-Chief, McClellan, put forward. His project was for an invasion down the line of the Atlantic coast with Richmond as the first objective.

Three years later even, this was still unattained. McClellan's was certainly the shortest and most direct route, but in war, as in life generally, the longest way round is often the shortest way there. This route was not only beset with natural obstacles which cramped manœuvre and canalized the invading flow, but by taking Richmond as its obvious objective encouraged the enemy to concentrate his strength for its defence and simplified his "lines of expectation." To move along the natural line of expectation is to consolidate the opponent's equilibrium, and by stiffening it to augment his resisting power. In war as in wrestling the attempt to throw the opponent without loosening his foothold and balance tends to self-exhaustion, increasing in disproportionate ratio to the strain put upon the opponent's resistance. For even if at the outset successful, it rolls the enemy back in snowball fashion, towards his reserves, supplies and reinforcement.

The habitual military argument for thus leading through strength is that if successful it annuls all other factors and by overthrowing the strongest resistance of the enemy ensures the collapse of all other parts of his resistance. In theory it should, but in experience how rarely has such a result been attained? And an incomplete result merely weakens the attacker and fortifies the defender. It is one more illustration of the divergence between idealism and realism.

Even if Richmond had been attained, it is highly questionable whether at this stage of the war, or at a later, the effect would have been decisive. For although, on Virginia joining the Confederacy, the seat of Government had been transferred from Alabama to Richmond, rather as a general moves to an advanced headquarters for battle, Virginia was not the real seat of the Confederacy's hostile will and power. To reach and strike at the real seat was not a practicable possibility in 1861, or 1862, either by McClellan's way or any other. But it was practicable to strike at the Confederacy in its weakest parts and by detaching these to ease the way of approach to an opponent thereby weakened morally and materially. Kentucky, Tennessee and Missouri gained, there were alternative lines of approach to Mississippi or to Alabama and Georgia. And then to Louisiana or South Carolina. Always an alternative strategic course, distracting to the opponent.

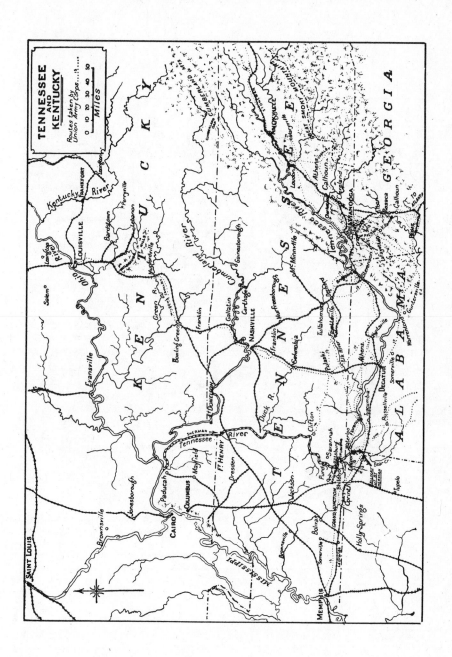

TENNESSEE
AND
KENTUCKY

Routes taken by
Union Army Corps........

Miles
0 10 20 30 40 50

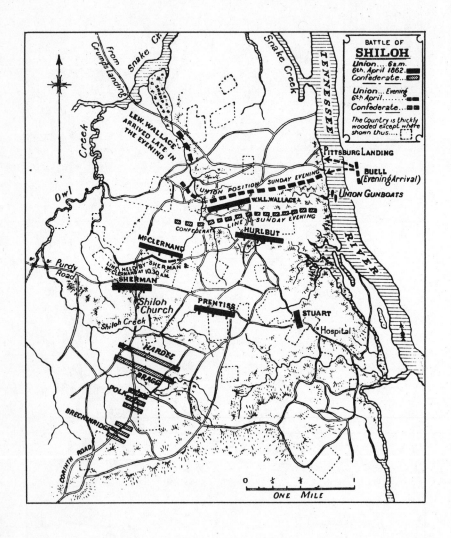

BATTLE OF
SHILOH
Union.... 6 a.m.
6th. April 1862.
Confederate....
Union.... Evening
6th April.
Confederate....
The Country is thickly
wooded except where
shown thus....

from Crumps Landing

Snake Cr.

Snake Creek

TENNESSEE

PITTSBURG LANDING

BUELL
(Evening Arrival)

UNION GUNBOATS

LEW. WALLACE
ARRIVED LATE IN
THE EVENING

Owl

Creek

UNION POSITION SUNDAY EVENING

W.H.L. WALLACE

CONFEDERATE LINE SUNDAY EVENING

McCLERNAND

HURLBUT

Purdy
Road

LINE HELD BY SHERMAN &
McCLERNAND AT 10.30 A.M.

SHERMAN

Shiloh
Church

PRENTISS

STUART

Shiloh Creek

Hospital

HARDEE

BRAGG

POLK

RIVER

BRECKENRIDGE

CORINTH ROAD

0   ¼   ½   1
ONE MILE

man's idea was that of cutting off the outer roots,
ring the deeper roots beneath the trunk, so that the
ations undermined, fell by force of gravity, McClel-
to begin at the top in Virginia and chop successive
s. And to do this he had to mount a precariously
off which he and a series of successors were toppled
rk.

plan prevailed, and even in preparation absorbed
the forces already raised, the West had to "forage" for itself. And
in Kentucky, the immediate problem was to hold the State for the
Union. Dreams of offence had to be put aside for cares of defence.
The external danger was not light, for the rival government at
Richmond had shown true strategic insight in establishing unity of
control west of the Alleghanies, giving the command to Albert Sidney Johnston, then commonly considered the ablest general of the
Confederacy.

Already a Confederate force under Polk—the bishop turned
general—had invaded the western fringe of Kentucky which lay in
the southern angle of the "K" at the junction of the rivers. Happily his further advance was blocked by the initiative of Brigadier
Ulysses S. Grant and his Missouri troops in stretching their grip to
hold both Cairo and Paducah. The bulk of Kentucky lay in the
eastern angle, between the Cumberland and Ohio Rivers, and in
mid-September Johnston pushed two forces upwards from the Cumberland into Kentucky, one on the left under Buckner to seize the
railway junction of Bowling Green, and the other on the right under
Zollicoffer to occupy Somerset. If these encroachments spurred the
Kentucky legislature to abandon neutrality, overriding the Governor and the Confederate-minded youth of the State, their support
to the Union was for long more vocal than physical. Thus the external menace, itself distracting, was aggravated by the internal
dissension and inertia. Anderson and his assistants had been sent
to make war without troops, and it is harder to make with men of
straw than to make bricks without straw.

Sherman was hurriedly despatched by Anderson as a personal
"SOS" to the Governors of Indiana and Illinois. But he found
that their troops were being drawn off to the wings, to McClellan
and to Frémont, who commanded in Missouri, and he could obtain

none to support Kentucky, although it was really their own "front line." "The world is a bundle of hay, mankind are the asses who pull, each tugs it a different way"—so the jingle runs, and in this case Kentucky had the misfortune to be the bundle of hay, tied up with straw. So as a last resort Sherman went on to see Frémont at St. Louis. He found the troublesome "Old Pretender" of California now enthroned with the resplendent pomp and inaccessibility of an Eastern Shah, and his court filled with an appropriate aroma of "baksheesh." Old Californian friends were welcome however—most of them busy making golden hay while the sun shone in its splendour—and Sherman at least got the privilege of a prompt audience, if nothing more profitable to his mission than flowery phrases of help.

He returned to Louisville to find the city a scene of alarms due to the Confederate incursions. Buckner's force, the most threatening, although only five thousand strong, was magnified by rumour, and at Louisville there were only a brigade of Home Guards and a collection of volunteers under training known as Rousseau's Legion. Collecting eighteen hundred of the former and twelve hundred of the latter, Sherman entrained them at midnight and pushed south with them to the Muldraugh Hills, thirty miles out, which formed a natural rampart covering Louisville. Finding that the Confederates were still at Bowling Green, consolidating their position in preparation for an eventual advance, he went into camp on the Muldraugh Hills, and laboured to organize his troops into an effective force.

It was in this emergency that he acquired the first of a changing series of nicknames. The story told of its origin is that when, on the journey out, he appealed to the ill-equipped and blanketless Home Guards, proposing to muster them into the United States service for thirty days, a number of them jibed at the suggestion, whereupon Sherman giving vent to his temper, called them "a paltry set of fellows" for haggling over such a small sacrifice. The men, now possessed of a double grievance, complained among themselves that it was a bitter pill to have to serve such a gruff and bearish commander, and coined the nickname "Old Pills" for him. When, however, they found how he exerted himself to look after their comfort and to get up blankets and tents for them, they modified their

first opinion, and changed his nickname to "Old Sugar-coated Pill."
Even their own local historians have recognized that they were
"rather a motley crew." As motley in quality as in raiment. In the
last irregularity they had an excuse in example. For Sherman,
ever careless of his dress, was at this time also curious in his head-
gear, wearing a battered "stove-pipe" hat. We have to thank this
hat, however, for at least one amusing anecdote.

The camp was in a district of Confederate sympathies, and Sherman's attention was attracted to a suspicious-looking young fellow
in civilian dress. He was promptly told to give an account of himself and explained that he had been called out too hurriedly to
change into uniform. As he quitted Sherman's presence he mut-
tered something to an officer near by, and Sherman promptly demanded to know what he had said. "Well, General, he said that
a general with such a hat as you have on had no right to talk to him
about a uniform." Sherman pulled off his hat, looked at it, burst
into a laugh, and called out—"Young man, you are right about the
hat, but you ought to have your uniform." Sherman was certainly
no connoisseur of buttons, no expert in pipeclay. Now and always,
as long as his men could shoot, march, obey orders, and best of all
use what was inside their heads, he cared nothing as to what was
outside their bodies. Economy of force was his ruling law, and none
have ever realized better that, with troops raised in and for war,
concentration on essentials must take precedence of incidentals.

It was well that Sherman could find a little light relief in the
situation, for the two months that followed were perhaps the darkest
of his career. On October 5, soon after he had been reinforced by
several regiments, from Indiana, he was summoned back to Louisville, to find a superior who said "he could not stand the mental
torture of his command any longer." Broken down in health and
spirit, he relinquished the command three days later, leaving Sherman to assume it by compulsion of seniority and against his own
wishes. Anderson's breakdown had been a happy release to himself,
but he left a legacy even more inconvenient than he had inherited.

Not only was Kentucky threatened from two directions, but the
difficulty of countering these threats was increased, indeed multiplied, by non-strategic factors. Kentucky aptly illustrated the
paradox that a State can be both unquiet and too passive. While

she was weak and unready, her opponents were weak but ready. Further, Sherman's few troops were not capable of matching his opponent's mobility if the latter chose to employ it. Cautiously, he never did. Lastly, Sherman had not only taken over a situation in which his small force was distributed in two parts, with some 80 miles of difficult country between, but he was fettered in making any redistribution. For Lincoln was pressing him to send early assistance to East Tennessee, where the people were strongly Unionist in sympathy. And to Lincoln's voice was added McClellan's.

Thus when he was even doubtful of holding Kentucky, and constantly expecting Johnston to strike concentrated at one of his two factions, he was being urged into a divergent offensive. Excusably, he felt that Washington's neglect was now drifting into wilful negligence. "If the Confederates take St. Louis and get Kentucky this winter you will be far more embarrassed than if Washington had fallen into their possession, as whatever nation gets the control of the Ohio, Mississippi, and Missouri Rivers will control the continent." Yet, in face of this warning, he was now asked to throw Kentucky's handful of guardians into a venture that, strategically, led nowhere, leaving his trust exposed everywhere.

To augment his difficulties, the political pressure from Washington was reinforced by the local pressure of politicians, notably Senator Andrew Johnson (later Lincoln's successor in the presidency), who spent their time in the camps making fiery speeches to the men and wasting time that should have been spent in training. Even Thomas, who was in command of the force facing Zollicoffer and the East Tennessee front, became irate at this—"speech-making." For although a strong advocate of the East Tennessee expedition he knew that his troops were not fit nor yet had any transport. But in such a politically heated atmosphere Sherman's restraining hand was resented, and the regiments of East Tennessee volunteers in Thomas's force became so mutinous that Thomas seriously thought of putting Senator Johnson under arrest. The blame does not fall on the dupes, but this ever-present interference with military movements has an unpalatable flavour of the French revolutionary armies and their commissaries. And the political outcry was reinforced by the local press.

Never a lover of either politicians or press since his California days, Sherman's dislike of both was so intensified by his Kentucky trials, which he saw as a reflection of the general misconception of the war problem, that it became deeply ingrained in his mind, until it went deeper than the stratum of conscious thought and became an irrational complex. Thus it was that he never missed an opportunity of scoring off the press, even in official letters. One of the cruellest is his report, "We have picked up the barges, and will save some of the provisions, but none of the reporters 'floated.' They were so deeply laden with weighty matter that they must have sunk . . . but in our affliction we can console ourselves with the pious reflection that there are plenty more left of the same sort." Equally characteristic of his attitude, and more offensive, was his rebuff to a correspondent who in 1864 sought a pass to Chattanooga—"I have as much as I can do to feed *my soldiers*." In this case, however, the laugh was on Sherman, for the correspondent had already a superior pass from Grant, and only asked Sherman's assent out of courtesy. Still less happy were his occasional "sermons" to the war-correspondents. "Now I am again in authority over you, and you must heed my advice. Freedom of speech and freedom of the press, precious relics of former history, must not be construed too largely. You must print nothing that prejudices government, or excites envy, hatred and malice in a community. Persons in or out of office must not be flattered or abused."

Sherman sarcastic is better than Sherman sententious, and Sherman the realist preferable to Sherman the idealist. For the final judgment must be that he gained as well as suffered from the press. If his sufferings came first, and his retaliation was never quite forgiven, the originality and unconventionality of his manner made him too good "copy" for any newspaper to ignore. Nor does his assertion ring quite true that "I never see my name in print without a feeling of contamination, and I will undertake to forego half my salary if the newspapers will ignore my name." True to a mood, but not true to the man. For the final reflection must be that the force of his revulsion against the press was due to the strength of his conviction of its importance, as the mould and mouthpiece of public opinion. The antithesis is well known in psychology.

No general has better transcended the limits of the military sphere. As his hatred of politics and politicians was due to his

insight into, and valuation of, the political sphere, so his hatred of
the press and pressmen was due to understanding of and belief in the
power of public opinion. And, in consequence, it irked him that he
could not wield this power or see it wielded according to his will.
The sternest censor of the press is frequently the man who graduated as a journalist—because he gauges best the strength of the
influence and the dangers of its reaction. Mussolini is the latest
example. Sherman's trouble was not merely that its words ran
counter to his opinions, but that he felt a professional contempt for
the way it was used by inferior journalists. One of the happiest
ripostes, the retort courteous, from the subjects of his abuse was
when a correspondent suggested that he had missed his vocation
and that "Any of the principal papers of New York will be glad to
give him double the pay of a major-general to act in the capacity of
war correspondent."

If his power of descriptive and expository writing justified the
"offer," he was qualified still more by a deeper sense—that in the
long run honesty and a fearless research for truth are both the best
journalism and the best policy.

But in the autumn of 1861 these virtues were at a discount; as
unpopular as the emergency which begot the need for them. Moreover, his intense absorption with the problem, of maintaining the
Union and holding Kentucky, and his vehement way of expressing
his disgust at the careless attitude of others were a combination
which encouraged misinterpretation. And to this, two incidental
factors unfortunately lent themselves. First, that he lived on the
ground floor of a hotel, the Galt House, a situation which if symboli-
cally appropriate was in the centre of a natural circle of gossip.
Men capable of such concentration of thought as to be able to isolate
themselves from their surroundings often choose to meditate in
pandemonium, but to ordinary men such a choice seems peculiar.
Second, he spent his evenings in the heart of the profession he so
heartily despised.

For in default of an adequate signal service the government and
the military authorities were utilizing the chain of agencies of the
New York Associated Press to transmit their telegraphed messages.
Every evening Sherman was at the Louisville agency, staying often
till 3 A.M., when the closing of the office drove him back to the hotel.

All these hours he paced up and down the room, only sitting down to make a note or compose a telegram, and any remark which interrupted his train of thought was either ignored or vigorously rebuffed. Even a direct question had often to be repeated before it could penetrate the walls of his concentration.

In a land where the only familiar form of warfare was political, and where action was by custom plentifully diluted with gossip, Sherman was as pleasant a companion as a tiger in a cage. Lacking Lincoln's flow of small talk and stories, and still more his patience, Sherman was too novel a type of leader to blend with his environment. Sherman of course could talk copiously, when action was not needed, but he talked in bursts, like the rat-a-tat-tat of a machine gun. And smoked like the ejector of one. For although he had frequently complained that smoking aggravated his asthma, and resolved to give it up, his resolution as regularly waned. The harder the problem he had to solve, or the more active his thought, the more furiously he smoked, puffing at his cigar as if he was shooting at the foe, not embracing a lover, while his little finger flicked off the incipient ash with quick automatic repetition as if to complete the machine-gun analogy. Repeatedly relighted these cigars were never finished, and an observer records that after an evening at the agency on the table were arrayed a chain of eight or ten stumps, which the porter aptly called "Sherman's old soldiers."

There is another story, again of that emergency journey out to the Muldraugh Hills, which tells how when his cigar went out he took another from his pocket and asked a sergeant for a light. The sergeant proffered him his own newly lighted cigar for the purpose, and Sherman, after lighting his own, took a few puffs to assure himself that it was alight, lapsed off into thought, and automatically threw away the sergeant's unsmoked cigar, too abstracted to notice either the mistake or the laughter which greeted it. The story is merely amusing, but its sequel also "offers a light." For when, long afterwards, the incident was recalled to him, he replied: "I was thinking of something else. It won't do to let to-morrow take care of itself. Your good merchant don't think of the ships that are in, but those that are to come in. The evil of to-day is irreparable. Look ahead to avoid breakers. You can't when your

ship is on them. All you can then do is to save yourself and retrieve disaster. . . ." Then, coming back from the philosophic
lesson to the sergeant's cigar, he added, laughing, "Did I do that,
really?" As his method of smoking was a symbol of his character,
so also was it true to his character that he should make the incident
a peg for a parable.

When his fame was assured this compound of abstraction and
vehemence was regarded admiringly as the eccentricity of genius—
it would be truer to call it the concentricity of genius. But when
he was unknown and unproved, save in a small circle, the compound
was regarded with less admiration and equal incomprehension, as
the symptoms of insanity. A human volcano, the deeper and fiercer
seethed the internal fire of thought the more violent and frequent
were the eruptions of lava-like words or gestures. And a human
volcano cannot help attracting publicity when it chooses a public
site. If an office of the pressmen he derided was an unwise site, no
wiser was the public quarters of a hotel. Yet as Villard relates:
"He paced by the hour up and down the corridor . . . smoking and
obviously absorbed in oppressive thoughts. He did this to such
an extent that it was generally noticed and remarked upon by the
guests and employees of the hotel. His strange ways led to gossip,
and it was soon whispered about that he was suffering from mental
depression."

By ill-luck, as this back-wash of rumour was spreading, a gust
struck Sherman's bark, already rocking, and, each reacting on the
other, almost capsized it. The gust was the tempestuous arrival of
Cameron, the Secretary of War, on his way back from St. Louis.
It was not auspicious that his visit there had been to investigate the
extravagant contracts and disbursements of Frémont, which resulted in Frémont's subsequent supersession. Nor, anxious to get
back to Washington, was he pleased at Sherman's unfortunate desire to detain him for a full discussion of the situation in Kentucky.
Like all weak men, too, he preferred to hide trouble by hiding his
eyes from it in the proverbial way of the ostrich, and was thus dis-
agreeably surprised to be told that the situation was full of trouble.
Frankness is always unpalatable.

The discussion took place at the Galt House and opened badly by
Sherman objecting to begin it in the presence of Cameron's party,

which included six or seven reporters. He was, however, overruled by Cameron, who testily said: "They are all friends, all members of my family." Then Sherman, taking the precaution to lock the door, gave a full exposition of the weakness of his force, the lack of arms, and the number of armed Confederates among the population. After Cameron had given instructions to the Adjutant-General, who accompanied him, for the despatch to Kentucky of any troops that were available, the discussion lapsed into a general conversation. In the course of this Sherman took a large map of the United States to illustrate his view of the general strategic problem. He pointed out that McClellan on the Union left had a hundred thousand men for a frontage of less than a hundred miles; that Frémont on the right had sixty thousand for a similar frontage; and that he himself had only been allotted eighteen thousand men despite the fact that he had to cover three hundred miles of frontier.

He then argued that, to safeguard this and drive out the Confederates, sixty thousand men were needed at once, and that to undertake a wider offensive two hundred thousand would be necessary. Whereupon Cameron threw up his hands and exclaimed: "Great God! Where are they to come from?" Sherman replied that the sources of man-power in the North were scarcely tapped as yet, and that it was notorious that the Government had refused offers of service from regiments raised in the Northwestern States, on the ground that they would not be needed! He further contended that the merely passive defence of so wide a frontier with inadequate forces on divergent lines, and with the rear communications liable to be cut by Kentuckian partisans of the South, was a policy ineffectual for defence and dangerous to the defenders. As he subsequently telegraphed in response to McClellan's request for an appreciation: "Our forces too small to do good, and too large to sacrifice."

According to the evidence of Brigadier-General Wood, the only other soldier present besides the Adjutant-General,. Sherman supported his broad alternative estimates with detailed reasoning, and his estimate of two hundred thousand for an offensive was based on the proposition that, the Government having undertaken to suppress the rebellion, the offensive was the only logical strategy and that, as a corollary, this number would be necessary to conquer the

Mississippi Valley down to the Gulf of Mexico. And history records that, paying instead on the instalment plan, the Union expended far more than his estimates to clear Kentucky and to conquer the Mississippi.

But by Cameron, in his memorandum on the interview, the estimate was termed an insane request. And to the adjective which, in his blindness, he carelessly employed, an unmistakeable significance was soon attached. There were germ-carriers in his own party of reporters, to whom his opinion of the estimate must have been divulged, if they did not violate the confidence placed in them at the original interview with Sherman. But there was also an outside germ-carrier with whom Sherman had an unlucky encounter that same night. In a bad temper over the interview, Sherman went as usual to the press agency, there to meet the correspondent of a New York paper, who asked for a pass through the lines to the South. Sherman refused him permission, whereupon he impudently said he would get a pass from the Secretary of War. Then Sherman exploded. Giving the correspondent two hours to remove himself from the limits of his department, he violently swore that if he was still there after they had expired the military "would hang him as a spy." Like the officer whom Lincoln jocularly warned, the correspondent believed that Sherman might fulfil his threat, and hurriedly caught the train. Once safely away he revenged himself by spreading the report that Sherman was crazy. According to one witness, to this correspondent fell the congenial task of writing up the account, soon divulged, of Sherman's interview with Cameron. Before long the Eastern papers, copied by the Western, were echoing with the vivid news of a mad general, and Sherman's lunacy became a popular theme. Naturally, also, his estimate was distorted to that of a demand for two hundred thousand men for the mere defence of Kentucky.

For all his contempt for the press, Sherman was acutely sensitive, and, deeply wounded, aggravated rather than allayed the popular impression by his bitter resentment of these stories. This soreness was increased when he found that the Washington authorities gave tacit countenance to the criticisms of his extravagant estimate, and did nothing to controvert the worse imputations. They seemed to him to be utilizing personal doubts of his judgment as an excuse for postponing any effort to remedy the dangerous situation in Kentucky.

In a report to the Adjutant-General, following up the Louisville interview, he mentioned that "You know my views that this great centre of our field is too weak, far too weak, and I have begged and implored till I dare not say more." But deeply as he felt the danger to the cause and strong as his resentment at the press scurrilities, his letters, both to his superiors and privately to his brother, wherein it would have been easy to make mischief, are impeccable in their tone. A subsequent report of November 4 contains the only hint of his personal grievance, a very gentle hint that he has heard that his estimate "has been construed to my prejudice, therefore leave it for the future." But he decided to give them an opportunity to change the commander if they had lost confidence in him, and concluded his report of the 6th with the sentence: "It would be better if some man of sanguine mind were here, for I am forced to order according to my convictions."

A week later General Buell arrived to relieve Sherman of a command which he had assumed against his own wishes and protests. At the same time he received orders transferring him to the Department of the Missouri, the other of the two departments into which the Western theatre was divided. A note to his brother reveals his mood: "I know that others than myself think I take a gloomy view of affairs without cause. I hope to God 'tis so. . . . For myself I will blindly obey my orders . . . but till I can see daylight ahead I will never allow myself to be in command." After taking leave of his old troops, now in camp on the far side of the Muldraugh Hills, he departed for St. Louis.

But before we take leave of the Kentucky phase of his war career, it is worth noting that he had intervened successfully with the Secretary of War to save his subordinate, Thomas, from being superseded in command of the East Tennessee front.

He himself had still some months of purgatory before he could live down his reputation for insanity. As usual with rumour, the ripples were still widening, and lapped the lips of St. Louis in time to greet his arrival there. He found officers and men looking at him rather askance, and with this irritation coming on top of the strain in Kentucky his highly strung nervous system threatened to snap. He was unpleasantly close to what would now be called a nervous breakdown.

Soon after reporting to Halleck, his old California companion of '46, who had taken Frémont's place, Sherman was sent out westwards to inspect the camp of Sedalia, and the detachments along the road back to Jefferson City. There were rumours of a Confederate attack on Sedalia, and he was given a contingent authorization to assume command over these troops. Finding them scattered and out of touch with each other, he issued preliminary orders to remedy this and sent a message advising Halleck to concentrate these forces in a single camp on the La Mine River, and there organize them into brigades and divisions. The advice was sound and was soon adopted, but it somewhat exceeded his brief. Halleck, according to his own rather contradictory statement later, had more recent information which negatived the idea of an immediate attack, and did not wish any movement which might dissuade the enemy from an advance.

Perhaps also, even more so, he was nettled at the implication that his forces were left open to surprise. In such a mood Halleck was ever as suspicious as he was sensitive. Sherman now, like many others later, suffered from a commander who, when crossed, lent his ear to any camp-talk which coincided with his mood, and lent his tongue to carry it to Washington. In this case Halleck seems to have accepted at their face value—he certainly passed on to Mc-Clellan—the complaints of sundry outlying officers that Sherman was "stampeding" the troops. If Sherman did not know his Halleck, neither did they know their Sherman and, resentful of interference, were the less inclined to appreciate the manner in which he shook them out of their slumbers.

Whatever the real cause, Halleck wired Sherman to make no movement without orders, and two days later sent him a message that his wife had come to St. Louis, and that he was to return and report his impressions. So Sherman, his actual duty completed, returned to find at St. Louis a wife who, distressed at the newspaper reports, had come to meet an insane husband. It was almost a wonder that although she did not find one, she did not soon have one. For he had no sooner returned from Sedalia than the papers came out with stories that his recall was due to some freak act of lunacy

at Sedalia.   To rest his own nerves and in the hope that the papers
would find another topic, he asked for three weeks' leave and went
back to his old home at Lancaster.   Only to find that the ripples had
spread eastwards, to Ohio, as well as westwards.   The *Cincinnati
Commercial* was especially malicious, and when one of his wife's relations protested to the editor, the latter cheerfully replied that it was
one of the news items of the day, and he had to keep up with the
times.

So at the end of his short leave Sherman returned to St. Louis,
hoping that work would be a better tonic than rest.   So it proved,
and with the opening of offensive operations the newspapers discarded him for a more topical news item.

CHAPTER VII

THE FIRST OFFENSIVE IN THE WEST

THE fact that it was the Union forces and not the Confederates who first developed an effective offensive in the West, seems outwardly to throw doubt on Sherman's "appreciation," and to suggest that his outlook was unjustifiably pessimistic. But the unfulfilment of certain general predictions which were merely offshoots of his basic appreciation of the situation does not prove that the appreciation itself was illusory. The failure of events to support him was primarily due to the decision of the Confederate President, Jefferson Davis, against strategical advice, to maintain a strictly defensive policy. The chief motive in this policy was the hope of foreign recognition and intervention, a hope inspired by the misplaced belief that "cotton was king," and that the cotton famine due to the blockade of the Confederate ports would compel Britain and France to take action. Thus, ironically, it was the enemy's delusion which gave to Sherman's view the semblance of a delusion.

Moreover, a study of the conditions in 1861 in the light of later knowledge, strengthens the opinion that the Confederacy missed its best chance alike in the East and in the West. If its forces were slender, they were superior in quality, mobility and command to their still more unready opponents. The North was far stronger in resources, but it was both a sleepy and recumbent giant, and if a lightweight has to tackle such a giant, his best chance, almost his only chance, is to strike before the giant has bestirred himself.

Politically, the occupation of Kentucky, where sympathizers were as numerous as opponents, and more active, promised the Confederacy all that Sherman feared. Strategically, its occupation and the control of the Ohio River, would have given the Confederacy a hold on the Middle West that would have been extremely difficult, if not impossible, to break. The grip would have been reinforced by the advantage, for switching troops, of possessing the one lateral railway—from Louisville through Bowling Green to Memphis, with its branch to Columbus and Paducah in the southern angle of the "K." Instead, by the policy actually adopted, the Confederates were only in possession of this railway as far east as Bowling Green, and it skirted the front so closely that it might easily be lost and the advantage forfeited. This happened.

But the Union offensive, which struck the Confederate front and the lateral railway at its most vulnerable point, in the centre, although brilliantly successful in upsetting the Confederate dispositions, was undertaken as a spasmodic local effort, and thereby its first fruits were ungarnered. Only after another weary winter and excessive expense was the second crop harvested.

Buell, Sherman's successor in Kentucky, had proposed to Washington, independently, a similar plan. Despite his large accession of force, that Sherman had pleaded for in vain, Buell had come to share Sherman's view of the folly of the "blind alley" advance into East Tennessee which Lincoln and McClellan desired. Without river or railroad for its communications this movement over country roads, soon impassable in winter, would be in constant peril of a thrust against its rear flank from a foe who had both a railway and a river from which to launch it. In contrast, Buell perceived that, further west, the Tennessee and Cumberland Rivers, the "split-nib" finishing stroke of the "K," offered an easy approach into the Confederate territory, and that even a short advance would sever the railway, splitting the enemy dispositions in twain. We should not overrate the perception, for it was obvious to any strategical mind—not least or last to Sherman's!

Buell accordingly proposed that Halleck should send two flotilla columns up these rivers to break the Confederate centre, while he himself took advantage of their "shouldering" action to advance due south and converge with Halleck's forces on Nashville. But this combined movement was rejected by McClellan and the idea of combination made no appeal to Halleck. So Buell instead let his forces lie fallow in scattered passivity except for one petty success on the East Tennessee front, in which only four thousand were employed.

And in the East, McClellan, despite his still growing strength of nearly two hundred thousand, felt that they were still unready for an advance, and pursued the policy of slow preparation which

eventually drew from Lincoln the delightful remark that if Mc-
Clellan did not want to use this army he would like to borrow it.
If there was any justification for McClellan's doubts, how much
more for Sherman's earlier?

Thus, in January, 1862, the situation in all theatres might be
epitomized as that of mass minus motion. Two of the three "sector"
commanders were unwilling to move, and the third, Buell, unable
because of their unwillingness. With dramatic suddenness a change
occurred.

Grant, still in Cairo, was yet another of those who perceived
the strategic value of the approach up the Cumberland and Tennessee. And, his perception reinforced by reconnaissance, he had
proposed to Halleck early in January such a move, only to be rebuffed in much the same way as Sherman previously. He renewed
his attempt, however, at the end of the month and found Halleck
now ready and willing. Halleck was always singularly prompt in
acting on opinions which he had rejected rebukingly. What he was
unwilling to do as part of a concerted and combined movement he
was now agreeable to do "off his own bat."

The immediate objective was the capture in turn of Forts Henry
and Donelson, lying parallel on the Tennessee and Cumberland respectively, which the Confederates had built to cover the lateral
railway and to guard the waterways into the heart of Tennessee.
On February 3, Grant moved off, with 15,000 men and a gunboat
flotilla, to attack Fort Henry. Overlooked both from its own and
the opposite side of the river it was untenable against a serious attack, and most of the garrison was evacuated before this began.
The fort surrendered on the 6th, and its capture, although an easy
success, had a wide moral effect.

The immediate strategic effect was to induce Johnston to retire
from Bowling Green, which was a hundred miles east of Fort Henry,
and to fall back to Nashville with half his force, sending the other
half to reinforce Fort Donelson. Had he used the railway to concentrate the bulk of his force against Grant, the latter might have
been discomfited, if not imperilled. But, as it was, Johnston merely
put another 12,000 men in the safe-deposit which Grant was soon
to unlock. Curiously, this number was approximately the total of
prisoners taken on the 16th when the garrison, after an abortive

attempt to break out, surrendered unconditionally to Grant, who thus completed a brilliant ten days' work, during which the flotilla had made their way first up the Tennessee, then down it and up the Cumberland. Only some 6,000 of the garrison succeeded in escaping by steamer or road before the surrender to a force smaller than their own. Nor was the result evidence of the inferior quality of the Confederate troops. It was rather an illustration that disparity of generalship often outweighs a difference of numbers, and that psychological incalculables are apt to make statistical calculations valueless—to the sore perplexity of military pedants, whose minds are fed on "balance-sheet" history.

Grant's coup unlocked the gate into Tennessee, closed the gate into Kentucky, and caused the Confederates to make a further slight withdrawal of their right wing, back from Nashville, which was now open to a water approach up the Cumberland, to Murfreesborough.

But Halleck, having sprung a surprise also on his own Government and on his neighbour, Buell, was now unable to exploit his success except for personal advantage. He lost no time in telegraphing to McClellan, "Give me the command in the West. I ask this in return for Forts Henry and Donelson." The exploitation of the military advantage was less prompt. Indeed, rather scared as to the recoil, Halleck feared that Beauregard, commanding the Confederate left wing on the Mississippi, might seize the chance to seize Cairo and Paducah behind Grant's back. Thus he neither allowed Grant to pursue nor spared him reinforcements from Missouri to safeguard his position. It is fair, however, to mention that the Confederate forces west of the Mississippi, which were threatening an advance on St. Louis, were not defeated and driven back to Arkansas until March.

By his own fault, Halleck's appeal for help from Kentucky took Buell unawares, and found him rather indisposed to give up part of his forces—if not indisposed to give up the East Tennessee expedition. Hence he sent only one division direct to Grant, and marched overland with the rest on Nashville. Although this was occupied on February 24, the time for an effective pursuit of Johnston had passed.

Although the Union forces thus missed the chance of overwhelming Johnston, they still had the strategic advantage of lying between the two separated wings of the weaker Confederate forces. The next lateral railway, and the last, which the Confederates could use for communication was the Memphis and Charleston railway, which spanned the Confederacy from the Mississippi to the Atlantic. From Memphis it ran eastwards to Corinth, near Shiloh and the bend of the Tennessee, where it intersected the line running north from Mobile on the Gulf of Mexico into the southern angle of the "K." And from Corinth it continued eastwards parallel with the Tennessee to Chattanooga, whence it passed through the mountain gap into Georgia and then by way of Atlanta to Charleston on the Atlantic.

If the Union forces could occupy Corinth they would sever the rail link not only between Johnston and Beauregard, but between the Eastern and Western States of the Confederacy, leaving Western Confederates no option but to remain in perilous isolation, or to retreat south on the Gulf States. The more rapid the Union advance the more difficult for the Confederates to counter such a deadly thrust. Their forces in the zone of operations were much weaker and, for the moment, their two separated wings could only coalesce by a long detour on a single-track railway. Furthermore, this railway skirted the Tennessee River which the Union gunboats dominated, and by which the Union troops might approach to within striking distance of the railway.

The moment passed, the best chance was forfeited—once again. The underlying reason was that the Union command was not only divided but too distant. Halleck was right back at St. Louis, sending his instructions by telegraph to Cairo, and thence relayed on by a "rickety telegraph-line" from Paducah to Fort Henry which was constantly breaking down. The further his forces under Grant proceeded, the further his power of control receded—and with it his equanimity. Grant at the other end was impatient to press on after the fall of Donelson, but could get no answer to his repeated requests. This was not entirely the fault of the wire, for the operator later deserted to the enemy.

Thus Grant took only tentative steps, and those in a direction different to Halleck's intention—sending part of his force up the Cumberland towards Nashville. For Halleck, after oscillating violently, at last settled, by March 1, on a plan to push Grant up the Tennessee, and strike at the railway at Corinth and other points. Less wisely, in view of the enemy's situation, he ordained that these blows should merely be "prick and run," and fettered the commanders on the spot by insisting that they must "avoid any general engagements." Buell came to a more discerning view—his idea being to unite with Halleck's force and place the combined forces across the railway. But his discretion was, in effect, more powerful than his imagination, and during the days of opportunity he was anxiously holding his troops back at Nashville, and calling Grant's advanced troops to his aid, from a groundless apprehension of an enemy offensive. Thus no effective action was begun until after the problem of command had been solved in part, and aggravated in part, by the satisfaction on March 11 of Halleck's desire for unity of command—with himself as the unit. But with such a unit real unity was impossible.

Just before he gained control over Buell he lost control over himself in dealing with Grant. Discovering on March 4 that Grant was still on the Cumberland, and not on the Tennessee as he had supposed, he sent a peremptory order to the victor of Donelson to hand over his command to Major-General C. F. Smith, without trying to discover or make allowances for possible hitches in the long-stretched chain of communication. And in telegrams to Washington he had painted Grant so blackly that McClellan had authorized Grant's arrest. "I have had no communication with General Grant for more than a week. . . . His army seems to be as much demoralized by the victory of Fort Donelson as was that of the Potomac by the defeat of Bull Run . . . satisfied with this victory, he sits down and enjoys it without any regard to the future. I am worn out and tired with this neglect and inefficiency." Halleck even passed on rumours to Washington that Grant was resuming "his former bad habits"—heavy drinking.

The one bright spot was in the relations between Smith and Grant. Smith had been Commandant of Cadets when Grant and Sherman were at West Point; one officer to whom both ever looked up with affectionate admiration, their soldiery ideal, mellowing their memories of the harsh system. Yet, the tables turned, he had served loyally under Grant at Donelson, and in nowise encouraged Halleck's desire to give him the credit of the victory and the command. Grant, unfortunate in his superior, was fortunate in his assistants, for similar self-abnegation was shown by Sherman.

On returning to duty at Christmastide Sherman had been assigned to the command of the large training camp at Benton Barracks, St. Louis, and close contact led Halleck to revise his first dubious impression of Sherman. When the news came of Grant's capture of Fort Henry and move on Fort Donelson, Sherman was hurriedly despatched to take command of the Cairo district, which Grant had just quitted. He was thus in fact, if not in name, in charge of the lines of communication, and he established himself at Paducah. Here he was the human regulating centre not only for supplies and reinforcements to Grant, but for the water connections with Halleck in Missouri, and Buell in Kentucky. The value of this experience may be traced in the reputation he later established as a commander whose strategy was ever based on a sure grasp of the factors of supply and transport, a foundation which ensured the security of his most audacious moves. Sherman was a master strategist because he was a born quartermaster.

Grant pays an illuminating tribute to his assistance in February, 1862. "At that time he was my senior in rank and there was no authority of law to assign a junior to command a senior of the same grade. But every boat that came up with supplies or reinforcements brought a note of encouragement from Sherman, asking me to call upon him for any assistance he could render, saying that if he could be of service at the front I might send for him and he would waive rank." For this there was soon no need, as both Grant and Smith were promoted major-generals after Donelson's capture. An ironical turn of fortune's wheel, for when, after the fall of Fort Henry, Sherman was offering to waive his seniority in order to serve under Grant, Halleck was proposing to McClellan that Sherman might be given charge of the Tennessee operations over Grant's head. Sherman, however, soon had his wish to be at the front—with the division which he had created out of the troops at Paducah.

On tiptoe to seize any opportunity for helping the operations, he was active in exploring the situation of the Confederate left wing at Columbus on the Mississippi. While the Confederates were feverishly preparing to evacuate Columbus and save their guns,

Halleck was obstinately faithful to his fearful belief that the forces at Columbus were being reinforced and were preparing an attack on him.   The assurances of McClellan and Buell, from the detached view-point of distance, that the piercing of the Confederates' centre would compel the withdrawal of their left, made no impression on Halleck.   And he was almost as impervious to the confirmatory evidence which Sherman supplied by direct reconnaissance and investigation.

Sherman urged in vain that something should be done to prevent the Confederates evacuating their guns, and suggested a threat in force to the railroad in rear of Columbus.   But Halleck was not convinced of the reality and opportunity—then the lost opportunity— until a cavalry detachment sent by Sherman from Paducah had occupied, on March 3, the deserted works of the "Gibraltar of the West."   This detachment narrowly forestalled a reconnaissance in force from Cairo by a gunboat flotilla, escorting an improvised brigade, which was led by Sherman himself.   When the ships arrived off Columbus, the cavalry were already in possession, but could not be seen, and, rather than launch his troops into a possible ambush, Sherman embarked on a tug and made a dash towards the shore under the muzzles of the water batteries.   With exceptional aptness one may say that he "had the courage of his convictions."

CHAPTER VIII

SHILOH

On March 10, a week after the occupation of Columbus, Sherman embarked his newly organized division at Paducah and steamed up to Fort Henry where he reported to Smith, who was already suffering from a poisoned leg which caused his death a month later. From Fort Henry Sherman steamed up the Tennessee another hundred and twenty miles, roughly double the distance, to Savannah, where Smith's first four divisions assembled on the 13th. Next day Sherman was despatched to land above the Shiloh bend, but below Eastport, and cut the lateral railroad between Corinth and Tuscumbia.

Tied by the orders to avoid a serious engagement, and baulked at several points by the presence of Confederate detachments, Sherman eventually made an unopposed landing late at night near the mouth of Yellow Creek. Thence it was nineteen miles to the railroad and, in order to strike before the enemy could be aware of the move, Sherman sent his cavalry detachment ahead, following on with his division through the rain and darkness. After some hours he met the cavalry returning, as their passage had been blocked by the rain-swollen streams. From behind, too, reports were coming in that the river was rising six inches an hour. With both his road and his landing under water, he took the only possible course— to give up the attempt. And was barely in time to avoid abandoning his guns.

He then steamed back to Pittsburg Landing, on the shore below the log chapel called Shiloh, where he found Hurlbut's division anchored and left his own while he reported to Smith at Savannah the information he had gleaned. He suggested that under cover of a move in force on Corinth the railroad might be successfully cut to the west. Smith ordered him to disembark the two divisions at Pittsburg Landing, leaving room for the rest of the force. Thus somewhat fortuitously the fateful point of disembarkation was chosen.

On the evening of the 16th Sherman made a reconnaissance in force towards Corinth, but on meeting Confederate cavalry in position he was constrained, by Halleck's fettering orders, to give up his subsidiary idea of seizing a chance to cut the railway. The care for security and march discipline shown in the orders for this reconnaissance are, however, a useful sidelight to history—in view of the controversy which has raged round the "insecurity" of the Shiloh operations. Moreover, in his report, Sherman not merely estimated with accuracy the Confederate force then concentrating at Corinth, but suggested that the Union forces should be disembarked not only at Pittsburg Landing, but at Hamburg Landing and Tyler's above it, and Crump's below it, and then "move concentrically on Corinth" or "on any other point along the railroad."

This suggestion recalls Napoleon's wide and loose grouping which was a snare for his opponents, a net which baffled their sight and entangled their limbs. For by its very width it distended their vision and distracted their forces. They were uncertain which route to defend and had no obvious target against which to concentrate. The several landings which Sherman suggested would have had an enhanced advantage—for each landing force would have been based on a river, controlled by the Union gunboats, which enabled a secure retreat at need and the lateral switching of forces.

This report ought to be read in conjunction with his other of the same day, which has been so often quoted and in which he stated that he was "strongly impressed with the importance of the position, both for its land advantages and its strategic position." The second report was strictly a local one on the Pittsburg Landing. Both were sent to Grant who had been restored to command and, on this day, had relieved the mortally sick General Smith.

Unfortunately Grant paid more attention to the second than to the first report, and decided to concentrate his forces at Pittsburg Landing. His action showed that, like most post-Napoleonic soldiers, he shared the general misunderstanding of the lessons taught by the master, a misunderstanding which originates from a linguistic mistake. For while Napoleon took care that his forces were "réuni" before taking the offensive, they were united in the sense of a net and not of a block. In contrast, his successors interpreted the words as meaning "concentrated" in a physical sense, and have regarded a strategical concentration as the essential preliminary to any strategical operation.

If Grant's decision to concentrate at one point was an error in obviousness, it was made worse by the point being so close to the enemy. Grant intended to march direct on Corinth, and his opponents could have no doubt of his intention. As he explained, with unconscious humour, in his memoirs: "I regarded the campaign we were engaged in as an offensive one and had no idea that the enemy would leave strong intrenchments to take the initiative when he knew he would be attacked where he was if he remained." Condemning the enemy, he condemns his own plan, for if Shiloh was only a qualified victory, his own plan would have incurred an almost certain repulse, from which the "unexpected," but most calculable, Confederate offensive saved him. Indeed the crowning irony of Shiloh is that Grant offered a perfect bait but omitted to set the trap.

Here, however, we anticipate events. Grant's plan was the outcome of Halleck's decision to change his "prick and run" strategy for a heavy punch at the Confederate forces gathering at Corinth. To this end, Halleck ordered Buell to move from the Cumberland to the Tennessee, at Savannah. Meantime Grant marked time—and became a marked target.

For within a few days of his resumption of command the bulk of the Confederate forces in the West had come in from the wings to concentrate at Corinth, reknitting their broken centre. Johnston had brought 20,000 men from Murfreesborough on the right, Bueauregard had drawn in his troops from Columbus, and the combined forces had been reinforced by Bragg with 10,000 fine troops from Mobile and Pensacola in the extreme south. A total of nearly 60,000 men were thus assembled in the neighbourhood of Corinth, and Johnston, stimulated by President Davis, decided to attempt the overthrow of Grant's forces before it could be joined by Buell's.

Unfortunately, the Confederates forfeited much of the time which their opponents were allowing them. Johnston had not been as quick as Beauregard to appreciate the value of concentrating at Corinth, and was seemingly dubious both of the risk and of his own power to retrieve the situation. The earlier set-backs and the popular clamour appear to have damped his spirits, and were the most probable cause of his offer to leave Beauregard in command, an offer which Beauregard declined. Even then Johnston waited in the hope of additional reinforcements.

But, at last, on April 3rd, he marched out with an effective strength of some 40,000 towards Pittsburg Landing. He had only twenty miles to cover before reaching the enemy's outpost line, and yet the clash did not occur until the fourth morning. Bad roads, thickly wooded country, and inexperienced staff work fettered the advance, but are only a partial excuse for the conduct of the offensive. We do not wonder that on the 5th Beauregard advised its abandonment on the ground that surprise was no longer feasible. For only a surprise, crowned by a complete success, could rationally justify this plan of a direct assault on an enemy of almost equal numerical strength in a naturally strong position.

Johnston, however, felt that it was "better to make the venture"; that the tame abandonment of the enterprise might forfeit the confidence of the troops and their confidence in him. This habit of gambling contrary to reasonable calculations is a military vice which, as the pages of history reveal, has ruined more armies than any other cause. Cromwell was one of the rare generals who had the strength of will to resist the temptation; even Marlborough succumbed once and Malplaquet was the apple which preceded his fall. If the first phase of Shiloh seemed to controvert calculations, the ultimate issue, and its effect, confirmed them.

Although surprising success attended the first phase of the attack, is it true that an actual surprise was obtained? Numerous historians have come to such a conclusion. Their strongest point, and most frequent, is contained in Grant's report to Halleck on the 5th —"I have scarcely the faintest idea of an attack (general one) being made upon us, but will be prepared should such a thing take place."

This was written after receiving a report from Sherman of an outpost skirmish in the afternoon; in reporting it Sherman said: "I infer that the enemy is in some considerable force at Pea Ridge" —about ten miles out towards Corinth. Among other evidence commonly cited is Grant's casual rejection on the 5th of the idea of ferrying across Buell's leading division which had just reached Savannah, the fact that Grant's headquarters were still downstream at Savannah, and the fact that the Union position was not entrenched. But Grant's very failure to set the trap after providing the bait is sufficient proof that the enemy offensive was a strategic surprise to him.

There is, however, a wide difference between a strategic and a tactical surprise—between the deduction that the Confederates' action in taking the initiative was unexpected by him and the conclusion that the Union troops were taken by surprise. For in the early morning of Sunday, April 6th, the first contact was made, not by the Confederates but by the Union pickets which, reinforced overnight, began to probe the enemy's picket line as soon as it was light. Although they were eventually driven back—the main Confederate advance following on their heels—the alarm was thus given in ample time for the Union divisions to form up and move into position. This they did; and it is clear from the reports of the Confederate regimental officers that there was no tactical surprise. If the struggle later began to show some of the characteristics of a surprise, the effect was due to the inadequacy of the Union troops and their dispositions—which in turn was due to the "offensive" obsession of the higher command.

Grant had some 45,000 men, distributed in six divisions. Of these, five, totalling some 33,000 effectives, were at Pittsburg Landing, and the sixth at Crump's Landing, some five miles downstream. The position at Pittsburg Landing was ideal for resistance, except that the woods were liable to cause confusion. The junction of Snake Creek with the Tennessee River formed a triangle of land which was squeezed into a peninsula by two tributary streams—Owl Creek on the west and Lick Creek on the east. Like incurving horns, these protected the flanks and narrowed the frontage to defend.

Along this frontage, some three miles wide and two miles inward from the landing, were disposed the camps of Sherman's and Prentiss's division, the two rawest divisions in the force. Sherman lay on the right, next to Owl Creek, with Prentiss on his left. Beyond Prentiss, on the extreme left, adjoining Lick Creek and the Tennessee, was Stuart's brigade of Sherman's division—which comprised four brigades, one more than the others. In close support behind the right centre of the front lay McClernand's division, and further back near the landing were the divisions of W. H. L. Wallace and Hurlbut in reserve.

Much ink, and more vitriol, has been expended in criticizing the position taken up by the Union force, but in fact the frontage was certainly not excessive for the numbers, and the reserve divisions were handily placed. As for the objection that there was no land line of retreat, this seems somewhat strained in view of the equality of forces, and of the fact that the expedition had been transported by and was based on the river, which the Union gunboats controlled. Many expeditions in history have maintained themselves on the tip of a peninsula with less strength, less chance of escape by water, and a far wider frontage to defend. But in the possible comparison between Shiloh and Torres Vedras there is one essential difference—the absence of the "Lines" which enabled Wellington to defy a superior foe despite his extended and thinly held front. In 1862 the art and value of entrenching, so repeatedly despised by peace-trained soldiers, had yet to be relearnt.

But the greater cause of the neglect to fortify the Shiloh position, or even to practise the troops in taking up defensive dispositions, was a surfeit of offensive spirit in the Union command. Subsequently, Grant's argument, loyally supported by Sherman, was that he had come to take the offensive and that defensive preparations would have damaged the spirit of his raw troops, besides wasting time better spent in drill.

History curiously repeats itself—for a similar argument was popular among the military leaders of Europe in 1914, until bullets and their troops removed the argument to a different plane—the bottom of a trench. Nevertheless, it was re-echoed by the American leaders in the last year of the war, a war which ended too quickly for them to discover that it is the bullet, not the trench, which damps the offensive spirit, and that an excess of trenches is merely the natural sequel to an excessive disregard of precautions against bullets. The more raw the troops the more necessary it is to safeguard their morale—by trenches on the defensive, by insuring surprise in the offensive. And the more morale is safeguarded, the easier it is to induce any troops to leave their trenches.

Atlanta was to show that Sherman, at least, learnt the lesson of

Shiloh, notwithstanding his protestations, and the thoroughness of his moral safeguards in 1864 was to be measured by the pace at which his "mobile entrenchments" advanced—thereby proving that trenches and mobility are not irreconcilable. If the example is almost unique, it is because the recognition of reality is equally rare. In the early part of the war such regimental titles as "Fire Zouaves" symbolized the spirit of the offensive which filled the mind of leaders and led alike. But the "fireguards" of later years were carried forward consistently, whereas the "Fire Zouaves" had too often gone backward.

The fundamental cause of the initial collapse at Shiloh was not that the Union forces were surprised by the enemy, but that they themselves were surprised at having to stand on the defensive. For this they were physically ready but mentally unready. Filled with the idea of hitting, they had never entertained the idea of guarding. The result which followed disillusionment at Bull Run was repeated, and came earlier, at Shiloh. For the careful student of the Shiloh records who has also experienced war soon realizes that the initial Union failure was due little to faulty generalship on the field, still less to superior Confederate generalship, but mainly to the unsteady morale of the Union troops. Hence the frequent panics and the thick crowd of stragglers on the river bank which gave Buell, on arrival, an exaggerated idea of the gravity of the situation. In all battles, the percentage of human failure is far higher than history ever records, but at Shiloh it was abnormal. Making all allowance for the confusingly wooded country, the lack of entrenchments, and the rawness of the troops, there is no adequate military reason; only a psychological one. And the scarcity of bayonet wounds is indirect evidence to this effect. For the psychological failure, however, the original blame lies with the command.

Now to outline the course of the battle. At about 5 A.M. the pickets became engaged and an hour later Prentiss's advanced troops had been driven back on his main body, which he had moved forward in the interval. Owing partly to this move and partly to the tendency of the Confederate first line to crowd inwards on the centre, Prentiss was bearing the first shock of the attack an hour before Sherman was engaged, and even before the alarm had been given in his division.

Prentiss seemingly did not think of sending word to Sherman, although he warned the reserve divisions. Arrangements for communication appear to have been deficient. But, in any case, Sherman would have been unwise to move, for the front of his two right brigades was protected by Shiloh Creek, a tributary of Owl Creek. Of this he took prompt advantage when his retiring pickets brought news of the enemy's approach and, with his right and centre brigades strongly posted to cover the valley, opened fire on the advancing masses of the enemy which were surging obliquely across his front on the heels of Prentiss's troops, who had fallen back to the line of their encampment.

Soon after eight o'clock Prentiss, unable to withstand the pressure, gave the order to fall back on the divisions of Wallace and Hurlbut which, in response to his appeal, had begun to come forward—in time to receive the fugitive swarms whom Prentiss was gallantly striving, with but partial success, to rally.

The tide of battle, flowing past Sherman's inner flank, did not leave him unscathed. For his left brigade, next to Prentiss, was caught by the enemy's advance before it was effectively posted, and the flank regiment bolted, led by its colonel. The other regiments, to whose support McClernand had sent a brigade at Sherman's request, made a longer stand, but eventually joined in the rearward drift. But with his two other brigades he maintained himself in his advanced position behind Shiloh Creek and covering Shiloh until after 10 A.M., although to the direct onslaught on his front, and a frustrated attempt to turn his outer flank, was added a constant erosion of his inner flank. When this was enfiladed by artillery he was at last compelled to withdraw his two brigades to the Purdy road on a line with the right of McClernand's division, which was now bearing the brunt of the Confederate attack.

During this stand Sherman was visited by Grant, who had come up hurriedly by boat from Savannah, and it was doubtless his bearing here which led Grant to single him out for unique mention in his subsequent despatch, as displaying "great judgment and skill in the management of his men. Although severely wounded in the hand the first day his place was never vacant. He was again wounded and had three horses killed under him."

Neither in his report nor in his memoirs does Sherman refer to his wounds, although there is a casual mention in a letter to his brother that "my right hand is temporarily disabled by inflammation from a wound." We learn from Grant that the second wound was a slight one in the shoulder, and also that a third ball passed through his hat. But the modesty of Sherman's report, and the absence of any personal claims, is in marked contrast with the self-adulation of McClernand who, not content with a colourful report, sent a boastful letter to the President.

Sherman's chief work in the battle was, however, accomplished in these first hours when his resistance on the advanced flank formed an invaluable brake on the Confederate advance during its original impetus. After the withdrawal to the Purdy road his brigades gradually dissolved, and though he strove indomitably to hold them together, only a remnant, augmented by a regiment and odd companies from other divisions, remained under his direct control. This remnant really formed an appendix to the line of McClernand's division, now also a mixture, and sustained its outer flank during the successive fighting withdrawals which ended shortly before dark on a line covering the River road across Snake Creek to Crump's Landing.

By this road Lew Wallace's division now arrived, belatedly, having taken all day to cover a distance which, directly, was only five miles. But he had marched originally by the Purdy road, and was within short reach of the battlefield when a staff officer from Grant overtook him with the news that the Union right had fallen back. This had caused him to retrace his steps in order to start afresh on the River road. When so far committed to the other road he might, with more profit, have gone on. He appreciated too much the risk of fighting isolated and too little the enemy's feelings when a fresh division appeared on their rear flank, and thus forewent the opportunity of an early afternoon intervention which might well have been decisive.

For, high as the élan of the Confederates, and fierce the vigour of their attacks, their advance became disjointed as they pressed on, and in the confusion of the woods hundreds of stragglers drifted back out of the disordered ranks. Then, about 2.30 P.M., Johnston fell, after playing the rôle of a gallant combat leader rather than a supreme commander. A belated attempt was made by his successor, Beauregard, to turn Grant's left flank and cut him off from the river—too late to be effective—because there was now too little room and too few reserves for such a manœuvre. Thus the Confederates wore down their own strength and endurance in repeated frontal assaults. For a time they minimized the strain and magnified the effect by penetrating between the disconnected bodies of the defending side, threatening their immediate flanks, and so hastening their withdrawal. But by pressing the defenders back into the apex of the triangle, they inevitably compressed the resistance into a more solid and shortened line—until it was little more than a mile wide and rested behind a ravine covering the Landing.

At six o'clock, with his troops disorganized by their efforts and darkness falling, Beauregard decided to suspend a battle that neither he nor his divisional commander could any longer direct. Spasmodic efforts were continued by Confederate units out of reach of this order, but they failed to make any impression on a defence which, although weak, had shed all its weaker members and was now reinforced by the arrival of the leading brigade of Buell's army from across the river.

The spent and shaken troops of the two armies lay confronting each other—at a distance—in the darkness of the woods, the men chiefly intent to snatch rest, while the commanders strove to restore order out of chaos. In such a situation the real advantage was with the defender and, as if in silent acknowledgment of the verdict, a swelling number of the Confederates snatched the friendly cloak of darkness to cover their individual retirement, until by morning the Confederate ranks had heavily shrunk in the wash—of several thousand stragglers now on their way home to Corinth. The martial ardour that had burnt so brightly on the first day had burnt itself out through an unwise heaping up of the fuel.

On the Union side the divisions of W. H. L. Wallace and Prentiss had disappeared, save for a few fragments, and the much mixed fighting line into which Sherman, McClernand and Hurlbut brought a measure of order during the night numbered barely 7,000 men. But Lew Wallace with an intact division of 5,000 was now in line on Sherman's right, and by daylight two of Buell's divisions and one brigade of another had arrived—a total of nearly 20,000 fresh troops (some estimates, without any clear warrant, put it at 23,000). These were now to be thrown in against the tired and hungry Confederates who numbered barely 20,000. And it says much for the way in which Beauregard managed to reorganize his divisions during the night, and for his control next day—if not so much for the Union direction—that the Confederates were able to make an unendangered fighting retreat.

In later years controversy became bitter among the chief actors on the Union side, so that the actual battle reports are a better guide. The impression left is that neither Grant nor Buell appreciated the opportunity on the second day, exercised much direction, or hoped to do more than drive the enemy back. Buell, of course, was handicapped by ignorance of the ground, although the handicap was partly retrieved when he met Sherman who, characteristically, was able to supply him with a self-drawn map.

But the light casualties in Buell's two divisions which led the morning counterstroke, although it was a frontal advance, do not suggest a greater impulse than that required to remind the enemy that retreat was the path of discretion. More energetic, if equally direct, was the advance of McCook's division which came into the action later, on their right. The sturdy pressure of this division, especially Rousseau's brigade, pushing straight up the Corinth road towards Shiloh chapel, was the main factor in leading Beauregard, early in the afternoon, to give the order for retreat.

Rousseau's finely trained brigade was composed of the same men whom Sherman, in the previous October, had hurriedly rushed out to the Muldraugh Hills. Now they were the means of bestowing upon him a fresh title. For, coming abreast of a smoke-blackened officer, with torn clothes and his arm in a sling, who was rallying his own cluster of men for a fresh effort, their commander recognized him and reported with the words—"Rousseau's brigade, your old troops, General Sherman." Rousseau's well-ordered ranks caught the name, and broke in a cry "There's old Sherman," followed by three ringing cheers. The title stuck until in the last year of the war it was superseded by the still more affectionate "Uncle Billy." At the moment Sherman was in no mood for compliments and ignored the cheers, but he appreciated it more than his honours, and in sending his wife an account of the battle he said: "One thing pleased me well," and then, after relating the meeting, added "such shouting you never heard. I have since visited their camp and never before received such marks of favor." In his report, too, he paid a tribute to his old troops who had followed up the compliment with a practical proof of their spirit in the finest assault of the day. Rousseau's was not the only "outside" body of troops to whom he gave mention. Indeed, Sherman's generous tributes to good work by brigades other than his own is in marked contrast to the reports of other commanders, which, in the reading, seem too intent to monopolize credit for themselves. And to the enemy, too, he gave credit that they "treated our wounded well and kindly." His chivalrous words were supplemented by at least one deed. After the battle he recognized in a ragged prisoner one of his old Louisiana cadets and fitted him out with new clothing. It was the first of many acts of kindness which he did, both during and after the war, for his former friends in the South.

Curiously, the battle ended near Sherman's original camp. Yielding the Shiloh chapel ridge which they had so stubbornly held the Confederates drew off under cover of feint counterattacks, whereupon Buell halted his advance, content to have regained the old front line. Grant was at least equally content, and discountenanced any pursuit until next morning on account of the fatigue of the troops. It was unfortunate that before the last attacks were delivered he had left the field—his ankle had been badly injured when his horse had fallen on the 4th, and thus ceaseless pain was added to the strain of his unsparing exertions during the two days of battle.

Next day a further division of Buell's had come up and two brigades of this as well as two brigades which Sherman had reorganized were sent forward to discover the enemy's position. Sherman was in command of this reconnaissance and pushed out for five miles, past the abandoned camps and litter of the Confederates, until he came in contact with their cavalry rearguard. This charged, whereupon the leading infantry regiment bolted, although they had admirable ground for defence. The Confederate cavalry were, however, soon repulsed, and after carrying the reconnaissance a further mile forward Sherman marched back to camp at nightfall. His news that the Confederate army had retired out of reach was grateful to the ears of the Union command. Grant's army was in no state to follow up the Confederates, and Buell's was not under his command.

Indeed, an uncertain duality of command reigned until the 11th when Halleck at last arrived. But he was in no greater hurry to advance than to arrive, and did not begin an excessively cautious move on Corinth until nearly three weeks later. With this in view he recalled Pope who, with 21,000 men and Foote's fleet of gunboats, were sweeping down the Mississippi. Thereby Halleck forfeited an opportunity of loosening the Confederate grip, far more hopeful than any direct pressure on Corinth. Pope's arrival brought Halleck's total strength up to 100,000.

Halleck also reshuffled his army—and his commanders. After the battle Grant had written to Halleck: "It becomes my duty again to report another battle fought between two great armies, one contending for the maintenance of the best government ever devised, the other for its destruction. It is pleasant to record the success of the army contending for the former principle." And in congratulating his troops on having "routed a numerically superior force" he had declared: "No such contest ever took place on this continent; in importance of results, but few such have taken place in the history of the world." Nemesis followed as swiftly on this grandiloquent pæan, probably due to his staff, as it did on the joy-bells which rang for Cambrai in 1917. In 1862, however, as the Confederate troops were unable to administer the rebuke, the Northern public did it for them, and with no less strategic effect.

If the Northern troops in 1862 had only been as mobile as the Northern news they would have been irresistible in manœuvre. The stragglers who had not found time for fighting had found ample on the river bank to relate, to correspondents and camp-followers, lurid stories of disaster—of an army overwhelmed by surprise in their tents and of careless and incompetent leadership. These reports soon filled the press and resounded in the main streets of the North. The first impression was the more difficult to change, because it contained a measure of truth, although not so much as a half truth, and because the official reports, as is their habit, went to the other extreme in ignoring truth. The impression, too, seems to have been aggravated by the freely sprinkled comments of Buell and some of his subordinates. No self-delusion is more natural, nor so commonly repeated in history, than for an army which arrives on the scene when the enemy has shot his bolt to believe, and proclaim, that this result is solely due to the latest arrivals.

Halleck was receptive to this widespread impression even though he contradicted it in his official reports. If he had superseded Grant before without justification, he was unlikely to forego the chance of repeating it now that there was a reason. Thus in his redistribution Buell's army became the centre; Pope's disembarked at Hamburg Landing, the left; and Grant's the right—but without Grant. G. H. Thomas was taken from Buell and given command, thus becoming Sherman's superior, a reversal of their old positions in Kentucky and one that ere long was to be reversed again.

This step was a little curious, as Sherman was now in better favour with Halleck who, indeed, had written specially to the Secretary of War on reaching Pittsburg Landing: "It is the unanimous opinion here that Brig. Gen. W. T. Sherman saved the fortune of the day on the 6th instant, and contributed largely to the glorious victory on the 7th. He was in the thickest of the fight on both days. . . . I respectfully request that he be made a major-general of volunteers. . . ."

This promotion duly followed, and was a just tribute to his spirit and energy, if the terms of the recommendation perhaps over-estimated the extent of his influence on the battle, except in the first phase. Thus, to signalize one of the few occasions on which his vision was at fault was, however, in accord with the habitual irony of military authority in rewarding gallant atonement more than the vision which makes it unnecessary. But if it had been Sherman's view that the encounter on the 5th only portended a "strong demonstration," on the ground that "Beauregard was not such a fool as to leave his base of operations and attack us in ours," this view coincided remarkably with Beauregard's own state of mind on the same day. Sherman's mistake was that while he projected himself into the enemy's mind he estimated their moral courage by his own. If his vision was thus at fault, even Buell when, stung by later controversy, he sought to exalt his own share at the expense of Grant and his assistants, could not forget the impression of Sherman's bearing in the hour of crisis. "There was the frank, brave soldier, rather subdued, realizing the critical situation in which causes of some sort, perchance his own fault chiefly, had placed him, but ready, without affectation or bravado, to do anything that duty required of him."

The sequel yields another sidelight, different, but equally significant, on Sherman's character. Grant had been deposed from any active command and left in gilded isolation as "second in command." There was a curiously prophetic aptness in the fact that Halleck borrowed the idea of this vice and vicarious post from French practice, for he ignored his unwanted deputy as assiduously and ostentatiously as did Joffre half a century later.

Slighted by his fellow generals, assailed in the press, and knowing that he was the subject of disparaging gossip among the soldiers, Grant suffered deeply in spirit but said little, staying in comparative seclusion with a few loyal members of his staff. Outside this tiny circle he turned for sympathy and understanding to only one man in the camp—Sherman. Slight as their previous acquaintance, these two—the one who had gained fame and the one who had lost it—drew together rapidly in friendship. Beneath the fiery energy which had won Grant's admiration in the crucial hours of Shiloh, there was in Sherman an almost feminine tenderness, which now manifested itself in greater sensitiveness to Grant's hard lot than to his own new laurels. Shiloh had been a spiritual tonic to Sherman by proving to him, the severest judge, his own capacity to rise to an emergency. The effect is shown by a remark, in a letter to his father-in-law, which strikes an entirely new note—"I am not in search of glory or fame, for I know I can take what position I choose among my peers." April 6 had been the way and day of revelation, to himself. Thus he was now, as he says, "in high feather." Yet heightened confidence instead of taking the common form of conceit set him free to be more, rather than less, considerate of others, having suffered himself. These bonds of sympathy between Grant and Sherman had vital consequences some weeks later when they alone intervened to hold Grant fast to the service.

For Grant, growing weary beyond endurance, asked permission to return home, an act which would have been tantamount, as with so many other officers, to resignation. Sherman happened to call at Halleck's headquarters and, hearing him mention casually that

Grant was going away next morning, guessed the meaning. He rode at once to Grant's camp, to find him packing. To a direct enquiry as to the cause, he replied: "Sherman, you know. You know that I am in the way here. I have stood it as long as I can, and can endure it no longer." He added that he was going to St. Louis, and when Sherman asked him if he had any business there, answered "Not a bit." Sherman, however, argued with him, recalling how he himself had sunk to rise again, and finally won Grant's promise to reconsider the decision. Soon afterwards Sherman received a note to tell him that his advice had been taken.

Sherman's efforts on Grant's behalf were not confined to direct sympathy and advice. As he had earlier urged his brother not to lend himself to the political clamour against McClellan, so now he took up the cudgels for Grant in Washington through the same useful channel. He was indignant that the blame should be thrown on Grant by "the common soldiers and subordinates" who "ran away." "The scoundrels who fled their ranks and left about half their number to do their work have succeeded in establishing their story of surprise, stuck with bayonets and swords in their tents and all that sort of stuff. *They* were surprised, astonished and disgusted at the utter want of respect for life on the part of the Confederates, whom they have been taught to regard as inferior to them, and were surprised to see them approach with banners fluttering, bayonets glistening and lines dressed on the centre. It was a beautiful and dreadful sight and I was prepared for and have freely overlooked the fact that many wilted and fled, but gradually recovering, rejoined our ranks." For those who did not recover his contempt is blazing, and the prophetic realism—still unchanged—of his conclusion is in contrast to the declarations of Grant and others as to the consequence of the battle—"that the war is ended or even fairly begun I do not believe."

In a subsequent letter of May 12 he remarks of his men that "They are all green and raw. . . . Last evening I had to post my own pickets and came under the fire of the enemy's pickets. Came near being hit. Of course being mounted and ahead, I and my staff always get an undue share of attention. . . . I have been worried to death by the carelessness of officers and sentinels . . . with as much idea of war as children. . . . Too many of the officers are sick of the war and have gone home on some pretence or other." If this was the condition a month after Shiloh we can better understand the course of that battle. And the rare modesty of Sherman's reports, the lack of all suggestion of personal achievement even in intimate letters, the generosity of his tributes to good work wherever he finds it, and the invariable recognition by others of his courage, are strong if indirect corroboration of his judgments, as true to the facts.

A week after the battle Sherman conducted a raid which he does not even mention in his memoirs, but which, temporarily and potentially, had a greater strategic effect than the ponderous operations which followed. Embarking with a hundred cavalrymen and an infantry brigade on a couple of transports, one appropriately named *Tecumseh*, he steamed up the Tennessee to the now unguarded landing near the mouth of Bear Creek. His cavalry headed up the road to Juka, twenty miles east of Corinth, and west of Bear Creek, driving back the Confederate pickets, who themselves obligingly set fire to the Juka road bridge over the Creek.

With the flank of the raiding movement thus safeguarded, the cavalry swerved away from the Juka road and dashed up the east bank for the railroad bridge. Driving off the detachment guarding it, they began the work of destruction which was completed with the aid of the infantry on arrival. Then, with the bridge and 500 feet of trestle work, over the swamp on either side, ruined, the force retired unmolested, thanks to the rapidity and deceptiveness of their dash. Thus the Memphis and Charleston railroad, the lateral railroad, was broken, only for the strategic advantage to be forfeited by Halleck's prolonged delay in getting up steam in his "steam-roller." Two more weeks passed before it moved and six before it reached Corinth.

CHAPTER IX

THE CAMPAIGN OF 1862 IN THE EAST

THE first week of April, 1862, was a fateful week of the war. It is noteworthy how often, by curious coincidence, turning points came simultaneously in the East and in the West. For the day after the Western Confederate army had moved out temerariously from Corinth and three days before it reeled back from Shiloh, precariously shaken by its repulse, a Union advance began in the East which seemed still more ominous for the Confederate cause. McClellan had conceived the plan of utilizing the Union control of the sea to avoid the well-barred and narrow direct approach to Richmond, and instead to transfer his army on to the enemy's strategic flank, close to Richmond.

The conception was rich in promise. But the infant plan was marred in delivery by ignorant midwifery—and too many midwives. Lincoln and his government interfered repeatedly and harmfully with McClellan, and their impatience was aggravated by the stubborn and unconciliatory disregard shown by McClellan. Rightfully desirous to prepare his forces adequately for their next spring and to risk no more Bull Runs, he unduly ignored political factors in his obsession with the military, and failed to appreciate that military power can only be generated from a public dynamo.

Thus the irritated and uneasy President repeatedly overstepped the borders of McClellan's sphere and ultimately confined him to the command of the expeditionary force—the Army of the Potomac— alone. But even here the President interfered by compelling him to choose the least suitable and least favoured of his three suggested points of disembarkation—at Fort Monroe near the end of the long and cramped Yorktown Peninsula, confined between the York and James Rivers. It is likely that the restriction was inspired by the desire to compel him to discard the indirect oversea approach for the the direct overland route to Richmond, a line of approach which, if it covered Washington, was foredoomed as a way to gaining Richmond—because it followed the line of most resistance.

McClellan wisely persevered with his plan, even as restricted. While three corps, totalling some 58,000 men, landed at Fort Monroe, McClellan planned to use McDowell's corps on the north side of the York River as a lever to loosen the resistance facing himself. But the chance of success was further marred by Lincoln's reluctance to accept a calculated risk, in consequence of which he kept back McDowell's corps for the direct protection of Washington and so deprived McClellan not only of part of his strength but of the element of distraction essential to the success of his expedition.

On April 4, the day on which his advance towards Richmond began, he received this bitter news, in effect a stab in the back—indeed in the backbone, for it seems to have paralyzed his nerve and energy. In fairness it must be said that he had in part provoked it by misleading his own Government as to the force he was leaving for the direct protection of Washington. Although he had more than four times the force of the Confederates facing him he allowed his force to become rooted, and lost a month in the siege of Yorktown.

The delay enabled the Confederate main army under J. E. Johnston to be withdrawn from Manassas in the north and brought to meet him. And, ironically, the Union Government was constrained to send him more reinforcements, in the hope of accelerating his progress, than they had originally detained. Further, they allowed McDowell's corps to co-operate so long as it advanced overland by a route which did not uncover Washington. This permission caused McClellan to stretch his own force northwards, astride the Chickahominy River, towards McDowell's intended line of approach —so that the advance would become convergent or semi-direct.

In war, time lost is rarely regained. On May 24, two months after his force had landed, McClellan heard that McDowell's share in the plan had been again suspended—owing to the fright over Washington's security caused by "Stonewall" Jackson's advance northward down the Shenandoah Valley. Rarely has so small a force by mobility exercised so great a moral influence.

Thus handicapped, McClellan was still able to force his way slowly forward until, on June 25, his outposts were only four miles from Richmond. But by then Robert E. Lee, who had replaced

Johnston—severely wounded on May 31
federate army, was strong enough to i
reinforcements drawn from the Atlantic c
the paralyzed McDowell and bring "Ston
Shenandoah Valley to strike against McCl
For by altering his course to run nearer to
route, McClellan had exposed his flank and com.
a thrust.

But the Confederate thrust miscarried and the tactical flesh-
wound inflicted on McClellan in the Seven Days' Battle merely drove
him to seek shelter in a better vantage point, by a flank march
southwards. By switching his base to the James River he not only
secured his own communications, but placed himself menacingly
close to Petersburg and the enemy's communications from Richmond
to the South—the same position which Grant so painfully and
expensively regained two years later. Thus McClellan still had the
strategic advantage, perhaps more than before, of position for
approach.

The advantage, however, was forfeited by a change of strategy,
which was precipitated by his exorbitant demands for fresh troops
—his "constitutional" weakness. He was ordered on August 3 to re-
embark his army and withdraw it northwards in order to unite with
Pope's army—composed of McDowell's corps and two more from
the Shenandoah Valley—in a closely convergent and direct overland advance southwards on Richmond.

As so often in history, a direct doubling of strength by concentration—that popular panacea for all military ills—meant not a
doubling but a halving of the effect through simplifying the enemy's
"lines of expectation." This fresh change of strategy led first to a
loss of time and relaxation of pressure, so that Pope was nearly
trapped in Lee's net while McClellan's army was being transported
back. After an escape from being cut off on the Rapidan Pope
was hoodwinked by Lee's calculated daring in dividing his army
for a wide indirect approach; Pope's communications cut and his
supplies destroyed, his badly mauled although numerically superior
army escaped from the battlefield of Bull Run, now doubly of ill-
omen to the Union arms, to seek shelter on September 1 within the
fortifications of Washington.

The sequel was that the Union, despite its superiority of numbers, had to suffer the indignity and political danger of invasion. For Lee, slipping past the flank of Washington, swept across the Potomac into Maryland on September 4. But his pause to safeguard his communications by capturing Harpers Ferry, and McClellan's initiative in moving west—if not moving quick—forestalled his intention to press on into Pennsylvania. And, accepting battle at Sharpsburg on the Antietam, the stalemate end of a costly struggle compelled Lee to withdraw his weak and weakened force across the Potomac.

Three days later, on September 22, Lincoln issued his Edict of Emancipation, by which all slaves in States still in insurrection after the New Year were to be recognized as free by the Union Government. If this act gained him sympathy abroad and kindled much enthusiasm in the North, especially in the large Abolitionist party, it antagonized the Democratic party. This was dangerous in view of the autumn elections and Lincoln, sensitive to the currents of feeling, felt a quickened anxiety for a timely military success. McClellan, as stubborn as ever in responding to political pressure or needs, took his usual time in preparation. Already distrusted as a Democrat, this delay caused his final downfall, and just as he was beginning his advance in November he was replaced by the charming and charmingly complaisant Burnside. Recasting the plan and starting from Acquia Creek, forty miles below Washington on the Potomac, Burnside determined to march straight on Richmond. And, attacking without any hope of surprise, the futility of the strategy of direct approach was finally attested, for 1862, by the bloody repulse at Fredericksburg on December 13.

CHAPTER X

THE PARALYSIS OF THE NORTH

A YOUTHFUL giant stricken with paralysis—such is the symbolical story of the North in 1862. The immobility to which it was reduced came first from internal causes, and only later was aggravated by external causes. Growth had outstripped strength, and the overgrown body was handicapped by weak limbs and a weaker brain. Thus prone to infection, the strategic bacilli of the direct approach—whose symptoms are obviousness and slowness—fastened on it and multiplied in its blood. In consequence, an excess of blood in the head was followed by a dangerous hæmorrhage. From midsummer onwards it suffered from the stings of a swift-moving and elusive foe, but its own immobility was manifested before the mobility of the enemy was developed.

In the West the paralysis set in more rapidly than in the East. It was, indeed, the only rapid feature of the campaign. Both sides spent April in carrying concentration to the pitch of absurdity. Halleck collected a hundred thousand men into a human sheepfold round Shiloh, and the military result of the earlier victory of his lieutenant Curtis over Van Dorn's Confederate force west of the Mississippi was to enable Beauregard to swell his own mass at Corinth with Van Dorn's 15,000 men, so that he had now present for duty 53,000—and 18,000 in the hospitals.

While Beauregard entrenched himself, losing men steadily from sickness in this marshy area, Halleck began a painfully cautious advance across the twenty mile interval with his cumbrous mass, like a reluctant hippopotamus forsaking its river-side haunts. The commanders in the van were solemnly warned "not to bring on an engagement." Leaving on April 29, and entrenching each night, his line at last came in touch with the Confederate advanced troops, driving them back to the Corinth defences two miles behind, on May 18. Twenty miles in twenty days—surely a record slow march! As a Tennessee man asked of Sherman, "If it took us a month with no opposition to make a day's march, how long's it going to take us to get in yonder if they show fight?" But the Confederates were not inclined to fight for a swamp-surrounded village which had already lost its strategic importance once the Union forces could command the lateral railroad.

On May 25, Beauregard issued his orders for the evacuation and the withdrawal of his army southward, down the Mobile and Ohio Railroad. It was well staged. On the same day Halleck was wiring the Secretary of War that if any reinforcements were to be sent "I would wait for them; if not I would venture an attack." On May 28, three reconnoitring columns were sent to feel the enemy's position. Sherman, on the extreme right of the line, directed one column and carried a ridge overlooking the enemy's parapet, taking a Confederate brigade by surprise and repulsing their counterattack to regain the ridge. The next day was spent in getting heavy batteries into position ready to overwhelm works now filled with dummy guns and stuffed gunners. Some war correspondents were apparently the only members of the mighty Union host who suspected what was happening, having talked with railroad men who, putting their ears to the rails, had declared that loaded trains had been going out and empty ones coming into Corinth.

In the early hours of the 30th, General Pope, commanding the left wing, informed Halleck that "The enemy are reinforcing heavily in my front. . . . I have no doubt I shall be attacked in heavy force at daylight." Halleck thereupon ordered the centre and reserve to stand ready to reinforce to support Pope. Then soon after daylight a series of explosions were heard, and clouds of smoke seen rising over Corinth. Sherman at once telegraphed the news to Halleck, and was instructed to advance and "feel the enemy." His division, with others, pressed over the abandoned parapets and into the burning town.

Later there was an acrid controversy, in which Sherman took no part, as to which division had entered first, and certain of Buell's commanders protested against the credit being popularly given to Sherman's division. Sherman's comment is more to the point—"There was some rather foolish clamor for the first honors, but in fact there was no honor in the event. Beauregard had made a clean retreat to the south. . . . The advance on Corinth had occupied all of the month of May, the most beautiful and valuable month of the year for campaigning in this latitude." The only profit, he felt, was that it had been a "magnificent drill" for his half-trained troops.

Other commanders, Pope especially, were more boastful, and Halleck's despatch drew from Stanton, now the Secretary of War, the reply: "Your glorious despatch has just been received and I have sent it into every State. The whole land will soon ring with applause at the achievement. . . ." Lincoln's was more apt: "Thanks for the good news. . . . Have you anything from Memphis or other parts of the Mississippi River? Please answer."

For Halleck's money-lending strategy of "no advance without security" had imperilled the future of his own business, and thereby caused greater insecurity to the Union. By too brazen and too narrow an approach he had defeated his own object, and had allowed, indeed impelled, the fly to walk out of his parlour. A consequence all the more unfortunate because the Confederate forces had been conveniently attracted to a single point, whereas now they could again spread out and carry the germs of trouble into other and wider areas. Actually, they were slow to do so, although eventually with excessive success, and their delay gave Halleck a fresh chance to keep the initiative, which in turn he forfeited.

He has often been blamed for his failure to follow up the Confederates southward when they fell back to Tupelo. But the real fault was in the approach, not in the pursuit. They had gone down the railroad and could, as they did, destroy the bridges on their way through the swampy districts.

From the viewpoint of strategy, and also of war policy, Halleck's better way would have been the one indicated in Sherman's note to his brother the day after the occupation of Corinth. "I hope all this army with some exceptions will be marched forthwith to Memphis. A part could be spared for Huntsville, Ala., and Nashville, but as to pursuing overland it would be absurd. We want the Mississippi now in its whole length and a moment should not be lost." He sees, too, that "the greatest danger is that they will scatter," although this scattering did not take the form which he feared of a wide-spread diffusion into guerrilla bands. The note contains another significant comment: "Our people must respect the well-established principles of the art of war, else successful fighting will produce no results."

Conditions were ripe for the Mississippi move which he advocated. Already in April Farragut's squadron had run past the forts guarding the mouth of the Mississippi, and thereby gained the bloodless surrender of New Orleans, which was occupied by General Butler. Then on June 6, the "other end" fleet of Union gunboats and rams, which had been pushing down the Mississippi from Columbus, gained Memphis. Coupled with Farragut's achievement it was the thin end of a strategical wedge which ultimately split the Confederacy along the line of this great river, the "Father of Waters." But Sherman's vision was to be more than a year in fruition.

For Halleck turned his gaze eastwards, after securing Corinth with a chain of fortifications which were never used—and would have needed a hundred thousand men to occupy them. Drawn by the old East Tennessee magnet, once more dangled by Lincoln and McClellan, he despatched Buell with his Army of the Ohio along the broken Memphis and Charleston railroad to move on Chattanooga.

Not only was an overland advance on Chattanooga more difficult for speed and supply than an advance down the Mississippi, but Buell was sent by the most difficult route thither. He was ordered to repair the Memphis and Charleston railroad as he advanced and to use it as his line of supply—a line which left the ever-extending flank of his communications exposed to raids from the south. As a result his advance grew slower and lost weight as it went, for the danger of his life-line being cut by the Confederate cavalry or guerrilla bands was ever present.

While one-third of Halleck's strength had thus been sent off divergently to a different theatre of war which it could only reach belatedly, the remainder were relegated to a passive rôle as trench diggers and railway guards along the Memphis and Charleston railroad, through Corinth and Tuscumbia. Sherman was first sent, with his own and Hurlbut's division, from Corinth westwards to Chewalla to salve trains—and to contract a touch of malarial fever from the swamps. He found the stretch of line between Corinth and the intersecting north and south line at Grand Junction so badly broken that he advised Halleck not to attempt its repair, but to rely on the route from Corinth back to Jackson and forward to Grand Junction.

He was then sent to repair the line between Grand Junction and Memphis, and, "in the belief that I could better protect the railroad from some point in front than by scattering our men along it," despatched two brigades to Holly Springs, twenty miles to the south. Soon afterwards he had word from Halleck of a Confederate threat, and promptly moved out the bulk of his force towards Holly Springs, only to receive a telegram from Halleck ordering him "not to attempt to hold Holly Springs, but to fall back and protect the railroad,"—a hundred miles of railroad!

But, as always, having put forward his own view, Sherman obeyed instantly and without murmur. It is significant, in a man so impulsive and vehement, that complaints of his own difficulties are so rare in his correspondence with headquarters—in contrast to other commanders. Once, after weeks of salving trains for others' use, and hauling his own supplies, he asks, "Cannot I have a locomotive? I have never had an hour's use of one even for supplies. . . ." And when Halleck replied: "We are very hard pushed. . . . Don't get angry . . . ," Sherman, changing as rapidly to contrition, wired, "Excuse my growl. I feel and appreciate the burden you carry. . . ."

In mid-July Halleck was summoned to Washington, to be placed over McClellan's head, as General-in-chief of all the armies, and to signalize his appointment by ordering McClellan's withdrawal from the James—from the enemy's rear to the enemy's front. Sherman, the most loyal of subordinates, "deeply deplored" his going. So, in a different sense, but with more sense if less loyalty, did those to whom he came. Even Sherman was consoled as soon as he found that to Grant fell the succession in the West.

But Grant took over a situation already compromised and was powerless to alter the conditions radically. For not only was he without control over Buell but he was ordered to hold two divisions ready to reinforce him. And by early September, Grant had to send more. In his own sphere he did what he could to redistribute his strength, abandoning Grand Junction and the railroad thence to Memphis and constructing fresh fortifications on a smaller scale at Corinth, so that he could hold a larger reserve in hand. Even so, he was still reduced to a defensive rôle. And in fulfilling it the position of Memphis was a source of possible danger. Sherman, however, had been sent thither to command, and Grant's comment is illuminating: "Memphis . . . was practically isolated from the balance of the command. But it was in Sherman's hands." If Sherman had still to wait for the opportunity of making his reputation as a strategic artist, he had gained the confidence of his superiors as a thoroughly competent workman.

At Memphis he stayed from July until November, and his work was mainly that of an administrator of conquered territory, although there were frequent alarms and incessant activity against guerrilla bands. These he justly regarded as the worst menace to the effectiveness of the Union advance, not least because their depredations embittered the struggle. For they plundered Union and Confederate homes alike, and among a population either sympathetic or cowed were difficult to track down. The problem has vexed many commanders and has usually ended in the same unsatisfactory and inequitable solution—that of indirect retaliation against the inhabitants.

If Sherman was ultimately driven to this course, he only did so when the guerrillas turned from firing on troops to firing on noncombatants. Then he tried by one swift lesson to check this ominous extension of guerrilla methods. On September 23, one of the regular river steamships was fired on from the town of Randolph, and next day Sherman despatched a force to destroy the town "leaving one house to mark the place." "Let the people know and feel that we deeply deplore the necessity of such destruction, but we must protect ourselves and the boats which are really carrying stores and merchandise for the benefit of secession families. . . . If any extraordinary case presents itself to your consideration you may spare more than one house. . . ."

He followed up this act of retribution by publishing an order that for every further boat fired on ten families would be expelled from Memphis, to be drawn by lots from a list of secession sympathizers and to be given three days to arrange their departure. When, however, two more ships were fired on next month, he strained the quality of mercy so far as to suspend the expulsion order for fifteen days, while the prospective sufferers and their friends sent an appeal to the nearest Confederate commanders for an official disavowal of these acts, and a ban on their repetition. Moreover, he had shown himself equally indignant and energetic to restrain pillage by his own troops—although the evil was too widespread and discipline too lax for any orders to be wholly effective. In an order early in July he had declared "stealing, robbery and pillage has become so common in this army that it is a disgrace to any civilized people. . . . This demoralizing and disgraceful practice of pillage must cease, else the country will rise on us and justly shoot us down like dogs and wild beasts."

To enforce this order he had detailed patrols with instructions to fire upon any party found pillaging, and to arrest any men found outside the lines, who were to be put "on bread and water until relieved by the commanding general." The frequency of these robberies, and even outrages, is confirmed by the reports of other generals, some of whom, however, seem to have allowed or even encouraged them. But in the district of Memphis the evil was steadily curtailed.

There was little precedent and less regulation to guide Sherman in his administration, but his path was illumined by his own vision of grand strategy—which is true statesmanship. That vision, though not always perfect, led him to temper the asperities of war, and to work for the re-establishment of confidence and security among the people of the occupied area as a means to the security of the occupation. "We know the people are generally united in spirit and feeling against us, and must not count on any reaction until the safety of property changes their feeling, their political opinions and Southern prejudices." He came to a dead town, and by encouraging the reopening of shops, churches, and theatres caused the life-blood to circulate afresh. So also he sought to strengthen the arm of the municipal authorities and the jurisdiction of the civil courts, leaving to them the maintenance of order among the population. And when a judge introduced political questions into his address to the jury, asserting State law against Congress on slave property, Sherman could make time, despite his multitudinous cares, to write him a temperate but firm and closely argued letter of over two thousand words supported by legal quotations.

This judicial indiscretion caused an outburst of fury in Union circles, and to counteract it Sherman wrote a calming letter to the president of the newly formed Union Club, pointing out that "The Union people are not yet able to compose the necessary courts and machinery of Government. . . . These you must have, before you can make county courts, district and supreme courts, and it behooves Union men to think of these things, for it is far more easy to destroy than to build up a government. . . .". This far-sighted realism foreshadowed one of the most debated points in his provisional peace treaty three years later.

To the United States Commissioner he commented: "Let the gabbling fools of Memphis draw their own conclusions as to our seeming concessions to the people. . . . We have confidence enough in our power to allow a little blowing off of surplus steam." But his wise forbearance did not find favour with rabid Unionists, and his brother, writing late in August, remarks: "the only criticism I notice of your management in Memphis is your leniency to the rebels," and implied that this was contrary to the sentiment of the people in the North. In this letter, too, John foreshadowed the coming Edict of Emancipation, regretted the failure to use the negroes "as *allies* in the war," and gently impugned William's failure to encourage slaves to quit their masters.

To the first charge William replied, with logic and satire: "The people are always right. Of course in the long run, because this year they are one thing, next year another. . . . 'The People' is a vague expression. Here the people are not right because you are warring against them. People in the aggregate may be wrong. There is such a thing as absolute right and absolute wrong. And people may do wrong as well as right. *Our people* are always right, but another people may be and always are wrong." As for the second charge—caused by his order that escaped slaves should be supplied with food and clothing in return for work, but not paid until the courts had determined their freedom—he pointed out that "you or Congress may command 'slaves shall be free,' but to make them free and see that they are not converted into thieves, idlers or worse is a difficult problem and will require much machinery to carry out. . . . If the women and children are to be provided for, we must allow for the support of, say, one million. Where are they to get work? . . . if we are to take along and feed the negroes who flee to us for refuge it will be an impossible task. You cannot solve this negro question in a day."

But Sherman's attitude on both questions had made him a fresh target for the press. He had certainly not taken his brother's advice—to be "polite to everybody, even a newspaper reporter. They are in the main, clever, intelligent men, a little too pressing in their vocation."

For on arrival in Memphis, one of his first acts had been to damp the enthusiasm of the local "Union Appeal," whose editor had eulogized him, by writing: "Personalities in a newspaper are wrong and criminal. Thus, though you mean to be complimentary in your sketch of my career, you make more than a dozen mistakes of fact, which I need not correct, as I don't desire my biography to be written till I am dead. It is enough for the world to know that I live and am a soldier, bound to obey the orders of my superiors, the laws of my country and to venerate its Constitution. . . ." The letter concluded on a minatory note, with the suggestion that he regarded pressmen as one degree worse than rebels.

That his feeling, if accentuated by personal memories, had a deeper source, is shown by a letter to his wife on June 6, when he had fiercely declared: "I will get even with the miserable class of corrupt editors yet. They are the chief cause of this unhappy war. They fan the flame of local hatred and keep alive the prejudices which have forced friends into opposing hostile ranks." Embittered the struggle, too, by lurid tales of atrocities until in "North and South each radical class keeps its votaries filled with the most outrageous lies of the other." Sherman, knowing the Southern people intimately, knew better than to believe such yarns; for travel and direct contact with other peoples is the great antidote to the poison which spreads so rapidly through the international system. Sherman's letter was written during Grant's unhappiest days, of fallen greatness, and it is perhaps characteristic that the indignant Sherman should blame the press as a soldier's loyalty forbade him to blame Halleck. "Grant . . . is not himself a brilliant man and has himself thoughtlessly used the press to give him éclat in Illinois, but he is a good and brave soldier . . . sober, very industrious and kind as a child. Yet he has been held up as careless, criminal, a drunkard, tyrant and everything horrible."

It was thus with keen satisfaction that a few weeks after Sherman's arrival in Memphis, he was able to report to Grant that he had fulfilled his order to arrest a correspondent, adding: "I regard all these newspaper harpies as spies and think they could be punished as such." There is often a contradiction between Sherman's tempestuous outbursts and his considered opinion, but his "press complex" ousted his reason. Thus it is not surprising that he soon suffered a counter-blast, the press charging him with cruelty to the sick because he had refused to allow the Sanitary Committee— a volunteer Red Cross organization—to take away a shipload of sick.

His ban was part of a campaign which he was waging to check the alarming growth of "absenteeism"; his idea was that the sick should be nursed in the regimental or district hospitals "where as they convalesce they can join" their regiments again. "There are hundreds trying to get their brothers and sons home. I know full well the intense desire to get home, but any army would be ruined by this cause alone. McClellan has 70,000 absent from his army."

Sanitary committees and other civilian societies he disliked heartily, and expressed his dislike with his usual vehemence. To the ladies who sought permission to "comfort" his troops or to intercede for secession friends, his gruffness often extended to rudeness.

Yet the same man could publish an order to his troops: "Generosity and benevolence to the poor and distressed are characteristic of good soldiers. I tell you that there are many poor families in and about Memphis who, unless aided, will suffer for wood, clothing, and provisions. Government provides all these to our soldiers bounteously and I know that, by the exercise of reasonable economy, every company can and does save a proportion of their allowance. . . . I recommend all who have spare bread, flour, meat, rice, coffee, sugar, or anything needed by poor and sick families, that they send it to . . . be . . . distributed. . . ."

On another occasion he relaxed the usual rules against trading in cotton in order to allow a number of needy farmers to obtain the money to buy supplies for their families. This act was doubtless dictated not only by kindness but by policy. For in impressing on his subordinates the wisdom of consideration and moderation in their dealings with the people he had emphasized that "every opportunity should be given to the wavering and disloyal to return to their allegiance."

Sherman had an uncommon appreciation of the truth that military power rests on a civil foundation. If he shared the common professional incomprehension as to how this public support could be tactfully developed on his own side—although seeing the need— he had an exceptional insight into the ways of weakening the war-will and undermining the civil foundation of the other side not only psychologically but economically.

As he reported to Grant on July 30: "I found so many Jews and speculators here trading in cotton, and secessionists had become so open in refusing anything but gold, that I have felt myself bound to stop it. This gold has but one use—the purchase of arms and ammunition." He was equally keen to check the shipping of salt— "If we permit money and salt to go into the interior it will not take long for Bragg and Van Dorn to supply their armies with all they need to move. Without money—gold, silver, and Treasury notes— they cannot get arms and ammunition out of the English colonies; and without salt they cannot make bacon and salt beef." He had, however, to relax the ban on the trading of cotton on orders from Washington, as it was contrary to the existing Government policy.

But he felt so deeply what he regarded as the blindness of authority to the economic basis of the enemy's resistance that he took up the argument with Chase, the Secretary of the Treasury. And he concluded by saying: "I may not appreciate the foreign aspect of the question, but my views on this may be ventured. If England ever threatens war because we don't furnish her cotton, tell her plainly if she can't employ and feed her own people, to send them here, where they cannot only earn an honest living but soon secure independence by moderate labor. . . . She has more reason to fight the South for burning that cotton, than us for not shipping it. To aid the South on this ground would be hypocrisy which the world would detect at once. . . . Of course her motive is to cripple a power that rivals her in commerce and manufactures, that threatens even to usurp her history. . . . Therefore finding us in a death-struggle for existence, she seems to seek a quarrel to destroy both parts in detail. Southern people know this full well, and will only accept alliance of England in order to get arms and manufactures in exchange for their cotton. The Southern Confederacy will accept no other mediation, because she knows full well in *Old* England her slaves and slavery will receive no more encouragement than in *New* England."

Sherman's view of the consequences of "Free trade" and fettered blockade in his own theatre of war was pithily and pungently emphasized to his wife. He tells her that the enemy "were nearly out of bacon and salt meat, but the desire of our people to trade has soon supplied this. Cincinnati has sent enough salt to supply all their army for six months. In like manner the Jews and speculators have sent in enough gold to get all the cartridges, so the two wants of the army are supplied, a whole year lost to the war, and some Jews and speculators have made ten per cent. profit." A very suggestive light, by reflection, on a similar objection, by American speculation, to England's blockade of Germany half a century later.

But civil administration and economic measures did not absorb all his energies during these months at Memphis. He constructed a strongly fortified position, as a legacy to his successors, and by constant training sought to forge his division into a strong thrusting weapon. It is particularly significant to note how much care he devoted to march discipline, and his orders as to pace, halts, protection, the regulation of transport, are in accord with the best modern practice. He also emphasized the need of study, instituted examinations, and penalized ignorance of the principles laid down in the text-books. But the most characteristic activity is, once more, his unremitting search for information from every quarter and promptness in communicating it to his neighbours. Perhaps the very thoroughness with which he ransacked the Southern press helped to increase his distrust of his own.

Again, directly he hears that a new commander has been appointed on the other side of the Mississippi, in Arkansas, he writes to him to suggest that they "should keep up a correspondence of ideas." He determined that co-operation should prevail, although he would have preferred co-ordination from above, and had earlier urged on Grant that "the lines of the Mississippi must be under one command." He was indeed constantly harping on the need for strategic unity of direction, and it even creeps into a congratulatory letter of October 29 to Rosecrans, who was going to replace Buell in Kentucky: "I do not like departments; each line of operations should be intrusted to one mind."

Events had endorsed Sherman's opinion. For during the past few months the situation in the West had changed kaleidoscopically. Buell's "slow motion" towards East Tennessee, and Grant's no motion in West Tennessee, had allowed the Confederates ample leisure to collect their forces and thoughts. Late in June Bragg had succeeded Beauregard in command and, leaving Van Dorn and Price at Tupelo to hold Grant in play, Bragg had forestalled Buell at Chattanooga. While Bragg's infantry were switched by rail south to Mobile, on the Gulf of Mexico, and then north by Atlanta to Chattanooga, his cavalry under Forrest and Morgan hamstrung Buell.

Forrest made a dashing sweep which, on July 13, cut the Nashville-Chattanooga railroad at Murfreesborough—Buell's new temporary line of supply. This was not repaired until July 28, and on August 12 Morgan, sweeping further north, cut the Louisville-Nashville railroad, Buell's rearward link with his main base in Kentucky. Coincidently Kirby Smith, the local Confederate commander in East Tennessee, who had been reinforced by Bragg, outmanœuvred the rival Union force guarding Cumberland Gap and drove deep into Kentucky. On August 30 he installed himself at Lexington, whence he threatened Cincinnati, to the north, and Louisville, to the west.

Then, in turn, Bragg with the main force slipped across the Cumberland Mountains, and past the flank of Buell, who perforce turned back to head him off in a race northward towards Louisville. But Bragg got astride the Louisville-Nashville railroad at Munfordsville, not far from the Muldraugh Hills, when Buell had only reached Bowling Green.

Unfortunately for the Confederates Bragg and Kirby Smith held independent commands. In consequence, Bragg, who was short of supplies, did not summon to him Kirby Smith, who had ample. And as Buell cautiously held back from throwing himself onto Bragg at such a strategic disadvantage, after a week Bragg had to move off the railroad eastward, and allow Buell to regain Louisville unopposed—before the latter had to fight his way thither under strategic compulsion. Meantime Kirby Smith was solemnly inaugurating a Confederate governor at Frankfort, the capital of Kentucky.

On October 1, Buell, having recruited his strength in Louisville, moved out to meet Bragg, and on the 8th a partial and indecisive encounter took place at Perryville. Buell was, wisely, too cautious to attack the combined Confederate forces in their chosen position, and when further reinforcements reached him the Confederate invaders, with equal discretion, withdrew into East Tennessee—the brief tenure of their new Governor of Kentucky having already, and abruptly, been terminated.

But the invasion had inflicted a deep moral wound on the North and Buell was sacrificed to serve as a healing ointment for a sore public. And after an indecisive battle near Murfreesborough on New Year's Day, 1863, the Unionists, now under Rosecrans, settled down in winter quarters—at a point less advanced than they had occupied in the early summer of 1862.

Rosecrans's promotion had been a reward for his success in repulsing the subsidiary Confederate advance by Van Dorn and Price on Corinth, an advance which had been made as a distraction, to the Union forces, in aid of Bragg. Grant, however, regarded the transfer of Rosecrans as a relief, to himself, rather than a reward. For when Price advanced first and occupied Iuka on September 14 —without waiting for Van Dorn, whose forces were still scattered and unready to move—Grant planned to grip him in a pair of pincers and destroy him while isolated. But the Rosecrans half of the pincers did not close properly, and Price slipped safely away to join Van Dorn. Thereafter the combined Confederate force moved up the Mississippi Central Railroad from Holly Springs into the hundred-mile gap between Corinth and Memphis, and then swerved suddenly eastwards on Corinth, which was held by Rosecrans. On October 3 he was driven back to the entrenchments, but the Confederate assault next day was repelled after about an hour's fighting, when two fresh divisions approached to the aid of Rosecrans who, however, made no attempt to follow up his success or to hold the Confederates while the new arrivals moved to cut off their retreat.

Although no direct share in these operations was taken by Sherman, and although he was weakened by sending Hurlbut's division to Grant, he had used one of his brigades to threaten Van Dorn's base at Holly Springs, and his small cavalry detachment to raid the railway, thereby helping to hinder Van Dorn's concentration and to distract his attention while Grant was converging on Price at Juka.

During this period Sherman and his brother indulged in a vigorous interchange of views. Sherman had led off by saying: "It is about time the North understood the truth. That the entire South, man, woman and child are against us. . . . It will call for a million men for several years to put them down. . . . I guess you now see how, from the very first I argued that you underestimated the task. . . . We ought to hold fast to the Mississippi as a great base of operation. I should regard the loss of St. Louis as more fatal to our future success than the capture by them of Harrisburg and Philadelphia. . . . The passage of the enemy north of us, leaving us among a hostile population, was a bold and successful movement and will give them great credit in Europe. You doubtless, like most Americans, attribute our want of success to bad generals. I do not. With us you insist the boys, the soldiers govern."

To this John Sherman retorted with a shrewd thrust: "As one of the bad signs I regret to notice so many quarrels between officers," and then continued, "The feeling among the people is general that the regular officers are indisposed to treat with decent civility those who, like most of the great military men of history, are educated in the field rather than in the school. And it is feared that habits of education and association make them feel indifferent of the success of the war—fighting rather from a pride of duty than an earnest conviction . . . persistently efforts are being made to separate the class of high regular officers to which you belong from civilians. Whenever that separation is effected all important commands will gradually be transferred to such officers as Banks, Sigel, Morgan, Nelson, and to such regular officers as show a sympathy with the Radical faction. . . . I earnestly deprecate such tendencies. I want the war conducted regularly according to the tenets of civilized warfare . . . but if the time shall come when emancipation of blacks and civilization of whites is necessary in order to preserve the unity of this country, then I would prefer a fanatic like John Brown to lead our armies and an abolitionist like Chase with brains and energy to guide our counsels."

Ignoring this warning, Sherman replied: "I knew and know yet that the northern people have to unlearn all their experience of the past thirty years and be born again before they will see the truth. . . ." But John Sherman was not in a mood to recognize it, for in November the elections were disastrous for the Republican party, and in telling William how public dissatisfaction with the war had contributed, he complained that Lincoln "put and kept in those slow generals and we shall be punished for it by having an organised opposition limiting appropriations."

CHAPTER XI

THE FIRST ATTEMPT ON VICKSBURG

If October, 1862, was a month of baulked opportunities for the armies of the North, it nevertheless marked their release from the long summer's paralysis and the definite ebb of the sudden Confederate tide of invasion—in all theatres. In the East Lee withdrew from Maryland; in the centre Bragg from Kentucky; in the West, Van Dorn's retreat from Corinth marked not merely an ebb of the tide but a permanent recession of the sea from West Tennessee. Then in turn, a Union wave surged southwards everywhere, but by the first weeks of the New Year it had been dammed in the east and the centre. In the west it flowed further, over virgin soil, and although it was not merely dammed but flowed back, from its main objective—Vicksburg, its backwash carried away another stronghold of the South.

Vicksburg, roughly midway between Memphis and the mouth, was the main key to the Mississippi. Not only did it stand on high ground overlooking the river, the first high ground below Memphis, but it was the only rail and river junction between Memphis and New Orleans. From Vicksburg a line ran eastward through Jackson, forty-five miles distant, where it intersected the main north and south (to New Orleans) line and then continued east through Meridian where it intersected the parallel line which ran from Corinth down to Mobile. And on the west bank of the Mississippi opposite Vicksburg, a line ran westwards towards Shreveport in western Louisiana. Thus Vicksburg was not only the nodal point of the communications in the Southern States but the navel cord which connected the newer Trans-Mississippi area of the Confederacy with the parent body.

When the war began the naval and industrial inferiority of the Confederates had led them to strengthen their hold on the Mississippi by building a chain of fortified posts between New Orleans and Columbus. One by one these had fallen to the two-ended Union pressure until at the beginning of May, 1862, only Vicksburg blocked the Union fairway. And the work of fortifying Vicksburg had only been begun late in April.

There is a curious parallel between Vicksburg and Gallipoli half a century later, not only because each controlled the bloodflow along a vital economic artery. In time and in method the Union effort to open this artery anticipated the British effort to open the Dardanelles—above all, in arousing the defender's anticipation of the move.

While Halleck's army of a hundred thousand men was creeping cautiously southwards on Corinth, Farragut's fleet, having taken New Orleans, pressed north up the Mississippi and appeared off Vicksburg on May 18. It was a useless demonstration, although useful to the Confederates as a warning. For Farragut brought only 1,500 troops with him, and as their commander, Williams, considered his force too small to co-operate, the expedition returned to Baton Rouge and New Orleans. A month later Farragut returned, with a mere increase to 3,000 troops, who were landed on the west bank opposite Vicksburg. They stayed there ineffectively for a month, which sufficed to show that the fleet was powerless to overcome the land batteries, and that the troops were too few.

Following up Farragut's withdrawal, the Confederates re-occupied the river as far south as Baton Rouge, and established a fresh block just above it by emplacing batteries at Port Hudson to command the river. Batteries were also established at Natchez and Grand Gulf, between Port Hudson and Vicksburg, while above Vicksburg a fort and gunboat base was created on the Arkansas River, off the Mississippi, as a hidden menace and impediment to any hostile approach to Vicksburg from the north. By this time also the Vicksburg defences were complete. Meantime Halleck's great army was allowed to disperse and stagnate.

Only after the repulse of the Confederate attempt on Corinth in October was the project revived of a Union advance on Vicksburg. Reinforcements had brought Grant's strength to nearly half what Halleck had early disposed of and dispersed.

The two natural and parallel lines of approach to Vicksburg were down the Mississippi and down the railroad—from Grand Junction through Holly Springs, Oxford, and Grenada (where the

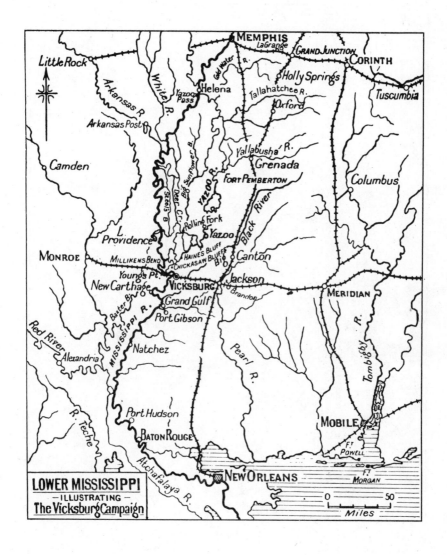

LOWER MISSISSIPPI
—ILLUSTRATING—
The Vicksburg Campaign

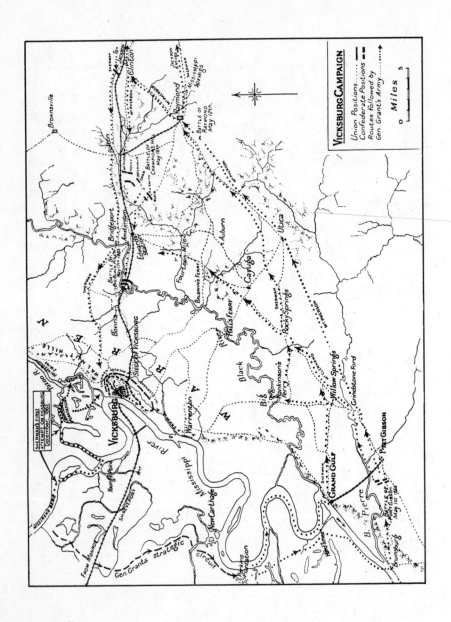

VICKSBURG CAMPAIGN

Union Positions......
Confederate Positions....
Routes Followed by
Gen. Grant's Army.....

0   Miles   5

branch from Memphis joined) to Jackson.   Between these two
lines of approach the Yazoo River ran diagonally downwards.   In
its higher reaches the Yallabusha and the Tallahatchie flowed into
it from the east, themselves serving to obstruct Grant's line of
approach down the railroad; another tributary, the Coldwater, came
down from the northwest near Memphis.   The Yazoo flowed into
the Mississippi eight miles above Vicksburg, and the country between the two was low-lying and swampy—a black vegetable mould
criss-crossed by innumerable streams and bayous, their banks overhung by dense foliage.   If, in consequence, this two-hundred-mile-
deep belt of country between Memphis and Vicksburg offered many
potential avenues of surprise approach, they were so extraordinarily
difficult that surprise could too easily be nullified by slow progress,
and each was so confined that, when once committed, a force could
not vary its route.

Only less difficult was the line of approach down the railroad,
barred both by the enemy's army (now under General Pemberton)
and by successive rivers.

The Mississippi route was easily the quickest and simplest, and
only suffered the drawback that a move down it would be quickly
reported.   Speed of approach would diminish the inconvenience,
provided that the enemy's main force remained as a block across
the other route, and that the immediate approach to the attack of
Vicksburg was not direct.

During the months on the defensive Sherman had viewed with
impatience the outpouring of force on inland expeditions, and the
neglect of the opportunity to gain control of the Mississippi.   "This
is my hobby," he wrote to Grant, "and I know you pardon me when
I say that I am daily more and more convinced that we should hold
the river absolutely and leave the interior alone.   Detachments inland can always be overcome or are at great hazard, and they do
not convert the people . . . with the Mississippi safe we could land
troops at any point, and by a quick march break the railroad, when
we could make ourselves so busy that our descent would be dreaded
the whole length of the river."

When reinforcements foreshadowed a change to the offensive,
his constant research for information of the topography and enemy
dispositions bore fruit in a report to Grant on September 29, 1862—

"I feel certain that the two railroads that branch from Grenada northward can and should be broken preliminary to operations against any part of the Yazoo near its mouth.   Almost the entire force of the enemy about Vicksburg has been moved north. . . ." His idea was, clearly, to hamstring their main forces so that they could not interfere with a blow against Vicksburg in their rear.   It is also clear that he thought the latter move should be through the back door to Vicksburg, for he got in touch with Admiral Porter, commanding the gunboat flotilla, in order to find out if the Confederates had done anything to bar the mouth of the Yazoo.   And when, to his disappointment, he discovered that they had begun fortifications there, he was so anxious for prompt action that he wrote to Halleck, on November 17.   In it he tactfully hints that action should be taken to forestall the completion of these fortifications, and also that co-ordinated action is essential.   For, as he had told Porter the day before: "My opinion is that a perfect concert of action should exist between all the forces . . . operating down the Valley; and I apprehend some difficulty may arise from the fact that you control on the river, Curtis on the west bank, and Grant on the east bank."

A further complication was that McClernand had been carrying on an intrigue in Washington with the object of obtaining from Lincoln independent command of an expedition against Vicksburg. His proposal was for a direct advance down the river in great force. And newspaper rumours warned both Grant and the Confederates that his suit was prospering.

On the same day that Sherman wrote to Halleck he received a summons from Grant, who explained that he was about to begin an advance down the railroad and wished Sherman, from Memphis, to converge inwards and join him in a combined advance on Pemberton.   So on November 24 Sherman marched out from Memphis as Grant's right wing, while Grant's centre and left moved straight down the railroad.   The move frightened Pemberton into a prompt retreat, almost a stampede, and, giving up his position on the Tallahatchie he fell back to Grenada, behind the Yallabusha—110 miles north of Jackson and 140 from Vicksburg by the direct route.

Halting to repair the Tallahatchie bridges, Grant sent for Sherman on December 8 in order to discuss with him his two alternative plans. One was to despatch two divisions back to Memphis and thence down the Mississippi against Vicksburg while Grant himself held Pemberton firmly in front. The other was to continue the advance down the railroad, repairing it as he went and then, at an opportune moment, cut loose and strike for Jackson. After the consultation Grant decided on the first plan, and despatched Sherman to Memphis to assume charge of the river move on Vicksburg.

Sherman took away only one division, but from reinforcements already sent to Memphis he was able to organize a force of 20,500 men, in three divisions, with whom he steamed down the river on December 20, a week after his arrival. At Helena he was joined by another division, 9,500 strong, from the west side of the Mississippi. At that time the Confederates had only 6,000 men at Vicksburg, while 24,000 faced Grant.

Speed and surprise were essential, not only to success, for Grant has told his memoirs that "my object in sending Sherman back was expedited by a desire to get him in command of the forces separated from my direct supervision. I feared that delay might bring McClernand, who was his senior and who had authority from the President and Secretary of War, to exercise that particular command—and independently. I doubted McClernand's fitness and I had good reasons to believe that in forestalling him I was by no means giving offence to those . . . above both him and me." For Halleck was enamoured neither of McClernand's ambition nor his plan.

Unhappily the foundations of Grant's plan were destroyed by his own action—if this was the sequel to Confederate intervention. For on the same day that Sherman's force steamed down the river from Memphis, Van Dorn with 3,500 cavalry, having passed round Grant's flank, seized Holly Springs in his rear and there destroyed his secondary base of supplies. Simultaneously, Forrest with 2,500 carried out a still longer range manœuvre and destroyed many miles of his 180 mile long life-line—the railroad by which Grant drew his supplies from Columbus, Kentucky. Cut it, moreover, close to Columbus. For over a week Grant was cut off from all communication with the North, and was constrained to fall back to his starting point and release his hold on Pemberton, without being able to tell Sherman, now committed to a forlorn venture.

Grant yielded to this constraint the more readily, perhaps too readily, because he had received orders from Washington placing McClernand in charge of the Vicksburg expedition although under his superior direction. Indeed, McPherson had suggested to him on the 20th, "I would, if in your place, proceed to Memphis and take command of it myself. It is the great feature of the campaign, and its execution rightfully belongs to you." And Grant had only received the first news of the break in his rear when he decided to adopt this suggestion, and withdraw his forces. He was perhaps a little hurried, in view of the consequent danger to Sherman. Moreover, for two weeks Grant's forces had "lived" on the local supplies of the country and could, as he admitted later, have done so for two months.

Actual surprise had never been possible for Sherman's attempt, with spies lining the banks of the Mississippi, and the other condition of success—the enemy's inability to turn and meet his move—had disappeared with Grant's disappearance. It was a sorry turn of fortune that in default of the adoption of Sherman's own idea of hamstringing the enemy by an indirect move against the railroads, the enemy should have hamstrung Grant, upon whom he depended. Moreover, by the fact of Grant stampeding the enemy back from the Tallahatchie to the Yallabusha, they had all the less distance to cover in order to get back to Vicksburg. Pemberton, indeed, had been falling back hurriedly and was able to concentrate 12,000 men to close the door in Sherman's face. A door so strong in itself that little weight of men was needed to hold it.

Sherman's idea was, first, to disembark a brigade above Vicksburg on the west bank to cut the railroad to Western Louisiana; then to turn into the mouth of the Yazoo, land some miles up it and cut the railroad to Jackson; finally, when Vicksburg was thus isolated on both sides, to attack the town from the landward, or rearward side, while the gunboats assailed it from the river. Once Vicksburg had fallen, his intention was to move north-eastwards to co-operate with Grant's expected approach, and with this aim, to cut the north and south railroad in Pemberton's rear. To secure the smooth execution of his first step, he issued copies of his own map, complete with the latest information, to his divisional commanders, telling them to have copies made for their subordinates, "so that no mistakes or

confusion need result from different names of localities." And it
is no less characteristic that in his instructions he described the general strategy of the campaign so that his officers might realize that
their action was but one "part—an important one of the great
whole."

On Christmas day, 1862, the imposing armada reached Milliken's
Bend, just above the mouth of the Yazoo, and A. J. Smith's division landed on the west bank, sending one brigade, marching light
without transport, to break the Shreveport railroad. Next day the
other three divisions landed twelve miles up the Yazoo, at Johnson's
Plantation, a broad flat shelf beneath the steep clay cliffs, two hundred feet high, of the Walnut Hills, on which the town of Vicksburg
stood. But the shelf between the banks of the Yazoo and the foot
of the bluffs was an alluvial swamp covered with dense undergrowth
and intersected by bayous. And as it was some three miles wide, the
gunboats could not cover the attack on the bluffs.

On the 27th and 28th the troops pushed forward, skirmishing
with the enemy's pickets, until they reached a last and broader
bayou, athwart their front and almost at the foot of the bluffs—
Chickasaw Bluffs. Beyond this a strip of firm ground was lined
with rifle-pits and batteries, which also crowned the bluffs behind.
Sherman had intended that while two divisions pushed inland from
Johnson's plantation, A. J. Smith's division, now arrived, should
move direct towards Vicksburg as a diversion, and the fourth,
Steele's, advance from a landing a little higher up the Yazoo—
separated from the centre divisions by Chickasaw Bayou. But personal reconnaissance convinced Sherman that A. J. Smith's route
was too exposed to fire from the Vicksburg batteries, and Steele
found the natural obstacles impassable. Thus Sherman had to
draw in the bulk of these divisions and trust to a narrow frontal
assault in the centre, hoping to widen the gap once a footing was
gained on the bluffs.

Eagerly and vainly Sherman waited for some news or sound of
Grant—but only heard enemy troop-trains steaming into Vicksburg.
Delay would have forfeited the bare chance that remained, and so
on the morning of the 29th Sherman decided to launch the assault.

From his personal reconnaissance he had come to the conclusion
that the bayou was only crossable at two points, and the best of

these he pointed out to General Morgan, who was to lead his division, receiving the confident answer: "General, in ten minutes after you give the signal I'll be on those hills." To cloak this real drive and form a funnel for it, Sherman ordered the attack to begin on the flanks and then, at noon, gave the signal for Morgan's advance. One brigade rushed forward, crossed the bayou—and went to ground behind the sheltering bank. Morgan neither crossed himself, nor sent forward his other brigades; Blair's brigade of Steele's division which advanced in support swept forward to the foot of the bluff but then, itself unsupported and severely enfiladed, drifted gradually back. To retrieve the check Sherman had already sent forward a regiment from A. J. Smith's division and directed it towards the only other crossable point. But this could not advance beyond the far bank and the men hung on beneath the enemy's muzzles until darkness enabled their withdrawal. Although Sherman felt, and always felt, that Morgan's original attack should have succeeded if driven home—a feeling that perhaps had more faith than realism—he was too sane to renew the effort when the enemy's attention had already been drawn to the only two feasible crossing places. Too sane also, to anticipate the World War habit of digging in and clinging on to a depressed and depressing foothold under the enemy's "command."

When the assets of surprise and mobility have once been dissipated "reculer pour mieux sauter" is the sound military maxim and course, save sometimes in a formal siege.

Next day Sherman arranged to make a fresh landing below Haines's Bluff, further up the Yazoo, and enlisted Admiral Porter's support to cover the landing. As the bluffs here came close to the river, and although strongly fortified were further from Vicksburg, the site was at least more favourable than the first. Sherman had proposed it originally, but naval opinion was against it, owing to torpedoes which the enemy had laid in the river. Now, however, the navy had fitted a prow to a ram to explode these, and were willing to risk the passage.

On the night of December 31, one division and one brigade— 10,000 men in all—were withdrawn after dark and embarked. Sherman waited to attack at Chickasaw Bluffs as soon as the sound of cannonading reached him, but as the first dawn of the New Year came he received a message that a dense fog on the river had stopped the movement of the ships. The attempt was at first postponed twenty-four hours, but the Admiral reported that the moon would compel a daylight landing, which he considered too hazardous. Sherman felt that it was equally hazardous and vain to wait longer —with increasing masses of the enemy appearing on the heights, the chance of surprise gone, rain falling heavily, and watermarks on the trees ten feet above the ground. He took his decision swiftly and that night, January 1, the whole force was safely re-embarked under cover of darkness, having lost altogether 1,776 officers and men to the Confederates' 207.

Soon after dawn he heard that McClernand had arrived at the mouth of the Yazoo, and, running down in a tug to meet him, was shown the orders placing McClernand over his head. McClernand informed him that the force was to be renamed the Army of the Mississippi and divided into two army corps, of which Sherman was to command one and Morgan temporarily the other.

In a hurriedly scribbled note to his wife, Sherman said—"Well, we have been to Vicksburg and it was too much for us and we have backed out. McClernand has arrived to supersede me by order of the President himself. Of course I submit gracefully. The President is charged with maintaining the Government and has a perfect right to choose his agents." If Sherman felt his supersession more deeply than his note showed, his attitude was impeccable, and in announcing the fact to the troops he said: "A new commander is here to lead you. . . . I know that all good officers and soldiers will give him the same hearty support and cheerful obedience they have hitherto given me. There are honors enough in reserve for all and work enough too. Let each do his appropriate part, and our nation must in the end emerge from this dire conflict purified and ennobled by the fires which now test its strength and purity."

To Halleck, enclosing his official report of the operations, he simply said, "I reached Vicksburg at the time appointed, landed, assaulted and failed, re-embarked my command unopposed and turned it over to my successor." If this brevity recalls Cæsar's "I came, I saw, I conquered," it is harder to resist the temptation to excuse a failure than the temptation to embroider a success. All that Sherman added was a detailed description of the topography of the Vicksburg neighbourhood as a guide to further attempts. And far from sulking Achilles-like in his tent, Sherman immediately suggested to McClernand a new move which would crown the new command with laurels, and leave his own brow the barer by contrast.

As a sedative to the enemy's exhilaration, a restorative to the spirits of the Union troops, and for its own strategic advantages, Sherman proposed that the army, instead of lapsing into immobility, should retain and utilize its water-borne mobility by an immediate move against the Confederate post up the Arkansas which, so long as it remained, was a constant threat to the Mississippi communications of any expedition operating against Vicksburg. A steamer loaded with ammunition and supplies had just been captured by a raiding ship from this post.

McClernand agreed to consult Admiral Porter about the practicability of the scheme. Sherman had already suggested it to Porter on the night of the withdrawal from Chickasaw Bluffs, before McClernand's arrival, but now Porter was inclined to make difficulties because of an old prejudice against McClernand which his present manner aggravated. But on Sherman's intervention Porter relinquished his objections for unstinted helpfulness. His reluctance, indeed, had been due to his dislike of McClernand's offensively patronizing manner towards Sherman and to his disgust at McClernand's cool pretence that he had originated the scheme. To indicate his rating of McClernand, the bluff sailor had finally declared—"I'll tell you what I'll do, General McClernand. If General Sherman goes in command of the troops, I will go myself in command of a proper force, and will insure the capture of the post." While McClernand was trying to conceal his anger in study of a map, Sherman called Porter aside and reproachfully said—"Admiral, how could you make such a remark to McClernand? He hates me already, and you have made him an enemy for life." "I don't care, he shall not treat you rudely in my cabin, and I was glad of the opportunity of letting him know my sentiments." Sherman's self-sinking tact, however, brought the two men together again for a practical discussion of details and so saved the scheme from shipwreck.

Without loss of time, the armada left Milliken's Bend on January

5, and on reaching the mouth of the Arkansas River, continued up the Mississippi, as a deception, to the mouth of the White River, ascending that and regaining the Arkansas near the Post by a "cut-off," or connecting channel. On the evening of the 9th it reached Notrib's Farm, some three miles below the fort on the same bank—the north bank—and there the troops disembarked next morning.

The riverside approach to the fort was contracted into a defile by inland swamps, and an advanced line of earthworks had been constructed covering the narrowest part. Somewhat prematurely the enemy abandoned this and fell back to the fort and to a line of earthworks half a mile long between the fort and an inland bayou.

Twenty-four hours later the four Union divisions, Sherman's two on the right and the other two nearer the river, were assembled opposite this line for a frontal assault, while the gunboats bombarded the fort at close range. Guns from the other bank also enfiladed the defences. Despite McClernand's impatience, Sherman waited until the bombardment had well begun before he gave the order for the troops to assault, soon after 1 P.M., across the stretch of ground some six hundred yards wide, which separated them from the enemy. Even so, after three hours' fighting they had not succeeded in crossing the enemy's parapet, when white flags were hoisted on it opposite Sherman's left division—by a regiment of a dismounted cavalry.

Sherman, who was close up, immediately sent his aide-de-camp forward, and as soon as he saw that the latter had been allowed to mount the parapet, followed him and received the surrender of Colonel Garland, commanding the Confederate brigade in that sector. Firing now ceased, except opposite Sherman's right, and Morgan's troops took unopposed possession of the fort and the line adjoining it—the Confederate commander, General Churchill, seeing that it was useless to disavow his subordinates' action when once his position had been entered. On the inland flank, however, the local brigade commander refused to let his men lay down their arms until Sherman brought Churchill to overrule him.

This completed the capture of a force five thousand strong, for an expenditure of one thousand casualties.

But the long check to the assault, despite a superiority of six to one, is a more than ordinarily significant illustration of the drawbacks of a frontal attack. McClernand had originally, on the 10th, ordered one of Sherman's divisions to move by a detour behind the swamps on to the rear of the fort but, discovering that it would have to make a circuit of seven miles, he had countermanded the move soon after the start, from a fear that the division would be too far separated from the rest of his force. If the natural difficulties of the swampy country were formidable, the fear of separation seems exaggerated.

According to Sherman, McClernand was more than content with the result, exclaiming to him: "Glorious! Glorious! My star is ever in the ascendant!" The tone of his proclamation to the troops certainly suggests a somewhat extreme exultation and exaltation. Sherman, however, hungry and exhausted, was perhaps more than usually intolerant of such pæans. Having borrowed a meal, he returned to his own sector of the captured position, there to meet Garland who, uneasy at the hot feeling against him among the Confederates, asked permission to spend the night with Sherman. Borrowing some coffee, a battered coffee-pot and some scraps of hard bread from a soldier he shared this evening repast with Garland, and the two sat talking politics beside a fire until late at night, and then lay down together to sleep on a heap of blood-soaked straw.

It was characteristic of Sherman that he should choose the roughest quarters, among his men. So also before and during an action he was ever as far forward as was possible while still retaining control. Indeed, reports of his boldness drew an anxious protest from home, to which he replied—"As for exposing myself unnecessarily, you need not be concerned. I know better than C—— where danger lies and where I should be. Soldiers have a right to see and know that the man who guides them is near enough to see with his own eyes. . . ." His desire to be forward was also inspired by a reasoned preference for the "front" as the best atmosphere in which to make not only prompt but sound decisions. As he explains in his memoirs—"I never saw the rear of an army engaged in battle but I feared some calamity had happened at the front—the apparent confusion, broken wagons, crippled horses, men lying about dead and maimed, parties hastening to and fro in seeming disorder, and a general apprehension of something dreadful about to ensue; all these signs, however, lessened as I neared the front. . . . Although cannon might be firing, the musketry chattering, and the enemy's shot hitting close, there reigned a general feeling of strength and security that bore a marked contrast to the bloody signs that had drifted rapidly to the rear; therefore, for comfort and safety"—of morale, if not perhaps of person!—"I surely would rather be at the front than the rear. . . ."

On January 17, after dismantling and levelling the fort, the army re-embarked and steamed down river in a heavy snowstorm to a rendezvous off Napoleon at the entrance into the Mississippi.

McClernand had contemplated a further move up the Arkansas River in order to pounce on Little Rock, the base and headquarters of the Confederate forces operating in northern Arkansas, which still threatened Missouri. Although not mentioned in Sherman's memoirs—probably out of deference to Grant—it would appear from the records that this move was suggested and advocated by him. Such an exploitation of the army's water-borne mobility promised, if successful, to extinguish the Trans-Mississippi effort of the Confederacy, and also the danger of interference with the Mississippi communications of the Union army while operating against Vicksburg, a danger already damped down by the capture of Arkansas Post. At the least a pounce on Little Rock would distract the Confederates' attention, now concentrated on Vicksburg. In assessing the merits of this still-born project it is just to remember that the Union army, after reverting to a rigid maintenance of their main objective, lay confronting Vicksburg ineffectively for nearly six months, and that the Trans-Mississippi forces continued to be a thorn in the Union side even after the capture of Vicksburg.

The execution of the project was momentarily delayed by Admiral Porter's doubts whether the rise in the river would be maintained, and was definitely annulled by the receipt on the 14th of an angry message from Grant, who did not even know of it. But on hearing of the first move he had wired to Halleck—"McClernand has . . . gone on a wild-goose chase to the Post of Arkansas," and written to McClernand, "I do not approve of your move on the Post of Arkansas while the other is in abeyance. It will lead to the loss of men without a result." When he discovered the result, however, he modified his opinion, and admitted that it was "very important" —none the less because Sherman had inspired it.

But his intervention was the spark to a powder trail. McClernand had already shown an acute sensitiveness to his dignity, and certainly had just cause for suspecting that Sherman had been sent off hurriedly on the original expedition in order to forestall his arrival and assumption of command. Now, stung at Grant's rebuke, he wrote direct to the President—"I believe my success here is gall and wormwood to the clique of West Pointers who have been persecuting me for months. How can you expect success when men controlling the military destinies of the country are more chagrined at the success of your volunteer officers than the very enemy beaten by the latter in battle?"

On the 18th Grant came down from Memphis to the armada at Napoleon, receiving fiery complaints from Porter of McClernand's attitude, and from there wrote to Halleck saying that he intended to assume command in person as he neither had nor found sufficient confidence in McClernand's leadership. He ordered McClernand to take the force down river again to Young's Point, on the west bank below Milliken's Bend. And on the 29th he himself followed to assume command.

By orders from the War Department the forces in the Mississippi Valley had been grouped in four army corps. The existing Vicksburg expedition was divided into the 13th [McClernand's] and the 15th [Sherman's], while the forces still with Grant were distributed into the 16th [Hurlbut's], and the 17th [McPherson's]. The missing number, the 14th, was allotted to Thomas's corps in middle Tennessee. McClernand had already entitled the first two as the 1st and 2nd of the "Army of the Mississippi" under himself and, galled at descending to be one of four co-equal corps commanders, found a fresh grievance when Grant assigned to the 13th corps the duty of garrisoning the Arkansas bank of the Mississippi, which suggested to him that he would be relegated to a subsidiary rôle in the forthcoming attack on Vicksburg. He now made formal complaint through Grant that this arrangement contravened the personal order he had obtained from the President and the President's wish, conveyed through Halleck to Grant, that he should have the imme-

diate command of the Vicksburg expedition under Grant's higher
direction.   But Grant had a higher trump, having obtained from
Halleck, on January 12, authority to supersede McClernand
either by himself or the next in rank.   And in passing on Mc-
Clernand's complaint he remarked: "If Sherman had been left in
command here, such is my confidence in him that I would not have
thought my presence necessary.   But whether I do General Mc-
Clernand an injustice or not, I have not confidence in his ability as
a soldier to conduct an expedition of the magnitude of this one successfully."   Thus McClernand not only failed to get satisfaction
but had a growing cause of dissatisfaction.

The episode and its sequel leaves an unpleasant taste, not wholly
caused by McClernand.   If he had gained his appointment by his
political influence as one of the more whole-hearted Democratic
Congressmen—hence much valued—and was sensitive, self-centred,
and bombastic, he had nevertheless been displaced by means which
savoured of sharp practice.   It is not surprising that he ascribed his
treatment to the clan spirit of the Regular officers and, if their
doubts were honest, their acts show traces of having been swayed
subconsciously by an instinctive "trade-unionism."   The feeling, at
least, is revealed in Sherman's letter to his brother from Napoleon—
"Mr. Lincoln intended to insult me and the military profession by
putting McClernand over me. . . . I never dreamed of so severe a
test of my patriotism as being superseded by McClernand, and if
I can keep down my tamed (?) spirit and live I will claim a virtue
higher than Brutus."

Moreover, and much further, it is at least clear that Grant gave
up his original plan—of manœuvring overland against Jackson and
the rear of Vicksburg while the enemy was distracted by a Mississippi threat to Vicksburg—mainly because of McClernand's arrival
on the scene.   Yet both Sherman and McClernand favoured this
plan, which was probably the best strategic approach.   Once committed to the frontal move on Vicksburg from the Mississippi Grant
was reluctant to revert the other for fear of the popular effect of
what might appear a step backward, even though it was for a better
jump forward.

Not for the first time, or the last in history, was strategy sub-
ordinated to the human nature of the strategist.   And in this war,

as in the West so in the East. We do not wonder, except at the candour, that John Sherman replied to his brother—"If we recover from the folly of our legislators and the quarrels of our generals, it will be evidence of vitality, remarkable in the history of any nation."

The aftermath of the first attempt on Vicksburg also produced a controversy in which Sherman was more directly concerned. As usual in his case it was a press case. Before leaving Memphis he had issued orders forbidding civilians to accompany the expedition and adding that any one "found making reports for publication" would be "treated as a spy." Nevertheless an indomitable correspondent of the New York *Herald*, Knox by name, travelled on one of the steamers, which also carried General Steele and his divisional staff. But from fear of being arrested if seen on the battlefield, he had stayed aboard when the landing and attack were made, and gathered his information from the returning soldiers of Steele's division, alone, if also from conversation with Steele and with Blair—who was naturally incensed at the failure of Morgan's division. Thus Sherman's very precautions recoiled on his own head. Knox in his report to the *Herald* naturally dished up a purely one-sided account of the attack, inaccurate in many of its details, seasoned with some fair criticism and more unfair, and covered with a fiery sauce—of comment on Sherman. The report was the keynote for a fresh harmony in the Northern press, singing tunefully in malediction of Sherman.

The echoes naturally came back last to the front, so that not until the end of January did Sherman hear them and discover the source. He then sent for Knox, who admitted his mistakes of fact and frankly said that it was his business to collect news, true if possible, but only if possible. He might have retorted that if research for the truth had not been possible it was owing to Sherman, and it at least says something for his courage that, in ominously hostile surroundings, he only retracted the parts of his criticism which were proved false by the orders and reports now shown him in full. But, in excuse for his scathing comments on Sherman's own leadership, he ingeniously said: "Of course, General Sherman, I had no feeling against you personally, but you are regarded as the enemy of our set, and we must in self-defense write you down." He quoted Blair, in particular, as his authority for some of the criticisms. Sherman called to Blair to answer a long string of written questions, saying, "I do not design it for publication, but propose to send your answer to my brother, John Sherman, that he may partially protect me from the effect of the base accusations and slanders published to the world. . . ."

Sherman here shows himself more sensitive to his reputation than he normally admits and, even though Blair was an old friend, this method of a questionnaire is rather undignified—in contrast to Blair's reply, which disavowed many of the criticisms but sturdily maintained his independence of judgment as to the choice of landing and the conduct of Morgan's troops under his own eyes. Sherman's acknowledgment, wherein he explains that the submerged torpedoes prevented him landing originally near Haines's Bluff and admits the failure of Morgan's division, shows him in a happier light—"I may be and am too reckless of public opinion, but I am not of my officers and men. I would not have them think or feel that I am reckless of their safety or honor. . . . I know General Morgan's enthusiasm and devotion to the cause . . . and assume to myself the consequences of failure rather than throw it off on any generous or brave man or set of men." This he had certainly done in his report. And in excuse for his outburst it must be remembered that the secluded life of the military profession is apt to make its members more sensitive to criticism than other servants of the community and to instil in them an exaggerated, indeed almost morbid, fear of the effects on the army. He, like others, might have profited from a course of the "stump-speaking" for which he had rebuked his brother—if only for its hardening value.

But if he had made it up with Blair, he had not forgiven the source of the trouble. Not content with denouncing Knox as "a spy and an infamous dog"—far more slanderous expressions than that of which he complained!—and "hoping that the day will come when every officer will demand the execution of this class of spies," he brought him before a general court-martial on a capital charge as a spy and for giving intelligence to the enemy. Much to Sherman's disgust the court acquitted Knox of the more serious charges and merely sentenced him to be sent away. Although Sherman told his brother that he had not seriously intended that Knox should be shot, his declamations against the press continued in letter after letter, and he was so incensed that he spoke of resigning. When his brother wrote to calm him and urged him to be more reasonable in dealing with correspondents, he retorted, "I know they will ruin me, but they will ruin the country too. Napoleon himself would have been defeated with a free press."

If Sherman changed his mind about resigning and his prophecy was disproved, his cup of bitterness overflowed when Knox returned in April with a special letter from Lincoln revoking the expulsion order subject to Grant's assent. Grant, however, declined unless Sherman agreed, and the latter replied to Knox—"Come with a sword or musket in your hand . . . and I will welcome you as a brother and associate, but come as you now do . . . as the representative of the press, which you yourself say makes so slight a difference between truth and falsehood, and my answer is, Never." Sherman's back tuft of hair must have become vertical with the exhilaration of deliving the *coup de grâce*.

While the incident has a strong flavour of farce, there was serious substance in Sherman's complaint that the indiscretions of the press were a constant source of information and warning, if also of distraction in a dual sense, to the enemy. Sherman relates several vivid examples, and remarks, "The only two really successful military strokes out here have succeeded because of the absence of newspapers, or by throwing them off the trail. Halleck had to make a simulated attack on Columbus to prevent the press giving notice of his intended move against Forts Henry and Donelson. We succeeded in reaching the Post of Arkansas before the correspondents could reach the papers." As an exponent of mobility he might, however, have recognized that the press gave generalship an extra incentive to that speed of action which is so essential to success! In siege warfare this advantage was lacking. In April a number of batteries were being brought into position with great secrecy close to Vicksburg, but as a Confederate officer who came under a flag of truce was parting from Sherman he casually asked Sherman—as a parting shot—not to open the batteries that night as he was going to have a party and did not wish to be disturbed.

It is, however, to his wife that Sherman reveals and relieves his mind most clearly—leaving us in no doubt as to the main cause of his grievance against the press and as to his view of the campaign.

"How painfully it begins to come home to the American people that
the war which all have striven so hard to bring on and so few to
avert is to cost us so many thousands of lives.   Indeed do I wish
I had been killed long since, better that than struggle with the
curses and maledictions of every woman that has a son or brother
to die in any army with which I chance to be associated.   Of course
Sherman is responsible.   Seeing so clearly into the future I do think I
ought to get away.   The President's placing McClernand here, and
the dead set made to ruin me for McClernand's personal glory would
afford me a good chance to slide out and escape the storm and
trouble yet in reserve for us.   Here we are at Vicksburg on the wrong
side of the river trying to turn the Mississippi by a ditch, a pure
waste of human labor. . . . We must carry out the plan fixed up
at Oxford.   A large army must march down from Oxford to Grenada and so on to the rear of Vicksburg, and another army must be
here to co-operate with the gunboats at the right time.   Had Grant
been within sixty miles of Vicksburg, or Banks (from New Orleans)
near, I could have broken the line of Chickasaw Bayou, but it was
never dreamed by me that I could take the place alone."

His own affliction was soon lightened by having Grant as companion in adversity, and although his plan was not adopted he soon
forgot the pain, as well as his idea of resignation, in whole-hearted
execution of Grant's plan.   For, with him, disagreement of view
made no difference to loyal co-operation of action, and in action he
ever found solace of spirit.

CHAPTER XII

THE MANŒUVRES AGAINST VICKSBURG, 1863

ALTHOUGH Grant had placed himself and his forces in face of Vicksburg on the direct Mississippi line of approach, it is just to recognize that he endeavoured to avoid a frontal assault, and sought instead to find a way to its backdoor by manœuvres which, if narrow, were at least ingenious. Perhaps too ingenious. The double chain of creeks and bayous which flanked the Mississippi on both sides between Memphis and Vicksburg were fetters on any overland advance which grew heavier with the heavy rains. So high did the water rise that winter, spreading over the land, that Grant's primary difficulty was to find room for the camps of his troops. Hurlbut's corps had been left behind for the passive protection of the Corinth-Memphis line, but even McPherson's corps could not be brought down to Young's Point, and its camps were placed near Lake Providence some sixty miles above, and likewise on the west bank of the Mississippi. Even so, the water was rising so steadily that early in March McClernand's corps had to be moved back from Young's Point to higher ground at Milliken's Bend. And Sherman's was forced to seek a refuge on the narrow levee, only about ten feet across, which was parcelled out in constricted camp sites, and yet was insufficient, so that part of the troops had to live on the transports. He himself stayed in a water-surrounded house, which was connected to the levee by a plank bridge.

Meantime Grant had been striving to turn the height of the waters to his advantage. Below Young's Point the river made an acute turn eastwards before reaching Vicksburg, and thus formed a narrow peninsula on the west bank opposite the fortress. The work of cutting a canal across this peninsula had already been begun during Farragut's abortive expedition of 1862, and now Grant renewed and pressed the effort, as a means to slipping his transports past the Vicksburg batteries and attacking the fortress from the south.

Although energetically carrying on the work Sherman had no faith in the project, and told Grant that it was labour lost, as it was so slow and obvious that the enemy would have ample warning to emplace fresh batteries to command the exit just below Vicksburg. The excavations, however, went on until March 7, when the protecting dam at the northern end gave way, and the river rushed in to swamp the workings. Dredgers continued the attempt for three weeks until they in turn succumbed to the fire of the enemy batteries which had now been emplaced in accordance with Sherman's expectation.

Meantime, Grant had begun a still wider attempt to "circumnavigate" the enemy's position. At the beginning of March McPherson's troops had started to clear channels through a series of bayous which connected Lake Providence with the Red River which flowed into the Mississippi 170 miles below Vicksburg; certainly a long way round, for this passage would have meant a circuit of nearly six hundred miles. By the end of the month a navigable channel was almost complete, when Grant abandoned it for a shorter move round the enemy's western flank, now feasible over land.

Before he resorted to this, two further water movements had been tried. Both were intended to get round the enemy's eastern flank and both traversed the network of creeks and bayous between the Mississippi and the Yazoo.

The first was made by way of the Yazoo Pass, a ten-mile bayou connecting the Mississippi, nearly opposite Helena, with the Coldwater, and thence by the Tallahatchie into the Yazoo. Once the Yazoo was reached a force might steam down it and land near, but above, Haines's Bluff, the extreme end of the Vicksburg defences on the east, thus not only turning their flank but also interposing between Vicksburg and the Confederate force at Grenada.

A passage through the pass was opened and a detachment sent by McPherson passed through, only to be blocked on March 11 at the junction with the Yazoo by a fort recently constructed by the Confederates from Grenada. The flooded country prevented any overland attack, and although a fresh reconnaissance in stronger force was made at the end of the month, the expedition was abandoned on receiving orders of recall from Grant.

In the interval the fourth attempt to find a waterway had been made and had failed. This was prompted in part by Porter's initiative, and in part by Grant's fear for the safety of McPherson's detachment if the Confederates utilized their Grenada force to overwhelm it while isolated. And it produced the most romantically coloured adventure of the campaign. It was made from the opposite or Vicksburg end of the swamp belt, and in order to circumvent the obstructed and Confederate-commanded lower reaches of the Yazoo below Haines's Bluff Grant plotted a zig-zag course across the swamp belt. Starting from the Mississippi, the expedition was to steam up Steele's Bayou for forty miles, then by a six-mile lateral bayou into Deer Creek, thirty miles up this to another connection, Rolling Fork, and so into the Big Sunflower River. Then, turning southwards, the expedition would follow this river until it flowed into the Yazoo sixty miles above the mouth.

Porter, accompanied by Grant, steamed up Steele's Bayou on March 15, but the gunboats became entangled in the fallen and overhanging trees which obstructed the cross channel, called Black Bayou, into Deer Creek. Grant thereupon returned, and sent an urgent call to Sherman who, taking a regiment and a detachment of pioneers, set off next day to the aid of the flotilla. He also dispatched the rest of Stuart's division in transports up the Mississippi to a point where one of the turns of the much-winding Steele's Bayou came within a mile of the Mississippi. They then crossed the isthmus and embarked on tug-drawn coal barges in which they were ferried in relays to Black Bayou, which the first regiment was now helping to clear.

The gun-boats, released, had gone ahead once more, up Deer Creek; but where these iron vessels could force a way the wooden ones with the troops could not follow, until the channel was clearer. Before reaching the Rolling Fork channel into Big Sunflower River, the gun-boats were blocked by newly felled trees and any men who exposed themselves on deck were sniped by skirmishers lurking in the dense undergrowth along the banks. This fire came from a Confederate battalion which, with six guns, had been hurried up Big Sunflower on the first news of Porter's advance. Soon Porter, with his gun-boats blocked, was seriously endangered. At 3 A.M. on the 20th a negro reached Sherman, carring an urgent appeal, written on tissue-paper which was concealed in a lump of tobacco.

It was fortunate that Sherman, alone in a tug without an escort, had been exploring the country ahead of the troops. For everywhere it was under water save, as he had discovered, for a strip near the Creek, across which he had found and repaired an old bridge. Up this Sherman dispatched eight hundred men, all that he had at hand, under his leading brigade commander. Thereby he was left alone in a hostile district. Taking a canoe he paddled back along Black Bayou until, luckily, he met a shallow-draught transport, the *Silver Wave*, coming up with a fresh load of troops. Darkness had now fallen and movements along the winding and treacherous bayou would, under normal conditions, have been too hazardous to attempt. But the need was urgent. So the *Silver Wave* drove ahead, despite the slashing blows of the tree branches which carried away pilot-house, funnels, and everything above deck. Progress was desperately slow, and as soon as they reached the first strip of ground above water, two and one-half miles from his deserted headquarters, Sherman disembarked the troops, sent back for fresh boat-loads, and led the men through the dense canebrake—an eerie procession as they picked their steps by the flickering light of candles held aloft.

On reaching the banks of Deer Creek they lay down in the open cotton fields to rest for a few hours and then at daylight pursued their forced march. To set an example, so that no man could complain, Sherman was himself on foot, and kept his men moving at the "double-quick" save for occasional rests, and also when they had to wade through the swamps, where the slimy water reached the men's hips while the drummer-boys carried their drums on their heads. By noon twenty-one miles had been covered under pressure of the appealing gun-fire from ahead, calling ever louder as they hurried to reinforce the hard-pressed flotilla and advanced party.

For, parallel to this up the Big Sunflower had raced a Confederate brigade by boat, and so had nearly twenty-four hours' grace in which to overwhelm the slender Union detachment. Before Sherman's reinforcing troops reached their endangered comrades they came upon two Confederate regiments which had descended the Creek with the intention of blocking the gun-boats' line of retreat. These were driven back and then the advance reached a long open vista of cotton fields beyond which they could see their gun-boats. Mounting bare-back a horse which had been found, Sherman galloped forward alone along the levee until he reached the gun-boats, the sailors coming out on deck to cheer his daring ride.

Porter had been so critically placed that he had thought of blowing up the gun-boats and trying to make his escape on foot through the swamps with his men. When Sherman reached him he was in course of backing down-stream, a slow process which took three days before Black Bayou was regained, while Sherman and his troops covered the retirement of the gun-boats. The enemy made no serious attempt to close with them. The whole Union force was then withdrawn to its camp opposite Vicksburg, reaching it on the 27th.

That same day Grant, to his chagrin, had been forced to abandon the original canal scheme. He had confidently promised the Washington authorities that he would be in Vicksburg before the end of March, and now his credit had fallen. With 130,000 men at his disposal, and over 50,000 immediately at hand, he seemed to be, and geographically was, further from Vicksburg than Sherman's 30,000 had been at Christmas. Lincoln and Halleck began to show signs of impatience even though they took account of his difficulties. The despondency induced by the multiple checks was not lessened for Grant by the suspicion that his subordinate, McClernand, was again at work to oust him. Sickness, too, of a malarial type, was rampant among the troops after the wet and trying winter in this flooded country. And Grant, in consequence, was now being energetically chased by press and public as a scapegoat for prospective sacrifice. Meantime he was nourishing a new-born design. This, indeed, had been in embryo early in February, when in telling Halleck of his first and second projected routes round Vicksburg, he had mentioned an intermediate route—on the same west bank of the Mississippi—between the short canal and the immensely long circuit to the Red River. By joining up a series of bayous a passage could be opened from Milliken's Bend to New Carthage, thirty miles below Vicksburg, but this project was postponed until the others had failed, because much of the country along the route was under water in February. Moreover, even if a channel deep enough for barges could be made, it was vain to move troops below Vicksburg on the west bank unless their passage to the east bank and subsequent supply could be protected by the Union fleet. Hence, when his mind revived the idea, he sought the assistance, on March 29, of

Porter, who undertook to run the gauntlet of the Vicksburg batteries.

Porter's fleet was lying off the east bank just above the mouth of
the Yazoo, shrouded by the dense forests which here came down to
the water's edge.   These and the swamps prevented scouts prying
into its preparations from the land side and reconnaissances by
river had little hope of success.   One day a small skiff was seen moving quietly and mysteriously up-stream towards the fleet, and on
being overhauled a tiny white flag was found covering the presence
of an ex-cabinet minister and, less successfully, his purpose.   He
and his companions were brought to Grant who, however, pretended
to take the flag of truce at its small surface value and, after a
pleasant discussion of trivialities, allowed the skiff to bear its occu-
pants back to Vicksburg no wiser than they came—as to the fleet's
place of concealment or as to any desire to conceal it.   Meantime the
vulnerable boilers of the ships were being protected and their tell-
tale fires hidden from view by stacking bales of hay and cotton and
sacks of grain round them—thereby fulfilling a double purpose, for
the forage and grain would help to maintain the army when it arrived below Vicksburg.

All was at last ready and at ten o'clock on the night of April 16,
Porter's flagship led the stealthy procession of seven gunboats and
three transports, the latter towing coal barges.   Discovery was not
long postponed and the passage soon became pyrotechnical, lighted
up by bonfires from the bluffs and by the blazing cotton of one of
the transports, the *Henry Clay*, which had been disabled by the
Confederate fire.   But the rest of the fleet came through with little
damage.   Thus although the shore between Vicksburg and Port
Hudson was held by the Confederates the river was now dominated
by the Unionists.   Porter's success consolidated the precarious ascendency gained just previously by Farragut who, in his flagship,
had run northward past the Port Hudson batteries while Banks's
army of 20,000 men was still held in check on the far side.

On the night of the 22nd six transports, loaded with supplies and
towing twice as many barges, ran the Vicksburg gauntlet with the
loss of only one of their number, and so provided Grant with an adequate reserve of food ready for his army.

If these successful passages were naval feats, Sherman contributed his share in a way which helps us to realize his popularity with the sailors. For, anticipating a heavier loss, he had four yawl boats hauled across the swamp to the reach of the Mississippi just below Vicksburg and, manning them with soldiers, lay out on the river ready to succour any disabled ships which might drift down. In this way he was the first to greet Porter after the passage had been achieved, and one of his boats rescued the pilot of the *Henry Clay*.

On March 29, the same day that he enlisted Porter's aid, Grant had begun filtering McClernand's corps down towards New Carthage. It was a slow process. Although the winter floods were beginning to recede, the wagon road to New Carthage was as yet barely above the water—and beneath it for a couple of miles at the further end, owing to a break in the levee. Across the submerged interval the troops had to be ferried in boats collected locally, and thus the leading division only reached New Carthage on April 6, and the others were still strung out far behind. And although the land route was drying too slowly, the water route was drying too fast. For, as a further complication, the shrinking level in the bayous soon nullified the original hope of ferrying troops and supplies in barges by the inland waterway to New Carthage. But by the ingenuity of the engineers, in bridging a succession of bayous, and by thus opening a new and better road, all obstacles were eventually surmounted.

The new road reached the Mississippi at Perkins's Plantation, eight miles below New Carthage and forty from Milliken's Bend. Along it, McClernand's four divisions were moved in turn, and after them McPherson's three; with Sherman's corps under orders to follow. Grant himself went on to New Carthage, leaving Sherman in charge at the other end, entrusted with the safe-custody of the base and with the task of improving the hazardously slender and unstable line of communication on which the south moving army depended.

Even when McClernand's corps was at last assembled at Perkins's Plantation, no suitable high ground was discovered for a landing on the east bank above Grand Gulf, twenty miles further down, and so on April 27 McClernand's corps began a further move in transports, down to Hard Times, nearly opposite the fortified Confederate position at Grand Gulf. McPherson's corps also moved thither by land. And at 8 A.M. on April 29 Porter's gun-boats opened fire on the Confederate batteries while 10,000 of McClernand's men waited in transports and barges for a favourable chance of making a landing. The bombardment continued until the afternoon, but still the Confederate batteries were unsilenced, so that the landing had to be abandoned, and the troops disembarked once more on their own west bank.

Grant wasted no time in vain regrets but marched his troops during the night several miles further south, while the gunboats and transports slipped down-stream under cover of darkness past the Grand Gulf batteries. By dawn the troops were re-embarking, and by noon McClernand's whole corps, nearly 20,000 strong, was safely on the east bank six miles below Grand Gulf, while McPherson was preparing to follow. And out of about 52,000 Confederate troops under Pemberton in Mississippi, only some 4,200 were near Grand Gulf to counter the menace—thanks largely to Sherman's activities.

For a month had been spent in switching the Union forces sixty miles south of their camps above Vicksburg, and the time thus forfeited to nature's troublesome claims would probably have been fatal to success but for the distraction of the Confederate commander's mind and attention. To this distraction the abortive expeditions towards the Yazoo had contributed, as also a repeated rumour that part of Grant's troops were being withdrawn to reinforce Rosecrans near Nashville. Then, while McClernand was beginning his southward move, a division of Sherman's had been sent on March 29 across the Mississippi to occupy and harass the upper reaches of Deer Creek—a menace to the Yazoo line which worried the Confederate command throughout April, not least because of the piteous lamentations of the local inhabitants whose lands were being stripped of their produce.

This particular campaign against civil resources yields a sidelight on Sherman's views, in a letter which he wrote to the divisional commander—"I most heartily approve your purpose to return to families their carriages, buggies, and farming tools, wherewith to make a crop. War at best is barbarism, but to involve all—children, women, old and helpless—is more than can be justified. Our men will become absolutely lawless unless this can be checked. . . . The destruction of corn or forage and provisions in the enemy's country is a well established law of war, and justifiable as the destruction of private cotton by the Southern Confederacy. . . . Still, I always feel that the stores necessary for the family should be spared, and I think it injures our men to allow them to plunder indiscriminately the inhabitants of the country."

In addition to this constant irritation of his Yazoo flank, Pemberton was much worried, though not seriously deceived, by a Union cavalry raid round his rear. Leaving La Grange, near Memphis, on April 17, three regiments under Colonel Grierson rode down past Jackson, damaging the railroads and causing incessant alarms, and finally joined General Banks at Baton Rouge on May 2, after traversing the state of Mississippi from north to south. The moral damage was immense. Lack of mobile troops prevented Pemberton intercepting this raid, as later owing to that same deficiency he had to forfeit the vital chance of harassing Grant's advance inland from Grand Gulf.

The final attempt at distraction to Pemberton came once more from Sherman. Late on the night of April 27 he received a message from Grant saying: "If you think it advisable, you may make a reconnaissance of Haynes's Bluff, taking as much force . . . as you like. . . . The effect of a heavy demonstration in that direction would be good so far as the enemy are concerned, but I am loth to order it, because it would be so hard to make our own troops understand that only a demonstration was intended, and our people at home would characterise it as a repulse. I therefore leave it to you whether to make such a demonstration."

If Grant's reluctance was natural, and well meant, it left Sherman with the hard responsibility of deciding whether he would bear the appearance of being driven off from the same approach where he had suffered a real repulse at the year's eve. Militarily he did not believe in its value, regarding it as too late to be a fresh cloak to the landing at Grand Gulf. In order to pin down more forces at Vicksburg than were already detained by his own obvious presence at Young's Point the demonstration would have to be developed into a real landing and attack, "and until we know that Grant had secured a base at Grand Gulf it would be bad war for us to make a foothold on the Yazoo." For that foothold might be easier to gain than to relinquish, and the troops there would be dangerously sepa-

rated from the rest of Grant's army. Nevertheless the fact that
Grant considered it of service was reason enough for Sherman.
Taking Blair's division, formerly Stuart's, he steamed into the
mouth of the Yazoo on the same day, April 29, as Porter's fleet was
ineffectually bombarding Grand Gulf.

Next day, while his attendant gunboats kept Haines's Bluff
under a heavy fire, Sherman artistically staged a very pretty by-
play of feeling for a good landing point and preparing the disembarkation of the troops. This was continued on May 1, and then
at dusk they slipped away swiftly and quietly to their camp at
Young's Point, whence they marched up-stream to Milliken's Bend.
Here Sherman left Blair's division to guard the base and continue
a demonstrative performance, while he himself hurried on to catch
up his other two divisions which had already started on their way
southward to join Grant.

Although the demonstration did not cause such confusion and
consternation as Grant's glowing comment suggests, it had an ap-
preciable effect. Pemberton, still back at Jackson on April 30, had
his attention already fixed on Grand Gulf—as Sherman surmised—
and he continued to order troops from Vicksburg thither. But the
first day's demonstration alarmed the local command at Vicksburg
sufficiently to cause the recall of a reinforcement already on its way
to Grand Gulf and to discourage any excess of unselfishness. Thus
Bowen, the commander at Grand Gulf, after moving his slender
forces south and successfully checking McClernand's advance inland during May 1, was constrained to give up Grand Gulf next
day and fall back north towards Vicksburg. And it was not until he
reached Hankinson's Ferry on the Big Black River that he met
the reinforcements from Vicksburg, which raised his strength to
17,000.

Twenty-four hours earlier such a force might have shaken Grant's
foothold on the east bank. Now both McClernand's and McPherson's corps were across and Grand Gulf was secured to Grant as a
base. Grant's bold move had succeeded thus far, but the worst risk
was still ahead. Supplies were limited, the troops already on short
rations, and almost without transport until Sherman, arriving on
May 6, brought the first part of a train of several hundred wagons
stacked with provisions from Milliken's Bend.

His rapidity over bad roads was not his least contribution to the success of the campaign, and with his keen insight into the supply factor he had ordered Blair to "keep . . . hauling stores forward," and likewise instructed all his regimental commanders that "every ounce of food must be economised." He restricted the transport of his men to two wagons per regiment, exclusively loaded with provisions and ammunition, and even ventured to send Grant a friendly hint that he should take measures to regulate supplies and to control the "everyone for himself" competition between the different corps and divisions. "Stop all troops till your army is partially supplied with wagons, and then act as quickly as possible, for this road will be jammed as sure as life if you attempt to supply 50,000 men by one single road." Grant laconically replied that he did not propose such an attempt, but intended instead to get up what he could and then depend on the country.

For his plan of operations was now crystallized. He had at first intended to stay at Grand Gulf and send McClernand's corps down river upon the rear of Port Hudson, so releasing Banks as a reinforcement to himself, and then with combined forces march on Vicksburg. But he had now heard that he would have to wait nearly a month for Banks, and then only profit by an extra 10-15,000 men. Delay would be hazardous to his prospects and would ensure stronger opposition.

He had now about 41,000 men, with Blair's division due in a few days, and he decided to move north-east on to the rear, or inland side, of Vicksburg, which would thus be cut off from supplies and reinforcements. His plan was favoured by the lie of the country. For the Big Black River, parallel to the Yazoo, formed with it two slanting strokes from the north-east, with only the difference that the Yazoo joined the Mississippi just above the Vicksburg, and the Big Black, just below.

Thus, while Grant was moving north-east on Jackson the enemy would be kept in constant doubt whether Jackson or Vicksburg was his real objective and whether he might not at any moment swerve due north against Vicksburg. He was in the happy position of being able to do what in football language would be called "selling the dummy." At the same time the line of the Big Black, along which his left was moving, would cover and protect this more threatened flank from any interference from Vicksburg. And he had now high ground and dry ground for his operations.

After the capture of Grand Gulf reconnaissances towards the Big Black were made, and Hankinson's Ferry seized in order to strengthen the illusion of a direct advance on Vicksburg. Meantime the troops waited in bivouac for three days for the arrival of Sherman and supplies. Then on May 7, with three days' rations in their haversacks, McClernand's and McPherson's corps moved off, the first on the left and the second on the right. Meanwhile Sherman, ferrying the whole of his command across to Grand Gulf, marched it inland next day to Hankinson's Ferry, eighteen miles distant, where he took over the responsibility of guarding the exposed rear flank of the advance. He had already summoned Blair's division to join him as quickly as possible from Milliken's Bend, where it was replaced by troops sent down from Memphis by Hurlbut who, significantly, wrote to Grant's headquarters—"I respectfully ask the major-general commanding to attach them to General Sherman's corps, as they and I have the fullest confidence and largest acquaintance with him and his command."

On the 10th Sherman broke the boat-bridge at Hankinson's Ferry and moved swiftly in the wake of McClernand, almost catching him up that night. McPherson had reached Utico on a parallel road and ridge to the right.

Two days later Grant's advancing line reached a geographical line parallel to and barely seven miles south of the Vicksburg-Jackson railroad, the corps being in echelon from right to left. McPherson's on the right had gained Raymond, eighteen miles west of Jackson, driving back a Confederate brigade newly arrived from Port Hudson; Sherman's corps had pushed up into the centre and was aligned along Fourteen Mile Creek; McClernand's corps on the left was also on Fourteen Mile Creek with its right facing Edward's Station but with its left thrown back to hold the crossings over Big Black River and the several roads to Vicksburg.

The advance, apart from Sherman's corps, had not been fast, even the right wing which had gone furthest, having covered only about forty miles in six days. Grant's primary concern was to hold his forces well together rather than to move swiftly. Now, however, he accelerated his pace.

His original intention had been to place himself astride the railroad midway between Vicksburg and Jackson, and then to wheel westwards down it against Vicksburg.   But the encounter at Raymond, and other indications that strong enemy forces were concentrating at Jackson, led Grant to decide that he would first make a further spring east and seize Jackson in order to secure his own rear during the subsequent advance west on Vicksburg.   Accordingly on the 13th McPherson was directed to continue his northeasterly advance to Clinton on the railroad and then due east along it to Jackson; Sherman was to turn and move due east through Raymond and straight on to Jackson, so that instead of being on McPherson's left he came up on his right; McClernand was to follow on and cover the rear with three divisions well spaced out, while the other and Blair's newly arrived division still guarded Fourteen Mile Creek and the Big Black crossings near by.

If Grant's force, by these new dispositions, became a loose-linked chain it was not insecurely linked.   For although it stretched over some forty-five miles the intervals were not excessive, while the lie of the rivers and the nature of the country increased its capacity for resistance.   Moreover, the incalculable direction of advance helped to paralyze the enemy's counter-offensive impulses and to tire out his troops in marching and counter-marching.   Pemberton did, indeed, start on the 15th with three divisions, totalling some 18,000 men, to march south-eastward across Grant's communications.   But there were none!   For when Grant decided to pounce on Jackson, he determined to forestall any such danger by cutting himself loose from his base.   And Pemberton's blow, as we shall see, recoiled on his own head because of the quickness with which Grant had moved. A further advantage of Grant's act was that he cut himself off from communication with Halleck who, ever cautious, desired him to unite with Banks before attempting any offensive move.

On the night of the 13th McPherson was at Clinton and Sherman at Raymond, and despite torrential rain all night and roads sometimes a foot deep in water, Sherman, with the longer distance to go, was within three miles of Jackson by 10 A.M., almost simultaneously with McPherson.

Although Pemberton had ordered all his outlying forces in Mississippi, including that at Grenada, to concentrate at Jackson, only two brigades were as yet present to meet the attack.   Two more were expected during the day—one from Port Hudson and one from the East—but even then there would only be about eleven thousand men available.   And until then there were only two brigades to withstand two army corps.

In consequence, when the Union approach was reported early on the 14th, J. E. Johnston, who had just arrived to assume supreme command in Mississippi, felt that he had no option except to quit Jackson before he was pulverized and, accordingly, sent the two brigades to the outskirts to delay the Union advance while he prepared for an emergency departure and loaded a train with stores. And in the early afternoon the two brigades retired northwards, one of them losing three field-batteries and two hundred prisoners to an outflanking movement by Sherman's corps.

So quick was the Confederate withdrawal and Union occupation that Grant and Sherman, walking into a factory, found the looms still at work weaving tent-cloth marked "C.S.A." and their presence hardly noticed until Grant suggested that work might stop, as he wished to set fire to the factory.   That evening he sent out orders for McClernand's and McPherson's corps to turn about and move west on Vicksburg, so forestalling any attempt by Johnston to circle round north of the railroad and join hands with Pemberton.

But the swiftness and unexpectedness of the Union movements had dislocated the mental balance of the Confederate command. Pemberton was groping his way south-east from Edward's Station, while Johnston, delayed by the troops' fatigue, was preparing to go north-west to meet him!

The luck of being blocked by a swollen creek prevented Pemberton from diverging as far as he intended in a thrust against Grant's non-existent communications, and so prevented Grant having an open path across Big Black River to Vicksburg.   Even so, Grant's quickly converging columns caught Pemberton mentally unready and undecided at Champion's Hill—just south of the railroad—on the 16th, swept him back westwards, and reached the Big Black River, the one strong natural barrier, on his heels next day.   Beyond burning the bridges, the Confederate troops were too disorganized and demoralized to defend the river, which was crossed by the Union forces early on the 18th.   But for McClernand's inertia in allowing his four divisions to be held in play by one Confederate division on the 16th, the Confederate line of retreat would have been cut off and their army almost certainly overwhelmed. The division which thus thwarted him successfully slipped away southward, and after a circuit joined Johnston.

When the other Union corps moved west on the 15th, Sherman's had been left at Jackson to make the place useless as a railroad and munition centre. This he did by destroying the rails and bridges for several miles on all four sides, as well as the arsenal, foundries and cotton factories. Before he sternly checked them, unauthorized pillagers had destroyed other property—and some ex-convicts, not to be outdone, burnt the gaol. Early on the 16th Sherman had an urgent summons from Grant in view of the battle that had begun, and within an hour he had dispatched one division westwards, following with the other later in the day as soon as his task was complete. He was then directed to swing out north to turn the enemy's anticipated resistance on the Big Black River and although this proved unnecessary he was, nevertheless, the first across the river on the 18th, and the first to reach the fortifications of Vicksburg on the 19th. It was an odd and, for the South, ominous coincidence that a house where he happened to pause casually for a drink during this rapid march was one belonging to President Jefferson Davis.

By falling back within the fortifications of Vicksburg the Confederates had given up their hold on the Walnut Hills overlooking the Yazoo, and as Sherman's troops moved forward from the Big Black in the morning of May 19, he despatched a cavalry regiment on to the rear of the battery at Haines's Bluff with orders to seize it. Attack was unnecessary, for it was found already abandoned save for a hospital full of sick and abandoned. And from the bluff up to which Union eyes had so long and so vainly been strained, the cavalry commander looked down on the waters of the Yazoo, sighting some miles downstream a Union gunboat. To this he signalled, and his signal seen, the gunboat steamed up past the deserted batteries to meet and greet him.

It was a moment almost comparable with the "Thalassa" cry of the Ten Thousand, for it meant not only the completion of a strategic circuit and circle round Vicksburg, and the occupation from the rear of those long-defiant bluffs, but the reknitting of the self-severed lines of communication, so that a hungry army was assured of supplies more grateful to stomach and teeth than "hard tack."

None certainly felt the significance of the event more deeply than Sherman when later in the day he rode with the foremost skirmishers of his right wing on to Chickasaw Bluffs, thus completing his own strategic circle and effacing the bitter memories of the old year's end. To Grant, who accompanied him, he turned with the remark that up to this minute he had felt no positive assurance of success, but that now the end of a great campaign was sealed.

For when he had first heard of Grant's intention he had gone privately to dissuade him if possible, arguing that Grant was placing himself in the enemy's jaws and in the very way that the enemy would most desire. Sherman had then urged Grant to switch the bulk of the army back through Memphis and down again east of the Yazoo, in order to base himself on Grenada for a thrust at Jackson, while the fleet and a force of not more than ten thousand troops attracted and distracted the enemy's attention on the Mississippi and stood ready to pounce on Vicksburg as soon as the main army arrived in its rear. Communication between the two forces should be developed by holding and fortifying the lateral route by the Yazoo Pass. By this plan, in Sherman's opinion, Grant would gain all the advantages of an approach to the enemy's rear without risking his security of supply.

Grant had replied that public opinion in the North was already too discouraged for him to risk the appearance of going back, even temporarily, and although Sherman elaborated both his plan and his arguments in a memorandum on April 8, Grant had gone resolutely on with his own. But without reassuring Sherman, whose feelings are well illustrated in a letter to his brother on the eve of his own departure to follow Grant—"I feel in its success less confidence than in any similar undertaking of the war, but it is my duty to co-operate with zeal and I shall endeavour to do it." He kept his word. In the execution of Grant's plan it had been Sherman's zealous energy that had largely contributed to minimize the initial danger of the army's dependence "on a single road, narrow, crooked and liable to become a quagmire." So, also, it had been on his zealous rapidity that the success of the later phase had largely hinged.

Yet in the hour of fulfilment, and later, Sherman forgot his own share in his anxiety to make atonement for his doubts. So anxious that he constantly sought to publish to the world his confession of error. Thus when a party of official visitors came soon after to Vicksburg Grant was surprised to hear Sherman declaiming "Grant is entitled to every bit of the credit for the campaign. I opposed it. I wrote him a letter about it." Grant had not even preserved the letter, yet when the history of his campaigns was being written, Sherman hastened to send in a copy so that the facts and his own misjudgment might be recorded! This desire to perpetuate the truth at his own expense is the more praiseworthy because of the slightness of his error. For his judgment was certainly not at fault in estimating the risks of Grant's plan, but only in under-estimating the psychological effect of a move which by its very audacity perplexed and paralyzed the counteracting forces. Like all his experiences—save with the press—that psychological lesson was later turned to profit.

CHAPTER XIII

THE FALL OF VICKSBURG AND ITS SEQUEL

By the morning of May 19 the Union forces were in contact with the Vicksburg defences, although not so close on the other corps fronts as on Sherman's. Hoping to carry the defences before the garrison had recovered its order and morale, Grant ordered a general assault for 2 P.M. But the shelter of stout entrenchments gave new heart and life to the defenders and the assault was repulsed. None the less easily because it came in a straightforward fashion along the main roads, the natural avenues of approach. Indeed, for want of time for reconnaissance and preparation, it was not pressed vigorously save on Sherman's front.

But a deeper cause of failure was one inherent in the strategic situation. Until now Grant had benefited from the dislocating effect of being on the enemy's rear and across their communications. But once they had been definitely driven back into Vicksburg, with their "backs to the wall" that effect faded and the Union advance re-acquired the disadvantages of a frontal attack. Like snow which is squeezed into a snowball, direct pressure has always the tendency to harden and consolidate the resistance of an opponent, and the more compact it becomes the slower it is to melt.

Grant allowed two days for further reconnaissance and preparation and then ordered, for 10 A.M. on the 22nd, a combined assault, preceded by a bombardment from all the batteries now in position. The result was a second and more emphatic repulse. Any other result would, in the nature of war, have been a fluke, for with about 45,000 men Grant was trying to carry the strong fortifications and entrenchments of a superb natural position manned by only ten thousand less. A position which Sherman, after seeing Sevastopol in later years, declared to be the stronger of the two. The fact that the attacking troops reached the ditch and momentarily planted their flags on several points along the parapet was illusory.

The loss, 3,000, was partly due to this illusion. For after the

193

first failure, McClernand sent a series of messages to Grant; that he was hard-pressed; that his troops had entered the enemy's entrenchments; that reinforcements and a renewal of the assault were needed to confirm the success. Grant was with Sherman at the time and showed strong disbelief in McClernand's assertions, but Sherman offered to renew the attempt as a diversion in aid of McClernand and, accordingly, an extra division was sent to the latter while Sherman and McPherson launched fresh assaults. Thereby the loss was doubled without profit.

This illusion, also, sealed the fate of McClernand. Throughout the expedition, he had ceaselessly grumbled and procrastinated in carrying out orders. The slowness of his movements at the start had exasperated Porter into writing to Grant, "I wish twenty times a day that Sherman was here." The bluff sailor's indignation is the more intelligible when we discover that the steamers were not only burdened with the excessive amount of officers' baggage which McClernand insisted on taking, but one of them delayed in order to carry his new bride and her servants. He showed increasing resentment at the most trivial orders, and at last exploded to Colonel Wilson, of Grant's staff, who brought an order to strengthen his corps outposts on Big Black—"I'll be God damned if I'll do it. I am tired of being dictated to! I won't stand it any longer and you can go back and tell General Grant." And then he abused Wilson as the bearer until Wilson's vigorous protest led him to apologize in the words, "I was simply expressing my intense vehemence on the subject matter"—a phrase which soon became a popular euphemism for cursing. Grant had borne his complaints with wonderful patience, but the fiasco of the assault finally exhausted it and he reported to Halleck that "looking after" McClernand's corps "gives me more labour and infinitely more uneasiness than all the remainder of my department." Grant had so many justifiable military occasions on which to remove McClernand that it was perhaps unfortunate that he tarried so long, and even now postponed the act for several weeks until McClernand published a bombastic address to his troops in which he implied that his corps had won all the successes with some slight assistance from the other corps, and had really captured Vicksburg only to lose the prize through the failure of the others to support it. Graciously, however, the "Thirteenth

Army Corps, acknowledging the good intentions of all, would scorn indulgence in weak regrets, and idle criminations."

Coming on top of their unnecessary losses in the second assault, incurred owing to what Sherman called "a mere buncombe communication," this address drew violent protests from McPherson and Sherman, and as McClernand refused to retract Grant promptly relieved him, laconically reporting to Washington that "The removal of General McClernand . . . has given general satisfaction, the Thirteenth Army Corps sharing, perhaps, equally in that feeling with the other corps of the army." Yet for all his faults McClernand had an apt wit, and even though his subsequent protests were wearisome in their exuberance, his first comment when he received the order removing him was—"Well, sir, I am relieved! By God, sir, we are *both* relieved!"

As for the snowball, Vicksburg, Grant had at once decided to let it melt by the force of nature—empty stomachs—with the gentle assistance of harassing fire and mines. The Union entrenchments were extended until they enclosed the fortress except on the Mississippi front, where the fleet did its share. The one danger to this method lay in the intervention of a relieving force; but June had come before Johnston could gather 20,000 men at Canton, twenty-five miles north of Jackson, and even then he was fettered by lack of transportation. The destruction of the railroad at Jackson had ensured Grant's security for his rear during the critical weeks, for a large force could not operate against him and a small one was ineffective.

It is an illustration of the change in strategical conditions caused by the development of the railroads. For when Napoleon had aimed to isolate an enemy army by getting astride its rear and at the same time to protect himself against a stab in the back from a fresh army, he had commonly utilized a river or a range of hills as his strategic back-plate or barrage. In contrast, Grant's strategic barrage was primarily constituted by a single point, a railroad junction, being made useless to any intervening army.

Long before Johnston was capable of intervening effectively, Grant's strength was raised to over 70,000 by reinforcements sent from Memphis and also from the other theatres by Halleck. And when, on June 29, Johnston at last moved forward from Canton in the hope of releasing Pemberton's force—not of relieving Vicksburg—Grant had already provided a new shield for his own rear. Drawing troops from all corps Grant had formed a special covering force of seven divisions, out of his sixteen, and placed it under Sherman who, after careful reconnaissance, posted his force from Haines's Bluff to the bridge which carried the Jackson railroad over Big Black River. South of the railroad he relied mainly on the line of this river and his own powers of quick concentration.

On July 1, Johnston's advanced troops came up and spent the next three days in vainly exploring Sherman's front for a weak point. However desperate the need of Vicksburg, Johnston was too intelligent a commander to risk the inevitable result of a direct assault on Sherman's entrenchments, realizing that it was useless to sacrifice two armies for an illusory hope of saving one. He had determined to swing south of the railroad and probe cautiously for an opening there when, on the evening of the 4th, news came that the garrison of Vicksburg, hungry and hopeless, had surrendered.

The doubly demoralizing sensation of isolation from outside and emptiness within had done its work and Pemberton felt that his troops were not equal even to an attempt to break out. If he hoped that Grant would be willing to purchase the chance of occupying Vicksburg on July 4 by easier terms, he was disappointed, for once the white flag of negotiation was raised the act was a morally irrevocable lowering of the "Stars and Bars." Thus the anniversary received the most significant commemoration by the physical splitting of the Confederacy. Henceforth "the Father of Waters went unvexed to the sea"—for Port Hudson, the only remaining Confederate obstruction, already undermined and sapped of its strength indirectly by Grant's move behind Vicksburg, capitulated as soon as the news came from Vicksburg. Henceforth, the Confederacy was deprived of supplies, both of men and of food, from the States west of the Mississippi—without hope of regaining this source. Loss of hope is worse than loss of men and land. It was the moral effect, above all, which made Vicksburg the great turning point of the war.

That effect was all the greater because of the Confederates' reaction from their efforts to hold it, efforts which first induced a dangerous confidence and then impelled them to an additional moral buffet at Gettysburg. Sherman, indeed, had found discerning consolation for the failure of the earlier Union attacks in the reflection that "Vicksburg is not only of importance to them, but now is a subject of pride and its loss will be fatal to their power out west." A similar expanding moral value was later to make the loss of Atlanta irreparable and, later still, caused the Confederacy to sacrifice the whole South to Sherman rather than sacrifice Richmond—thereby completing its fate.

On hearing of the negotiations Sherman had wired to Grant—"Telegraph me the moment you have Vicksburg in possession, and I will secure all the crossings of Black River, and move on Jackson or Canton, as you may advise. . . . If you are in Vicksburg, glory, hallelujah! the best fourth of July since 1776. Of course we must not rest idle, only don't let us brag too soon."

In return Grant sent him orders to drive Johnston out of Mississippi, breaking up his force as far as possible and also the railroads, as a strategic barricade against fresh interference. Thus unleashed, Sherman pressed hard on the heels of Johnston, who had made a timely retreat towards Jackson, and on July 9 closed it against the entrenchments covering the town. Johnston expected that he would make an immediate assault and calculated on inflicting a heavy repulse, but with a common-sense respect for the defensive capacity of entrenched troops and the knowledge that Johnston was short of supplies, Sherman invested the town on three sides, bringing up his batteries to goad Johnston into evacuation.

But Johnston had already decided that discretion was the better part of strategy and on the night of the 16th, before the fire of the Union batteries had become uncomfortable, he slipped out of the town and away eastward towards Meridian. Sherman made no attempt to pursue beyond sending a division in the enemy's wake to destroy the railroad bridge at Brandon, fourteen miles out. Sherman's attitude was indicated in his despatch to Grant three days before, "I think we are doing well out here, but won't brag till Johnston clears out. . . . If he moves across Pearl River and makes good speed, I will let him go. By a flag of truce to-day I sent him our newspapers . . . ; that, with our cannon to-night will disturb his slumbers."

This restraint was due in part to the broiling heat and lack of water in the country, but equally to the restraining note of Grant's instructions. For these convey the impression that he was more anxious that the Confederates should be driven out of Mississippi, and their return blocked, than that they should be destroyed—if destruction meant a serious expenditure of life and energy. If this was not a heroic policy it was sound military psychology—to refrain from demanding an immediate further sacrifice from troops who had been through a hard campaign and had gained their real goal. For by such supplementary demands the keen edge of many good weapons has been blunted. A wise commander knows that the moral and physical "drive" of a body of troops is akin to the spring of an alarum clock, and that once it has "gone off" it must be wound up and set afresh.

The need to conserve these well-tried troops was the greater because they were being dissipated by the government's-man-power policy—if such it can be called—of raising new regiments instead of grafting the draft on the experienced body of the old. Even during the siege of Vicksburg an order came on which Sherman comments sarcastically in this letter to his wife—"I did think our government would learn something by experience if not by reason. An order is received to-day from Washington to consolidate the old regiments. All regiments below 500 . . . are to be reduced to battalions. . . . Instead of drafting and filling up with privates, one half of the officers are to be discharged. . . . If the worst enemy of the United States were to devise a plan to break down our army a better one could not be attempted. Two years have been spent in educating colonels, captains, sergeants and corporals, and now they are to be driven out of service in order that governors may have a due proportion of officers for the drafted men [of their new regiments]. Last fall the same thing was done, and the consequence was those new regiments have filled our hospitals and depots. . . . It may be the whole war will be turned over to the negroes, and I begin to believe they will do as well as Lincoln and his advisers."

The last sentence was inspired by Sherman's dislike of the recent decision to raise negro regiments in the conquered territory, for, regretting any step which would embitter the struggle without adequate compensation, he had said emphatically, "I would prefer to have this a white man's war—and provide for the negroes after the time has passed."

With the capture of Vicksburg a wide swathe had been cut right through the Confederacy to the Gulf of Mexico, Grant's army was far in advance of any other, far from its home bases, and before it could transfer its weight to another theatre it would have to be switched back to Tennessee. The immediate need was to fasten the Union yoke on the conquered valley of the Mississippi. In fulfilment of this object Sherman destroyed the railroad for some fifty miles north and south of Jackson, completed the wreck of the town, and devastated the country over a radius of 30 miles. Then with the comfortable feeling that "Jackson will never again be a point where an enemy can assemble and threaten us" Sherman withdrew his troops to camps near Vicksburg for a well-earned rest.

A rest, however, not in the sense of idleness, for his first idea was to organize camps of instruction and to get experts in training sent down to him so that he might sharpen his tools for the next campaign. He also grew impatient of the air of relaxation which spread, and was allowed to spread, throughout the army as a whole. For although the capture of Vicksburg had been for Sherman "the first gleam of daylight in the war" that daylight was merely the signal for a hard day's work, and welcome because it promised the chance of a full day's work to bring the task to completion. His grimly practical and level-headed view was expressed, in the hour of general elation, to his wife—"We have ravaged the land, and have sent away half a million negroes, so that the country is paralyzed and cannot recover its lost strength in twenty years. Had the eastern armies done as much war would be substantially entered upon . . ."

The sudden coming of spring with its rise in the temperature of opinion carried with it a danger to moral health, even in the higher command. In reward for Vicksburg Grant had been made a major-general in the Regular Army, while Sherman and McPherson had been given two brigadier-generals' vacancies—in preference to sundry strong candidates in the East. But popular recognition was still stronger, having all the force of a swift reaction. Grant, at a bound, became the hero of the public and press, with Sherman a close second. An already keen insight into Grant's susceptibility to such influence had led Sherman with surprising candour, to write Grant on the day that Vicksburg fell—"as a man and soldier, and

ardent friend of yours, I warn you against the incense of flattery
that will fill our land from one extreme to the other. Be natural
and yourself and this glittering flattery will be as the passing breeze
of the sea on a warm summer day." Sherman was usually less poet-
ical and more terse when discanting upon the plaudits of the people
—"vox populi, vox humbug" being a favourite comment. His great
fear was that the man whom he regarded as the one solid asset might
be unbalanced by adulation. To his wife also he revealed his
thought—"I thank God we are free from Washington and that we
have in Grant not a 'great man' or a 'hero,' but a good plain, sensible kind-hearted fellow."

But Sherman was slow to realize that he himself had become a
popular idol, if also slower to be affected directly by it, and he
still continued to talk of himself as the butt of the press with bland
disregard of the fact that they were singing his praises. A discerning brother, however, could detect in this an underlying sense of
hurt pride and gently rebuked him with the remark "it is now unnecessary for you to care for defenders." A sense of success was
undoubtedly causing in Sherman a further subtle egocentric
change—"the press, my standard enemy, may strip me of all popular applause, but not a soldier . . . but knows the part I have
borne in this great drama, and the day will come when that army
will speak in a voice that cannot be drowned. . . . In the events
resulting thus, the guiding minds and hands were Grant's, Sherman's and McPherson's, all natives of Ohio."

There is significance even in the order, and still more in the third
person. When a man begins to view himself as a character on the
world's stage there is a dawning danger to his sense of reality, or
at least of a dissociation of his public from his private character.
Such dissociation may be unfortunate, for himself and for others,
by removing an essential check on his exercise of power. For it is
only through the eyes of his private character that a man can retain
the self-righting ability to see himself as others see him. Lacking
it, he lacks the counterpoise to the tendency of his public character
to identify might with right.

In a domestic event, a stroke of misfortune, not of fortune, which
marked this period of Sherman's career we can perhaps trace an-

other symptom suggestive of the same tendency to view himself from outside. Although most of the other generals, and many of the men went on leave—or took it—during these sultry summer months, Sherman would not quit his post, lest training suffer, and in compensation arranged for his family to come down on a visit. His eldest boy, Willy, now aged nine, developed an ardent martial enthusiasm and, not content with accompanying Sherman on horseback during parades, attached himself to the one regular battalion, the Thirteenth Infantry, who treated him as a regimental mascot, teaching him the manual of arms and bestowing on him the "rank" of sergeant.

Just as Sherman was quitting Vicksburg with his corps at the end of September, Willy developed typhoid fever and died on reaching Memphis. The loss of his favourite child was a shock to Sherman which only his urgent duties could in part assuage. For weeks it preyed on his mind during every interval of rest, and filled his letters to his wife—"Sleeping, waking, everywhere I see poor little Willy." A peculiarly sympathetic trait in his character is that in his own affliction he did not forget the feelings of others, or lapse from his essential justice of outlook—"Poor Doctor, although I have poured out my feelings of gratitude to him he seems to fear we may have a lingering thought that he failed somehow in saving poor Willy." Indeed, he put all blame on himself for taking the boy to that "fatal climate."

Yet for all the depth of his grief his personal note of thanks to the commanding officers of the Thirteenth, which had given Willy a military funeral, reads like a platform peroration—"Consistent with a sense of duty to my profession and office, I could not leave my post, and sent for the family to come to me in that fatal climate . . . and behold the result. The child that bore my name . . . now floats a mere corpse, seeking a grave in a distant land, with a weeping mother, brother, and sisters clustered about him. For myself, I ask no sympathy. On, on I must go, to meet a soldier's fate, or live to see our country rise superior to all factions, till its flag is adored and respected by ourselves and by all the powers of the earth. . . ."

Such unreserved treatment of private sorrows is usually reserved for royalty—and royalty is a state of mind as well as of blood. That state of mind can exist in the most respectable republican circles through a simple sense of self-divine right in *res publica*.

Nor was it the only psychological change one can trace in Sherman during 1863. There is a hardening of his attitude towards the war and the South. Exceptionally free from personal venom, undeflected by popular passions, he was more and more developing a logical ruthlessness, which was fostered by his increasingly acute sense that the issue of the struggle rested in the wills of the Southern people and not in the bodies of their troops. The divorcement of his public from his private personality helped to loosen the counteracting influence of his warm-hearted human impulses and allowed his mind to rise to a more remote judicial plane. He did not merely transcend the plane of every man, and of every man's representative, the politician, but rose beyond normal statesmanship to the plane of the philosophic historian. No historian examining the ant-heaps of past humanity could have been more detached in his view. But the difference with Sherman was that he aimed at application as well as examination. And for both purposes his mind was formed by inherited as well as personal experience—by a Puritan ancestry and three generations of judges. From such a line no Cæsar could be born. Rather was Sherman, notwithstanding his lack of religious instinct, akin to the Old Testament prophet and law-giver. The land must be purified by fire; and in this purification he would bear a torch, but without dream or desire of a sceptre.

His clarified philosophy, one of slow evolution, is expressed in a letter of August 3 to his brother—

"A government resting immediately on the caprice of a people is too unstable to last. The will of the people is the ultimate appeal, but the Constitution, laws of Congress and regulations of the executive departments subject to the decisions of the Supreme Court are the laws which all must obey without stopping to enquire why. All *must* obey. Government, that is, the executive, having no discretion but to execute the law, must be to that extent despotic. . . . There are about six millions of men in this country all thinking themselves sovereign and qualified to govern. Some thirty-four governors of States who feel like petty kings. . . . I treat all these as nothing, but when a case arises I simply ask: Where is the law? Supposing

the pilot of a ship should steer his vessel according to the opinion
of every fellow who watched the clouds above or the currents below,
where would his ship land?   No, the pilot has before him a little
needle; he watches that, and he never errs.   So if we make that our
simple code, the law of the land must and shall be executed; no matter what the consequences, we cannot err. . . .   We have for years
been drifting towards an unadulterated democracy or demagogism,
and its signs were manifest in Mob Laws and Vigilance Committees
all over our country. . . .   I saw it, and tried to resist it in California, but always the General Government yielded to the pressure.
I say that our Government, judged by its conduct as a whole, paved
the way for rebellion. . . .   I doubted whether our government
would not yield . . . and die a natural death.   I confess my agreeable surprise. . . .   No great interest in our land has risen superior
to Government, and I deem it fortunate that no man has risen to
dictate terms to all.   Better as it is.   Lincoln is but the last of the
old school Presidents, the index (mathematically) of our national
existence. . . .   Our Government should become a machine, self-
regulating, independent of the man."

The logical corollary of this view was that the State governments
should be weakened to the strengthening of the central Government, and Sherman soon had an opportunity to give point to his
view.   At the end of August he was consulted by Halleck, for the
President's information, as to the reconstruction of the conquered
States, starting with Mississippi, Louisiana and Arkansas.   Sherman, in a closely reasoned memorandum of immense length, argued
strongly against any revival, even later, of the State governments.
He first touched upon his favourite theme of the economic interde-
pendence of the different parts of the country.   Then analyzed
and classified the different strata of society in the South, pointed
out the dangers of reviving the obstructive power of any section or
area until the whole was subdued.   He implied that from the viewpoint of the nation's economic future it would have been better to
replace than to reconstruct the class of large planters, and wished
that "the war could have been deferred for twenty years" so that
a surplus of efficient producers might have been available in the
North to flow in and replace it.   As for the class of "young bloods
of the South . . . who never did work and never will . . . but the

best cavalry in the world . . ." they must either be exterminated or "employed by us." His suggestion to divert their energy into the post-war military service of the Government recalls Wolfe's scheme for the Highlanders a century earlier and subsequent British policy on the Indian frontier.

Next, turning to the immediate problem, he said: "It seems to me . . . that all the people of our country, North, South, East and West, have been undergoing a salutary political schooling, learning lessons which might have been acquired from the experience of other people; but we had all become so wise in our own conceit that we would only learn by actual experience of our own. The people even of small and unimportant communities, North as well as South, had reasoned themselves into the belief that their opinions were superior to the aggregated interest of the whole nation. . . . I think the present war has exploded that notion, and were this war to cease now, the experience gained, though dear, would be worth the expense."

"Another great and important natural truth is still in contest and can only be solved by war. Numerical majorities by vote have been our great arbiter. . . . . The South, though numerically inferior, contend they can whip the Northern superiority of numbers, and therefore by natural law they contend that they are not bound to submit. This issue is the only real one. . . . I would not coax them, or even meet them half way, but make them so sick of war that generations would pass away before they would again appeal to it. . . . Obedience to law, absolute—yea, even abject—is the lesson that this war, under Providence, will teach the free and enlightened American citizen. As a nation, we shall be better for it."

And in telling Grant of his reply, he explained—"I know that in Washington I am incomprehensible, because at the outset . . . I would not . . . rush headlong into a war unprepared and with an utter ignorance of its extent and purpose. I was then construed *unsound;* and now . . . I am supposed vindictive. You remember what Polonius said to his son Laertes: 'Beware of entrance to a quarrel; but, being in, bear it, that the opposed may beware of thee.' What is true of a single man is equally true of a nation. Our leaders seemed at first to thirst for the quarrel, willing, even anxious, to array against us all possible elements of opposition; and now, being in, they would hasten to quit long before the "opposed" has received that lesson which he needs. I would make this war as severe as possible, and show no symptoms of tiring till the South begs for mercy; indeed, I know, and you know, that the end would be reached quicker by such a course than by any seeming yielding on our part."

Here we have the key, now finally cast, to Sherman's attitude during the remainder of the war, and at the end of the war. Moral law is the best compass, but moral law has many interpreters and varying interpretations. Religion and sentiment are the most frequent moral compasses, but he distrusted both from seeing so many ships that had relied on them now drifting as derelicts on the surface of history. Hence his logical mind chose instead a certain compass—the law of the United States Constitution. At least he could steer straight, even if he steered to an amoral haven, and to do that was better than to drift.

That law, like all law in a democracy, was founded on the natural law that might is right. The action of the South was in itself a logical recognition of this fact, and their challenge merely a question as to which was by natural law the right might—the superior might. To postpone a settlement of it or to compromise the issue in any way would only lead to a renewal of it later. And to settle it, the war must be not only carried to its logical end but carried out in its logical extreme. This, on the surface, would seem to mean extermination—no quarter. But dead men cannot acknowledge that their might has not proved right; if the acknowledgment is to be effective and remain effective it must be wrung from living men, who can pass on the lesson.

To subdue men without killing them is possible in two ways. First, by holding them in physical bondage, which is trying for the warder—like a master who has to stay in himself in order to keep boys in as a punishment. Second, by the threat or act of destroying their possessions, which is to place them in economic bondage. Sherman appreciated the superior advantage of this method and with relentless logic was now to apply it. Moreover, embracing the doctrine of the survival of the fittest, he was even ready in theory, as his letter reveals, to fulfil it by economic sterilization of the unfit. That his practice stopped short of this was because it was not practicable to replace them by more fit producers. Accepting, therefore, the need to preserve them his aim was to press them to the point, and not an inch further, that would suffice to wring an acknowledgment of defeat.

In this philosophy of war there was no room for vindictiveness and no excuse for post-war penalization. To the mass of his countrymen Sherman appeared a bundle of contradictions; they could not reconcile his objection to the war with his ruthless conduct of it, nor this again with his "peace terms" of 1865. Actually, he was the one man who in the path of policy never deviated by a hair's breadth from his compass-bearing.

That compass he had before Vicksburg and if he relied on it more rigidly afterwards, it was because he had then for the first time been able to take soundings—to know what depth of water was beneath him. As he expressed it, the summer of 1863 brought to him "the first gleam of daylight," and by this he could see his lead. "I see much of the people here—men of heretofore high repute. The fall of Vicksburg has had a powerful effect. They are subjugated. I even am amazed at the effect. . . ." That effect had come not from the result of combat, for there had been little fighting compared with other and earlier campaigns of the war. Battles, indeed, had been insignificant. The effect came from the sense of helplessness caused by the unchecked progress of a hostile army through their country, and from the burden of its presence.

To that burden, unofficial destruction contributed in no small degree, but Sherman was true to his compass-bearing. Here, for example, are his remarks in forwarding to Grant the proceedings of a court-martial on a private, a sergeant and a captain for being concerned in the burning of a cotton-gin:—

"The amount of burning, stealing and plundering done by our army makes me ashamed of it. I would quit the service if I could, because I fear that we are drifting to the worst sort of vandalism. I have endeavoured to repress this chaos of crime, but you know how difficult it is to fix the guilt among the great mass of an army. In this case I caught the man in the act. He is acquitted because his superior officer ordered it. The superior officer is acquitted because, I suppose, he had not set the fire with his own hands, and thus you and I and every commander must go through the war justly chargeable with crimes at which we blush."

"I should have executed the soldier on the spot . . . but he pleaded his superior orders." Sherman concludes by asking that the commanding officer should "be dismissed summarily and in disgrace" and further that a general order should be issued that "our province is to maintain good law, and not to break it." Furthermore, although he laid his hand so heavily on the town of Jackson, as soon as he saw that the will of the people to resist was really subdued, he supplied their wants, in provisions, even to the extent of incurring a rebuke from Grant.

But that will must be subdued, and in making his iron grip felt not merely by the combatant but by those who fed and fanned the flame of resistance he showed his inexorable logic. Not least formidable and fierce among these combative non-combatants were, and always in history have been, the women who, in the very excess of their emotions over their reason, drive the sword deeper into their breasts. If his history was at fault Sherman's perception was sure when, shortly before the fall of Vicksburg he had written to his wife—"I doubt if history affords a parallel to the deep and bitter enmity of the women of the South. No one who sees and hears them but must feel the intensity of this hate. Not a man is seen; nothing but women with houses plundered, fields open to the cattle and horses, pickets lounging on every porch, and desolation sown broadcast, servants all gone and women and children bred in luxury, beautiful and accomplished, begging with one breath for the soldiers' rations and in another praying that the Almighty or Joe Johnston will come and kill us, the despoilers of their homes and all that is sacred. Why cannot they look back to the day and the hour when I, a stranger in Louisiana, begged and implored them to pause in their career, that secession was death . . . and that their seizure of the public arsenals was an insult that the most abject nation must resent or pass down to future ages an object of pity and scorn? Vicksburg contains many of my old pupils and friends; should it fall into our hands I will treat them with kindness, but they have sowed the wind and must reap the whirlwind."

CHAPTER XIV

BACK TO TENNESSEE—CHATTANOOGA

WHEN Sherman's impatient desire for renewed action was at last gratified in the autumn, it was not, as he had hoped, to exploit a success but to retrieve failure. For only in the Mississippi Valley had the chequered course of the 1863 campaign been capped by a solid crown. Elsewhere there had merely been proofs that all that glitters is not gold, and for the generals the discovery that laurels are not enduring.

In the East, Burnside's had withered after the "horror of Fredericksburg," and Hooker had taken his place. Hearing the news, Sherman told his wife—"I know Hooker well and tremble to think of his handling 100,000 men in the presence of Lee. I don't think Lee will attack Hooker in position because he will doubt if it will pay, but let Hooker once advance or move laterally and I fear for the result." Hooker had fulfilled this foreboding, only too accurate, by taking the initiative, in yet another direct approach towards Richmond, and with the now customary result. Not that his actual approach to Lee's army had been direct, for while the two corps of his left wing were sent across to Rappahannock, below Fredericksburg, the four corps of his right made what was tactically a wide manœuvre by the upper fords round Lee's flank. But strategically it was no more than an overlapping and followed the line of natural expectation, so that Lee was able to exploit his central position to hold one wing in check while he struck at the other, and thus throw back each in turn. Stonewall Jackson's life was part price of this victory, in the first days of May. A victory which, however brilliant in tactical execution, had no real effect on the strategic situation of the war as a whole.

Vicksburg was then imminently menaced, and Longstreet proposed to Lee a plan of indirect approach to its relief, utilizing the central position of the Confederate armies in relation to the enemy's. This plan was to leave two of the three Confederate corps to hold

Hooker in check, take the other to join Bragg in Tennessee, drawing in also Johnston's force from Mississippi, and then seek to overwhelm the isolated forces of Rosecrans. Victory would be exploited by a prompt invasion of Kentucky, a root of the Union so sensitive that a stroke against it would compromise Grant's success in Mississippi, compelling him perhaps to loosen his hold on Vicksburg.

But Lee was unwilling either to leave Virginia or to divide his army. His plan was a narrower one, a renewal of his luckless attempt to invade Pennsylvania. By it he might re-equip his army at the enemy's expense, scare the politicians at Washington, and prevent reinforcements being sent to Grant. But such a move could hardly have the immediate effect on Grant as one against Kentucky, nor even as profound a political reverberation. Sherman knew his Union more acutely than Lee.

Lee, however, was skilfully deceptive in his actual approach to Pennsylvania, slipping down the Shenandoah Valley and across the Potomac into Maryland. And the lead he thereby obtained from Hooker enabled him to penetrate further than in 1862—almost to Harrisburg and the Susquehannah. But through Jefferson Davis's refusal to supply troops for a separate detaining force, Lee had lost time by having to sidle away instead of springing away from in front of Hooker. And, with nothing to detain or distract him, Hooker was quick to follow Lee. Too quick for the peace of mind of Lee, who let himself be "lassoed" and pulled back southward by a groundless fear of a Union threat to his communications, on which he depended for ammunition if not for subsistence.

In consequence the two armies (the Union now under Meade) collided at Gettysburg in blindfold fashion, and Lee, the expert in ripostes, was induced to lunge directly, and continue lunging, at an opponent whose defensive parries grew steadily stronger and surer. After two days of effort, bruised and spent by his own vain exertions, Lee retreated on July 4, the same day that Vicksburg was surrendered. And Meade, too careful to give him the opportunity of a riposte, was stripped of his laurels like those who had. By the end of the month the two armies were back again glaring at each other behind the familiar bars of the Rappahannock, and so continued until the end of the year, apart from occasionally shaking the bars.

If Gettysburg damped the spirit of the South, it was only a cocktail to the North, and even in moral effect was inferior to Vicksburg, which in material effect—both strategic and economic—was far the greater.

While the campaign of 1863 in the East was thus another violent see-saw, brought back to rest on the now familiar line of the Rappahannock, the campaign in the middle or Tennessee theatre was a more static stalemate. For the first six months the armies of Rosecrans and Bragg remained facing each other south of Murfreesborough, both in part paralyzed by the threat and effect of cavalry raids on their respective communications, and both content if their mere presence prevented the other sending reinforcements to Mississippi. Rosecrans, indeed, argued with some reason that to drive Bragg back out of Tennessee was the most likely way to drive him towards Mississippi. But to use a superior force for no more than this passive purpose was hardly an economic use of force.

Ultimately at the end of June, when the fate of Vicksburg was sealed, Rosecrans advanced with his Army of the Cumberland, and Bragg, foiling his manœuvre, made a timely retirement to Chattanooga, the gateway into Georgia. It was a strong strategic position with the Tennessee River in his front, a five-layered mountain belt on his left close behind the river, and the great mountain belt of Northern Georgia behind his right—although this belt was considerably further behind the Tennessee River and further away, than that on his left, from the Chattanooga-Atlanta railroad on which he depended for his supplies and for reinforcements. In consequence, as buttress or as shield it was less helpful. Further, this flank was exposed to an advance down through East Tennessee by Burnside's army—"of the Ohio"—from Kentucky.

The natural assumption was that Rosecrans would move round this flank. Bragg proceeded to dispose his army accordingly, and Rosecrans, having confirmed his natural delusion by feints, moved the opposite way—crossing the Tennessee unopposed south of Chattanooga, while Bragg's army was concentrated above it. But Bragg discovered the danger before Rosecrans could get across his line of communications and, falling back from Chattanooga on September 7, retaliated by setting a trap for Rosecrans who, too ready to believe that the Confederate retirement was a panic flight, pressed on eastward across the five-layered mountain belt with his army strung out over a front of nearly sixty miles. Tucked away in the middle of it lay Bragg, waiting for a chance to fall on and smash any separated part of Rosecran's army. Bragg, moreover, had been reinforced by two divisions from Johnston's army in Mississippi, and two more were on their way from Virginia.

But the very width of Rosecran's advancing front puzzled and confused the Confederates so that the chance was forfeited. Rosecrans had time to close in his army on his left centre in the Chickamauga Valley. Thither Bragg marched and thence Rosecrans was driven, after one of the bloodiest battles of the war, into Chattanooga. The Confederates had for once enjoyed the asset of larger numbers and also suffered the debit of larger casualties even though they broke the right of the opposing line. This adverse balance can largely be traced to the continuance of direct pressure on the unbroken Union left, under Thomas, which thus became solidified.

Bragg then followed Rosecrans's army to Chattanooga—the "Eagle's Nest," and there invested it, drawing his lines round from Missionary Ridge on the north to Look-out Mountain on the South. In such a position Rosecrans had difficulty in supplying his large army, and would soon have to choose between starving or going back across the Tennessee. And even going would be difficult.

His plight aroused Washington to action, and reinforcements were hurriedly drafted both from the East and from the Mississippi. Since the capture of Vicksburg Halleck had let Grant's army lie idle or dissipated it in his now characteristic way. One corps was sent back to Kentucky, another sent down to New Orleans for a contemplated move—rather, a drift—west towards Texas, and Grant's own desire for a move against Mobile, the only important Gulf port still in Confederate hands, was rejected by Halleck. Grant himself went down to New Orleans and was badly hurt in a fall from his horse—naturally and popularly ascribed to drink.

During his absence Sherman declined to assume the command in name, letting Grant's appear in all orders, although he actually controlled those issued by the headquarters of the army. Sherman's motive appears to have been to frustrate any idea of leaving him in Grant's place, and Grant again on the shelf. Before the war ended he was to receive and refuse such a proposal.

While Grant was still on a sick bed he received orders from

Halleck to despatch all available forces to the rescue of Rosecrans. One of Sherman's divisions was immediately sent off on September 23, one of McPherson's followed, and Grant quickly decided to send Sherman in charge of the expedition, with two more. On October 2 Sherman reached Memphis, but his move eastwards to Chattanooga was hampered by orders from Halleck to repair the railroad as he went. These orders were due to a desire to open up a fresh line of supply, as the Nashville-Chattanooga railroad was already burdened with the supply of Rosecran's army. But Sherman had three hundred and thirty miles to cover, with Confederate cavalry and guerrillas constantly trying to destroy the railroad as he repaired it, so that it was not surprising that by October 27 his two leading divisions had advanced no further than Tuscumbia, while he himself was at Juka.

There he had just received notice that Grant, who had now gone in person to Chattanooga, had been given the supreme command in the West and that he himself would succeed to the command of the Department and Army of Tennessee, which included his own corps, Hurlbut's at Memphis and McPherson's at Vicksburg. But it was to be some time before his new dignity could become more than a name or his new army anything beyond the four divisions he had with him.

For on the 27th an urgent call, brought by a ragged messenger who had paddled alone down the Tennessee, came from Grant, telling him to drop all work on the railroad and hurry forward along the north bank of the river. So, sending McPherson and Hurlbut general directions for their interim guidance, and selecting an extra force of 8,000 men from Hurlbut's corps to follow on, he left Juka on November 1 to catch up his own divisions which he had already despatched across the Tennessee at Eastport and thence eastward. On the 13th, despite a detour north by Fayetteville owing to the Elk River being impassable, he reached Bridgeport with his troops hard on his heels.

Leaving them to assemble there he himself went upstream by boat to Chattanooga, there to meet Grant, who was only waiting for Sherman's divisions before launching an attack on the investing Confederate army. If this had been weakened by the despatch of

Longstreet's two divisions up river to Knoxville, the detachment not only bottled up Burnside there and prevented him intervening at Chattanooga, but gave Grant another starving army to succour. And caused him the worry of repeated telegrams from Lincoln telling him to send aid to Burnside. Grant, however, went doggedly on with his first task of relieving the Army of the Cumberland—in command of which Rosecrans had now been replaced, at Grant's instigation, by Thomas.

The sight which greeted Sherman's eyes was more unpleasant than he had anticipated. The Army of the Cumberland was lying down in the hollow just outside the town, overlooked in front and flank by the Confederates on the heights. For one layer, the thousand-foot Missionary Ridge, ran straight across the front of Chattanooga, leaving barely half a mile of low ground between it and the Chickamauga River, which flowed behind and round the northern end of the ridge into the Tennessee—thus forming a protective girdle for the defenders of the ridge. And behind the southern edge of Chattanooga another layer—the ridge known as Look-Out Mountain, over two thousand feet high—reached, and broke off abruptly at, the Tennessee just where it began to make a hairpin bend northward.

Thus any tactical manœuvre was immensely handicapped, for there was only a tiny gap through which the Confederates' northern flank could be turned and the summit of Look-Out Mountain would have to be crossed before their southern flank could be turned. And any wide strategic manœuvre was prevented by the urgency of the need to drive the Confederates back from Chattanooga as a preliminary to sending aid to Burnside.

Nevertheless, Grant determined to hoist Bragg out of his position by using such narrow leverage as he could obtain on either flank. Hooker, who was already facing Look-Out Mountain with the three divisions he had brought from Virginia, was to demonstrate against this sky-scraping flank and then be ready to switch the bulk of his force across the river to back up either Thomas or Sherman. Sherman with three divisions was to move up from Bridgeport, cross the Tennessee on Thomas's left and gain a lodgement on the northern end of Missionary Ridge. Thomas in the centre was to close in on his left and "co-operate with Sherman . . . moving as near simultaneously as possible" and forming a "juncture" on the ridge.

This plan was the outcome of a reconnaissance made on November 7 by W. F. Smith, the Chief Engineer, accompanied by Thomas. Grant, reluctant to wait for Sherman because of Burnside's plight, had ordered a crude and certainly suicidal attack to be made by Thomas. But the view of Missionary Ridge obtained from a high hill on the west bank above Chattanooga showed that Bragg's lines extended too far north for Thomas's advance to have any chance of overlapping them. On Smith's emphatic report, Grant countermanded the attack and decided to wait for Sherman, who might be able to turn the key in the lock, although his problem was difficult —to arrive unseen across the river on the narrow skirts of the ridge and get on top of its northern end before Bragg could concentrate an adequate force to stop him.

On the 16th Sherman rode out with Smith to the hill where the plan had originated, and with great care studied the intervening river valley and the lofty ridge behind. Then, shutting his long glass with a snap, he turned to Smith and crisply said, "I can do it."

After Grant had settled that the attack should be made on the 22nd, an excessively narrow margin of time, Sherman hurried back to Kelly's Ferry below Chattanooga, only to find that the steamer had gone. Not to be delayed he procured a row boat, manned it with four soldiers and, himself taking turns at the oars, reached Bridgeport by daylight. He at once sent one of his divisions, as arranged, to threaten the Confederates' extreme southern flank along Rosecrans's old pre-Chickamauga route—the route, incidentally, by which Bragg was expecting Sherman's advance.

With his other three divisions Sherman set out for his real objective on the other flank, but torrential rain and bad roads delayed his troops, so that Grant had to postpone the attack until the 24th. Sherman's movement across the "back of the front" was inevitably observed from Look-Out Mountain, but he disappeared out of sight behind the hills west of Chattanooga, and troops which were crossing the river direct to Chattanooga as a reinforcement to Thomas were mistaken by the Confederates for Sherman's "reappearance."

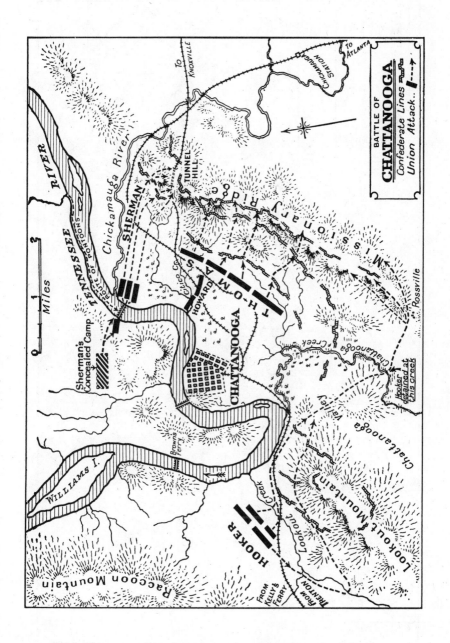

BATTLE OF
CHATTANOOGA
Confederate Lines
Union Attack

Miles
0   1   2   3

TO
KNOXVILLE

TO
ATLANTA

CHICKAMAUGA STATION

TENNESSEE RIVER

Chickamauga River

ROUTE OF PONTOONS

Sherman's
Concealed Camp

SHERMAN

TUNNEL
HILL

Missionary Ridge

Citico Creek

HOWARD

THOMAS

Rossville

CHATTANOOGA

Chattanooga Creek

Hooker
detained at
this creek

Brown's Ferry

WILLIAMS I.

Chattanooga Valley

Citico Creek

HOOKER

Lookout Mountain

Lookout Creek

FROM
KELLY'S
FERRY

FROM
TRENTON

Raccoon Mountain

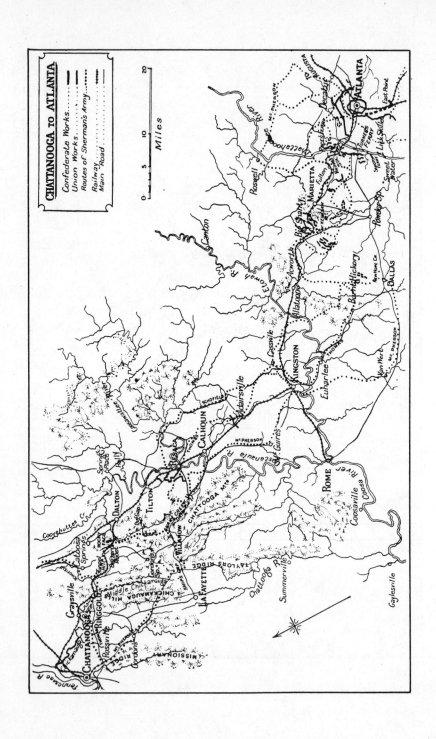

Unfortunately the future was somewhat prejudiced by Grant ordering Thomas to "feel" the Confederate position on the 23rd. This preliminary attack captured the first line of rifle-pits at the foot of Missionary Ridge, and thereby put Bragg on his guard as well as drawing his attention to his right wing, if not yet to his extreme right. In consequence he recalled two divisions which were just being sent to Knoxville, and brought over another from his extreme left.

By the evening of the 23rd Sherman's troops were concealed in woods near the river and at 2 A.M. on the 24th a brigade in (one hundred and sixteen) pontoon boats dropped quickly with the current across stream, surprised the enemy picket and gained a secure footing on the far bank. More troops were ferried across in the pontoons while the pontoon-bridge itself, 1,350 feet long, was being laid for the artillery. Soon after noon the whole force was across and at 1 P.M. Sherman moved against the ridge in drizzling mist which helped his surprise and so helped him to gain the northern extremity of the ridge without opposition. This was about 3.30 P.M., and in conformity with his instructions to secure this position, Sherman dug himself in.

But the view from the captured height brought an unpleasant discovery. Instead of the ridge being continuous as shown on the faulty maps given him, there was a deep saddle between the ridge he had gained and the main ridge, christened Tunnel Hill.

Thomas had remained quiescent all day despite his original instructions and despite orders from Grant at 1 P.M. to "attack at the same time" as Sherman's attack began. Thomas's attack of the previous day had carried him close to the foot of the ridge, and presumably he was reluctant to launch his troops at this towering obstacle until he was sure that the defenders' attention had been distracted. Nor was it easy to tell when an attack began which never became one—owing to Sherman reaching the ridge unopposed. Grant's vague order was here the measure of his abnegation of control.

The low clouds and mist had also aided Hooker on the other flank. Nor was this advantage the whole of their "silver lining," for it was to prove a happy mishap that the swollen river prevented his lateral switch, and so caused his preliminary demonstration to be converted into a real attack on Look-Out Mountain. In this "battle above the clouds" he had carried the end of the ridge and pressed forward to the eastern slope, until halted by the thickness of the mist.

That evening the weather cleared and a bright moonlight night heralded a brilliantly clear second day of battle. The menace of Sherman's lodgment had already led Bragg to send thither his one reserve division, and another drawn from Look-Out Mountain. Meantime Grant, impatient for victory in order to send aid to Burnside, sent orders to Sherman to attack at dawn. Sherman accordingly pushed skirmishers forward at 7 A.M., but did not launch a real attack until 10.30 A.M. There was only room for one brigade to advance along the saddle between the two crests, and over this fire-swept stretch Corse's brigade, with another brigade on each flank, working along the lower slopes, pressed forward to meet the repulse which was calculably certain for whichever side took the offensive against the other's commanding position.

Two more brigades were then thrown in convergently against the weak face of the ridge to help the right flank brigade but, thus passing across the enemy's front, were trapped and thrown back by a counterstroke against their own exposed flank and rear. The three original brigades had been held up short of the enemy's position, and although they renewed their efforts they failed to dislodge the defenders of Tunnel Hill and its lower spurs.

Nor was there any sign of the "simultaneous" attack which Thomas had been ordered to make to check the flow of Confederate reinforcements against Sherman. Thomas preferred to wait for Hooker's expected arrival on the other flank to turn the scales, rather than risk his troops in a direct attack. And Grant apparently agreed.

But Hooker had been detained by a flooded creek and at last, about 2 P.M., Grant ordered Thomas forward to gain, as a first step, the line of rifle-pits at the foot of the ridge. The order was slow in percolating downwards to the four divisional commanders, and not for another hour and a half did the advance begin. Then it easily carried its immediate objective, and the men stopped as ordered and lay down. Above them rose the rough and precipitous slope—some five hundred feet high.

Suddenly, as if by an electric impulse, and without superior orders, the troops leapt to their feet, moved forward and began to clamber up the slope. Its very roughness and steepness were probably assets, by affording cover to those who could exploit it and by lulling the defenders into a false sense of security. Thus the attackers gained the crest in places before their close approach was realized by the defending commanders, and as they wheeled inwards to sweep the ridge a panic seized the defenders, and many of them broke in flight.

The best of the Confederate troops had been sent to face Sherman, and the sound of battle all day on their flank was not good for the nerves of those who remained in the weakened centre. And although Sherman's attack had now subsided, Hooker had at last arrived and was sweeping along the other end of the ridge to the menace of their other flank. The combination of effects is sufficient to explain the cause of the collapse to those with any knowledge of battle-psychosis.

Unfortunately darkness intervened and the pursuit was not general, nor the success generally realized, although Sheridan's division, like a knife cutting through butter, continued to advance until after midnight. The collapse of the Confederate centre forced the right, facing Sherman, to give way and retire during the night. Next day an organized pursuit was begun and continued far enough to hustle the Confederates back to Dalton on the Atlanta railroad, breaking up the branch line by which Bragg might have switched troops to Knoxville.

Grant had already despatched Granger with two divisions to the relief of Burnside in Knoxville, but finding that Granger was moving with distressing slowness, he sent a message to his invariable handyman to take his corps and take charge of the expedition. Grant's message reached Sherman late on the 30th as he was riding into the town of Charleston, where his troops were being withdrawn from the pursuit. Seven days before, they had left their camps west of the Tennessee with only two days' rations and without a change of clothing; only a single blanket or coat apiece to protect them in the bitter winter nights, and Sherman by choice no better off than his men. Now, just as they were hoping to rejoin their transport and rest, they were called on for a fresh effort.

The message said that Burnside had only enough rations to hold out for a few days. And they had eighty-four miles to cover! At Loudon their shortest route to Knoxville across the Tennessee was barred by an enemy brigade which destroyed the bridge. Rather than delay to repair it Sherman swerved along another route, ordering a cavalry detachment to push on at any cost of life and horse-flesh and tell Burnside he was coming. Again, the main body was blocked by an unfordable river, a bridge was improvised, and broke.

Nevertheless, on the night of December 5 Sherman's force arrived at Maryville, only eighteen miles from their goal, to receive the glad news that Longstreet had given up the siege on their approach and begun a retreat to Virginia. Next morning Sherman rode on to Knoxville—to find a well-stocked town and Burnside's staff ensconced in comfort! Perhaps it was as well for the continuance of that comfort that Sherman had not brought his troops with him to greet their "starving" comrades.

Thereafter, leaving Granger's divisions with Burnside, Sherman began a more leisured return to Chattanooga with the rest and then, sorting out his own 15th Corps, marched west to winter quarters between Stevenson and Decatur, on the north bank of the Tennessee. Thus in momentary peacefulness the year of 1863 passed out.

.   .   .   .

Chattanooga brought fresh fame to both Grant and Sherman, yet like Shiloh the controversy over it has waged almost more fierce than the battle. Both generals, loyal to each other, indulged too ingenuously in the "general" habit of talking as if all had gone according to plan. And they suffered like other generals on the rebound. Napoleon said that the best general was the one who made least mistakes, and everybody knows that amid the uncertainties of war mistakes must be made. But nobody knows the general who admits that he has made one.

Sherman has been criticized for trying to get on to Missionary Ridge rather than getting round it on to the Confederate line of retreat. But this too direct direction was implicit in Grant's plan and rather shadowy instructions, while any movement round the enemy's flank was necessarily confined to a narrow corridor which was itself commanded by Missionary Ridge. And to fulfil either purpose it was essential that the Confederates' attention should be distracted. Instead, Thomas's preliminary attack on the 23rd drew their strength to a handy point for blocking Sherman's way. On the 24th Sherman's approach, owing to mist and good execution, attained a greater measure of unexpectedness than Grant had any right to expect in these deteriorated conditions, but during the critical hours nothing was done to help Sherman. It was not necessary for Thomas to launch his troops direct at the forbidding slopes of Missionary Ridge, as his original instructions had given him the order, and those of the day the option, to move his troops to the left and thus converge with Sherman against the end of the ridge. When Sherman gained this and found that a depression still separated him from the main ridge, the early darkness of a misty day was at hand. His troops were barely on the heights before a Confederate counter-attack, which they repulsed, indicated that the end of the main ridge was effectively held by the enemy. A further attack at this late hour would mean that his troops were launched over unknown ground into an unknown position, and even if successful would have to spend the night in the midst of the enemy.

An alternative was to push on round the enemy's flank. Here again the slender margin of time and space—between the ridge and the Chickamauga River—made such a move hazardous. For if the enemy, who knew the ground, held Thomas in check—and this did not seem difficult—they could come down from the heights to close the narrow corridor between ridge and river and isolate Sherman's force while it was groping in the darkness. Unless Thomas was vigorously pressing the Confederates at the same time it was unlikely that their resistance would collapse—indeed, the obscurity would hinder their perception of the danger. And men do not give way unless they are acutely conscious of danger. Moreover, even if such a success had crowned the Union attack the darkness would have prevented it from being exploited.

Next morning, however, the case was somewhat different. Sherman had three alternatives. To attack the main ridge directly; to hold on to his own in the expectation that Bragg would attack in order to dislodge him from such a threatening position; to move on to the enemy's rear by squeezing through the "corridor" which, however, was now guarded by two brigades disposed in depth, while two more brigades were on the other side of Chickamauga River and covering the railroad bridges across it.

Sherman adopted the first course but with mental and physical reservations. For it is clear, both from his orders and from his dispositions, that he had no delusions as to its direct result, and only developed it in order to tempt the enemy to attack, and so give him an opportunity to follow the second course. Indeed, he stretched Grant's orders far enough to give the enemy several hours in which to attack him. When he saw that they showed no sign of accepting the invitation, he made it more pressing by launching three brigades against their position. But his real desire is unmistakably established by the fact that he kept three brigades to hold his own ridge, with five more in reserve behind. And when Howard's two divisions were sent from Thomas to join him during the morning—a procession across the front well calculated to impress the Confederates that the real attack was coming on their northern flank—Sherman used one brigade to support his right flank attacking brigade, and moved the other four round to his left to "squat" in the corridor between his own hill and the Chickamauga River. Thus, in all, only six brigades were used offensively out of sixteen.

The common criticism is that Sherman failed to carry out his "mission" of capturing Missionary Ridge, and that he failed to throw his weight into the attempt. This criticism misses the point. He did not fail—because he deliberately abstained from trying. All that he sought was to hypnotize the enemy into the belief that he was trying. An analysis of his action, or relative inaction, fully confirms the statement, in his subsequent letter to his brother, that "The whole philosophy of the battle was that I should get, by a dash, a position on the extremity of the Missionary Ridge from which the enemy would be forced to drive me, or allow his depot at Chickamauga Station to be in danger. I expected Bragg to attack me at daylight, but he did not, and to bring matters to a crisis quickly, as time was precious, for the sake of Burnside in East Tennessee, Grant ordered me to assume the offensive."

Theoretically it may seem that to make the "suggestion" stronger Sherman should have pushed more strongly. But the solid fact remains that although he did not, the weakened Confederate centre collapsed. This fact cannot be explained away by treating the success of Thomas's men in breaking through the centre as a miracle. The miracle has been repeated too often in history. It was, indeed, the favourite tactical method of Napoleon, and a century later the Battle of the Marne furnished a fresh proof of its efficacy, all the more convincing because the effect was unintentional and the fighting infinitesimal. Even more than Chattanooga, the Marne was an apt illustration of a new conundrum—"when is a battle not a battle?" And the answer is "when one army gives way because it is psychologically unhinged."

Let an army, as at Chattanooga, be kept on the rack for hours or days by the repeated strain to its nerves and reserves of threats to its flanks, which tax the elasticity of its dispositions. Sooner or later the elastic will normally break somewhere in the middle if, fortuitously or otherwise, it receives a sudden blow. The result is only a miracle to those who calculate military strengths in terms of numbers instead of in terms of nervous endurance. The four divisions of Thomas's which performed the "miracle" at Chattanooga lost only 14 per cent. of their strength in the whole five days' fighting, including the preliminary attack and the eventual pursuit.

It would be temerarious to say that Sherman by pressing his diversion more forcefully could have contributed more than an increased casualty list. To throw more men directly at Missionary Ridge would have been to throw away more lives, with little hope of dislodging an expectant enemy. And to throw his weight along the corridor would not only lead them to a well-blocked end but would have massed his troops along a defile under the fire of the Confederate guns on the heights and on other heights beyond the river. Compressed cannon-fodder, indeed. Even if those who survived had forced their way slowly through they would only have forced the Confederates back along their natural line of retreat, which ran not due east, but south-east along the Atlanta railroad. The flank on which Sherman was operating was a good one to dislodge the enemy, but not the one on which success would jeopardize his retreat, and no one is more likely to have realized this than Sherman.

The one valid criticism is that Sherman had more troops than he could effectively employ in his distraction, and perhaps more than were needed to ensure his own security, awkwardly as he was placed between the Confederate devil and the deep river. But for this surplus, which would have been more useful on the other flank, Grant and not Sherman was responsible. Sherman, indeed, on hearing that Grant had sent him Baird's division as an additional reinforcement, immediately replied that it was unnecessary, and thus enabled this division to be recalled in time to take part in the "miracle."

It was perhaps natural that Grant, seeing Confederate columns moving northward, should have been alarmed for Sherman's security, but there is no historical warrant for his opinion that Sherman's position was "critical," and no excuse for repeating it in his memoirs. The conviction grows on the student of the Grant-Sherman partnership that Sherman's interpretation of his superior's mind was clearer and more definite than that mind itself. For Grant had more inspiration than precision of thought. Even at Chattanooga it was fortunate that the rain-swollen river rose so fast as to compel him to revert to his original inspiration of letting Hooker advance across Look-Out Mountain and against the Confederates' southern flank instead of switching him north to support Sherman or Thomas.

CHAPTER XV

THE COMMAND IN THE WEST, 1864

As the Vicksburg campaign had cleft the Confederacy asunder
down the line of the Mississippi, so the Chattanooga and Knoxville
campaign had cut off a fresh section west of the Alleghanies. But,
further south, Alabama was still intact save for the northern edge,
and the railway from Mobile to Georgia, the one remaining link between East and West, enabled the Confederacy to keep in touch with
their scattered forces in the West. The severe winter weather in
East Tennessee and the need to recuperate the Union forces called
a halt in the operations, and this interval before the spring campaign began gave Sherman a chance to oversee in person the affairs
of his new Department, from which he had been summoned away even
as he was summoned to its command. But, less content than others
to enjoy a breathing space, he proposed to Grant a plan whereby to
utilize this to the enemy's detriment and the Union's profit.

Although the Confederacy had been permanently severed down
the Mississippi line the cut had not been wide enough to prevent
the Confederate edges closing in while Grant was operating anew
along the Tennessee line. Vicksburg itself was immune from Confederate encroachments, but in eastern Mississippi the Confederate
forces based on Meridian had drawn in close enough to the Mississippi to be unpleasant company and an ever-present menace to
the free navigation of the great river. Sherman's idea was now to
strike a quick blow at these forces and roll them back eastward, while
Banks from New Orleans similarly rolled back the Confederate
forces west of the Mississippi. By thus widening the gap through
the Confederacy the Mississippi would be made more secure and the
force devoted to its close protection could be released for service elsewhere. Further, by breaking the communications as far east as
Meridian Sherman would "cut off one of the most fruitful corn supplies of the enemy."

After receiving Grant's prompt assent, he went home to spend

Christmas with his family at Lancaster, and from there travelled to Cairo, to find the Mississippi almost ice-bound. But he also found Porter, easier to thaw, and as Sherman was willing to risk his life the admiral risked a small gunboat to help him risk it in an adventurous trip amid grinding ice-floes down to Memphis. Here Sherman collected two divisions from Hurlbut's corps and also formed a cavalry force of about seven thousand men under Brigadier-General Sooy Smith, who had been sent by Grant to check the constant raids of the irrepressible Confederate cavalry leader, Forrest. Sherman promptly wove Sooy Smith, his force and mission into the pattern of his own scheme.

This was completed after a visit to Vicksburg, where Sherman instructed McPherson to prepare two more divisions and to send out spies to discover the strength and exact location of the Confederate forces. While Sherman himself would strike due east from Vicksburg for Meridian, and draw on himself the attention of the enemy's main force, Sooy Smith was to sweep down south from Memphis upon the strategic flank of Meridian, seizing any chance to overwhelm Forrest, who lay across his route with less than three thousand cavalry.

Having given Sooy Smith full instructions and warning of Forrest's methods, Sherman finally went down river on January 27, 1864, with Hurlbut and his two divisions, after being entertained at a banquet given by the citizens of Memphis in his honour. He told his brother that he dreaded this more than the assault on Vicksburg, but from his obvious if reluctant enjoyment his comment seems tinged with self-deception. He had been a popular target so long that when he became a popular toast he had a guilty sense of illicit indulgence. The "incense of flattery," against which he had warned Grant, tickled his own palate even though it turned his stomach.

The effect is amusingly revealed in a letter written to his wife on his voyage south from Memphis—"I was not aware of the hold I had on the people until I was there this time . . . every time I went into a theatre or public assemblage there was a storm of applause. I endeavoured to avoid it as much as possible, but it was always so good-natured that I could not repel it." In this letter he also explains, in apparent answer to a protest, why it was necessary for him to take personal charge of the Meridian expedition instead

of leaving it to one of his corps commanders who had not borne the
heat and risk of the day at Chattanooga. He would have liked to
give McPherson the chance of distinction but Hurlbut was the senior
of the two and neither Grant nor he had "confidence enough in his
[Hurlbut's] steadiness to put him on this expedition. He is too
easily stampeded by rumors. I have a better sense of chances. I
run two chances, first, in case the enemy has learned my plans or
has guessed them, he may send to Meridian a superior force. A
bad road may prevent my moving with the celerity which will command success. Would that I had the Fifteenth Corps that would
march in sunshine or storm to fulfil my plans. . . ."

On February 3, 1864, the expedition moved out from Vicksburg,
with only a bare minimum of transport, on its 150-mile pounce on
Meridian. Sherman's preliminary orders had sounded the keynote—"The expedition is one of celerity, and all things must tend
to that . . . not a tent, from the commander-in-chief down, will be
carried. The sick will be left behind, and the surgeons can find
houses and sheds for all hospital purposes." And Sherman sought
the advantage of "selling the dummy" by spreading the story that
his move was aimed against Mobile. To strengthen the suggestion
he asked Banks to "keep up an irritating foraging or other expedition in that direction," and in return promised, if Grant agreed,
to co-operate subsequently with Banks in a westward expedition up
the Red River against Shreveport. The doubly "mobile" move
so far imposed on the Confederate Government that J. E. Johnston,
who had succeeded Bragg in command at Dalton, was ordered to
despatch three divisions to help in opposing it. But by the time
they were on their way south Sherman was already on his way back
to Vicksburg, his mission at Meridian completed.

For, driving back a thin screen of Confederate cavalry, Sherman's two columns reached Jackson on the 6th, before the enemy
were fully awake to his coming. They had two infantry divisions,
one east and the other north of Jackson, but Sherman came up too
quickly for them to concentrate effectively to block him, a task the
more difficult because his columns were moving on two roads until
well past Jackson. As a result the enemy were hustled back
and through Meridian without a battle, the only trouble coming
from the Confederate cavalry who hung on Sherman's flanks.

He himself had a narrow escape from capture by these. On the last lap of the march the columns of Hurlbut and McPherson were moving on the same road, with a four-mile gap between them, and as nightfall was approaching Sherman himself halted at a cross-roads to await McPherson's column, detaching one of Hurlbut's regiments to guard the cross-roads until the head of McPherson's column came in sight. Meantime Sherman snatched a brief rest in a log-house—to be awakened by shouts and pistol-shots, and to find that Confederate cavalry were around the house. Worst of all the protecting regiment had disappeared, its commander having assumed that an approaching cloud of dust was sufficient evidence of McPherson's coming to justify him in moving on. Despatching his aide-de-camp to catch this vanishing guard, Sherman gathered a few orderlies and clerks to make a stand in defence of his temporary headquarters. Salvation, however, came from another quarter—the passing of some straggling wagons of Hurlbut's train and their escort, which diverted the enemy's attention, as an easier and richer prize, until the errant regiment returned to the rescue. There is humour in the fact that Sherman should have owed his preservation to faulty march discipline.

On reaching Meridian safely, Sherman set his men to work in destroying the arsenal, the supply depots, and the two intersecting lines of railroad, thus creating a new and more extended "safety curtain" for the Mississippi theatre. There was no sign of Sooy Smith, and after waiting five days, Sherman began his homeward march, making a circuit northward to feel out for Sooy Smith. But in vain, and only after Sherman's return to Vicksburg did he discover that Forrest had claimed yet another victim.

This was the only subtraction from his satisfaction, but he could forget this, if not forgive Sooy Smith, in the joy of a special addition to it. For as he gleefully wrote to his wife—"Had I tolerated a corps of newspapermen how could I have made that march a success? Am I not right? And does not the world now see it?" To have outwitted both the enemy and the press was balm indeed.

At Vicksburg also he found a letter from his old colleague Boyd, now a prisoner of war in Natchez jail. And, going down to New Orleans, Sherman stopped to release him on the way, taking him to New Orleans in his own steamer as a preliminary to arranging an exchange. The purpose of Sherman's visit to New Orleans was to discuss the Red River project with Banks, and although unfavourably impressed by Banks's fondness for spectacular ceremonial "when it seemed to me every hour and minute were due to the war," Sherman arranged to lend a force of ten thousand men for a period of a month, when they were to be returned to him for the forthcoming Atlanta campaign. Sherman emphasized the importance of close co-operation with Porter's fleet, but in the outcome Banks, himself late at the rendezvous, let his army be caught strung out on a single road, and after suffering defeat retreated independently of the fleet which, forsaken, narrowly escaped capture. And Sherman never saw his detachment again, although it was eventually returned to Tennessee in time to aid Thomas in the December Battle of Nashville—when Sherman himself was already on the Atlantic coast.

Banks's failure also nullified one part of the plan for the spring campaign. For it had been Grant's intention that while the force round Chattanooga pushed through the Georgian gateway towards Atlanta, Banks should combine with Admiral Farragut in an attack on Mobile and thus open an alternative gate into Georgia from the extreme south, besides completing the severance of the Eastern States of the Confederacy from the West. Now, Banks was so delayed in extricating himself that the Mobile project had to be postponed, and the advance from Chattanooga into the eastern half of the Confederacy had to be made without either the security to its flank or the possibility of varying its direction which the original plan promised. The consequences were far-reaching and might have stultified the whole plan of campaign if a leader more cautious or less farsighted than Sherman had been in charge. For to that rôle he was now called.

On his journey back to Memphis from New Orleans he was met by a letter from Grant which said that the grade of Lieutenant-General, last held by George Washington, had been revived, and that he had been summoned to Washington. The implication was obvious— that Grant, on receiving it, would be given the supreme command of the United States armies. The letter went on to express Grant's "thanks to you and McPherson as *the men* to whom, above all others, I feel indebted for whatever I have had of success. How far your advice and suggestions have been of assistance, you know. How far your execution of whatever has been given you to do entitles you to the reward I am receiving, you cannot know as well as I do."

Sherman's reply of March 10, was equally characteristic—no jam without a pill. After disclaiming the tribute to himself, he told Grant that his strongest feature was his "simple faith in success." "Also, when you have completed your best preparations you go into battle without hesitation . . . no doubts, no reserve; and I tell you that it was this that made me act with confidence. I knew wherever I was that you thought of me, and if I got in a tight place you would come—if alive."

Then, with delightful candour, Sherman added, "My only points of doubt were as to your knowledge of grand strategy, and of books of science and history; but I confess your common-sense seems to have supplied all this. Now as to the future . . . for God's sake and your country's sake, come out of Washington! I foretold to General Halleck before he left Corinth the inevitable result to him, and I now exhort you to come out West. Here lies the seat of the coming empire; and from the West, when our task is done, we will make short work of Charleston and Richmond, and the impoverished coast of the Atlantic."

The last sentence contains the germ, here first seen, of the great march which settled the issue of the war. A march which was made, and made by Sherman, because Grant reluctantly rejected the advice of the previous sentence, and went to the East. Any other course, indeed, was hardly feasible since in the East lay the seat of government.

Thus Sherman, summoned on arrival at Memphis to meet Grant at Nashville, was there greeted by the news that Grant was leaving the West and transferring to him the command of the "Military Division of the Mississippi," the supreme command in the West, embracing the Departments of the Ohio, Cumberland, Tennessee, and Arkansas. Grant, indeed, was already on the point of departure when Sherman arrived, and in order to have some chance of discussion Sherman accompanied Grant as far as Cincinnati. Before leaving Nashville, however, he issued orders formally assuming command, as from that date, March 18, and was also witness of the presentation of a sword of honour to Grant by the Mayor of Grant's native town of Galena. A ceremony more humorous than ceremonious, for when the time for reply came Grant fumbled in his several pockets until he at last found and pulled out a crumpled sheet of cartridge paper on which his reply was written, and handed it to the Mayor in lieu of a speech.

This final memory of Grant's rough simplicity was not calculated to make Sherman feel happier as to Grant's fate in the lion's cage of social Washington, and his subsequent letters to his brother reveal his acute foreboding—"Give Grant all the support you can. If he can escape the toils of the schemers he may do some good." And again, on hearing from his brother that "General Grant is all the rage; he is subjected to the disgusting but dangerous process of being lionized," Sherman repeats the admonition: "Grant is as good a leader as we can find. He has honesty, simplicity of character, singleness of purpose and no hope or claim to usurp civil power. His character, more than his genius will reconcile armies and attach the people. Let him alone. Don't disgust him by flattery or importunity. Let him alone . . . if bothered, hampered or embarrassed, he would drop you all in disgust, and let you slide into anarchy."

Sherman himself was suffering immersion in an almost equally warm bath of adulation, but his skin had become tough by long exposure to criticism. The warmth of public acclaim undoubtedly had an effect on him, but it was not the normal reaction. Instead of enervating it exhilarated. And by strengthening his weakest point, his self-confidence, so grievously shaken by past mischances, strengthened his capacity to fulfil the task he was now about to undertake.

A significant stage in the growth of his self-confidence is revealed in his outlook when undertaking the Meridian expedition—"Our armies are now at the lowest point, and so many are going home [on furlough] as re-enlisted veterans, that I shall have a less force than should attempt it; but this is the time and I shall attempt it. It seems my luck to have to take the initiative and to come in at desperate times"—just a trace of the old pessimism here—"but thus far having done a full share of the real achievements of this war, I need not fear accidents. . . ." And by the succeeding paragraph of the same letter, we can perceive how, in spite of himself, public support was at least one of his spiritual reinforcements.

"You who attach more importance to popular fame would be delighted to see in what estimation I am held by the people of Memphis, Tenn., and all along this mighty river."

He still maintained his old attitude of outward scorn of publicity, an attitude prompted more by a distrust of the consequences than by a dislike of the feeling, if also by a professional contempt for unprofessional opinion. But his consistency of action was at least greater than that of most public figures.

These several characteristics are illustrated in a letter to his brother at Christmastide—"I have been importuned from many quarters for my likeness, autographs and biography. I have managed to fend off all parties and hope to do so till the end of the war. I don't want to rise or be notorious, for the reason that a mere slip or accident may let me fall, and I don't care about falling so far as most of the temporary heroes of the war. . . . If parties apply to you for materials on my behalf, give the most brief and general items, and leave the results to the end of the war or of my career. . . . I know I stand very high with the army and feel no concern on that score. Today I can do more with Admiral Porter or the Generals than any general officer out West except Grant, and with him I am a second self."

Sherman certainly placed high value on the opinions not only of his peers but of his men, and if his cultivation of it was unconscious it is all the more tribute to his instinct for the art of popular leadership. Thus on arrival at Nashville to take up his new command he declined the offer of a private box in the theatre but, when he visited the theatre during his brief month's preparation for the new campaign, he sat in the pit among the soldiers—to the great delight of all except the manager who found that no officer would take, and pay for, more exalted seats in face of their commander's example of republican simplicity.

CHAPTER XVI

ON THE ROAD TO ATLANTA—THE RESACA MANŒUVRE

GRANT'S appointment as Lieutenant-General Commanding the Armies of the United States gave to them not merely a nominal unity of command, but a practical unity of idea and action. In itself his appointment was little more than a reversion to that suddenly given McClellan in November, 1861, and as abruptly terminated, while the distinction between it and Halleck's position as "General-in-Chief" was merely that between a chief in the field and a chief in the office. In now stepping down to be "Chief of staff of the Army," Halleck assumed in name the function he had fulfilled in practice.

Far more important than the title and authority, even more important than Lincoln's loosening of the rein, was the intimate understanding and sympathy between Grant, who was now personally to direct the armies in the East, and Sherman who—five hundred miles distant, and soon more—was to direct the armies of the West. Arbitrary control commonly breaks down unless it rests on the co-operation of minds attuned to the same key. Without this the first is but voice control. As Sherman wrote to Grant—"That we are now all to act on a common plan, converging on a common centre, looks like enlightened war." The convergence was more mental than physical. Plotted graphically the two armies, so far separated, became more separated as they moved on their respective courses, and the most deadly work had been done before they began geographically to converge. It is an illustration of the fallacy of confusing a common aim with a common target, a single object with a single objective.

On March 25 Sherman actually began his command, by a tour of the armies around Chattanooga, and on returning to Nashville received a letter from Grant, dated April 4. This contained Sherman's "commission" for the spring campaign, and the bareness of

Grant's orders is significant of the co-operation between the two men.   He first tells Sherman that he has ordered Banks to begin operations against Mobile as soon as possible—his faith was here misplaced—and that Butler will go up the James River with 33,000 men and strike at Richmond from the south.   He then comes to the two main moves:

"I will stay with the Army of the Potomac . . . and operate directly against Lee's army, wherever it may be found . . . you I propose to move against Johnston's army, to break it up, and to get into the interior of the enemy's country as far as you can, in- flicting all the damage you can against their war resources.   I do not propose to lay down for you a plan of campaign, but simply to lay down the work it is desirable to have done, and leave you free to execute it in your own way."

Between the purposes of the two moves there is a subtle but sig- nificant difference.   For Grant told Meade, in immediate command of the Army of the Potomac, that "Lee's army would be his objective point; that wherever Lee went he would go also."   But Sherman was given an economic as well as a military objective.   And in his acknowledgment of the commission there is a further subtle accen- tuation of the difference—"I am to knock Jos. Johnston, and to do as much damage to the resources of the enemy as possible."   The military cause is less emphatic, the economic more emphatic, while the term "resources" is broader.   Sherman's mind, following the evolutionary trend of his thought on the war, was set on the deeper object of uprooting the economic foundations of the enemy's will and power to resist.   And in regard to the military objective Sher- man, knowing the shrewdly cautious mind of his immediate oppo- nent, foreshadows the difficulty of breaking him up—"If Johnston falls behind the Chattahoochee—" the last of the three rivers astride the road to Atlanta—"as I believe he will . . . I will feign to the right, but pass to the left and act against Atlanta or its eastern communications, according to developed facts.   This is about as far ahead as I feel disposed to look, but I will ever bear in mind that Johnston is at all times to be kept so busy that he cannot in any event send any part of his command against you or Banks."

Then Sherman turns from the enemy's economic base to his own and once more casts a shadow before—the shadow of his great and decisive post-Atlanta move. "If Banks can at the same time carry Mobile and open up the Alabama River, he will in a measure solve the most difficult part of my problem, viz., 'provisions.' But in that I must venture. Georgia has a million of inhabitants. If they can live, we should not starve. If the enemy interrupt our communications, I will be absolved from all obligations to subsist on our own resources, and will feel perfectly justified in taking whatever and wherever we can find. I will inspire my command, if successful, with the feeling that beef and salt are all that is absolutely necessary to life, and that parched corn once fed General Jackson's army on that very ground"—here we see the practical value of Sherman's studies in the military history of the region. Its topography, too, was known to him from his subaltern reconnaissances, although better for the last lap from Allatoona to Atlanta than for the earlier stages. Further, he obtained and analyzed census and taxation returns whereby to calculate the population and resources of every county in Georgia. If there was any lingering doubt that Atlanta was the objective uppermost in Sherman's mind, or that he looked definitely to reaching it by a series of strategic points or stepping-stones, it would be dispelled by a letter of April 27 to his wife—"Dalton will be our first point, Kingston next, Allatoona and then Atlanta." On these points both his plan and his mind revolved, and evolved.

For Atlanta, the "Gate City of the South" had a three-fold strategic value—apart from its moral value, which grew with the effort to hold it. First, as one of the few manufacturing centres for munitions—a term wider than "ammunition"—in the agrarian Confederacy; its foundries and machine-shops furnishing a high proportion of the material without which the war could not be maintained. Second, as the greatest rail centre of the South; thither converged and thence radiated outwards the main lines connecting the Atlantic seaboard with the western parts of the Confederacy. If these were already curtailed, the value of Alabama's resources had increased thereby, and not least that of the newly created ordnance works at Selma. Third, because Atlanta was the inner back gate, as Chattanooga was the outer, to the Atlantic states of old foundation, which were the foundation of the hostile power and will. And the last line of nature's battlements was that which cov-

ered Atlanta. Once the Atlanta gate could be opened the heart
of the Confederacy would lie open to a mortal thrust.

Those battlements, however, were strong. The stretch of country, over a hundred miles wide, between Chattanooga and Atlanta
may be likened to an M. The left-hand stroke is formed by the
Tennessee River, with Chattanooga as a midway point. The two
oblique central strokes are the Oostenaula and Etowah Rivers, respectively, which join near Rome to form the Coosa. The right
hand stroke is the Chattahoochee, which constituted the final barricade covering Atlanta. These four strokes of the M form three
"pockets." The left-hand pocket was filled with a parallel series
of mountain ridges; the central pocket was comparatively flat, with
abundant wheat-fields and numerous iron mines; the right-hand
pocket was a wild forest region interspersed with hills. To reach
Atlanta Sherman would have to cut across the M from left to right.

The first, and greatest, problem to be solved was that of supply.
And on the solution Sherman stamped the hallmark of his genius,
here as brilliantly orthodox as in the next campaign he was brilliantly unorthodox.

Chattanooga, his starting point, was 151 miles in front of Nashville, his main base of supply, and this in turn was 185 miles from
Louisville, the main source of supply. This long and slender
"throat" might be cut at scores of points by enemy cavalry and
guerrillas and had to be guarded along its whole length, as also the
Cumberland River. Garrisons, too, had to be left to hold the occupied territory. But out of a total of one hundred and eighty thousand men in the three departments Sherman planned and contrived to form by the end of April a compact striking force of a
hundred thousand. For this, however, the means of supply were
inadequate and precarious when he took over, and as Grant had
fixed the starting date for April 30—subsequently postponed to
May 5—there was scanty time to make them adequate.

Sherman's first step was to take over supreme control of the railroads which had hitherto been controlled by the departmental commanders, with consequent friction and uneven distribution of supplies. His next step was to close the railroads to civil traffic, both
supplies and passengers; an act which at once caused a public outcry and appeals to Lincoln, who urged Sherman to relax his ban,

only to receive the blunt reply that as "the railroad cannot supply the army and the people too, one or the other must quit, and the army don't intend to, unless Joe Johnston makes us. . . . I will not change my order, and I beg of you to be satisfied that the clamor is partly humbug . . . and to test it, I advise you to tell the bearers of the appeal to hurry to Kentucky and make up a caravan . . . to relieve their suffering friends by foot, as they needed to do before a railroad was built. . . . We can relieve all actual suffering by each company or regiment giving of their savings." As soon, however, as he had built up a secure surplus of stores at the front, he judiciously loosened the restrictions, and meantime the traders rediscovered the use of wagon-roads. Moreover, Sherman was equally stringent in his regulation of the military use of the railroads, confining it to supplies and making all troops march, and beef cattle be driven, to the front.

Although he thus nearly doubled his daily delivery of stores at the front, it was still below his calculation of the need, which he put at one hundred and thirty ten-ton car-loads a day—in order to provide a reserve in case the railroad was temporarily cut. At the time only about ninety car-loads were being delivered, and the main difficulty was that there were only some sixty locomotives and six hundred cars available. Accordingly Sherman ordered all trains which reached Nashville from Louisville to be detained for use on the Chattanooga line. This drew a protest from the former railroad company, whereupon Sherman advised them to levy a forced loan of trains coming into Louisville from the north, and thus, before the campaign had ended, cars labelled with far distant northern railroad names were to be seen usefully "strayed" down in Georgia. And contemporary observers relate that Sherman showed more joy over the news of a small increase in car-loads than over a large reinforcement of troops—perhaps the best psychological testimony that he was truly a strategist and not merely a fighting general practitioner.

More forgiving than most commanders where tactical errors occurred, knowing that the enemy's resistance and counter-action is the most incalculable factor in war, he would rarely tolerate excuses for delays in movement supply, believing that by due foresight, preparation and initiative, material obstacles can always be overcome. And those who obstructed or clung to the letter of regulations suffered sharply from his tongue. One such officer who, still unacquainted with his Sherman, made difficulties was spurred to overcome them by the vehement retort, "If you don't have my army supplied, and keep it supplied, we'll eat your mules up, sir—eat your mules up." Later in the advance when there was urgent need to replace a burnt railroad bridge over the Oostenaula and the chief engineer, after methodical calculation, estimated that he would require four days for the task, Sherman is credited with the reply, "Sir, I give you forty-eight hours or a position in the front ranks." If the story was perhaps exaggerated the result at least proved that a day could be cut off the original estimate.

One of the fiercest partisans of Thomas and critics of Sherman, says of this preparatory period—"In such duty as this, General Sherman had no superior. Quick-eyed, ingenious, nervously active in mind and body, sleeplessly alert on every occasion, with a clear idea of what he wanted and an unyielding determination to have it, he made himself and everybody around him uncomfortable till his demands were gratified. . . ."

Sherman's research for mobility was equally intense in the organization of his fighting force—stripped like an athlete for a race. Each division and brigade was allotted enough wagons to form a supply train, but its size was curtailed owing to the fact that every man carried five days' rations on his person or horse. Apart from these supply trains only one wagon and one ambulance was allowed to each regiment, with a pack-mule for the mess-kit and baggage of the officers of each company. The transport was restricted to carrying food and ammunition, and tents were forbidden except for the sick and wounded, and one for each headquarters as an office. His views were pungently expressed in a letter to the "Q" branch of the War Department—"My entire headquarter's transportation is one wagon for myself, aides, officers, clerks and orderlies. I think that is as low down as we can get until we get flat broke, and thenceforward things will begin to mend. Soldiering as we have been doing for the past two years, with such trains and impediments has been a farce, and nothing but absolute poverty will cure it. I will be glad to hear Uncle Sam say 'we cannot afford this and that—you must gather your own grub and wagons. . . .' I think I see that period not far distant."

To the same end clerical work in the field was reduced to a minimum by the use of permanent offices in rear for the transaction and transmission of all routine correspondence.

This enabled a severe restriction of the size of the various headquarter staffs and herein, likewise, Sherman set the example by limiting his own to three aides-de-camp, one of whom, Captain Dayton, acted until the end of the war as his adjutant-general. Perhaps the recollection of his own Californian opportunity had some influence on Sherman's choice of such junior and juvenile assistants, while his belief in physical elasticity and the campaigning superiority of young men was an undoubted factor. But, above all, he had a deep-rooted conviction in the necessity of the commander being master in his own house and of his own organization, and to mark his distrust in the principle of a "chief of staff" he left his own behind at Nashville. Attached to his staff were the several heads of the specialized service—the chiefs of artillery, engineers, ordnance, the chief quartermaster and commissary, the medical director and three inspector-generals, and with these he dealt directly. Subsequently, in the "March through Georgia," a fourth aide-de-camp was added and a judge-advocate, whose duties were largely those of a private secretary—not least to deal with the torrent of congratulatory letters and gifts from known and unknown admirers, and to convert into suitable language such scribbled hints, from Sherman, as "Somethin' sweet you know, as the feller said—molasses and honey."

The ban on tents although exceptionally effective in reducing baggage was not, however, universally enforced, a failure due to example. For while Sherman himself and his staff had not a tent among them, Thomas was more dependent on comfort to maintain his efficiency, and as he moved with a headquarter-camp so generously tented and equipped that it was known as "Thomas's circus," or "Tom town," he could hardly, with decency, enforce the ban too stringently on his subordinates.

His Army of the Cumberland comprised more than half the force, totalling 61,000 men and 130 field-guns. It was divided into the

4th (Howard), 14th (Palmer), and 20th (Hooker) Army Corps, each of three divisions. There were also two weak cavalry divisions present, and a stronger one still to come. The Army of the Tennessee, in command of which McPherson had succeeded Sherman, numbered 24,000 with 96 guns, and was divided into the 15th (Logan) and 16th (Dodge) Army Corps, the last comprising only two divisions. The 17th Army Corps (Blair) did not arrive until June. The Army of the Ohio, which Schofield brought down from East Tennessee, was only 13,000 strong, with 28 guns, and comprised the 23rd Army Corps, and a cavalry division of 3,000 on its way to Kentucky. Thus the whole striking force totalled 98,000 men and 254 guns, the infantry alone numbering 88,000.

The scale of the forces and their dependence for supply on a single railroad ending just south of Chattanooga were inevitable fetters on freedom of manœuvre. Thomas was already in the centre at Chattanooga, McPherson on his right rear and Schofield on his left rear, so that any radical reshuffling would entail confusion and loss of time. The natural dispositions thus gave Sherman's forces the historical pattern order of battle with a strong centre and two mobile wings.

But Sherman's original plan was based on the idea of the widest manœuvre possible within these limits. While Thomas was to move straight down the Atlanta railroad from Chattanooga against Johnston, at Dalton, and Schofield converge on the same objective from Cleveland, McPherson was to slip behind the many-layered mountain belt which filled the stretch of country between the Tennessee and the Atlanta railroad below Chattanooga. Passing south of this belt McPherson would arrive at Rome and Kingston far behind the enemy's rear. To achieve this result he had merely to take a direct route eastward, little more than a hundred miles, from his winter quarters near Decatur, and on reaching Rome would not only have turned the line of the Oostenaula but be able to use it as a strategic barrage across the rear of Johnston, whose eyes and forces would be fixed on Thomas and Schofield. It was an ideal plan and in retrospect its abandonment is to be regretted, even under the conditions which led Sherman to drop it.

The vital change was due to the disparity between the size of Thomas's and McPherson's armies, which in turn was due to the ab-

sence from McPherson's of the two divisions loaned to Banks, and to
the late arrival of two more, constituting the 17th Army Corps,
whose men had gone on "veteran" furlough to the north—a good
illustration of the trials of a Civil War general. The cavalry division assigned to McPherson's army was also late, but Grant had
fixed May 5 for the start, in order to synchronize with his own advance in Virginia, and Sherman was too loyal a colleague to risk
marring the effect of the double offensive by postponing his own
share.

In the changed circumstances Sherman considered that it was too
risky to separate an army which had only five instead of nine divisions, and hardly any cavalry, so far from the support of the other
armies. He therefore decided on a narrower manœuvre, adopting
but adapting a proposal made by Thomas. This was to reach
Resaca, on the enemy's immediate rear and just north of the Oostenaula, by a detour round their western flank and through Snake
Creek Gap.

The country between Dalton and Resaca was a natural funnel,
fifteen miles long, formed by the Connesauga River on the east and
Rocky Face Ridge on the west. The railroad from Chattanooga
came slantwise into the west side of this funnel by a slit near the top
known as Mill Creek Gap. Snake Creek Gap was another slit near
the bottom.

Thomas suggested that his army should manœuvre to pass
through it while McPherson and Schofield engaged Johnston's attention at the mouth of the funnel. But Sherman preferred to
retain McPherson for the manœuvre rôle. In making this decision
he may well have felt a natural confidence in the aptitude of his
own old Army of the Tennessee, and a doubt whether either Thomas
or his army had an equal capacity. Whatever it might do in future
the Army of the Cumberland had as yet given no such proofs of
strategic mobility as had the Army of the Tennessee.

But, confidence apart, his decision was obviously justified on every
ground save one. To swing Thomas out to the right and pull in
McPherson, who was already "out," would mean a crossing of
routes and a probable entanglement of the lines of supply. And in
this spy-ridden country the sudden disappearance of Thomas's
army which had been so long facing the Confederates, would be

likely to put them on their guard. The one objection to Sherman's decision was that it employed but a quarter of his force in the rear attack, and left an excessively large force to contain Johnston in front. At the same time, however, this covered Sherman's own base, which was within unpleasantly close reach of the enemy, and the loss of which would ruin not only his plan but his army. Moreover, the turning movement had to be made by an uncertainly known route, and with a still greater uncertainty as to whether Snake Creek Gap would be blocked. Sherman would look foolish if two-thirds of his force found itself locked out in front of this narrow defile, with Johnston free to strike swiftly at the remaining third and at Sherman's precious base.

Thus, in sum, the one valid criticism seems to be that Sherman might have augmented McPherson's army from Thomas's. But Grant had previously discovered Thomas's sensitiveness and for Sherman, newly appointed and previously junior to Thomas, to have broken up an army of such jealous ésprit de corps would hardly have been the way to eradicate jealousies and to ensure harmonious co-operation. Nor is there any serious reason to believe that McPherson's army was inadequate in strength to the task of closing Johnston's line of retreat.

What were the Confederates planning and doing during the interval before the storm broke? After Chattanooga they had halted at Dalton, mainly because Grant had pursued them no further. And had remained there, despite Johnston's wish to fall back to a stronger defensive position behind the Oostenaula, because of the Confederate President's pressure on Johnston to renew the offensive. The plan suggested to Johnston was that he should strike across the railroad between Chattanooga and Knoxville, and press through the mountains into middle Tennessee, living on the country, the calculation being that he would thus compel the Union armies to fall back in order to save Nashville.

For this project he was offered reinforcements to bring his strength to 75,000 men. In his reply of March 18 Johnston said that he was fettered by lack of field-transport, being "destitute of mules," and declared his preference for awaiting the enemy's expected offensive, repulsing it, and then following up their retreat.

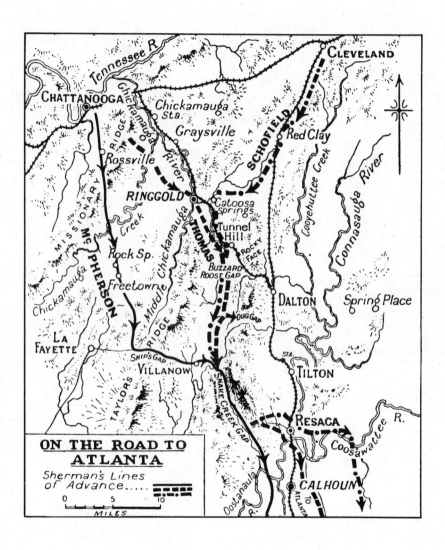

ON THE ROAD TO
ATLANTA

Sherman's Lines
of Advance.....

0   5   10

MILES

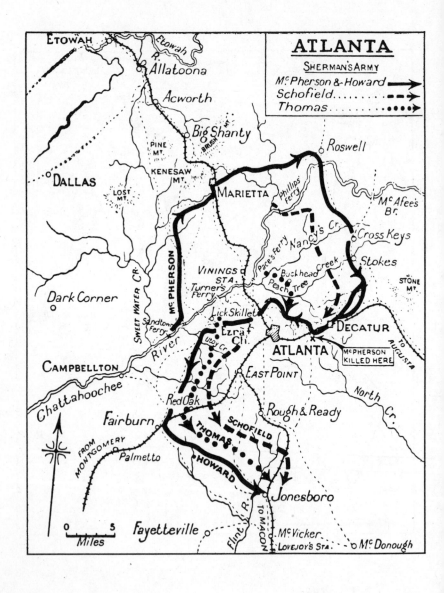

But he wanted and suggested reinforcements "*immediately*, otherwise we might be beaten, which would decide events." By the time Sherman's advance began Johnston's strength had been raised to about 60,000, while Polk's corps from eastern Mississippi was on its way to join him in response to his urgent pleas. A ratio of three to five was a comfortable strength for a defensive attitude in such naturally strong defensive country and by a commander so experienced in the art of defence as Johnston.

Moreover, although he would have preferred to retire to a still stronger line of resistance along the south bank of the Oostenaula, he had covered the mouth of the funnel near Dalton with stout entrenchments which bent well back on either flank, and as an additional barrier he dammed Mill Creek to form a deep wet ditch. Strongest of all, by nature, was the left flank where Mill Creek and the railroad from Chattanooga passed through the "slit"—the deep and narrow gorge in Rocky Face Ridge which was aptly called Buzzard Roost—and Sherman's direct approach would lead him to this mountain side-wall.

To hold this position covering Dalton, Johnston disposed his two corps (seven divisions), commanded by Hardee and Hood, with Wheeler's cavalry (8,000) farther out, watching the approaches. It seems curious that he should have concentrated so solidly and placed no part of his force to guard his rear near Snake Creek Gap. But apart from the lack of accurate maps of this tangled wilderness, Snake Creek Gap itself was so narrow and the mountain approaches to it so winding and difficult, that the Confederates did not seriously believe that Sherman would attempt such a manoeuvre.

Johnston knew that Sherman, like himself, was tied to a single line of railroad for his supply, and one has a strong suspicion that he regarded his opponent as both an impulsive and an orthodox professional soldier who would take the obvious and simplest course, relying on his superior weight to crush Johnston in a direct attack. Indeed, Johnston confesses as much in his subsequent explanation— "I supposed from General Sherman's great superiority of numbers, that he intended to decide the contest by a battle, and that he would make that battle as near his own and as far from our base as possible —that is to say, at Dalton. On general principles, that was his true policy." Oh! "principles," how often is thy name an excuse for obviousness—the deadly sin against the art of war, indeed, the very negation of the term.

In this case it is at least fair to recognize that Johnston, with the advantage of the central position, could switch his troops back to Resaca by a direct level and short route, along three parallel roads, whereas the outer approach to Resaca was by a single and circuitous road through the mountains. But this power of getting back to guard Resaca depended on time and warning. And in this event he failed to get warning and was lucky to get time, through Mc-Pherson's failure to fulfil Sherman's instructions.

These instructions, as contained in a letter of May 5, are so explicit that one can only marvel at the subterfuges to which in post-war controversy disgruntled partisans of Thomas were driven in their efforts to blame Sherman not merely for giving McPherson the task in preference to Thomas, but for McPherson's failure to execute it. "I want you to move . . . to the head of Middle Chickamauga, then to Villanow: then to Snake Gap, secure it and make a bold attack on the enemy's flank or his railroad at any point between Tilton and Resaca. I hope the enemy will fight at Dalton, in which case he can have no force there that can interfere with you. But, should his policy be to fall back along his railroad you will hit him in flank. Do not fail in that event to make the most of the opportunity by the most vigorous attack possible, as it may save us what we have most reason to apprehend—a slow pursuit, in which he gains strength as we lose it." Sherman had clearly grasped the truth that to roll the enemy back along their communications means that their resistance will be solidified and expended by accretions like a snowball. "In the event of hearing the sound of heavy battle about Dalton, the greater necessity for your rapid movement on the railroad. If once broken to an extent that would take them days to repair, you can withdraw to Snake Gap. . . ."

To Thomas, Sherman wrote—"The plan of action will be: you move in force on Tunnel Hill [an outlying ridge covering the Buzzard Roost slit in Rocky Face Ridge], secure it and threaten Dalton in front, but not to attack its defenses until further orders unless the enemy assume the offensive against either of our wings, when all must attack directly in front towards the enemy's main army and not without orders detach to the relief of the threatened wing." This last clause foreshadowed the truth learnt by the end of the World War—that support to a threatened or held up neighbour is better given indirectly by pressure on the enemy elsewhere than by reinforcing him directly.

Schofield, similarly, was instructed to converge on the enemy's front from the north—from Cleveland—inclining inwards to link up with Thomas. Sherman added, "We will not be able to detach to McPherson's assistance, but can press so closely from this direction that he [Johnston] cannot detach but a part of his command against him."

Where Grant's plan at Chattanooga had been to lever the enemy out of his position as if extracting meat from a tin by inserting a knife on each side, Sherman's plan at Dalton was to make a neat incision in the base of the tin so that the meat dropped out. He aimed to use the least possible pressure from the top, but to hold Thomas and Schofield "ready to rush in at the first appearance of 'let go,' and if possible, to catch our enemy in the confusion of retreat." And he calculated that this confusion would be greater because, with the railroad cut near Resaca and McPherson commanding the valley, the enemy would be forced to retreat along the rough and impracticable roads east of the valley. Consciously or sub-consciously the plan fulfilled the truth latent in historical experience that the object of the rear attack is not itself to crush the enemy but to unhinge his morale and dispositions so that his dislocation renders the subsequent delivery of a decisive blow both practicable and easy.

Sherman had arranged that his three armies should concentrate on the centre, Chattanooga, out of reach of the enemy, and move forward slightly to their starting line, a twenty-mile arc from Rossville on the west through Ringgold to Red Clay. McPherson was then to be given two days' start on his manœuvre march. By the night of May 4 Thomas was in position at Ringgold and Schofield at Red Clay, but McPherson was a day behind the time-table and only the head of his column had reached Rossville. On the 7th Thomas moved forward, as intended, on Tunnell Hill, with Schofield closing in on his left, and carried it without difficulty by a front and flank advance of his 4th (Howard) and 14th (Palmer) corps, while his 20th corps (Hooker) moved farther down across the road from Buzzard Roost to Villanow—as a safety curtain to McPherson's flank march.

On the 8th Thomas moved up to the foot of Rocky Face Ridge and Schofield overlapped its inner face, while Geary's division of the 20th corps, as a further distraction, brilliantly effective, made a demonstration against Dug Gap, a smaller slit in the ridge between Buzzard Roost and Snake Creek Gap. Sherman's orders forbade any serious attack on the enemy's immensely strong position unless they came out of their entrenchments. But skirmishers were ordered to probe boldly and ceaselessly for any sign of retirement.

Meantime, away to the west, McPherson had passed up the mountain valley of the middle Chickamauga, then turned east through the pass to Villanow and on that same night, the 8th, his leading division occupied Snake Creek Gap unopposed, while the main body bivouacked near the entrance. Distraction and "safety curtain" had cloaked the move perfectly. Thus far the plan had worked with a success beyond anticipation. The ideal and the reality had for once coincided.

What of the Confederates? Until the 7th Johnston's correspondence shows him convinced that Sherman was massing for a battle on his front, and without the least suspicion of McPherson's lurking presence and imminent approach. That day Johnston had a report of a Union force being near Lafayette. His supposition, however, was that it was aiming to push southwards across the Oostenaula between Calhoun and Rome, and he wired to Polk to hurry his arrival and concentrate at Rome. But as a brigade (Cantey) and the first part of another (Reynolds) had just arrived at Resaca—on their way from Mobile to reinforce him at Dalton— he took the precaution of halting them there and ordering a regiment (Williamson) to be sent to hold "Villanow Gap." Whatever he meant by this uncertain description, it seems clear from the records that Williamson went (with two regiments) to Dug Gap, where Geary's diversion gave it ample occupation, and thereby left McPherson's advanced guard a free passage through Snake Creek Gap. It is also clear that the Confederate command at Dalton was flustered during the 7th and 8th, by the variety of places at which the Union forces appeared, several times sending Cantey orders to come to Dalton followed by counter-orders to remain at Resaca.

Thus when, early in the morning of the 9th, McPherson's corps, 24,000 strong, debouched into the valley about 4 miles due west of Resaca, there were only Cantey's brigade and a fraction of Reynolds's, not more than 2,000 men, to stop it. After driving back a cavalry detachment, belatedly sent down from Dalton to watch this flank, McPherson came within sight of the frail line of Confederate entrenchments covering Resaca, and halted his army, taking up defensive dispositions with four divisions while he sent the fifth forward. This skirmished forward cautiously, and at 12.30 P.M. McPherson wrote a despatch to Sherman saying that it was probably "within 2 miles of Resaca," and adding "I propose to cut the railroad, if possible, and then fall back and take [up] a strong position near the gorge. . . ." The tone suggests that he was thinking more of the final clause of Sherman's order than of the earlier clauses about making "a bold attack."

At half past ten that night he sent a further and fuller report— "General Dodge's command moved up and skirmished with the enemy at Resaca this afternoon. While that was going on one company of mounted infantry [actually eighteen men] . . . succeeded in reaching the railroad near Tilton station, but were forced to leave without damaging the track. They tore down a small portion of telegraph wire. . . . After skirmishing till after dark . . . I decided to withdraw the command and take up a position for the night"—at the mouth at Snake Creek Gap. He then explained that his decision was due, first to the fact that there were several roads down which Confederate reinforcements from Dalton might arrive on his flank if he stayed out; second, that Dodge's division was "out of provisions." "I shall have to rest my men tomorrow forenoon, at least, to enable them to draw provisions." Lastly, he expressed regret that he had been unable to break the railroad owing to lack of cavalry, telling Sherman that Garrard's cavalry division had only reached Lafayette and that Garrard wished to wait there for his forage train.

This message tells the story of a missed opportunity which could never recur, and so frankly exposes McPherson's mind that no comment is necessary.

More than eight and a half hours passed before the message reached Sherman. For at 7 A.M. next morning he wired to Washington, "I believe McPherson has destroyed Resaca"—a highly logical deduction from the previous message, and one that for a time had been shared by the Confederate headquarters at Dalton. Then came the second message and disillusionment.

Sherman was never more bitterly disappointed in his life, and in acknowledging the message prefaced his fresh instructions by the remark, "I regret beyond measure you did not break the railroad . . . but I suppose it was impossible." Yet, in his evening despatch to Washington he generously covered McPherson's failure with the cloak of his own authority, saying that he had acted "according to instructions." So also in his subsequent report, and even in his memoirs, he goes no further than to say "at the critical moment McPherson seems to have been a little timid. Still he was perfectly justified by his orders." More accurately, if less kindly, he might have said that McPherson had only fulfilled the last few words of his orders. Yet Sherman's phrase in his memoirs was stigmatized as a base defamation of a man then dead! How sensitive to even the mildest criticism are some soldiers, usually those who are least discriminating in their own language, and least sensible of its extravagant violence. Warner relates that when they met Sherman greeted McPherson, sadly rather than angrily, with the words—"Well, Mac, you have missed the great opportunity of your life." But apart from this one comment Sherman carefully spared the feelings of his subordinate, and the sympathy between the two was rather strengthened than lowered by the misfortune.

The meeting came soon, for Sherman evolved a fresh plan immediately on receiving McPherson's message. This plan is succinctly defined in his evening despatch to Washington—"I must feign on Buzzard Roost, but pass through Snake Creek Gap, and place myself between Johnston and Resaca, when we will have to fight it out." These last words imply an acute appreciation that the chance of a sudden unhinging of Johnston's balance had passed. A movement on Johnston's rear would no longer have the shock of surprise.

Sherman continued—"I am making the preliminary move. Certain that Johnston can make no detachments, I will be in no hurry. My cavalry is just approaching from Kentucky and Tennessee (detained by the difficulty of getting horses), and even now it is less than my minimum."

On receiving McPherson's morning message Sherman had written to Thomas saying, "I think you are satisfied that your troops cannot take Rocky Face Ridge, and also the attempt to put our columns into the jaws of Buzzard Roost would be fatal to us," and had then invited Thomas's opinion, on two alternative plans which differed slightly. The first being to move Thomas's army rapidly down to reinfore McPherson, side-slipping Schofield into Thomas's place by night, and Stoneman's cavalry division on arrival into Schofield's. The second, "to cut loose from the railroad altogether and move the entire army on the same objective point [i.e., Resaca], leaving Johnston to choose his course."

Thomas, in a letter apparently crossing this, had volunteered to send one corps to support McPherson, saying, "I think General Hooker's corps will be sufficient to enable General McPherson to whip any force that Johnston can bring against him." Now he replied to Sherman, preferring the first, or more cautious, of the alternatives, but suggesting a more gradual side-slipping—"Hooker's corps might be sent at once to reinforce General McPherson whilst Palmer's corps could be placed in reserve, to march at a moment's notice, and Howard's corps placed in position . . . to hold the enemy in check."

Schofield, similarly consulted, preferred the more complete alternative, and expressed his fear that, if he was left, Johnston might fall on him when alone, and overwhelm him.

Sherman thereupon formulated a plan which, on the whole, was a happy compound of both alternatives: to leave one of Thomas's corps—"so light and so familiar with the ground that Johnston cannot strike him"—"to keep up the feint of a direct attack on Dalton," and Stoneman's cavalry to mask Schofield's disappearance, while moving Thomas's two other corps and Schofield's down to Snake Creek Gap.

This plan ensured an essential distraction in front to Johnston, and in fulfilment of it Hooker's corps was already on the move the same day. The criticism has been made that Schofield was not ordered to start until two days later. But, apart from the fact that Stoneman was not expected and did not arrive until then, Schofield's corps was even then obstructed on the march by Thomas's second corps. The roads were mere rough wagon-ways converging into a single narrow track in the last six-mile lap through Snake Creek Gap.

An army of a hundred thousand men, and the supplies necessary for it, cannot be moved with the ease of a small detachment. As well might one expect a cannon ball to be juggled with as lightly as a tennis ball. And a wise commander allows a margin, here proved necessary, for the possible delay in his subordinates' movements. Sherman's irritated sense of the handicap is revealed by the remark "I can't move about as I did with 15 or 20,000 men," in a letter ten days later to his wife. But the outstanding feature of the Atlanta campaign is the degree in which he overcame this and other fetters on manœuvre—heavy enough to reduce most armies to immobility.

A more valid criticism is perhaps that, in informing McPherson of the new plan, Sherman permitted him to stand fast. "I wish you to select near the 'débouché' [of Snake Creek Gap] a strong impregnable position," and "in the meantime mask your own force as much as possible." But he also urged him to be ready to strike Johnston in flank if the latter began retiring.

Sherman knew that the surprise had passed and that if McPherson brought on a general engagement Johnston could switch the bulk of his army against him by a quick march along the 15-mile chord while Sherman would have to travel by bad roads round the circumference of the arc in order to support McPherson. For to follow Johnston directly he would have to force his way across Rocky Face Ridge, and mere common-sense told him that he could be long delayed there by a small rearguard. Sherman's one hope therefor was that Johnston would stay at Dalton until he himself got round to McPherson.

It also deserves emphasis that McPherson had reported that the Confederates were in a "strong position" at Resaca and had "displayed considerable force." Until he had seen for himself, Sherman could not well override the judgment of the man on the spot, and in any case no order of his could have reached McPherson in time for the latter to develop a strong attack before the 11th.

Such arguments can be tested by the actual thoughts and action of the enemy. When late in the afternoon of the 9th Johnston had heard of McPherson's appearance near Resaca, he had hurriedly despatched three of his seven divisions down the Valley thither. They reached the outskirts of Resaca early on the 10th to find that the shadowy assailant had fallen back to Snake Creek Gap. They had then been recalled, although two were left midway at Tilton ready to support either the Dalton or the Resaca force, and within easy reach of both. And even up to the morning of the 11th Johnston was still induced to believe that the Resaca manœuvre was nothing more than a strong demonstration, and that Sherman was still making a serious bid, and his main effort, to force the Dalton position. He was comforted, moreover, by the knowledge that Polk's divisions, by his orders, were arriving to concentrate at Resaca, where Cantey had already been reinforced by two more brigades. But next morning Johnston had detected sufficient signs—by cavalry reconnaissance and signal-officers on the mountain curtain wall —of Sherman's movement south, inevitably a narrow circuit, to deduce the real direction of Sherman's aim, although he again guessed wrong as to its immediate goal—taking it to be a passage of the Oostenaula between Calhoun and Rome. His uncertainty did not matter, for, deciding to fall back in step with Sherman's march, he would have the shorter and easier line to march on, as well as the assurance that some part of Polk's troops, coming up through Rome and Calhoun, would be conveniently at hand to delay any attempt to cross the Oostenaula.

The result was that when, on the night of the 12th, Thomas and Schofield were lying in bivouac close behind McPherson, their long march completed, Johnston's army was evacuating Dalton and on the march down the valley to Resaca their rear covered by the cavalry. A dead heat. And next morning, stalemate.

At 6 A.M. McPherson advanced on Resaca, Thomas following in his wake and then inclining north to deploy on his left, and Schofield in turn on Thomas's left. Johnston's army was then just arriving at Resaca, and Polk held McPherson in check long enough for Hood's and Hardee's corps to get into position undisturbed on an arc covering Resaca on the west and north, its right resting securely on some low hills beside the Connesauga. The Union troops spent the 13th in feeling their way forward over the rough and unknown ground, and driving in the Confederate skirmishers. Next day they tested the strength of the Confederate position by attacks at numerous points, most vigorous on the left, probing for a weak point, but in vain. This probing also produced a humorous incident. General Howard relates how Sherman after working all night was sitting on a log, with his back against a tree, fast asleep. A column of troops passed, and some of them made typical soldier comments at the sight. Sherman, awakened by the noise, caught the remark, "A pretty way we are commanded!" Sacrificing dignity to the interests of morale he called out in retort, "while you were sleeping last night, I was planning for you, sir; and now I am taking a nap." And, as Howard remarks, the familiarity bred not contempt but confidence.

For with astonishing swiftness Sherman was already evolving a new combination. In the morning of the 13th he was still uncertain whether Johnston's whole army had reached Resaca, and was urging his own left wing forward to get across the railroad in the hope of hustling Johnston into a retreat eastward, while keeping his own forces closely knit in case Johnston attempted a riposte. At the same time, however, he was ordering the pontoon train to come up from Villanow to a ferry where he could cross the Oostenaula southwest of Resaca, for a fresh move on to the enemy's rear. That order was the first incision in Johnston's new position.

He had been manœuvred out of an impregnable position at Dalton and he had no intention of being manœuvred out of another which was only less strong. Indeed, it seems from the diary kept by his Chief of Staff that on the 14th he thought the moment and opportunity had arrived for a decisive counterstroke. Sherman's left wing had been working round towards the Connesauga, when about 5 P.M. Hood, who had been reinforced for the purpose, suddenly emerged from the trenches on the Confederate right flank and struck it in flank. Despite a temporary success the blow was quickly parried, and darkness brought the struggle to an end. Johnston ordered Hood to resume the attack at daylight and to wheel west with the idea of reaching the mouth of Snake Creek Gap and cutting Sherman off from his trains and line of retreat.

But after nightfall, Johnston heard that a Union division had crossed the Oostenaula, whereupon he despatched a division from

Calhoun to meet it, cancelled Hood's attack, and ordered a pontoon bridge to be laid across the river a mile east of the permanent rail and road bridges which were now commanded by Sherman's artillery. Next day, hearing that the enemy had gone back across the river, he ordered Hood to attack afresh in the morning, of the 16th. But a later report caused a further change of mind, and he ordered his army to evacuate the Resaca position and withdraw across the river during the night.

Their departure cloaked by a sudden and intense burst of musketry, sustained for an hour, the bulk of the troops began moving out shortly before midnight, the pickets following by 3 A.M., and, using all three bridges, the Confederate army was safely across to Calhoun by morning. The smooth and silent execution of the withdrawal, in which four guns were abandoned, was a masterly feat. But, with part of Sherman's army already across on his left, Johnston found no defensive position that satisfied him, and ordered a fresh retirement south to begin the following morning, the 17th.

The Union troops were quick to advance at daylight, on discovering the enemy had gone, but the burnt bridges delayed Thomas in the centre, and Schofield on the left had to feel out and find a crossing further east.

The effect of McPherson's previous crossing on the enemy's flank was, however, disappointing. On the morning of the 14th Sherman had ordered him to "send one division immediately . . . to effect a lodgement on the other side, and as the day develops send other divisions in order. . . ." But, after crossing, the divisional commander was alarmed by a false report of a threat to his rear and fell back to his own bank. Thus twenty-four hours were lost, and when it crossed afresh on the 15th it had an enemy division to oppose it. Only after the discovery of Johnston's retreat next morning did the rest of McPherson's army follow it. The crossing had been effective in compelling the retreat, but too slow to intercept it.

Once more one feels that McPherson's energy had fallen short of his reputation, a feeling reinforced by examination of his trifling losses during the whole of these operations. One feels that Sherman might have put more pressure on him, and that he might have detached a larger force for this manœuvre, especially as Thomas had volunteered to send part of his army. On the other hand, Sherman was in little known and difficult country in face of a wary and skilful opponent who, as we know, had no intention of retiring and was searching for an opening to strike back decisively.

But the most probable reason for Sherman's restraint was that, also on the 14th, he had despatched Garrard's cavalry division to cross the river far to the west near Rome and then break Johnston's railroad far to his rear near Kingston. Sherman would naturally desire to avoid alarming Johnston before this coup was delivered. Garrard, however, was slow, and Johnston's decision to continue his retreat southward from Calhoun stultified it.

With this retreat a new phase of the campaign opens. The chance, if a difficult chance, of trapping Johnston and breaking up his army had been narrowly missed. If this was a disappointment, it was nevertheless a brilliant achievement to have manœuvred so renowned a master of defence out of two strong positions against his will and his orders. And the cost had only been 6,800 casualties to the Confederate 5,000.

Henceforth, however, Sherman had a lengthening line of communications, Johnston a shortening and less exposed one. The two commanders had crossed swords and each now felt a heightened respect for the other's skill. The next phase was a masterly fencing bout, each striving for an opening without giving the other one. Johnston warily guarding himself but ready to lunge if his opponent exposed himself. Sherman repeatedly thrusting and taking the greater risk, yet so skilfully that the risk never matured. As shrewdly careful, also, to avoid blunting or breaking his weapon. But while neither could seriously wound the other physically, Johnston was being steadily forced back, with a depressing effect to the morale of the Southern people and a most valuable tonic effect to the Northern public—in view of the impending elections. Wars can be won and lost in the hustings as well as on the battlefield. And all the time, too, Sherman was drawing nearer to Atlanta, now more than ever the predominant goal in his mind.

CHAPTER XVII

THE OOSTENAULA–CHATTAHOOCHEE DUEL

WITH the passage of the Oostenaula the scene changed as well as the performance. Rugged mountain ridges gave way to open and slightly rolling country, with broad and fertile fields—soon to be ruined sources of supply to the Confederacy. Johnston's retreat was across the base line of a triangle formed by the Oostenaula and Etowah Rivers, Rome being in the apex where their streams joined.

Falling back from Calhoun on May 17 Johnston had hoped to take up a fresh position astride a valley near Adairsville, ten miles south, but on arrival found it too wide for his flanks to rest securely, and was thus forced to retire again on the 18th to Cassville, another ten miles.

At Adairsville the road south had forked, one fork going S.S.E. to Cassville, the other S.S.W. to Kingston alongside the railroad. It was Johnston's hope thereby to trap Sherman at a disadvantage. Calculating that Sherman's army would divide to move along both roads, Johnston lay in wait at the point where the separation of the two was widest, seven miles, and planned to crush Sherman in detail. The last of Polk's divisions had now arrived, so that Johnston's strength was probably 75,000—favourable odds for such a counterstroke. Early on the 19th he issued the general order, "You will now turn and march to meet the advancing columns. Fully confiding in the conduct of the officers, the courage of the soldiers, I lead you to battle."

But his plan was based on the supposition that Sherman's advance would fulfil the orthodox interpretation of Napoleon's maxim of moving concentrated. And it was upset because Sherman had adopted the unorthodox, but true, interpretation—that of moving in a wide loose grouping or net, which could be quickly drawn in round the point of contact with the enemy. The vital distinction arises from the subtly different meaning of the words *reuni* and *concentré*, so commonly confounded.

Only two of Thomas's corps had advanced down the road to Adairsville, McPherson's two moving on a line about six or eight miles to the west, heading towards Kingston, and Schofield with his own and Hooker's corps moving on a line about four or six miles to the east—the frontage naturally varying with the trace of the roads. Sherman ordered his columns to attack the enemy wherever met and deliberately used their separation to tempt Johnston to battle, confident that he could swing in his columns before Johnston could endanger any one of them.

Thus, just as Johnston was expecting to strike Sherman in flank he discovered that his own flanks were menaced, and likely to be enfiladed, by Sherman's still wider stretched flanks—that instead of catching a part of Sherman's army between his pincers, these narrow pincers were likely to be caught in a wide net. Once more he was driven to abandon his plan; coming on top of his general order the effect was depressing, and the fact that he had been overtrumped undisguisable, while correspondingly exhilarating to the Union troops. At 1 A.M. on the 20th the Confederate army began retiring south-east along the railroad to the Etowah and crossed it at Cartersville during the day—"a step," Johnston said in his autumn report, "which I have regretted ever since."

Once more, also, the scene changed. South of the Etowah the country again became hilly and wooded, intersected by numerous streams and less numerous dirt roads—much of it a tangled wilderness, little known and unmapped, rivalling the Wilderness of Virginia. Johnston took up his position behind the river, covering the steep and narrow gorge known as the Allatoona Pass, through which the Atlanta railroad ran. Ten miles to the south of this hill rampart another covered the approach to Marietta, which now became Johnston's advanced base.

As swiftly as before, the next plan took shape in Sherman's mind. Having ridden through the Allatoona Pass in 1843 he had no intention of following Johnston into such a trap, but instead, decided to push due south across the Etowah, leaving the railroad, and swing in on to it again in Johnston's rear if possible.

Twenty-five miles south of Kingston and about seventeen miles west of Marietta lay a little village and road-centre called Dallas. On the same day, the 20th, that Johnston had fallen back, Sherman wired to Washington—"I give two days' rest to replenish and fit up. On the 23rd I will cross the Etowah and move on Dallas. This will turn the Allatoona Pass. If Johnston remains at Allatoona I shall move on Marietta; but if he falls behind the Chattahoochee [the last of the three rivers covering Atlanta], I will make for Sandtown and Campbellton"—west of Atlanta and south-west of the direct approach by the bridge carrying the railroad.

Sherman was enabled to cut his halt so short by the amazing rapidity with which the railroad was being repaired in rear of his advance by Colonel Wright, a civil engineer, with a corps of two thousand men. Howard graphically tells how "while our skirmishing was going on at Calhoun, the locomotive whistle sounded in Resaca." The Resaca bridge was repaired in three days and the locomotives were bringing fresh supplies into Kingston, Sherman's new advanced base, almost on the heels of the troops. And nothing perhaps produced a more depressing effect on the enemy than the sound of locomotives whistling in rear of Sherman's front so soon after the railroads had been reported effectively broken for many days.

The impression, or depression, caused in the Confederate ranks is illustrated by a good story of the period. The report came that a tunnel on Sherman's communications had been blocked by a cavalry raid, but the exultation was damped by the sardonic comment of an intelligent Georgian, who growled, "Oh, stop your noise; s'posin' Forrest has broken in the tunnil—Sherman's got a duplicate of it, and it's fixed up 'fore this time!"

With this assurance Sherman was able to issue twenty days' rations, loaded on the wagons except for three days' rations carried on the person, and thus to cut loose from his railroad for a period which could be extended to more than double if necessary by economizing and foraging. Foraging, indeed, had been systematically organized since arriving in this fertile triangle of country, and was most successful in gathering food, if too successful in destroying private property, despite stringent orders. Flaming houses and barns already marked the beginning of the swathe of devastation which was soon to be cut through the centre of Georgia. Hooker's corps seems to have been especially full of the lust of wanton destruction.

Sherman still strove to check such abuses, as his orders and letters amply testify, but it is difficult for authority to instil in its servants the narrow distinction between authorized and wanton destruction, between authorized foraging and pillaging. Sorrowful yet unrelenting, as the appointed agent to fulfil the Old Testament of war, Sherman describes to his wife his impressions in the language of the "authorized version"—"We have devoured the land and our animals eat up the wheat and corn field close. All the people retire before us and desolation is behind. To realize what war is one should follow our tracks. . . . I know the country swarms with thousands who would shoot me and thank their God they had slain a monster; and yet I have been more kindly disposed to the people of the South than any general. . . ."

Perhaps the very thoroughness with which Sherman had curtailed baggage in his research for mobility contributed to the excess of desolation. If the troops themselves were to go without comforts they may have felt that those who were the cause should also go without. Or perhaps they wished others to share with them the pleasure of the simple life which they had discovered! Light fingers matched light feet, and light hearts, in the Grand Army of the West. Certainly no army ever marched more light. General Cox relates that "the mess at a division headquarters boasted that, beginning with nothing, they had accumulated a kit consisting of a tin plate, four tin cups without handles, three round oyster cans, doing duty as cups, two sardine boxes for extra plates, and a coffee pot. Pocket knives were the only cutlery needed, and for dishes nothing could be better than one of the solid crackers familiarly known as 'hard tack.' This outfit they declared was luxurious compared with the General-in-Chief." Sherman's contempt for luxury, manifest not only in his equipment but in his clothes, was well attuned to the mentality of the men he led in these armies of the West. As he had risen in dignity of position so he had increasingly discarded the trappings of dignity, and the greater his real cares the greater became his carelessness of outward appearance. The complete "workman," indeed—with his black felt hat, unbraided and untasseled, pulled bulgingly over his high forehead and rather long, unkempt hair; the outline of his well-chiselled chin, small but strong, obscured yet emphasized by the short bristling fringe of his reddish whiskers and beard; his faded and threadbare coat unbuttoned to disclose a uniform vest buttoned only at the bottom and stained with the ash or nicotine of his endless chain of "segars."

His appearance by day was at least more presentable than by night when he was seen, poking the camp-fire or prowling round a sleeping camp, with his bare feet in old slippers, his legs covered only by a pair of red flannel drawers, his tall, spare body wrapped in a travel-worn dressing gown, with sometimes a short blue uniform cape over all as a concession to convention and to cold. As odd a figure as the hours he kept. For he was the most restless man and lightest sleeper in his army and not only shared with other great captains the power to maintain his activity on a slender allowance of sleep but had the habit of waking finally in the fourth hour of the morning. At this hour he liked to be up and about, thinking or listening—the "best time," as he said, "to hear any movement at a distance." If he snatched any further sleep it was after daylight had come.

Here, as in almost all other aspects, the contrast with his chief subordinate was almost laughable. Where Sherman held his men in awe by personality, Thomas awed them by his dignity, although both won their men's hearts by consideration for their bodies. The portly and slow-moving Thomas, whose phlegmatic mien masked a curiously sensitive temperament, was ever a model of tidiness in his dress and equipment, and a lover of seemliness. While from habit he slept on a camp cot even when a comfortable bed was available, his camp mess was distinguished by negro servants, a good cook and silver tableware. And his military outlook was aptly illustrated by his historic rebuke to an officer, delivered with portentous solemnity: "The fate of an army may depend on a buckle." Another instance of this methodical habit of mind was when, on his way out to the critical battle-field of Nashville, he stopped to see that exactly fourteen bushels of coal were sent to a neighbour from whom he had borrowed that quantity.

Method is admirable, but it can be developed to the sacrifice of opportunity. There was more breath of understanding in Forrest's military panacea of "getting there fustest with the mostest" than in Thomas's emphasis on the importance of every buckle being correct.

Another aspect of Sherman's research for mobility was the appointment in each division of an officer as acting topographer, whose duty it was to accompany reconnoitring parties, to collect information as to distances and locations of hamlets and houses, and to sketch roads, streams, and other features. Their information was then co-ordinated at corps and army headquarters, and the complete maps were duplicated by a photographic process and distributed, new editions being issued periodically.

Promptly on May 23 Sherman crossed the Etowah and began his advance southward to renew his gladiatorial duel with Johnston. The metaphor has here a special illustrative value. For Sherman's dispositions were essentially those of the *Retiarius* with trident and net, and Johnston's those of the *Secutor* with short stabbing sword and shield—the natural shield provided by the hills. Sherman now cast his net round Johnston's left side.

Deducting casualties and small detachments necessarily left to guard his lengthening line of communications, Sherman's new advance was made with about 80,000 effectives, so that the two sides were more nearly equal during this phase than at any other in the campaign.

But the Confederate cavalry, far more efficiently led and manned than the Federal, was quick to detect signs of the circling move of Sherman's left wing, so that early on the 23rd Johnston had sufficiently penetrated Sherman's intention to lead him to begin moving Hardee's and Polk's corps south-westwards to block Sherman's path, and Hood's followed on the 24th. It is a fair criticism that Sherman, by moving his left wing, which was facing Johnston across the Etowah, lessened his chances of reaching Dallas before Johnston guessed his manœuvre; that surprise was sacrificed to the interests of security. From Allatoona to Dallas was only about fifteen miles. With an almost level start, no river to cross, and a shorter distance to cover, the Confederates had the advantage in the race. One severe handicap, however, was common to both sides—the blindness caused by the wild and wooded country.

Johnston, uncertain as to Sherman's whereabouts and progress, at first directed Hardee's corps to a point ten miles south of Dallas on the Atlanta road, Polk to a point midway between Dallas and Marietta, and Hood, the late starter, to New Hope Church four miles north-east of Dallas. The wide distribution worked out happily. For late on the 24th his cavalry discovered that Sherman's columns, groping forward, were still well to the north of Dallas.

Thereupon Johnston closed in his three corps to form an oblique defensive line from just north-east of New Hope Church to just south-west of Dallas, Hood staying where he was, Polk moving into position on his left, and Hardee coming back towards Dallas to be on Polk's left. The line ran along a series of wooded ridges with open valleys in front so that it formed a most effective barrier across the path of Sherman's wheeling advance.

Sherman had calculated on reaching Dallas by the night of the 25th, and that morning his right wing (McPherson) was at Van Wert, sixteen miles W.N.W. of Dallas, and about to begin wheeling inwards. To give it time, and also to safeguard his inner flank, Sherman held back his left wing, as the capture of a Confederate courier on the 24th had revealed to him that his plan was already penetrated by Johnston. But a division of Hooker's corps—the left of Sherman's centre, taking a wrong road ran into Hood at New Hope Church. Immediately Sherman heard the firing, he hurried to the front and directed Hooker to swing in his other divisions to the support of the one engaged. Perhaps less wisely he ordered Hooker to attack the enemy, an order probably inspired by the idea that Hood's corps alone had arrived on the scene, and that it might be overwhelmed while isolated from the rest of Johnston's army. To this end he hurried up Thomas's other corps. Nature then intensified the obscurity and the difficulty by a torrential downpour which lasted all night.

If Sherman had momentarily jumped to a mistaken conclusion it was not through "jumpiness." Cox, who headed the left wing when it came forward early next morning, relates how Sherman himself came to meet it and guide it into position. "Cheery and undisturbed, as if the most ordinary business were going on, the General sat on a log and sketched . . . a map of the supposed situation, for the use of the officer leading the column. Its firm delicate lines, and neat touches, even to the fine lettering of the names of houses and roads, showed how completely his nerves were unaffected by the night of battle and storm."

That morning also, McPherson had come up and found himself

blocked at Dallas, and Sherman realized that Johnston's whole army was astride his path. If Johnston had moved so far west and was expecting him on that flank, there might be an opening on the other flank, and Sherman accordingly pulled out two divisions from his centre and switched them to his left for an outflanking attack which, however, was repulsed.

Fierce skirmishing continued for several days and Johnston on the 28th struck heavily, and lost heavily, in an attempt to roll up Sherman's right. Sherman, on the other hand, had already decided to give up the attempt, so obviously expected, to get round Johnston's western flank, and was cleverly and imperceptibly side-stepping eastwards towards the railroad. Johnston soon appreciated the danger, and on the night of June 4 retired obliquely to a new line of entrenchments, hurriedly prepared, on a ten-mile arc along the hills covering Marietta—his right on Brush Mountain, his centre on Pine Mountain, his left on Lost Mountain.

Sherman was thus able to side-step freely to the railroad near Ackworth. If he had failed to reach Johnston's rear, and was still confronted by the second hill rampart covering Marietta, he at least manœuvred Johnston out of the first hill rampart, formed by the Allatoona Hills, and was once more sure of his supplies. Already, four days earlier, he had seized the deserted Allatoona Pass with a cavalry division, using it as a safety curtain to cover the repair of the railroad from Kingston forward. On the 11th the first locomotive whistled its exultant defiance in the ears of the Confederate defenders of Marietta.

The criticism can be, and has been, made that Sherman side-stepped to the wrong flank, and that by his desire to get back to the railroad he abandoned his original plan, and forfeited the chance of a speedy arrival at Atlanta. Certainly he had still a margin of supplies in hand, and in the outcome he was blocked before Marietta for a month. But the criticism seems to overlook one important fact—that Johnston lay immediately across his path. Once Johnston had frustrated his original manœuvre and the two armies were in close contact, it is almost inconceivable that Sherman would have been able to give his opponent the slip and get round his flank in time to reach the Chattahoochee before he was again blocked. It is far more probable that the two would have remained in a locked embrace until, with supplies running out, Sherman had to make a precipitate and difficult retreat to his starting point, even if Johnston had not found an opening for a crushing counterstroke.

For Johnston was resting on his base while Sherman was cut off from his and with his transport always in potential danger from Johnston's daring cavalry. Another strong incentive to be content with and make good the success he had gained, rather than play for higher stakes, was the heavy rain which had turned the dirt roads, under heavy traffic, into quagmires.

The need to temper his boldness of manœuvre with caution was the greater because he lacked the aid of any external distraction to his opponent. The influence on his thought of this lack is indeed revealed in a letter at this juncture to his brother—"All things are now as near our calculations as possible, save and except that the Red River failure has clipped from the general plan our main feature, a simultaneous attack on Mobile from New Orleans." This letter, too, shows his chief concern—"my long and single line of railroad to my rear, of limited capacity, is the delicate point of my game, as also the fact that all of Georgia, except the cleared bottoms, is densely wooded, with few roads, and at any point an enterprising enemy can, in a few hours . . . make across our path formidable works, while his sharpshooters, spies, and scouts . . . can hang around us and kill our waggoners, messengers, and couriers. It is a big Indian war. . . ." It is notable also, as evidence of his viewpoint and vision, that he lays less stress on his military achievement than on the fact that his advance has brought him possession of a large wheat-growing region and all the iron mines and works of Georgia.

In the first three weeks of his campaign Sherman had advanced over eighty miles across difficult country and two broad rivers, manœuvring the opposing army out of four strong positions, although its strength was growing till it almost equalled his own. And that army was commanded by a man who was recognized as the second general of the Confederacy, and by many even as the first. Some might complain of Johnston's caution, but none disputed his supremacy as a master of defence. Yet Sherman had forced him back all these miles without giving an opening, and at a cost which was but slightly more, and relatively less than that suffered by the defender. The achievement was the more significant because some had viewed Sherman's promotion with doubt, as a man too impulsive and temperamental. But now in command, as formerly in volunteering, the patience of this impatient man falsified all expectations. Not least the expectation of his opponent—a psychological effect which should not be overlooked.

The best augury for Sherman's continued patience and success in this prolonged strategic duel was in the balanced, unboasting tone of his most intimate letters—those to his wife. On the 12th he writes—"That it should have devolved on me to guide one of the two great armies on which may depend the fate of our people for the next hundred years I somewhat regret. Yet you know that I have been drawn to it by a slow and gradual progress which I could not avoid. . . . I think thus far I have played my game well. Had my plans been executed with the vim I contemplated I should have forced Johnston to fight the decisive battle . . . between Dalton and Resaca, but McPherson was a little over-cautious, and we cannot move vast armies of this size with the rapidity of thought or of small bodies."

Over eighty miles traversed, barely twenty-five to reach Atlanta, but the next stage was to be harder and slower. In it, the character of the campaign changed from mobile warfare to what might be called mobile siege warfare. This had developed during the lock, if not the deadlock, in front of Dallas and New Hope Church.

To the entrenchments of the Confederates on the defensive and the deadly fire of their skirmishers amid the trees, the veteran Union troops—like all veterans, grown wary and careful of their lives save when necessity called—had replied by a system of rapid fortification at every halt in the advance. The skirmishers would promptly convert logs, banked with earth, into a shield for themselves, and while the line of skirmishers was kept in front as a screen, the rest of a division would pile arms, and draw entrenching tools from the wagons. Then each company would prepare a breastwork of earth and logs covering its own front. Trees were felled and trimmed and the logs rolled into line to form a timber revetment usually four feet high, which was banked with earth from a ditch dug in front, to form a sloping parapet about seven to ten feet thick at the top and three feet more at ground level. On the top of the revetment, skids sustained a line of head logs, leaving a horizontal loophole about three inches wide through which to fire. The trees and bushes in front of the breastwork were then felled outwards to make an entanglement, which was sometimes elaborated by the use of chevaux-de-frise or sharpened palisades. So skilful and highly trained did the troops become in building these breastworks that a company could cover itself within a few hours of halting, and without engineer assistance.

The superiority thereby given to the side which awaited assault was such that it came to be a standard calculation that one man in a trench was equal to three or four in the assault, and dispositions and plans were regularly based on such estimates. The development, too, wrought a change in attack formations foreshadowing modern experience. For the customary deep columns were found both too vulnerable and ineffective, and were replaced by a single line of men with a second line, half its strength, kept under cover behind until the advance of the first line began to lose momentum. On the defence, too, the practice developed of holding a line of works with skirmishers only, and keeping the bulk of the men in reserve behind ready to reinforce a threatened point, or to counter-attack the flank of the assaulting enemy.

With the coming of June had come an almost unbroken sequence of wet days, downpours so torrential that the country became a morass which fettered every attempt to move. And every such attempt had to be made under the eyes of the enemy on the hills. Another wide manœuvre was out of the question until the roads dried, but in the meantime Sherman sought to loosen the enemy's hold by leverage on weak points. His eye for country showed him that such a point was formed by the projection of Pine Mountain in advance of the enemy's general line.

On June 14 the rain slackened momentarily, and Sherman pushed part of Thomas's army into the re-entrant angle east of Pine Mountain, while concentrating the fire of his batteries on it. Johnston, Hardee and Polk were there at the time reconnoitring and discussing the advisability of a retirement, and at the first volley hurried to take cover. But Polk, who was dignified and corpulent, walked back slowly rather than show alarm in the presence of the men, and was killed by an unexploded shell of the second volley. An intercepted signal message gave Sherman the news. That night the hill was abandoned and the Confederates drew back their centre to Kenesaw Mountain in consequence of the Union infiltration on the flank of the hill. And Sherman laconically reported the result in the words, "We killed Bishop Polk yesterday, and have made good progress to-day. . . ."

Lost Mountain, on the west flank, was now a projecting corner, and by leverage on this and other irregularities in the Confederate line Sherman induced Johnston to fall back and contract his line into a narrow semi-circle round Kenesaw Mountain, close to and covering Marietta on the north and west. If Sherman thereby compressed the defenders and made their task of direct resistance easier, he created for himself new freedom of manœuvre as soon as the roads should dry. And he had now been joined by Blair's corps, 10,000 strong, which reinforced McPherson, who, in the new movement, had been placed on the left flank—a reshuffle which might help to confuse the enemy but had also a more far-reaching motive.

Blair's arrival and other reinforcements fully balanced Sherman's losses during the previous month. Moreover, the menace of his alternating advances, foreshadowing 1918 tactics, brought a further, if indirect, contribution to his balance. No sooner had Johnston retired to his new line than Sherman began extending his right to threaten the edge of Johnston's new western flank, and to check this dangerous movement Johnston switched Hood's corps across to the other flank. It was a clever bid, but it was outbid. For the Union extension had gone further than was realized and Hood, expecting to outflank Sherman's right, dashed his men against the quickly made breastworks of the Union right, on June 22, and suffered a severe rebuff and a loss of about 1,000 men.

This fresh indirect addition to his balance Sherman now expended, and more, in a move which has been much debated and was his only direct assault of the campaign. Yet it was based on a shrewd psychological calculation, and if it followed the line of direct approach it avoided the line of natural expectation. Indeed, it was inspired by the idea not only of upsetting the enemy's calculations but of making it more difficult for him to anticipate Sherman's moves subsequently. Thus while its immediate and outward result was failure its ultimate profit was considerable, if not easy to measure.

Its one defect as an attempt at surprise lay in the reason which hastened it. Grant had impressed upon Sherman the need of gripping Johnston too tightly to allow him to detach troops to strengthen the Confederate army in Virginia, now all too successfully resisting Grant's advance. Hence Sherman, ever a loyal lieutenant thinking of his chief's need, was loath to let even bad weather and roads be a ground for relaxing the pressure on Johnston. As these conditions forbade a fresh wide manœuvre, he conceived a plan which is concisely expressed in his June 25 despatch to Washington—"I shall aim to make him [Johnston] stretch his line until he weakens it and then break through."

Thomas had suggested that they should make a regular siege approach to the enemy's line, but Sherman replied that when that slow process had carried one line experience showed that two or three equally strong would have been prepared behind it—a lesson that had to be painfully relearnt in the World War.

Instead, Sherman continued the extension of his flanks, helped by the improving weather (since June 23), in order to strain the enemy's resources and distract their attention. For 8 A.M. on the 27th he ordered an assault in the Kenesaw Mountain sector, calculating that as this was the strangest sector by nature it would be the weakest in numbers of defenders. Apart from many past proofs —the latest at Look-Out Mountain—that a naturally difficult, and therefore unexpected, line of approach is often the easiest to penetrate by, Sherman already knew that this sector had been weakened by the "switch" of Hood's corps. But for these very reasons he is open to criticism for making the assault on the southwestern skirts of the mountain instead of against the mountain itself. At the same time, however, he ordered the skirmish line facing the base of the mountain to attempt to seize the summit under cover of the assault on the skirts.

The actual choice of the points of assault he left to the commanders on the spot, and it was decided that one division of McPherson's should attack Little Kenesaw, while two of Thomas's assaulted the enemy's works a mile to the right. These assaults were made in the usual narrow-fronted brigade columns; they might have suffered less and succeeded better if they had cast the drill books aside as they had already done before. It is notable that McPherson's assault, which was on a broader front, suffered only 20 per cent. of the total loss. At least as a cloak to these assaults the skirmishers moved forward along the whole front, simultaneously, firing vigorously on the enemy's work.

But if the enemy was weakened according to Sherman's expectation, the superiority of a weak defence behind entrenchments over a strong attack was all too well attested. And his expectation was to some extent discounted because Johnston, though not really anticipating an attack on his centre, calculated that the bad roads would prevent Sherman stretching his flanks much further.

Both assaults failed, with a total loss of about 2,500, although the attackers succeeded in entrenching themselves close to the enemy's parapet. That they inflicted a compensating loss of even 800 on the defenders was almost entirely due to their artillery. General Howard has described the whole Confederate position as stronger, naturally and artificially, than the Cemetery at Gettysburg.

In his report Sherman said: "I perceived that the enemy and our officers had settled down into a conviction that I would not assault fortified lines. All looked to me to outflank. An army to be efficient, must not settle down to a single mode of offence, but must be prepared to execute any plan which promises success. I wanted, therefore, for the moral effect, to make a successful assault against the enemy behind his breastworks, and resolved to attempt it at that point where success would give the largest fruits of victory. The general point selected was the left centre, because if I could thrust a strong head of column through . . . boldly and rapidly two and one-half miles, it would reach the railroad below Marietta, cut off the right and center from its line of retreat, and then by turning on either part it could be overwhelmed and destroyed."

The reasoning contains much truth, if not all the truth. The unexpected is the key to victory, and it may well have been worth the price even of an unsuccessful assault to increase his future scope for it. But if we judge the operation purely on its immediate merits, the test is more severe. A direct assault on an unshaken enemy in position has no justification in history—although Sherman made it only once, whereas with many generals it has been a normal practice. Leaving aside the ultimate value, the historical test at Kenesaw is whether Sherman had done enough to unhinge the defence before releasing this assault. And here the answer is that he had done as much as was possible, but hardly enough to assure a justifiable anticipation of success. Being unsuccessful, the momentary effect was to depress his own troops and fortify the confidence of the enemy.

But the best tribute to Sherman is his comparative quickness to repair the one and exploit the other effect. With the assaulting lines so close to the enemy's parapet, he was perhaps too inclined to hope that a renewed effort at fresh points might succeed, but he forebore to put any pressure on the executive commanders and relied on their opinion. Deprecating a fresh assault Thomas suggested that they should work forward by regular saps, but Sherman had no belief in this method, and at 9 P.M. sent a telegraphic message to him—"Are you willing to risk the move on Fulton [on the railroad and close to the Chattahoochee], cutting loose from our railroad? It would bring matters to a crisis, and Schofield [now the right wing] has secured the way." After a rapid interchange of telegrams Sherman at 9.50 P.M. ordered preparations to be made.

But an inconvenient delay was imposed by the supply factor. Thomas, indeed, was very prompt and issued his troops with ten days' rations that night, but Schofield, further from the railroad, was less well supplied and Sherman, anxious though he was to lose no time, was careful that his imagination should not outstrip his stomach. Curbing his own impatience he withheld the order to move until he was assured that he had adequate provisions at railhead, that his railhead and the communications in rear were secure, and working smoothly.

The need of this assurance was then especially acute, for on the 14th he had heard that the redoubtable Forrest had taken yet another scalp—that of Sturgis, the cavalry commander who was covering Sherman's rearmost communications in Tennessee. Sturgis and his cavalry had been routed and driven back into Memphis. Sherman had acted promptly by sending orders to the two divisions now released from the Red River campaign to take the offensive and keep Forrest off the communications. But it was not until mid-July, when news came of Forrest's defeat, that Sherman's anxiety on this score was settled.

Satisfied, however, as to his immediate communications, he made the first of a rapid series of moves which baffled an opponent who had set another trap for him, and carried him triumphantly across the broad barrier of the Chattahoochee to the outskirts of Atlanta. The fact that events did not correspond with his preconception sheds the more lustre on the opportunism and speed with which he played his game.

On July 1 Schofield side-stepped further to the right, and on the night of July 2 McPherson slipped behind the backs of Thomas and Schofield, from the left flank to the extreme right. And Sherman slipped Garrard's cavalry division in to occupy McPherson's trenches.

McPherson was now only three miles short of the Chattahoochee and five miles west of the railroad. The move took into account the likelihood that Johnston might detect that Sherman was extending to his right. If he did not, McPherson could swing in and get outside the railroad in his rear. If he did, Sherman's plan had an answer for either of his possible countermoves.

There were two. First, that Johnston, thinking that Sherman had weakened his centre, by stretching to the right, would attack it. Sherman hoped that he would—and have a dose of Kenesaw medicine. Second, that Johnston would let go of Marietta, and move southwards and outwards from the railroad to cover his communications. In this case, Sherman was ready to swing his left wing [now Thomas and Garrard] down the railroad, hoping either to cut Johnston off from it or to catch him in confusion as he tried to retire across the Chattahoochee.

On the evening of the 2nd there was a suspiciously ostentatious advance by the enemy. Sherman deduced that this was a bluff to cover their retreat, and at earliest dawn of the 3rd he was up watching, through a large telescope, the slopes of Kenesaw for the first signs of the enemy's intention. Soon he could see his own skirmishers creeping cautiously up the slope. No bullet greeted them and they reached the crest safely. It was clear that Johnston had detected the danger and, taking the second alternative, had retired in the night.

Instantly, Sherman despatched his staff to all quarters with confirmatory orders for a vigorous pursuit by all roads, directing Thomas down the railroad, Garrard out to the east of it, McPherson and Schofield to swing inwards. By 8.30 A.M. the Union forces had passed through Marietta, and Sherman turned the whole current of his energy into propelling the pursuers forward, and became furiously angry at the excessive caution of the cavalry and Thomas's infantry. His indignation seems justified in view of the fact that at nightfall they were only six miles south of Marietta where they ran into a strong rear-guard position.

But, actually, energy of pursuit was vain energy. For while Sherman reckoned that Johnston would be hurrying to get across the river—on the ground that "no general, such as he, would invite battle with the Chattahoochee behind him"—Johnston, wisely or unwisely, had decided to adopt this last course. In taking the risk he had, however, prepared a surprise for Sherman—fortifying a large bridgehead with a six-mile entrenched line of immense strength. Above it and below, all the likely crossings for a dozen miles were covered by batteries and fortifications on the south bank, which was also watched by Johnston's cavalry.

Sherman's troops celebrated the 4th of July by a noisy engagement with the enemy's rearguard position, and then on the 5th came in sight of the massive bridgehead lines—an unpleasant sight. Sherman was disinclined to believe that Johnston was really making a serious stand on the near bank until he had seen the fortifications with his own eyes. Nine miles distant also he now caught sight of the roof tops of his goal, Atlanta.

But already on the 4th he had taken intuitively a step which fitted in with his new-born plan. This step was the despatch of Garrard's cavalry to Roswell, twenty miles up river to the north-east, where there was a bridge. This had been burnt by the Confederate cavalry, but Garrard secured the ford and was then told by Sherman to watch it closely, but to conceal his presence there. Meantime, Sherman used Stoneman's cavalry division, aided and abetted by McPherson, to create the impression that he was searching for a crossing below Johnston's bridgehead. This drew off most of Johnston's guardian angels on horseback. After a reconnaissance of the river on the 7th had discovered a possible and unguarded crossing, known as Phillips' Ferry, midway between Johnston's position and Roswell, Schofield's army corps was moved swiftly and stealthily from the right to the left on the 8th and concealed near the river, while the pontoons were being set up and launched in the mouth of a small creek.

All this was done under the unseeing eyes of a cavalry outpost, with one gun, on the far bank. Meantime a small Union detachment scrambled precariously across the river over the rocks of a fish dam, half a mile upstream, and came sweeping down the far bank as the pontoons shot out from their hidden launching place; simultaneously also, a brigade dashed out from cover and down to the near bank to cover the crossing with their fire. The enemy outpost, taken completely by surprise, fled, and within a few hours the whole of Schofield's corps was across and securely entrenched in a strong bridgehead.

Coincidently Garrard had crossed at Roswell and formed another bridgehead, where he was soon relieved by an infantry division. On the 9th Sherman suddenly moved Dodge's corps, which was "selling the dummy" on the other flank, from Sandtown Ferry to Roswell, thirty-one miles distant, where it crossed the river on the 10th.

But already, during the night, Johnston, finding himself outwitted and his opponent in secure possession of two strong bridgeheads behind his flank, took the only possible course—that of retiring to Atlanta before he was cut off from it. For this strategic defeat he had to pay a double penalty, for by it he had forfeited not merely his fortified position but the chance of using the Chattahoochee as his forward line of defence—the strongest possible. And the sequel to it was a third fine, although it was really paid by the Confederacy, which inflicted it.

On the night of the 17th, just as the advance of Sherman's army from its bridgeheads had been reported, Johnston received a telegram from Richmond saying—"as you have failed to arrest the advance of the enemy to the vicinity of Atlanta, far in the interior of Georgia, and express no confidence that you can defeat or repel him, you are hereby relieved from the command . . . which you will immediately turn over to General Hood." In complying, Johnston could not forgo the retort—"Confident language by a military commander is not usually regarded as evidence of competence." He was soon to be justified. Historians of to-day, recalling ruefully the vocal confidence of General Nivelle in 1917, can appreciate still better the justice of the retort.

Johnston was now to be replaced by a "real fighting soldier"; one by no means deficient of fighting competence, although his fiery belief in the virtues of attack was perhaps stronger than his strategic judgment. By his "will to victory" he had already twice helped Sherman to balance his casualty budget, and Sherman was duly appreciative of the change of command. The change was not the least of the fruits of his strategic success in manœuvre.

CHAPTER XVIII

"ATLANTA IS OURS AND FAIRLY WON"

SHERMAN within sight of Atlanta, the Union within sight of defeat. Such was the situation in July and August, 1864, by a psychological tide in the affairs of men, and upon Sherman reaching his end there rested the best hope of the Union avoiding its end. No other could do it. For these two months were perhaps the most critical of the war, certainly since 1862. Yet in the spring the Union had seemed at the heights of its powers, the Confederacy with its shrivelled breast bared to the mortal blow.

How had the dramatic change come? Not by military defeat, but by military failure—the failure to fulfil hopes that had been raised so high. Under the moral shock of this failure, aggravated by the extravagant and apparently vain losses, the will to victory of the Northern people had weakened, and by its weakness emboldened all the forces of "defeatism."

How had Grant set out to fulfil those hopes of spring? By the orthodox strategy of using his superior weight to smash the opposing army, or at least to wear it down by a "continuous hammering." Perhaps the very ease of his problem compared with that which he had so audaciously solved at Vicksburg seduced him into applying the obvious, and apparently easiest solution. Perhaps also it was due to the very superiority of his balance in the bank of manpower, and the strength of his credit. The delusive influence of both these comforting assurances is well attested throughout the pages of history.

He decided on the old direct overland approach down the Virginian corridor from the Rappahannock towards Richmond. But with a certain difference of aim, for the enemy's army was his essential objective, and the enemy's capital relegated to a secondary and subsequent place in his outlook. Yet, in justice to Grant, one should note that if his approach was direct in the broad sense, it was in no sense a mere frontal push. Indeed, he continuously sought to turn

Lee's flanks by manœuvre, although his manœuvres were narrow—outflanking rather than rear bestriding. Further, he fulfilled, too well, the orthodox canons of strategy, his army kept well concentrated and his objective maintained unswervingly. Even a Foch could not surpass his will to victory. As one of his officers ruefully remarked—"He habitually wears an expression as if he had determined to drive his head through a brick wall, and was about to do it." This bull-like determination was the less effective and bruised him the more because his horns were broken at the outset.

The advance of his weak right horn, the force first under Sigel and then under Hunter, up the Shenandoah Valley was chipped on May 5, and broken off short a month later. If it had usefully distracted thither a portion of Lee's army—Early's corps, it also encouraged Early to exploit the fracture in July by a tip-and-run invasion of Maryland, the third, and this threat to Washington on top of Grant's own failure to reach his objective aggravated the moral decline which became so marked in the North at this period.

The left horn was formed by the force of 36,000 men which was landed in the James River below Richmond, and which was placed under the political general, Butler, of New Orleans notoriety, apparently to keep him out of politics—a dubious reason for so important a choice. Butler disembarked on May 6 high up the river at Bermuda Hundred Neck and, as directed, moved direct on Richmond—when, with little chance of opposition, he could have seized Petersburg and the railroads below Richmond. In consequence he lost time in front of the fortifications at Drewry's Bluff, and after losing men also, was shepherded back to Bermuda Hundred and then safely "bottled up" by Beauregard with less than half his strength.

Meantime Grant, with 119,000 men against Lee's 61,000, had lost 17,700 in an abortive opening battle in the Wilderness, May 5-7, then hurled himself repeatedly on the Confederate entrenchments round Spottsylvania from May 8 to 19 until he had lost a further 18,400. Stubbornly Grant declared—"I . . . propose to fight it out on this line if it takes all summer." Those who practised his method in 1918 might well envy him the generous support given and unfailing confidence shown by his political chief, who capped Grant's declaration by the statement, "I say we are going through on this line if it takes three years more." But although a general and a president may propose, the people dispose—and their disposition under the strain of these baffled hopes and appalling losses turned increasingly towards a doubt of the value of continuing the war. The ripe fruit of victory had withered in their hands.

Despite his declaration, Grant spent the rest of May in trying afresh to move by his left and outflank Lee's right, and, when successively blocked, he abstained from vain assaults. But at Cold Harbor on June 3 his patience was exhausted, and an assault ordered without any assurance of the enemy being "loosened" lost several thousand men in less than an hour. The feeling of the doomed gladiators was shown by the fact that they pinned papers, with their names and addresses, on their backs so that their corpses might be identified. And when Grant ordered a renewal of the assault his troops simply disregarded it—in passive verdict upon its futility. In a month's campaign Grant had lost about 55,000 men, nearly half his original strength, and nearly double Lee's loss.

Then on June 12, Grant, drawing back out of touch, side-stepped southwards to a point below Richmond, changing his base to the James River, but the chance of stepping into Petersburg was missed, and Lee once more blocked Grant in fortified lines. It is an ironical reflection that the determination with which Grant had wielded his superior weight had utterly failed to crush the enemy's army, while the chief result—the geographical advantage of having worked round to the rear of Richmond—had been gained by the bloodless manœuvres which punctuated his advance. He had thus the modified satisfaction of being back, after disheartening loss, in the position which McClellan had occupied in 1862. If the commander had not lost hope, his men fought without it. In response to his orders they might still go forward to die, but such a fatalistic spirit is a weak impulse, and their increasing reluctance is revealed not merely in the ineffectiveness of their June assaults, but in the decreasing loss. Grant's offensive strategy had, indeed, ruined the offensive power of his own army, and the sequel was that from July onwards he lay paralyzed before Petersburg, save for a spasmodic effort in October which flickered and failed.

But the damage was more far-reaching. Soldiers too often forget that a military effort rests ultimately on the support and consent of the people. The Democratic party gave a lead to all those who wished for peace or despaired of victory. And, as a powerful impetus, dollars fell and wages rose until ordinary men began to feel that a continuance of the war would not "profit anyone but the profiteers." Even in Lincoln's own party, men began to look askance at his policy. The Presidential election was due in November, and in early June he had been renominated by the Republican Convention, but a section now accused him of spurning opportunities for negotiation in his wish to prolong the war from personal ambition. Soon this movement developed into a clamour for a fresh convention to reconsider Lincoln's nomination, and even his strongest supporters began to feel and say that the chance of his election was hopeless.

This, then, was the dark background to the final phase of Sherman's Atlanta campaign. Grant could do nothing, and any serious repulse to Sherman might have a fatal effect on public opinion. Caution was essential, yet success was equally so. Whether Sherman manœuvred or fought it would be with the Chattahoochee at his back, as a watery grave already dug by nature. And he was warned by Grant that Lee might be able to detach troops from his secure lines at Richmond to reinforce the Confederates at Atlanta. Sherman's chief advantage, but one to be utilized with care, was that the change of commanders on the enemy's side gave him a reasonable calculation that both Hood's own nature and probable instructions would compel him to take the offensive. It was Sherman's first business as a strategist to give him the chance under conditions which would ensure an expensive repulse.

His first problem was to decide his way of advance upon Atlanta. Even had Sherman been by mind inclined to a direct advance, a broken bridge lay before him with the enemy's army beyond, covering Atlanta, and a dangerously cramped space between. The choice, then, lay between an advance from the crossings south of Johnston's old position and one from those north of it, where Sherman had already established two bridge-heads.

The Chattahoochee ran from north-east to south-west obliquely in front of Atlanta, which itself stood on a plateau or watershed. South of Atlanta the country offered an easier way of approach, as the streams were short and ran at right angles into the Chattahoochee, so that they offered no barrier to an advance inland from the river. North of Atlanta the streams were longer and formed slanting strokes which an advance would have to cross.

From Atlanta the railroad through Decatur to Augusta, and thence to Charleston and Richmond, ran eastwards, and the line to Montgomery and Mobile south-westwards, parallel with the Chattahoochee. Six miles down this line, at East Point, a branch diverged south-eastwards through Jonesborough to Macon, where it connected with another line to the Atlantic at Savannah. The town itself had owed its birth and growth to the junction of these railroads; it was at least fitting that it should now owe its fate to the greatest of railroad strategists. These, then, were the main logistical elements of the problem, and may be shown diagrammatically thus:

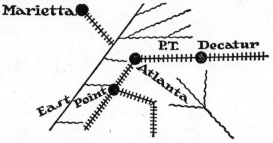

Sherman decided to take the longer and more difficult way round by the north. For by this route he could better cover his own communications, and by getting astride the Augusta railroad he would isolate the Confederates from the East, preventing both their reinforcement thence and their retirement thither. In view of Grant's warning of possible reinforcements from Richmond this argument acquired special force. It was a further asset that on the north Sherman had more room and two fortified bridge-heads at his back.

From July 10 to 15 he was accumulating supplies at his new railhead near the Chattahoochee bank, as well as at Marietta and Allatoona, while he was preparing fresh crossing places, and enlarging the bridges at those already made.

On the 16th, Blair's corps, which was guarding Turner's Ferry, directly facing Atlanta, was relieved by Stoneman's cavalry and marched north to join McPherson's army at Roswell. On the 17th,

Thomas crossed at intermediate points and formed up as the right wing and pivot of a line, some fifteen miles wide, completed by Schofield and McPherson. Sherman's purpose was to make a right wheel to the south, Thomas practically marking time and occupying the enemy's attention, while McPherson and Garrard's cavalry division on the extreme left swung swiftly across the Augusta railroad. Then, still pivoting on Thomas, the centre and left wing would make a further right wheel and converge inwards and westwards against Atlanta. To Thomas, the strongest army, the task of resisting any enemy counterstroke; to McPherson the mobile task of cutting the railroad and turning the enemy's flank while his attention was drawn by Thomas.

Deducting the detachments necessarily left to guard his now extended railroad, it is probable that Sherman's strength for the advance beyond the Chattahoochee was not more than 75,000. Casualties had reduced the Confederate army to 60,000 in the past month, but by falling back to Atlanta it had gathered in several thousand local reinforcements and militia, so that Sherman had but a slight margin of superiority. And his troops, unlike the Confederates, did not know the country.

Adopting the outline plan already formed by Johnston, Hood determined to await the Union forces on the line of Peach Tree Creek ("P.T." in the diagram) and to strike as they were in the act of crossing. In the hope of splitting Sherman's army and throwing it back on divergent lines of retreat, Hood ordered his right corps (formerly his own and now commanded by Cheatham) to hold on to the line of the Creek, while Hardee's and Stewart's (formerly Polk's) on the centre and left were drawn back ready to pounce on the enemy as soon as they had pushed across the creek. Unfortunately for Hood, Sherman's wide extension upset his plan, as at Cassville, although outwardly it seemed to endanger Sherman's.

On the morning of the 18th, Sherman began his wheeling advance from the Chattahoochee, and by the afternoon McPherson, moving swiftly along the circumference of the arc, arrived astride the Augusta railroad seven miles beyond Decatur, and fourteen east of Atlanta. Meantime Schofield, inside him, was approaching Decatur from the north and Thomas, the pivot, was feeling his way carefully forward to Peach Tree Creek.

On the 19th, McPherson turned westwards along the railroad to Decatur, destroying the railroad as he went. Sherman's orders even laid down how the rails should be torn up, laid on a bonfire of ties, and twisted, while red hot, into spirals. Only in case of "sounds of serious battle" was McPherson to leave this task incomplete and close inwards. Meanwhile Schofield occupied Decatur from the north, and the heads of Thomas's three corps, shouldering back the Confederate advanced troops, made their way across the marshy channel of Peach Tree Creek. All the time Thomas kept his troops in close-knit readiness for battle; indeed, a little too close, for he was tending to hug the Chattahoochee and crowd in on his own right. Several times during the day, as on the 18th, Sherman impressed on him that he should, instead, stretch out to his left in order to link up with Schofield.

In the evening Sherman ordered that at five o'clock next morning the converging final advance on Atlanta was to begin, Thomas moving down from "the direction of Buckhead" (due north), and linking up with Schofield's advance "two miles north-east of Atlanta," while McPherson pressed in from the east, down the railroad from Decatur. At 1.55 A.M. Sherman, still concerned that "your right will be too strong as compared with your left," instructed Thomas to send the two reserve divisions of his left corps (Howard's) to fill the gap between his left and Schofield's right.

Thomas's tendency, partly due to inadequate maps, to edge in to his right was all to well suited to Hood's plan, but fortunately the caution of his advance prevented Hood putting it into operation on the 19th, as he had hoped. And on the morning of the 20th the inward approach to his flank of Schofield and McPherson disturbed his mind and induced a change of dispositions which unhinged his plan. To ward off the flank menace, Cheatham's corps, the intended rock on which the Union advance should split, was ordered to side-step a "division front" to the right, and the other two corps to side-step also to fill the interval. This shuffling move caused confusion and delayed the Confederate counterstroke from 1 P.M. until 4 P.M.

By the paradoxical fortune of war the undesired side-step to the right was an actual advantage to the Confederates, because it placed them more on Thomas's flank and also helped to save them in the evening. Even the delay turned out to their advantage for it shortened the distance they had to traverse, and so prevented their two-counter-attacking corps advancing too far north, away from the Atlanta defences.

The counter-stroke was launched by divisions in echelon from Hardee's right, Stewart's taking it up in turn, so that if successful it might roll up Thomas's line and drive it into the Chattahoochee. And, by reason of Thomas's "rightward" tendency, its brunt was borne by Howard's one forward division and Hooker's corps, while Palmer's corps on the extreme right remained perforce a passive spectator. By their "shouldering" pressure the seven Confederate divisions made some initial progress as the Union divisions were forced to turn and face half left to meet them. From the tactical viewpoint Hardee's was the most dangerous attack, because it had the most chance of working round the Union flank. But this manœuvre was dislocated by indirect intervention.

For McPherson, converging inward from Decatur and driving back the Confederate cavalry, was now so menacingly close to the eastern side of Atlanta that at about 6 P.M. Hood was constrained to order off a division of Hardee's corps to help in checking McPherson. And the departure of this reserve division (Cleburne's), which he was about to use as the spearhead of a renewed assault, compelled Hardee to abandon his attempt. If Stewart's attack continued a little longer, its chances had already faded. The repulse cost Hood a loss which is varyingly estimated at from four to six thousand, while the Union loss was just under two thousand. It is significant that the one Union division which had covered itself with an improvised breastwork lost only 102 men—although it was the one on the exposed flank.

Although the enforced detachment of Cleburne's division ruined Hood's counterstroke, it probably saved him a worse disaster. For by Cleburne's verdict he only arrived on the eastern side just in time to prevent McPherson entering the inner defences of Atlanta on the heels of the Confederate cavalry. Thus, paradoxically Hood's series of errors, which in turn were the product of Sherman's manœuvre, were the means of saving him from the full effects of that manœuvre.

On the other hand, it would seem that Sherman's left wing missed a chance of gaining Atlanta while Hood's attention was occupied with Thomas. Neither Schofield's nor Howard's corps pressed in very vigorously from the north-east, where they had only Cheatham's corps to oppose them; and McPherson's three corps were held in play most of the day, in a running fight, by Wheeler's cavalry division.   Allowance, however, must be made for the difficult, densely wooded and little-known ground over which they were advancing—rather, groping forward in the fog of war.

Moreover, the Confederate counterstroke had been involuntarily delayed until so late in the day that there was time neither to hear of it nor to take advantage of it. At the outset Sherman's hope had been that the news of his advance from the Decatur direction would draw Hood's strength to the east side of Atlanta, so that Thomas might have a chance "to walk into Atlanta" from the north. Not until late in the afternoon did Sherman, who had placed himself on the left wing, receive a message, timed noon, from Thomas, telling him that the enemy were still in strength on the north side of Atlanta. His reply, timed 6.10 P.M., reveals his disappointment and also his annoyance—"I have yours of 12 M. I have been with Howard and Schofield to-day, and one of my staff is just back from General McPherson. All report the enemy in the front so strong that I was in hopes none were left for you, but I see it is the same old game . . . each division commander insists he has to fight two corps. . . . I will push Schofield and McPherson all I know how."

Even then he had no knowledge of Hood's counterstroke, and the possible chance it offered. He could hardly have received news in time to do anything before darkness intervened, but it seems strange, and somewhat remiss, that Thomas did not send off any message until 6.15 P.M., when the counterstroke was flickering out.

Perhaps the real clue to the day's partial disappointment is to be found eleven years before—in the fact that McPherson had passed out from West Point first on the list into the engineers, and that Hood had passed out forty-fourth. McPherson too technical in mind to be dashing and Hood too limited in mind to be caught. In another twenty-four hours the danger from the Decatur direction might have sunk into his mind and led him, as Sherman hoped, to switch and concentrate his strength to meet it. If this be a true deduction, the verdict would seem to be that Sherman's manœuvre fell short of full success because his new opponent was too insensitive to impressions, too slow in reaction, just as Johnston had been too quick for Sherman's taste.

On the 21st Hood, unable to cover both his flanks, prepared to withdraw his forces to the inner defences of Atlanta and to try the second alternative in the outline plan which Johnston had bequeathed to him. But with a difference. Johnston's idea had been, if unsuccessful in the Peach Tree Creek counterstroke, to fall back into the inner defences, and then, leaving only the state militia to hold them, slip out with his three corps to strike at whichever of Sherman's flanks was most exposed. Perhaps this plan was a little optimistic, and Hood found Sherman too close to attempt it in full. So, withdrawing Cheatham's and Stewart's corps into the inner defences on the night of the 21st, he despatched Hardee's corps to get round and behind Sherman's left flank. While he attacked it in rear, Cheatham and Stewart in turn would join the attack, seeking to roll up Sherman's line.

But McPherson's closer approach to the Atlanta defences during the day compelled Hardee to make a wider circuit to the south in order to get round, so that after a fifteen-mile night march he arrived at daybreak in the woods near McPherson's rear flank, but not behind his rear.

During the previous day Sherman had been closing in and contracting his semi-circular line round Atlanta, while getting his batteries into position to bombard the defences and the town. He ordered that each commander should seek to work forward "without a direct assault on the enemy's parapet if held in force" but ready to seize any opportunity provided by the repulse of a counter-attack to follow the enemy into his works. Quick as ever to look a step ahead he had already determined that if the enemy held on to Atlanta he would make yet another of his lateral "leap-frogs" and jump McPherson over to Thomas's right, using him to cut the enemy's remaining artery of supplies, the southerly railroad. The move would have the further advantage of covering his own railroad and its extension across the Chattahoochee.

His skirmishers, ripening in skill and cunning, were becoming remarkably quick to detect signs of an enemy retirement, so that the Confederates' after dark withdrawal from their outer defences was discovered on Thomas's and Schofield's fronts before 2 A.M. Anticipating that this might mean the evacuation of Atlanta Sherman promptly ordered his commanders to "satisfy" themselves on this point and pursue vigorously southward.

Although his anticipatory order was wise foresight, his anticipation was, as we know, incorrect, and as the sun mounted above the horizon the enemy were seen in the main defences. Sherman himself rode so far forward to reconnoitre that he and his staff drew the enemy's fire. Returning to his headquarters at the Howard House, he was joined on the way by McPherson who had ridden across to see him. Now sure that the enemy were holding onto Atlanta, Sherman explained to him his new project for the "leap-frog" to the other flank. As they were talking, the normal sound of firing to their front was supplemented by gun fire to the left rear in the Decatur direction. The time was about noon. McPherson hurriedly galloped off to discover the cause.

Hardee had launched his attack through the concealing woods, while Wheeler's cavalry, swinging further out, swooped down on Decatur, where lay McPherson's supply train, guarded by one brigade. Hardee's troops overran a battery and several hospital camps behind the Union front before their approach was known, obtaining an initial surprise due partly to nature and partly to Sherman. For after the capture of Decatur he had despatched Garrard's cavalry division to extend the destruction of the railroad another thirty miles eastward. At the same time, however, he had warned McPherson to safeguard his own rear and trains, and on the 21st had told him with accurate intuition "I think to-morrow Hood will draw from his left and reinforce his right." And a few hours before Hardee's then suspected attack developed McPherson had made the move which checkmated it.

The contraction of Sherman's semi-circular line had squeezed out Dodge's corps which was drawn back into reserve. At 8 A.M. on the 22nd, McPherson had ordered Dodge to move to the left in rear of Blair, the left flank corps, in order to strengthen and extend that flank. In consequence, Dodge's troops were on the march thither as Hardee's attack was launched and, turning outwards to meet it, were an invaluable shield to McPherson's rear, and an unpleasant surprise to Hardee. By repulsing his two right divisions they not only took the sting out of his attack but prevented it reaching the point where its effort would be most dangerous. For the assault of Hardee's two left divisions fell on Blair—on the flank instead of on the rear.

But, by penetrating into the gap between Blair and Dodge, the Confederates for a time made threatening progress, accentuated by the sally of Cheatham's corps from the Atlanta defences. Blair was thus pressed on three sides, but the attacks were fortunately not coincident and, utilizing his field entrenchments, he skilfully turned to parry each in turn. Hood undoubtedly waited too long before releasing Cheatham's attack. As the Confederates pursued their mistaken tactics of the 20th and repeatedly renewed their assaults long after the initial surprise and success were over, their casualties multiplied without profit, and their loss may have been as much as 10,000 men to the Union's 3,700. For 3,220 Confederate dead were buried by their foes, and 2,017 prisoners taken.

.　　　.　　　.　　　.　　　.　　　.

The Union loss, however, included one of great individual importance. After satisfying himself that Dodge could hold his ground McPherson had galloped across the gap to Blair. Alone save for an orderly he ran into the advancing Confederate skirmishers, who called on him to surrender. Instantly he wheeled his horse to gallop away, raising his hand as if in salute, but a volley brought him to the ground. The riderless horse came back into the Union lines and the news was sent to Sherman, who ordered Logan to take over the command, and to send a force to fill the gap. Within an hour McPherson's body was retrieved and brought to Sherman's headquarters. The pockets had been rifled and the pocket-book with Sherman's instructions for the next move was missing. Greatly to Sherman's relief he soon heard that it had been found in the haversack of a prisoner.

When McPherson had left him at midday, Sherman's first thought had been for the safety of his extreme rear and the trains at Decatur, and he had quickly drawn a reserve brigade from Schofield and despatched it to Decatur, where it arrived in time to beat off Wheeler's cavalry swoop. Threatening as was the attack on his actual flank, Sherman seems to have been both calm and confident that it could and would be repulsed.

The very fact that his own headquarters came under fire, and was

frequently struck, was the best of sedatives to one of his temperament.   For as General Cox relates, "he had the rare faculty of
being more equable under great responsibilities and scenes of great
excitement.   At such times his eccentricities disappeared, his grasp
of the situation was firm and clear, . . . and no momentary complication or unexpected event could move him from the purpose he had
based on full study of contingencies.   His mind seemed never so
clear, his confidence never so strong, his spirit never so inspiring,
and his temper never so amiable as in the crisis of some fierce
struggle like that of the day when McPherson fell in front of Atlanta."   When, about 4 P.M., Cheatham's attack was launched from
Atlanta and penetrated the front of Logan's corps Sherman himself was on the spot and met this second crisis of the day by changing from general-in-chief to gunner-in-chief.   With quick decision
and acute perception, he sent a call for the whole of Schofield's
artillery, and, as the batteries were brought up at full gallop, personally led them into position to enfilade the assailants' left flank.
This concentrated fire, directed by him, swept the captured parapets,
and to complete its effect he then threw in a counter-attack, rolling
the enemy up and back.

Trusting in the capacity of the Army of the Tennessee to check
the Confederate attack he had made no attempt to reinforce it directly from the other armies.   These had been ordered to press forward on their own fronts—an indirect but more effective form of
assistance.

With such excellent justification on military grounds for his
course it seems curious that in his memoirs he should suggest an
additional motive—"that, if any assistance were rendered by either
of the other armies, the Army of the Tennessee would be jealous."
There is no doubt that this jealousy between the armies existed, and
had existed when Grant was in command, but it was unfortunate
that a commander-in-chief should pander to it.   That he did, there
is also no question.   Sherman was not the first great man, still less
the first great soldier, to be blemished by such inequitable if human
prejudices.   It was human that he should have special affection
and trust in his own old troops, but even if justified on military
grounds it was unfortunate that to the Army of the Tennessee

should always fall the key task or the rôle of manœuvre. The coincidence went too far to be convincing. Time, however, brought its revenge, for from the staff of the Army of the Cumberland, equally if not more jealous of its laurels, came in later years the most prejudiced and irrational critics of Sherman. As compensation there was a third party—the Army of the Ohio—whose verdict is singularly untainted by prejudice.

Sherman's deeply ingrained sense of loyalty, both his strength and his weakness, may perhaps have influenced decisions of a different nature in the weeks which followed. The first was the choice of McPherson's successor. Logan had been given acting command in a crisis, and acquitted himself admirably. Like Blair, he had given up a political career to volunteer and had proved himself one of the ablest commanders in the army. Against his confirmation in command was the existence of a somewhat natural rivalry between him and Blair, a disposition to criticize orders—although he executed them whole-heartedly and brilliantly, and the fact that he was not a professional soldier.

Sherman goes so far as to admit that as Logan and Blair were politicians "it may be that for this reason they were mistrusted by regular officers like Generals Schofield, Thomas and myself." Still more ingenuous and illogical was his remark, in his memoirs, that "I regarded both Generals Logan and Blair as 'volunteers,' that looked to personal fame and glory as auxiliary and secondary to their personal ambition, and not as professional soldiers." The commonness of this "trade-union" outlook is certainly no excuse. If Sherman had had no better justification he would stand convicted of having placed his loyalty to the "trade-union" above his loyalty to the country's interests. For in choosing Howard instead he obtained a general, who was safe, cool and skilful, but lacked Logan's driving power. And thereby he was to hamper his own power of decisive manœuvre in the next stage of the campaign—a somewhat ironical comment on the remark that he "needed commanders who were purely and technically soldiers, men who would obey orders and execute them promptly." Sherman had not yet learnt that in other walks of life loyalty is regarded as compatible with criticism, and may often flourish the stronger for it. He was now to have a lesson, for Logan, though deeply hurt, relaxed not an effort—in illuminating contrast to some of Sherman's professional subordinates.

Sherman had, however, one better justification, that "it was all-important that there should exist a perfect understanding among the army commanders." And it would seem that he contemplated Logan's selection until Thomas remonstrated strongly. As Howard belonged to the Army of the Cumberland Sherman's decision may also have been inspired by a desire to conciliate feeling and to remove causes of grievance. If so, he was not entirely successful. For the sequel to Howard's selection was an instant protest from Hooker, the senior corps commander, who asked to be "relieved from duty with . . . an army in which rank and service are ignored."

Apart from Howard's youth—he was only thirty-three—his selection was peculiarly galling to Hooker because he had, with some justice, charged Howard with the major responsibility for the disaster at Chancellorsville which had led him to forfeit the chief command in the East. Vain and of an extremely critical mind, Hooker was nevertheless a capable soldier, as he had shown at Chattanooga and again in repelling Hood's counterstroke before Marietta. But his tongue was his own worst enemy in a society which does not care for criticism, even of a milder kind than Hooker's. No man could embitter the atmosphere of any camp quicker than Hooker with his caustic comments—"Hooker's opinions" as they were known throughout the army. Yet they carried with them their own antidote, for repetition dulled their effect, and those who knew the man best overlooked his words because of his deeds. It was unfortunate for him that he had come to an army whose chief prized harmony even above energy, sometimes to the sacrifice of results. It was still more unfortunate that Sherman knew him little, and did not care for what he knew.

Serious friction developed when Hooker, after repelling Hood's counterstroke near Marietta, reported that he had been attacked by three corps, instead of only one as in fact, and implied unfairly that Schofield had failed to support his flank. Sherman, after investigation, rebuked Hooker both for the insinuation and the sensational exaggeration. Henceforth with Sherman, latent prejudice became active dislike, and the sarcastic tongue of the chief vied with the bitter tongue of the subordinate. Schofield tells the story of how the two met on the battlefield and, coming under a heavy fire, there stayed because neither would withdraw to cover under the eyes of the other. But at least it must be said for Sherman that his relief was shared by most of his subordinates when Hooker asked to be relieved. Williams succeeded him temporarily until Slocum arrived from Vicksburg, and Hooker returned North to foretell an imminent disaster to the army before Atlanta.

The next important "casualty" was to be another of Thomas's corps commanders, Palmer, who marred the manœuvre of August 5 by refusing to obey instructions from Schofield, who had been placed in charge of it, on the ground that he was senior to Schofield. In military history, seniority has unfortunately been the most frequent excuse for disloyalty, as well as a fetter heavier than any other profession bears. The lot of a higher commander in the Civil War was not a happy one in matter of selection, for he had to contend not only with professional etiquette but with political intrigue.

Here Sherman is reflected in a happier light than in the Logan affair. News came that among recent promotions to major-general were two former divisional commanders, one who had gone sick and the other dissatisfied. As none of the serving commanders had yet received any advancement in rank this created much soreness among the officers, and Sherman promptly sent a scathing dispatch to Washington which concluded—"If the rear be the post of honor, then we had better all change front on Washington." The dispatch was shown to Lincoln, who wrote a tactful rejoinder. It was a shock to Sherman to find that the President had read his jibe, but he maintained his argument firmly if more respectfully, saying, "You can see how ambitious aspirants for military fame regard these things. They come to me and point them out as evidences that I am wrong in encouraging them to a silent, patient discharge of duty . . . as evidence that promotion results from importunity and not from actual service." Recognition of the justice of Sherman's complaint was at once made by a despatch which told him to nominate eight colonels for promotion.

.　　.　　.　　.　　.　　.　　.　　.

After the repulse of his counterstroke Hardee swung back his right so as to form a defensive flank south-east of Atlanta which

could be extended to block any attempt by Sherman to swing round
by his left against the Macon railroad. But Sherman, as we know,
had already decided to reverse his manœuvre and swing round by his
right. If the repeated indirectness of his approach was disconcert-
ing to his immediate opponent there is significant evidence that it
was also having an indirect effect on Grant's opponent. For on July
23 Lee, having only heard Hood's first highly-coloured report of his
initial success, wrote to the Confederate President, "relative to our
supply of corn," saying that "If the news of the glorious victory at
Atlanta . . . prove true it will again open to us Alabama and East
Mississippi, and remove a part of the great weight pressing upon
us."

Sherman's aim on his own front was now to give Hood the disagreeable sensation of an empty stomach in order to loosen his hold
on the sheltering defences of Atlanta. He had completely destroyed
the eastward railroad to Augusta, and earlier, while he had been
preparing his move across the Chattahoochee, a small cavalry force
under Rousseau had been improvised from scattered detachments
back in Tennessee for a long-range raid on the south-westward railroad to Montgomery. Leaving on July 9 Rousseau had reached and
made a temporary break in the railroad at Opelika, and then wheeled
north to rest his horses at Marietta. This, for the time, left Hood
only the Macon railroad as an artery of supply.

In contrast, Sherman's next move, or squeeze, was strengthened
by the anticipated reknitting of his own line of rail supply. The
great engineering feat of rebuilding the Chattahoochee bridge—
760 feet long and 90 feet high—was completed in four and a half
days, and the railroad then extended to reach Thomas's camps on
August 5. Early on July 27 McPherson had moved by successive
corps to Thomas's right, Schofield stretching out to the left and
utilizing the enemy's old entrenchments to cover his disappearance.
At daybreak McPherson's men had looked on Atlanta from the east,
at nightfall they had a new look at it from the west.

Simultaneously with this move Sherman had arranged a right and
left punch—pinch would perhaps be a more accurate term—with his
cavalry. McCook with 3,500 crossed the Chattahoochee low down
and, circling eastwards, made an incision in the Macon railroad near
Lovejoy's station, about thirty miles below Atlanta. But he did

not meet the other pincer as he had expected, and so returned by the route he had come with the consequence that he was intercepted and only extricated himself with considerable, and needless, loss.

At Decatur on the other flank the other pincer had been formed from an amalgam of Stoneman's division with Garrard's division, under the former, yielding a strong cavalry force of about 6,500. At a joint conference with Stoneman and McCook Sherman had explained their mission and instructed them to make their junction near Lovejoy's station on the night of the 28th, and then in concert destroy the railroad thoroughly. Subsequently, he gave Stoneman permission to push on south, after this task was accomplished, and attempt the release of the Union prisoners at Macon, and at the still larger prison camp at Andersonville. The sufferings of the 34,000 men at Andersonville had aroused great indignation in the North, and Stoneman let his desire for their rescue, or for the fame it would bring, divert him from his duty. Instead of swinging round south-westwards on a narrow arc towards McCook, he moved due south on Macon, leaving Garrard's tired men and horses behind as a reserve. Thus isolated, he became entangled with the enemy and, losing his head, lost his liberty. For, too quick to imagine that he was entrapped, he stayed behind with a third of his force to cover the "get away" of the rest, and was thus an easy victim. The result of this well-conceived but ill-executed cavalry stroke was to spoil two of Sherman's cavalry divisions and to shake what little faith he had left in them.

The only cavalry leader who had impressed him was Kilpatrick—whose aggressive nose, wiry build, and effective but ungraceful style of riding, aptly combined to express his personality—but when he asked Thomas to replace Garrard by Kilpatrick, Thomas demurred on the somewhat curious ground that Garrard was "an excellent administrative officer." Nobody valued such qualities more than Sherman, but he felt they were not all-sufficient in a cavalry leader, and tried to surmount the "Rock of Chickamauga"—Thomas—by regrouping his surviving cavalry in three small divisions under Garrard, McCook and Kilpatrick—in the hope that he might have one good unit.

The effects went further, for he was deprived of the chance, his best chance, of severing Hood's vital artery with his mobile arm, while using his less mobile arm to grip Hood by the throat. The only way now to sever it was by another swinging blow with part of his infantry.

For on the 28th Howard's swing in to the right had been foiled by Hood at the cost of another heavy repulse at disproportionate cost. That morning the last of Howard's three corps was just wheeling into line and taking up its position near Ezra Church on his extreme right, when Hood launched S. D. Lee's (formerly Cheatham's) corps to attack it. But Howard's men had time to cover themselves with a rough breastwork of logs, now so rapidly improvised, and the Confederate attack was held up. Renewals of the effort, and even a reinforcement of two divisions, only increased the vain cost—at least four thousand to Howard's six hundred—Howard estimated the Confederate loss at not less than six or seven thousand. The repulse might have degenerated into a rout if Davis's division, which Sherman had personally despatched from Thomas's army sector to the extreme right had come up in time to take the broken Confederates in flank. Unfortunately the divisional commander was taken sick, and his deputy led the division by a wrong road.

It was noticeable that even in the first onslaught the Confederates had lost their former élan, and in succeeding attacks some of the troops refused to follow their leaders and the others fought without hope. Indeed, the verdict of the troops on the "will to victory" of their new commander was aptly expressed when to the chaffing question, shouted by a Union picket, "Well, Johnny, how many of you are left," a Confederate across the interval retorted, wearily and grimly, "Oh! about enough for another killing." So great was the moral and material damage that a week later the Confederate President wrote admonishing Hood that "The loss consequent upon attacking him [the enemy] in his entrenchments requires you to avoid that if practicable." It was particularly, and bitterly, amusing that Jefferson Davis should be compelled to apply this check and rebuke, for to his dislike and distrust Johnston's supersession had been primarily due.

After repulsing this third abortive riposte by Hood, Sherman anxiously waited for news of his cavalry, holding his armies ready to exploit its anticipated success. For the idea underlying all his moves was not to shut the enemy up in Atlanta but "to draw the enemy out of Atlanta by threatening the railroad below" (letter to Thomas of July 29). No general ever had a more acute sense of proportioning the end to his means, and he knew that he had not a superiority of force adequate to invest the enemy effectively and safely. Without it he could not hope to enforce their capitulation. But if he could make them let go of the fortress by a threat to their stomach, he might hope to swing inwards against their retreating army while in motion.

At the same time it suited his purpose almost as well if the enemy continued their expensive attacks. Hence, even while awaiting news of the cavalry, he ordered the "utmost activity" on the flanks, so far as it could be done without disturbing his own dispositions for resistance or pursuit. Early on the 29th, he used two of Thomas's divisions, not to extend his line, but to operate as a mobile force against the railroad junction at East Point, while Schofield was to operate similarly from the other side of Atlanta. Sherman's intention, however, was foiled by the excessive caution of the two army commanders. For Howard had "refused," or bent back, his flank so much, instead of extending it towards the railroad, that Thomas was reluctant to let his two divisions go very far beyond the shelter of Howard's entrenched line, and they drew back as soon as they discovered enemy skirmishers astride the road.

On the 31st, Sherman was still without news of his cavalry, except that the discarded Garrard was coming back. Rather than wait longer, he decided to put into operation a project he had formed two days before. After dark next day Garrard's men, dismounted, were slipped into Schofield's trenches, and Schofield's corps began a night march round by the north to the right flank as a preliminary to a thrust against the railroad at East Point. To add weight to the punch, Sherman moved the rest of Palmer's corps to join Davis's division, which was already on the right flank, and placed this corps under Schofield's control so as to ensure a unified direction of the impending thrust. In conjunction with it, Thomas and Howard were to press forward, probing the enemy's defences along the whole front—now about ten miles, and almost doubled in length since July 22. "Any symptoms, however trivial" of a weak point or a weakening of the enemy's strength at any point were to be reported to Sherman, and special observers placed on watch.

Arriving on Howard's right late in the day, August 2, Schofield was about two miles from the railroad.   As a preliminary to his thrust he determined to gain a good jumping-off line next day by forcing his way across the north fork of Utoy Creek, held only by the enemy's skirmishers.   But Baird, of Palmer's corps, hesitated to obey Schofield, and his advance was delayed until late in the afternoon when Sherman came up in person and peremptorily ordered him forward.

Palmer was obstructing the movement to the best of his ability, and spent the 4th in sending complaints to Sherman and Thomas that he was senior in date of commission to Schofield.   Sherman had fixed the attack for daybreak on the 5th, and to accelerate the preparations replied to Palmer, "Co-operate heartily and the same result will be obtained."   But this Palmer refused to do because his dignity was hurt by receiving orders in Schofield's name, and replied to Schofield that he would "not obey either General Sherman's order or yours."   Sherman, meantime, had investigated the claim to seniority, based on a quibbling technicality; when he gave his formal decision that Schofield ranked Palmer the latter, at midnight, reiterated his refusal to comply with orders, and asked to be relieved. Accordingly Johnson, his senior divisional commander, was ordered to take over, but, in passive support to his chief. developed a passive immovability which paralyzed the attack next day.   And past operation had already shown that, with less excuse, Schofield was an easy subject for paralysis.

Sherman caustically suggested to Thomas that Johnson was no better than Palmer, and remarked, "I would prefer to move a rock than move that corps.   On the defensive it would be splendid, but for offensive it is of no use.   It must have a head that will give it life and impulse . . . if an enemy can be seen by a spy-glass the whole corps is halted and intrenched for a siege.   Unless it will attack I must relieve it in orders and state the reason."

His patience had certainly been strained, and he had stretched forbearance so far as to give Palmer two hours to reconsider his refusal and to withdraw his resignation—telling Thomas "I don't want General Palmer to make so fatal a mistake as he seems bent on committing."   And to Palmer he had written, "If you want to resign, wait a few days and allege some other reason—one that will stand the test of time. . . . I again ask you not to disregard the friendly advice of such men as General Thomas and myself, for you cannot misconstrue our friendly feelings toward you."

Palmer, both surprised and touched by this attitude, frankly confessed that in Sherman's place he would have been less tolerant to subordinates who were responsible for the execution of his plans, but still evidently considered that to uphold the sacred rights of seniority was a higher duty than to defeat the enemy. Admirable as was Sherman's kindly restraint, the result might perhaps have been better if he had been more tolerant to those who criticized his plans and less tolerant to those who marred them. He now decided to supersede both Palmer and Johnson, promoting Davis, an able leader, but even then it took four days to obtain sanction from Washington.

The time already frittered away could not be regained. Previous to the attempt the Confederate engineers and working parties had extended their entrenchments south to cover East Point, and when Sherman's menace developed, the delays in its execution gave Hood ample time to extend his troops to occupy and strengthen these works. A further attempt on the 6th to overlap his entrenched flank was repelled and wisely discontinued after the first assault had failed.

Thus blocked again, Sherman felt that he had stretched his lines to the limit of safety, in face of an enemy who held the shorter interior lines. The situation looked unpleasantly like stalemate, and Hood could no longer be tempted even to counter attacks.

Sherman's mind now turned to a fresh and more audacious manœuvre, first indicated in a message to Grant on the 10th— "Since July 28th General Hood has not attempted to meet us outside of his parapets. In order to possess and destroy effectually his communications I may have to leave a corps at the railroad bridge [over the Chattahoochee], well entrenched, and cut loose with the balance and make a desolating circle round Atlanta. I do not propose to assault the works, which are too strong, or to proceed to regular approaches." And the still greater extension of his thought was shown in a letter three days later—"If I should ever be cut off from my base, look out for me about St. Mark's, Fla., or Savannah, Ga.,—here we have a fresh hint of his march to the sea.

Sherman promptly ordered reconnaissances and preparations for the move, and meantime used his heavy rifled guns, just brought up from Chattanooga, to bombard Atlanta with the aim of straining the enemy's morale preparatory to his stroke. But just as he was ready to spring the enemy intervened by a stroke at his communications.

For on the 10th, Wheeler with almost all the Confederate cavalry had moved out on a long-range raid, and from the 13th onwards fragmentary and alarming reports came in over frequently broken telegraph wires of attacks on and cuts in the railroad from Marietta back to Dalton, which Wheeler surrounded on the 14th. Only three days before, Sherman had written to his wife, with just pride and revelation of his mental orientation, that "for one hundred days not a man or horse has been without ample food or a musket or gun without adequate ammunition. I esteem this a triumph greater than any success that has attended me in battle or strategy, but it has not been the result of blind chance. At this moment I have abundant supplies for twenty days, and I keep a construction party in Chattanooga that can in ten days repair any breach that can be made to my rear. I keep a large depot of supplies at Chattanooga and at Atlanta, two mountain fastnesses which no cavalry force of the enemy can reach, and in our wagons generally manage to have from ten to twenty days' supplies."

The news might well seem like Nemesis. Thomas advised him to despatch his own cavalry in pursuit of Wheeler—a rather vain hope. But Sherman, with confidence in his precautions, took a different view. While he decided to postpone the southward manœuvre of his mass until he had a clear idea of the damage which Wheeler might have wrought, his mind leaped to the idea of turning Wheeler's move to his own profit and the enemy's loss.

Prisoners had revealed the severe shortage of supplies and ammunition which the Confederate army in Atlanta was suffering, so that a short delay in his grand manœuvre might even be an advantage in weakening the enemy's grip while a lighter stroke might suffice to loosen it. If the enemy's cavalry was away the main obstacle to his own was removed, so why not use them to sever the enemy's artery and keep his infantry mass ready to strike as the enemy's body dropped down from Atlanta? The trend of his thought is

clearly shown in his instructions of the 17th to continue "preparations, but merely postpone. If the cavalry can do what we can
want, there is no need of moving the whole army."

A further strong incentive to this alternative course was the
great August heat, and his feeling that some of his senior infantry
commanders were not quick or enterprising enough to assure the
fruits of such a bold manœuvre. Indeed, he had candidly said to
Schofield—"I . . . despair of making a quick move. It takes two
days to do what ought to be done in one," and again, when Schofield urged the more cautious strategy of further side-stepping, "We
must act. We cannot sit down to do nothing because it involves a
risk." Sherman's dissatisfaction with the lack of "enterprise" of
some of his commanders was well founded, and it is equally characteristic of his self-exacting realism that when on the 12th he heard
that he had been made a major-general in the regular army as a
reward for his achievements he curtly replied to Washington, "I
would have preferred a delay until the close of the campaign."

Moreover, in adopting the idea of a new cavalry stroke, he fully
realized that this could only succeed if the execution was bold and
energetic. In Kilpatrick he felt that he had one such leader, but
that to tie him to Garrard would make the movement as slow as a
three-legged race. Hence he desired to take a junior colonel named
Long and place him in command of Garrard's division. But this
division belonged to Thomas's army, and Thomas objected to the
change. With delightful satire Sherman replied: "I am willing to
admit that General Garrard's excessive prudence saves his cavalry
to us, but though saved, it is as useless as so many sticks. Saving
himself, he sacrifices others operating in conjoint expeditions. I am
so thoroughly convinced that if he can see a horseman in the distance with a spy-glass he will turn back, that I cannot again depend
on his making an effort. . . . Wheeler is out of the way, and
when shall we use cavalry, if not now? If we wait till Wheeler
returns, of course an opportunity is lost, which never is repeated
in war."

The incubus of seniority again hampered Sherman's desire.
Warned by Thomas that if the division was given to Long without
him being promoted in rank, which would cause delay, there would
be a further trade-union strike among the colonels senior to Long,

Sherman achieved the best partial solution that he could by leaving Garrard in charge of one brigade to demonstrate on the Decatur flank while temporarily detaching his other two brigades under Long to join with Kilpatrick in the real stroke from the other flank. Meantime, Sherman had been remarkably quick and acute to diagnose that Wheeler was aiming for Tennessee. This cleared Sherman's communications, swiftly repaired, back to Chattanooga and relieved him of the anxiety of having only a fortnight's supplies left in hand. He cheerfully reported to Washington—"Wheeler . . . may hurt some of the minor points, but, on the whole, East Tennessee is a good place for him to break down his horses, and a poor place to steal new ones. All well." And to develop his advantage, Sherman concentrated his lines of communication troops, reinforced by McCook's cavalry, to form a barrage against any attempt of Wheeler to return before he had carried out his plan. In the issue Wheeler's departure not only failed to upset Sherman's strategy, but deprived Hood of his mobile arm and eyes during the critical and final phase of the campaign.

For Kilpatrick's stroke Sherman's orders were "It is not a raid, but a deliberate attack for the purpose of so disabling that road that the enemy will be unable to supply his army in Atlanta." On the night of the 18th Kilpatrick's force swung out southward from behind Sherman's front, crossed and broke first the Montgomery railroad near Fairburn and then the Macon railroad near Jonesborough, and on the 22nd reached Decatur, having made a complete circuit round the enemy's rear. Kilpatrick reported that he had broken four consecutive miles of the railroad and ten miles in patches. But boldly and skilfully as the force had been handled, the damage to the railroad was limited by the habitual distaste of the cavalrymen for the hard labour of destruction. Willing enough to engage in a dashing adventure, they scamped the task of fulfilling the thorough Shermanic method of rail twisting. In consequence, although Kilpatrick reported that the railroad was disabled for at least ten days, the Confederates had repaired it within two.

One man at least was not surprised. For, after searching cross-examination of Kilpatrick late on the day of his return, Sherman wired to Washington, "I expect I will have to swing across to that road in force to make the matter certain," and the next day, the

23rd, sent the cryptic message, "Give currency to the idea that I am to remain quiet until events transpire in other quarters, and let the idea be printed so as to reach Richmond in three days. You understand the effect."

He had already warned his commanders that the postponed grand manœuvre would begin on the night of the 25th, half of all baggage being sent to the rear and ten days' rations issued. The actual evacuation of the trenches was carefully graduated, the corps in turn from the left flank slipping out of their trenches behind a curtain of skirmishers, and moving round to gather behind the right flank ready for the spring. Such a withdrawal from close contact with the enemy and move to a flank across his front was a difficult and potentially hazardous operation; it was accomplished with a loss of one man wounded.

．　　．　　．　　．　　．　　．　　．

On August 23 Lincoln wrote and sealed this gloomy prophecy— "It seems exceedingly probable that this administration will not be re-elected. Then it will be my duty to so co-operate with the President-elect as to save the Union between the election and the inauguration, as he will have secured his election on such ground that he cannot possibly save it afterward."

．　　．　　．　　．　　．　　．

By the night of the 27th Howard's army, on the right nearest the Chattahoochee, and Thomas's army (less one corps), in the centre, were assembled facing south-west in the covered corridor between Schofield and the river. The previous night Slocum's corps had been drawn back out of its trenches to a newly entrenched position covering the Chattahoochee railroad bridge.

Early on the 28th the armies of Howard and Thomas began a grand left wheel to the southeast, pivoting on Schofield, and by afternoon were astride the Montgomery railroad between Fairburn and Red Oak—busily destroying it. A pleasant Sunday afternoon.

Hood was truly hoodwinked. On the 26th, he had discovered the movement so far as to telegraph to Richmond, "Last night the enemy abandoned the Augusta railroad, and all the country between that road and the Dalton railroad. . . . He has not extended his right at all." Twenty-four hours later he telegraphed again— "The enemy . . . have drawn back so that their left is now on the

Chattahoochee at the railroad bridge; their right is unchanged . . ."
Hood, indeed, jumped to the conclusion that Wheeler's raid had
so impaired Sherman's communications that the hungry Union army
was giving up the siege and withdrawing across the Chattahoochee
at Sandtown. Even when he discovered in the afternoon of the 28th
that the Montgomery railroad was being destroyed he seems to have
thought that Sherman was only raiding the railroads to cover a
withdrawal—for he merely despatched two brigades down the
Macon railroad to Jonesborough, and three brigades to Rough and
Ready, "all to co-operate with" the available cavalry "in repelling
raids."

Throughout the following day he remained passive, and as late
as 1 P.M. on the 30th did not think it was necessary "to send any
more troops to Jonesborough." At that hour Sherman's whole
force, moving on a six-mile front, had traversed half the interval
between the two railroads. The previous day had been spent by
Howard and Thomas in completing the destruction of the Montgomery line—with the thoroughness that Sherman ordained—
while Schofield evacuated his works and moved into position as the
left wing of the general advance, which was resumed early on
the 30th.

.   .   .   .

On August 29 the Democratic national convention, nominating
McClellan as its Presidential candidate, adopted the following
resolution—"After four years of failure to restore the Union by
the experiment of war . . . humanity, liberty, and the public welfare demand that immediate efforts be made for a cessation of
hostilities . . ." The significance of the resolution, whatever quali-
fying phrases might be used, was unmistakable in view of Jefferson
Davis's blunt declaration nine days earlier that "I shall at any time
be pleased to receive proposals for peace on the basis of your Independence. It will be useless to approach me with any other."

.   .   .   .

Not until 6 P.M. on the 30th—when Sherman's advance, after
another partial left-wheel, was within three miles of the Macon
railroad—did Hood allow his importunate and keener sighted subordinate to move his corps direct to Jonesborough, directing Lee
to follow down the railroad with his corps from around East Point.

Between East Point and Jonesborough the railroad made a sharp bend to the east following the line of the watershed between the confluents of the Flint and Ocmulgee Rivers. Sherman's immediate aim was to get his forces onto the railroad edge and into the triangle thus formed, so that he would, for a change, have the advantage of a central position, with the Confederates forced to move round the outside if they gave up Atlanta and sought either to retreat or strike at him.

When darkness intervened, the Union right wing was within a mile of Jonesborough, after sharp skirmishing, but the centre, although having a shorter distance to travel, had not come so close to the railroad, reporting the enemy to be in strong force and entrenched to cover it. The left, or pivot wing, had made but a narrow move to face East Point from the south, and then entrenched itself to cover the exposed inner flank of the wheeling line. Sherman had been with Thomas's army in the centre, and a remark to Howard next day clearly shows his dissatisfaction with its rate of progress—"I cannot move the troops 100 yards without their stopping to entrench, though I have not seen any enemy." For next morning, Sherman ordered a bold advance against the railroad, his idea being that once astride it his left wing and centre should turn south down the railroad, destroying it as they went, and close on his right wing near Jonesborough. Thus at the furthest point from the enemy he would be able to place himself comfortably astride their line of retreat with his arms outstretched to embrace them.

But at midday on the 31st, he received a message from Howard, sent three hours earlier, telling him that the enemy appeared to be concentrating for an attack. This seemed to Sherman to indicate that Hood had already left Atlanta and was facing him afresh; to ascertain the accuracy of this deduction he sent orders for Slocum "to feel forward to Atlanta as boldly as he can." If Hood had really slipped out of Atlanta, Sherman decided that he himself would swing out and in again below Jonesborough. It was characteristic of him that he instantaneously conceived Griffin, more than twenty miles below Jonesborough, as his next objective point on the railroad, whereas Thomas, a few hours later, suggested Lovejoy's station, seven miles below.

Meantime the enemy had obligingly launched yet another of their costly and vain counter-attacks. For this, Hardee used his own corps, temporarily placed under Cleburne, and Lee's corps. It was well-directed but ill-co-ordinated. For while it threw two strong corps against the Union right wing, the late arrival of Lee's corps caused a delay until three o'clock in the afternoon, giving Howard ample time to entrench in readiness, and then Lee's corps attacked prematurely before the other corps had arrived on the Union flank. Thus, both were repulsed and Lee's corps, suffering heavy loss, suffered excessive moral damage from its abortive effort.

The next step, however, was a move by Hood so incalculably irrational that it served to disconcert Sherman's plan—although rather through the effect on his subordinates' minds than on his own. For at 6 P.M. Hood, without awaiting news of the fight at Jonesborough, ordered Lee's corps to be sent back to Atlanta during the night, to help in resisting an attack on the place which he believed to be imminent. It is evident that he was still blind to the reality of Sherman's manœuvre, and thought that the Union forces near Jonesborough were only a detachment to divert attention from a main thrust against Atlanta. An order issued by his chief of staff, calling back the cavalry also, said "Sherman faces Atlanta from the west, crossing the Chattahoochee at Sandtown."

Hardee was given the detached mission of protecting Macon, so that instead of being tied to his ground to protect a general retreat south, he was encouraged to make an early and separate retreat. Fearful of the consequences to the main army, he telegraphed next morning, September 1, a protest to Jefferson Davis at Richmond, only to receive the rebuke, obviously based on Hood's information, "The enemy's movement is to gain Atlanta; we must endeavour to defeat his purpose. . . . If you can beat the detachment in front of you, and then march to join Hood, entire success might be hoped to result from the division which the enemy have made from his force." It is useful to note that while Hardee could communicate by telegraph with distant Richmond he was now cut off from Hood except by messengers, through the wires being cut along the railroad.

In contrast to Hood's delusion of a massed attack on Atlanta from the west, Sherman's army was closing in against Hardee at Jonesborough during the 1st. The previous afternoon his left and left-centre corps, Schofield's and Stanley's, had reached the railroad south of Rough and Ready, and, with the assurance that at least two of the three enemy corps were at Jonesborough, Sherman ordered his left and centre to turn south on the 1st, converging at Jonesborough. To ensure co-operation and eliminate friction, he had requested Schofield to waive the precedence due to his complimentary status as an army commander, and to take instructions during the combined movements from Stanley, who was his senior in date as a major-general.

But to Sherman's exasperation, Stanley merely sat on the railroad until late in the afternoon, awaiting a definite order from Thomas—in disregard of Sherman's emphatic instructions. Bitingly, Sherman wrote to Thomas that evening, "Now he (the enemy) has time to fortify. . . . If General Stanley lost a minute of time when he should have been in action, I beg you will not overlook it, as it concerns the lives of our men and the success of our arms."

The effect of Stanley's delay was that only a single corps was available before dark for a blow against the northern flank of the enemy facing Howard. This corps was Davis's, which had been guarding the trains in rear. While it was being hurried forward, Sherman, who met it, was impatiently sending first one and then another of his staff to hasten Stanley's arrival, finally despatching Thomas himself—"The only time during the campaign I can recall seeing General Thomas urge his horse into a gallop." Rather than lose the precious interval before darkness intervened, Davis was launched to the attack about 4 P.M., while Howard demonstrated against the enemy's works in his front and began moving Blair's corps round towards the enemy's rear. Despite an initial check, Davis's men carried the trenches covering the enemy's northern flank and captured nearly a thousand prisoners, but nightfall then intervened. If Howard's demonstration was not converted into a serious assault it should be remembered that two of the enemy's corps were thought to be confronting him—Thomas, indeed, was convinced that all three were there.

For the next day, Sherman ordered a double envelopment and triple attack on the enemy at Jonesborough. Thomas's army, now reunited, was to press south down the railroad; Schofield round the east, and Howard, round the west, were to press in from the flanks. To these wing armies he said, "I don't see any reason why the enemy should elect to hold Jonesborough defensively, as we have broken his road, so if you find him entrenched don't assault, but feel below the town. . . . But if fighting occurs, or you have a chance to attack, the orders are always to attack. We don't care about Jonesborough, but we want to destroy our enemy."

But the chance of immediate results had passed in the morning. Hardee, profiting from the Union delay on the 1st, had retired from his gravely menaced position at Jonesborough during the night and fallen back to a fresh entrenched position at Lovejoy's station. In view of his "detached" orders from Hood, there was no purpose in staying. Thus Sherman had to follow thither before he could again attempt to fold in his outstretched wings for a deathly embrace of Hardee.

But daylight had brought a greater change in the situation than merely the discovery of Hardee's retreat. Instead of sleeping, Sherman had spent the night in restless impatience, hourly expecting news of Slocum's reconnaissance at Atlanta—news which would have to be brought circuitously by messenger. Soon after midnight Sherman heard explosions from the direction of distant Atlanta, and these were repeated a little later. Did they mean an evacuation of the town, or had Slocum been trapped into a battle, perhaps against superior numbers? The situation was truly enveloped in the fog of war. In this anxious uncertainty Sherman took the wise course of adhering to his original purpose and orders, to concentrate on the enemy facing him, of whose whereabouts at least he was certain. But before daylight he gave orders that Garrard's cavalry which was in rear, as usual, should feel northward towards Atlanta to discover the situation there. And when daylight revealed the retirement of his immediate opponents, he posted Davis's corps to cover the rear of his advance south in pursuit of them.

Now, changing sides, let us look at the situation from Hood's viewpoint. When he had summoned Lee's corps back to Atlanta on the evening of the 31st, he was still ignorant of the result of Hardee's counterstroke. Not apparently until midnight did he hear of its disastrous repulse. This meant that he was cut off from the main railroad, his only line of supply, as also from his trains which he had previously sent south to Jonesborough for safety.

To hold Atlanta was no longer possible, bitter as the shock of having to yield it, and when morning revealed that his idea of Sherman's direct approach to Atlanta was an illusion he hurriedly made preparations to abandon the city. Lee was halted midway on his road back, ready to cover the withdrawal of Stewart's corps and the Georgia militia, and after nightfall on the 1st the retreat began, a rearguard staying to destroy, with incomplete success, the locomotives and ordnance material—the explosions which Sherman heard. Hearing them also, Slocum had pushed forward at daylight, and occupied the town, but his message did not reach Sherman until very late, and it was not until six o'clock next morning that Sherman sent to Washington the despatch which contained the ringing sentence, soon immortalized, "So Atlanta is ours and fairly won."

Whatever Hood's failure previously, the Confederate retreat was carried out with its usual skill. The bulk of their force marched by a wide circuit to the south-east through McDonough and once past Sherman's flank turned westward to join Hardee at Lovejoy's station, where it arrived during the night of the 2nd and the morning of the 3rd. A smaller part had withdrawn from East Point round the other flank.

Garrard was not the cavalry leader to obtain early information or to harass the enemy's retreat effectively, and a regiment pushed out to the McDonough road only arrived in time to discover the enemy's rearguard, whereupon it kept at a discreet distance. On the other flank Kilpatrick, who was covering the southern advance of Howard's army, reported at 4.30 P.M. that a column was passing outside him, too strongly protected for him to break through the flank screen, but his report was not received until after dark. This mattered little, for the enemy's night retreat had carried him so far towards safety that unless his columns had been located early in the morning they could not have been intercepted.

Sherman came quickly to the impression that the whole of the enemy army was now south of him, but in the faint hope of intercepting any remaining part, sent Schofield orders, at 8 P.M., to feel out to the McDonough road next morning, adding, "If he gives you a fair chance punish him." He supplemented this by another message at 11.20 P.M.—"What I want to know is, is the stand made at Lovejoy's a pre-arranged thing or a mere accident. If the latter, a junction should be prevented; if the former, it demonstrates a more formidable position than its mere appearance would indicate . . . try to prevent or delay a concentration of the rebel army in our front. Nothing positive from Atlanta, and that bothers me."

The morning reconnaissances brought clear information that the enemy's tail was moving to Lovejoy's station, and was too close to the shelter of Hardee's entrenched position for interception. Sherman promptly decided to discontinue his offensive, and his reasons are indicated in his despatch to Washington early on the 4th—"His [Hood's] position is too strong to attack in front, and to turn it would carry me too far from my base at this time. Besides, there is no commensurate object, as there is no valuable point to his rear till we reach Macon, 103 miles from Atlanta. We are not prepared for that, and I will gradually fall back and occupy Atlanta, which was our grand objective point already secured." It was an eminently wise decision, calculating end and means; at the best a continued advance would only press Hood further back, as there was no objective of such value as to make him hold on, and at the worst a continued advance with depleted forces and extending lines of communication would give Hood the chance for a counterstroke more effective than hitherto.

Hood's army was more seriously reduced than Sherman's by the abortive counterstrokes into which Sherman's manœuvres had lured it, but Sherman's had been weakened by a drain which Hood did not suffer. More than a month before, Sherman had been feeling this drain, as a letter to his wife on August 2 shows—"This army is much reduced in strength by . . . expiration of service. It looks hard to see regiments march away when their time is up. On the other side they have everybody, old and young, and for indefinite periods. . . . No recruits are coming [to me], for the draft is not until September." Actually, no less than twenty regiments had left for home and discharge by the end of August, and forty-three had necessarily been dropped to guard the communications.

Sherman might feel disappointment that he had only damaged and not broken up the Confederate army, but the capture of Atlanta, the goal uppermost in his mind from the outset, was more than a consolation. Even its military and economic importance as a great munition centre and the nodal point of the radii of communications in Georgia was a minor value in comparison to its moral value. When Sherman had declared that "its capture would be the death-knell of the Confederacy" his vision was more prophetic than was commonly appreciated. For if the effect on the South, although a severe moral blow, did not fully justify the prophecy, the effect on the North did. By reviving the hope of victory it revived the national will to victory, and this was fatal to the South.

In the popular enthusiasm created by the news of this tangible achievement, a sign-post clearer than any capture of prisoners, public and political opinion rallied in support of Lincoln, with the force and volume almost of a landslide, while the draft to fill the deficiency of volunteers came into effect on September 6 with scarcely an objection. Within a few weeks Lincoln's re-election was a certainty, and its confirmation by vote on November 8 only a formality. Sherman had saved Lincoln, and by saving him sealed the fate of the South.

Viewed purely as a military feat, Sherman's advance to, and capture of, Atlanta would earn him a permanent niche in the hall of fame. Although tied for his supplies to a single line of railroad, stretching out ever longer and more precariously, he had advanced one hundred and thirty miles through difficult and poorly mapped country in face of a stubborn and skilful foe little his inferior in strength, and had wrested from the enemy army the nodal point which it had been ordered above all to safeguard.

Although tied to a direct line of strategic approach he had manoeuvred so skilfully within the limits thus imposed on him as to gain each of the stepping stones on his way to the goal, and finally the goal itself, without committing his troops to a direct attack save once—at Kenesaw. And even that had been based on the calculation that it would be psychologically indirect, because of the suddenness of the change from his previous practice.

In contrast, the enemy army had been constrained twice during Johnston's tenure and four times during Hood's to throw themselves in vain assaults on the key positions in which Sherman's manoeuvres had placed him. And from each enemy failure to pierce his mobile shield Sherman had drawn the advantage of a fresh step forward.

An advantage not merely logistical but moral, for each had heartened his own troops while depressing both the enemy troops and the enemy public. As his men gained confidence in the invincibility of their progress, so the enemy acquired the hopeless sense of its irresistibility. Thus by manœuvre to draw an opponent acting on the strategic defensive into a series of costly tactical offensives, and at the same time to maintain an almost continuous progress, was a triumph of strategic artistry which of its kind is without parallel in history.

The report of the Medical Director of the Confederate army, which is certainly a minimum estimate and takes account only of wounded receiving treatment, returns the losses of the three Confederate infantry corps in the principal engagements up to Johnston's removal as 9,972 killed and wounded. During Hood's period of command, up to September 1, the killed and wounded in the same three corps are given as 11,816. The total is thus 21,788, to which must be added 12,983 prisoners taken by the Union forces—a grand total of 34,771. But as the total of dead reported as buried by the Union troops was more than double that given in the Confederate Medical Director's return, there is a strong suspicion that his total is an underestimate.

The total loss in Sherman's armies, similarly excluding cavalry, during the whole period from the beginning of May to the end of September is given in the Adjutant-General's return as 30,345 killed, wounded and missing (mostly prisoners). Making due allowance for a similar incompleteness in the returns, it is reasonably established that the loss of the side which was on the strategic offensive and reached its goal was actually less than that of the opposing side.

Impeccable security and economy of manœuvre were, indeed, the keynotes of Sherman's advance. Security, though of an active and not a passive type, may sometimes have been carried too far, with consequent loss of opportunity. Sherman's problem was not only to drive the enemy but to drive his own team, which included some slow horses. A study of the campaign amply confirms the shrewd judgment of Thomas's fellow cadets at West Point when they bestowed on him the nickname "Old Slow-Trot." As for Schofield, perhaps Sherman's private comment (recorded by Hitchcock), "Has large brain—larger than Thomas, but not so much the confidence of the troops," contains the explanation why Schofield, though bold in conception, sometimes appears slower still in execution. And although there were dashing subordinate leaders the average of talent was not as high as in the Confederate army. Nevertheless, their extreme caution must be viewed in the light of the fact that they were constantly engaged in offensive manœuvre, not in passive resistance, and must be weighed against the fact that no real opening was ever given to skilful and thrustful opponents. Above all, they never committed the folly of throwing their own weight into an assault on an enemy firmly in position. A good tribute and still better appreciation, was rendered to Thomas when, on a later occasion, Sherman remarked, "I wish old Tom was here! He's my off-wheel horse and knows how to pull with me, though he don't pull in the same way."

But between Sherman and his chief subordinates there was a subtle difference of outlook on the question of security. Equally careful to avoid the vain luxury of a direct attack, an indulgence most common among generals throughout history, he realized that the truest economy—productive economy—of force can only be obtained by taking calculated risks, and that mobility is the best insurance against them exceeding calculation. Hence he was ever desirous to push vigorously except against entrenchments, which cannot be pushed. His best results had come from movements on a wide front, and the only justifiable criticism against his generalship during the last phase of the Atlanta campaign is that still better results might have come if he had extended still wider, especially on the morning of September 2nd. Had he opened out his net after discovering Hardee's retreat it is unlikely that he would have intercepted any of the Confederate columns, for they had only to continue eastward for McDonough to be out of reach. But he might have prevented them reuniting with Hardee, and so have been able to close in his net again around Hardee. Even so it was only a chance, and a risk, in a situation that was perplexingly vague, and with a quarry in his front who had no longer any reason for staying to be netted. The best chance of netting Hardee had been, and been missed on the 1st, and no commander could have done more to stimulate the slow footsteps of his subordinates—even to converting a stout army commander into a galloping galloper.

CHAPTER XIX

THE BIRTH OF A PLAN

AFTER the fall of Atlanta Sherman's first step was to make his new base secure. With this purpose he made a breach with precedent as drastic as his action, of which he had given notice to Washington on September 4—"I propose to remove all the inhabitants of Atlanta. . . . If the people raise a howl against my barbarity and cruelty I will answer that war is war, and not popularity seeking. If they want peace they and their relatives must stop war." They could go south or north as they preferred, but go they must, for Sherman had seen and suffered too long the drain of strength due to garrisoning captured towns. Although on April 30 there were 207,000 troops in his territorial command, the Military Division of the Mississippi, he had been able to draw only half for his advance on Atlanta. For the larger the town, the larger the population, the larger the garrison required, the larger the area for it to control, the larger the chance for the larger proportion of potential spies and guerrillas, and so the larger consequent increase of the garrison to cope with them—truly a largening vicious circle. If this scale of garrisoning was to be continued as the Union advance progressed, the spearhead would soon be reduced to a pin-point. The *reductio ad absurdum* was apparent to Sherman's logical mind, and he unhesitatingly took the only possible remedy—a reduction of the cause.

Directly Sherman reached Atlanta he wrote to his enemy telling him of the decision, and asking him to provide transport from Rough and Ready to the other broken end of the railroad at Love-joy's. "If you consent, I will undertake to remove all the families . . . who prefer to go south to Rough and Ready, with all their movable effects . . . with their servants, white and black, with the proviso that no force shall be used towards the blacks." He suggested a two days' truce for the transfer.

In accepting the proposal, Hood concluded thus: "And now, sir, permit me to say that the unprecedented measure you propose transcends, in studied and ingenious cruelty, all acts ever before brought to my attention in the dark history of war. In the name of God and humanity, I protest . . ." However distressing for the citizens to quit their homes instead of remaining to be a target for shells in case of siege, Hood's remark confirms the witness of his place on the West Point graduation list and of his strategy—that his knowledge of the history of war was somewhat shallow!

His letter drew a lengthy reply from Sherman, replete with counter-charges. Its neatest thrust was that the Confederates "should scorn to commit their wives and children to the rude barbarians who thus, as you say, violate the laws of war, as illustrated in the pages of its dark history." Its most prophetic—"Talk thus to the marines, but not to me . . . who will . . . make as much sacrifice for the peace and the honor of the South as the best-born Southerner among you!" Its most sensible, "In the name of commonsense . . . if we must be enemies, let us be men, and fight it out as we propose to do, and not deal in such hypocritical appeals to God and humanity." Its weakest, the complaint that "you defended Atlanta on a line so close to the town that every cannon-shot . . . that overshot their mark, went into the habitations of women and children." For on approaching Atlanta Sherman had given orders that "If fired on from the forts or buildings of Atlanta no consideration must be paid to the fact that they are occupied by families, but they must be cannonaded without the formality of a demand."

Hood promptly retorted with a letter of thrice the length and irrelevancy, relieved by the one shrewd shot—"I have too good an opinion . . . of the skill of your artillerists, to credit the insinuation that they for several weeks unintentionally fired too high for my modest fieldwork. . . ." But he badly misfired when he accused Sherman of using negroes as allies, for Sherman had drawn on himself the wrath of many Northern politicians by his stubborn refusal to accept black regiments.

Sherman's next letter was short and hit Hood in a weak spot— "I was not bound by the laws of war to give notice of the shelling of Atlanta, a fortified town, with magazines, arsenals, foundries, and public stores; You were bound to take notice. See the books. That is the conclusion of our correspondence, which I did not begin, and terminate with satisfaction."

To similar protests from the Mayor and Council of Atlanta, he replied in memorable terms: "You cannot qualify war in harsher terms than I will. War is cruelty and you cannot refine it; and those who brought war into our country deserve all the curses and maledictions a people can pour out. I know I had no hand in making this war, and I know I will make more sacrifice to-day than any of you to secure peace. But you cannot have peace and a division too. If the United States submits to a division now it will not stop . . . until we reap the fate of Mexico, which is eternal war." Apart from the prophetic vision of the last phrase, the second contains the nearest recorded words to the saying which all know who hardly know the name of Sherman—"War is hell." Earlier still at Jackson he had used the words "War is barbarism," and the theme was so constantly in his mind and on his lips that he may well have used the more "historic" phrase in informal addresses. He gave enough to gatherings of his old soldiers after the war to incline us to accept the testimony of his hearers that he did. And he could hardly have done otherwise, for he had an artistic sense of phrase-making combined with a love of clothing an unvarying theme with ever-varying raiment.

But for all his stern logic, Sherman refined the actual conduct of the evacuation in such a way as to receive the grateful acknowledgments of those who suffered it. So far as a deportation could be humane this was, establishing a precedent which later deportations have not maintained.

Then he could breathe freely, the operations of his mind as well as of his army unfettered. For a letter to his wife suggests that his "military necessity" was a welcome relief to his masculinity—"by next Wednesday the town will be a real military town with no women boring me every order I give."

He had not forgotten his trials at Memphis, where he had at first wasted much time and paper in trying to appeal to the reason of charitably or enthusiastically inclined ladies of influence who sought to influence him, until he had lapsed from the reply courteous to the reply curt. Allied with his dislike of feminine interference was that, which he classed with it, of the voluntary aid societies who pressed their services upon him. Some of his pungent comments are famous. Thus, at the start of his Atlanta campaign when, as previously related, he had banned all civil usage of the railroad in order to pile up supplies at railhead, he had been requested to make an exception for the delegates and tracts of the United States Christian Commission. The moment was distinctly inauspicious, and the reply decisive—"Certainly not, crackers and oats are more necessary to my mind than any moral or religious agency." Evidently they did not cease their importunity, for when, on crossing the Chattahoochee, he was informed that civilian recruiting agents were to be sent to accompany him, he replied to Washington—"I must express my opinion that it is the height of folly. . . . The Sanitary and Christian Commissions are enough to eradicate all traces of Christianity out of our minds, must less a set of unscrupulous State agents in search of recruits."

To send recruiting agents to such a staunch Confederate State as Georgia certainly seems an apt practical definition of a "forlorn hope" and of "useless mouths." But the real core of Sherman's grievance was that they were to be State agents and not United States agents—thus accentuating the very division which was anathema to him. He soon found an opportunity of enforcing his vital principle, for, having authorized the admittance to Atlanta of a branch of the United States Sanitary Commission, he discovered one day an additional distributing store with the sign "Indiana State Sanitary Agent" hung out in front. He summarily closed it and seized the goods for general distribution, replying to agitated protests from Washington that he "hadn't any *Indiana* army down there but only a U. S. army," that he "wasn't going to have any man come there to make distinctions" among his men, and that he "wouldn't have one man nursed because he was from Indiana and his next neighbor left to long and pine for what *he* couldn't get" because he came from another State.

The completion of his campaign had sealed Sherman's confidence in himself, and although submissive as ever to the superior authority of Lincoln and Grant, he would be gainsaid by none others. Yet there is ample evidence that if his head rose higher it did not swell. His congratulatory address to his troops after the fall of Atlanta is a singularly modest specimen of such documents in the Civil War. The only approach to a boast was that "The crossing of the Chatta-hoochee and the breaking of the Augusta railroad was most handsomely executed by us, and will be studied as an example in the art of war"—and this was a just boast. Moreover, the dominant and concluding note was loftily simple—"I ask all to continue, as they have so well begun, the cultivation of the soldierly virtues that have ennobled our own and other countries—courage, patience, obedience to the laws . . . fidelity to our trusts, and good feeling among each other, each trying to excel the other in the practice of these high qualities—and it will then require no prophet to foretell that our country will in time emerge from this war, purified by the fires of war."

Sherman's confidence was of the type which is born of accomplished facts, not of mere conceit of his own qualities, and such a type of confidence prevents the possessor losing sight of his own defects however great his surprised satisfaction at his own achievements. Charming instances of this had been his comment on McPherson—"He is as good an officer as I am—is younger, and has a better temper"—and his lament "Oh! that poor Willy could have lived to take all that was good of me in name, character, and standing, and learn to avoid all that is captious, eccentric and wrong." So now on the morrow of his capture of Atlanta he revealed himself in a personal letter to Halleck—"I had allowed myself in 1861 to sink into a perfect 'slough of despond,' and do believe if I could I would have run away and hid from the dangers and complications that surrounded us. You . . . opened to us the first avenue of success and hope, and . . . put me in the way of recovering from what might have proved an ignoble end. When Grant spoke of my promotion as a major-general of the regular army, I asked him to decline in my name till this campaign tested us. Even when my commission came, which you were kind enough to send, I doubted its wisdom, but now that I have taken Atlanta as much by strategy as by force, I suppose the military world will approve it." How rare the generals who would have made that distinction!

Because he retained his balance he was equally resolute in spurning the first of many suggestions that he should aspire to a sphere for which he knew himself as unfitted, and true to himself in his rebuff of it. Its nature is indicated in this same letter to Halleck wherein he speaks of the nominations for the approaching Presidential election—"The phases of 'Democracy' are strange indeed.

Some fool seems to have used my name. If forced to choose between the penitentiary and the White House for four years . . . I would say the penitentiary, thank you, sir. . . . I doubt if I could have patience or prudence enough to preserve a decent restraint on myself, but would insult the nation in my reply. . . . We as soldiers best fulfill our parts by minding our own business." Here he was at least consistent both in thought and phrase, for a decade before he had refused the Democratic nomination for the post of City Treasurer at San Francisco with the unpalatably apt remark that he was ineligible because he had not "graduated at the Penitentiary," and now, in recalling this incident to his wife, he added, "I would receive a sentence to be hung and damned with infinitely more composure than to be the executive of this nation."

There was, however, an irony which he failed to realize in his remark about "minding his own business" as a soldier, for that was quite beyond his power or inclination. His incapacity to keep himself within those narrow limits was, indeed, the secret of his genius as a grand strategist, and the source of his worst trials as a soldier. Sharpest irony of all, it guided him to the supreme decision of his life and of the war—the choice of his next move.

This move, indeed, was no sudden inspiration, but rather the fulfilment of a purpose that had long previously taken form in his mind—although in an elastic form, ready to adapt to circumstances. It had taken form before he even began his spring campaign, according to the evidence of Colonel Warner, who reported for duty, as inspector-general, on the opening day, May 5. After Sherman had explained the outline of his plan, aiming at the capture of Atlanta, Warner somewhat dubiously remarked that if and when the army reached there it would be 450 miles from its real base of supplies, dependent on a single railroad, and that to protect this line would absorb the whole army. He asked what Sherman proposed to do then. "Stopping short in his walk and snapping the ashes off his cigar in a quick, nervous way he replied in two words—'Salt water.' I did not comprehend his meaning, but after a little further examination of the map I asked him if he meant Savannah or Charleston, and he said 'yes.'"

While this audacious conception had taken root in Sherman's mind, he hoped that the original plan of a conjoint move from

Alabama might be revived, as such double pressure seemed to promise the full profit with a minimum of risk. Hence on gaining Atlanta he had lost no time in renewing this proposal.

In his telegram of September 4 to Halleck, announcing his intention to fall back from Lovejoy's and occupy Atlanta, he had suggested that when the new draft arrived he should co-operate with General Canby, Banks's successor at New Orleans, in a convergent move on Columbus, a hundred miles south of Atlanta down the Chattahoochee, and then use this place as a base for a fresh move eastward into the heart of Georgia.

On the 10th he had a brief telegram from Grant with a rather different trend—"Now that we have all of Mobile Bay that is valuable, I do not know but it will be the best move to transfer Canby's troops to act upon Savannah, whilst you move to Augusta." In his reply, Sherman said: "I do not see that we can afford to operate farther, dependent on the railroad. . . . Macon is distant 103 miles and Augusta 175 miles. . . . If you can manage to take the Savannah River as high as Augusta or the Chattahoochee as far up as Columbus, I can sweep the whole State of Georgia."

But the outlook underwent a further change. For in a letter of September 12, and by the staff officer who bore it, Grant informed Sherman that Canby had his hands full in coping with fresh Confederate movements west of the Mississippi, adding: "What you are to do with the forces at your command, I do not exactly see. The difficulties of supplying your army. . . . I plainly see." Inviting suggestions from Sherman Grant then told him that his own intention was to wait until his army was restored to strength by an inflow of recruits and convalescents, and then to continue working round to the south of Petersburg. At the same time, however, a small expeditionary force would be sent down the coast of North Carolina to combine with the Navy in closing the entrance to the important port of Wilmington—as had already been done by Admiral Farragut, on August 5, at Mobile on the Gulf.

Sherman, in his reply of September 20, immediately fastened on to the Wilmington suggestion. "If successful, I suppose that Fort Caswell will be occupied, and the fleet at once sent to the Savannah River. Then the reduction of that city is the next question. If once in our possession, and the river open to us, I would not hesitate to cross the State of Georgia with sixty thousand men, hauling some stores, and depending on the country for the balance. Where a million people find subsistance my army won't starve; but, as you know, in a country like Georgia, with few roads and innumerable streams, an inferior force can so delay an army and harass it, that it will not be a formidable object; but if the enemy knew that we had our boats in the Savannah River I could rapidly move to Milledgeville, where there is abundance of corn and meat, and could so threaten Macon and Augusta that the enemy would doubtless give up Macon for Augusta; then I would move so as to interpose between Augusta and Savannah, and force him to give us Augusta, with the only powder-mills and factories remaining in the South, or [to] let me have the use of the Savannah River. Either horn of the dilemma will be worth a battle. I would prefer his holding Augusta (as the probabilities are); for then, with the Savannah River in our possession, the taking of Augusta will be a mere matter of time."

The Atlanta Campaign had brought Sherman's strategical mind to maturity, deepening his grasp of the truths that the way to success is strategically along the line of least expectation, and tactically along the line of least resistance, and that the general can best achieve the coincidence of the two by taking a line which provides a duality of objective—so that he has the baffling and unnerving power of being able to "sell the dummy" to his opponent, or, as Sherman put it, has his opponent on the horns of a dilemma. The conception of a single objective, and its unswerving pursuit are contrary to the very nature of war, and lead commonly to the impalement of oneself. In contrast, a duality of objective assures the essential elasticity whereby a commander can not only confuse and deceive his opponent but assure himself the opportunity of penetrating the opponent's guard and achieving at least one of his alternative ends. And Sherman's successive campaigns in Georgia and the Carolinas were to show that by his elasticity of plan he could even ensure that he gained in turn the objectives that he most desired.

The phrase "either horn of a dilemma will be worth a battle" is as true as any of Napoleon's much quoted maxims, and more universal a truth than the majority. In the Atlanta campaign Sherman had suffered, as he realized, by having only one geographical objective, and thereby simplified the task of his opponent in blocking his manœuvres. This limitation he now planned most ingeniously to avoid in his next campaign.

His letter then crystallized his ideas into a definite plan embracing all the armies—"The more I study the game, the more am I convinced that it would be wrong for us to penetrate further into Georgia without an objective beyond. . . . I will therefore give it as my opinion that your army and Canby's should be reinforced to the maximum; that, after you get Wilmington, you should strike for Savannah and its river; that General Canby should hold the Mississippi River, and send a force to take Columbus . . . ; that I should keep Hood employed and put my army in fine order for a march on Augusta, Columbia, and Charleston [i.e., the Atlantic coast] ; and start as soon as Wilmington is sealed to commerce, and the city of Savannah is in our possession."

He considered that the Confederate movements west of the Mississippi were "mere diversions" and that Canby's force should not be wasted in pursuit of them, but turned into the more profitable channel to Georgia. "The possession of the Savannah River is more than fatal to the possibility of Southern independence. They may stand the fall of Richmond, but not of all Georgia"—now the granary of the South since its severance from the Western States. "If you can whip Lee and I can march to the Atlantic, I think Uncle Abe will give us a twenty days' leave of absence to see the young folks."

Here Sherman had traced the complete circle of the plan he was soon to fulfil, but with one segment different. This segment was that before he jumped Grant should stretch out a hand to meet him and steady him as he alighted—by securing Savannah and the Savannah River. The hazard of this jump, away from his supplies, would thus be reduced to a minimum. But in the outcome Sherman was to cover the entire circle which he had traced. And it was the enemy who made it possible at a reduced risk, by throwing open the door. Sherman saw and seized the opportunity.

The first act in this vital change occurred two days before he had written his letter to Grant. For Hood then began to shift his army from Lovejoy's on the Macon railroad to Palmetto on the

Montgomery railroad, and his base from Macon to West Point, on the Chattahoochee. He was now south-west instead of south-east, of Atlanta and Sherman, and his intention was, as soon as he had accumulated supplies, to cross the Chattahoochee and move to Powder Springs, west of Marietta, as a menace to Sherman's communications.

On September 22, Jefferson Davis, who had himself hastened to Georgia in his bitter distress at the loss of Atlanta, delivered at Macon a fiery speech which gave Sherman sufficient clue to deduce Hood's intention—in another, six days later, he assured the people of Georgia that Sherman would be forced to quit Atlanta, "And when that day comes the fate that befell the Army of the French Empire in its retreat from Moscow will be re-acted." Unfortunately for his prophecy and his policy, Sherman chose to quit in the opposite direction.

On the 24th, the inimitable Forrest reappeared on the Tennessee River with a cavalry force from Mississippi, and frightened the garrison of Athens into surrender. Sherman had already sent a division back to Chattanooga and now ordered the despatch of another (Corse's) to Rome as an additional guard to the line of the Etowah. In reporting to Washington this apparent move of Hood, he said, "If I were sure that Savannah would soon be in our possession, I should be tempted to march for Milledgeville and Augusta; but I must first secure what I have." He was beginning to think of anticipating the outstretched hand. Next day he received a telegram from Grant—"It will be better to drive Forrest out of Middle Tennessee as a first step and do anything else you may feel your force sufficient for. When a movement is made on any part of the seacoast I will advise you. . . ." Sherman in reply urged that a reserve force should be built up at Nashville, and on the 28th heard from Grant that "I have directed all recruits and new troops from all the Western States to be sent to Nashville, to receive their further orders from you."

The Confederate movement came at a highly inconvenient moment for Sherman, as his forces had been further depleted by the discharge of time-expired regiments and veteran furloughs, while two of his best corps commanders, Logan and Blair, had gone home temporarily to take part in the presidential election campaign. On the 29th he sent another division back to Chattanooga, and Thomas to Nashville, to take charge of the safeguarding of Tennessee. At the same time he notified Cox, temporarily in Schofield's place, to prepare for a counter movement from Atlanta to the south and east.

Now certain that Hood was crossing the Chattahoochee westwards, Sherman crystallized his plan—one that should not merely counter Hood's plan, but turn it to Sherman's advantage. On October 1 he wired to Grant, "If he tries to get on our road, this side of the Etowah, I shall attack him; but if he goes to the Selma-Talledega road [i.e., to Alabama for a move against the Tennessee], why will it not do to leave Tennessee to the forces which Thomas has, and the reserves soon to come to Nashville, and for me to destroy Atlanta and march across Georgia to Savannah and Charleston, breaking roads and doing irreparable damage? We cannot remain on the defensive." The great project was now unfolded in full bloom. He communicated it in still more definite terms to his chief subordinates, including Thomas, telling the latter to "hurry down to Nashville the reserves ordered by Grant."

But during the 2nd reports came pouring in of threatening Confederate approaches to the railroad between Marietta and Allatoona, and on the 3rd Sherman began to move his army back across the Chattahoochee, leaving Slocum's corps to guard Atlanta and the bridge. Hood was then near Dallas, having sent Stewart's corps to break the railroad north of Marietta, and Stewart in turn sent a division to attack Allatoona, himself falling back to rejoin Hood on the 5th.

Sherman's weak cavalry, sent ahead, found the enemy on the railroad near Big Shanty, failing as usual to reconnoitre sufficiently wide to discover Hood's real position on the flank. Deducing from these reports that Hood was between the Kenesaw and the Allatoona range, Sherman planned to use these hills and the Etowah River as an anvil against which he could hammer Hood. To this end he had a message signalled from Kenesaw Mountain, over the heads of the Confederate force, to Corse to hurry to the support of the fort at Allatoona.

About 8 A.M. on the 5th he himself reached Kenesaw Mountain, and could see and hear the distant signs of battle at Allatoona. The signal officer reported that he had been unable to get any response from Allatoona, but at last the letters "C. R. S. H. E. R." were slowly spelt out, and interpreted as the comforting message "Corse is here." It was the assurance that Sherman wanted, and no subordinate could have wished a finer tribute than Sherman's comment— "I know Corse; so long as he lives the Allatoona Pass is safe." On Corse's stout defence and Sherman's signal of encouragement was later based the popular hymn—"Hold the fort, for I am coming."

Corse, another of the gallant and able volunteer officers thrown up by the war, had arrived in the nick of time. After receiving Sherman's message on the 4th he had wired to Kingston for a train to be sent, and filling it with a thousand men, all that could be carried, reached Allatoona at 1 A.M. on the 5th, his reinforcement doubling the strength of the garrison. Soon after daybreak the Confederates closed in and summoned him to surrender "to avoid a needless effusion of blood." Corse replied that he was "prepared for the 'needless effusion of blood,' whenever it is agreeable to you." He amply proved his word, and after repeated vain assaults the Confederates withdrew in the afternoon, leaving Corse to report his success in the words—"I am short a cheekbone and an ear, but am able to whip all hell yet!"

Meantime the cavalry had roughly located Hood, and Sherman, satisfied that Allatoona was adequately garrisoned, concentrated his now arriving army west of Marietta, ready for battle. But early next morning Hood slipped away to the north-west, his movements shrouded by the densely wooded country.

This plan of a progressive advance along the flank of Sherman's long and slender line of communication, with successive inward thrusts, was most admirably calculated to give the Confederates the maximum of advantage with the minimum of risk. For they could choose their points of approach to the Union communications, with a good chance of overwhelming isolated garrisons and detachments, and if interrupted by the arrival of Sherman's main army had only to draw off southward to be reasonably secure from pursuit. And with every successful break in the railroad they would add to Sherman's difficulties both of maintaining himself and countering them.

The broad conception and inspiration of the plan was, indeed, the best example of Jefferson Davis's strategy, and better than Hood's detailed fulfilment of it.

No one grasped its value quicker and more far-sightedly than Sherman. He had saved Allatoona and Marietta, besides preserving his hold on Atlanta, and even though the railroad was badly broken between Marietta and Allatoona his indefatigable engineers repaired it within seven days. Sufficient supplies were available to ensure a month's endurance. But Sherman realized the futility of any direct pursuit of Hood so long as Canby's paralysis left Alabama to the enemy as a secure shelter into which to retire whenever they chose. Merely to move back along his own lines of communication, in step with Hood's westward march, would play the enemy's game, and yield to them the very result which was the object of their manœuvre. Instead, his mind grasped the opportunity which the Confederates' move offered to turn their advantage into an advantage to himself. Just as Wheeler's similar move against his communications had inspired him to move through the open door to the rear of Atlanta, so now he would push through the open door into the "innermost recesses" of the Confederacy.

Hence on October 9 he wired again to Grant—"It will be a physical impossibility to protect the roads, now that Hood, Forrest and Wheeler, and the whole batch of devils are turned loose without home or habitation. . . . I propose we break up the railroad from Chattanooga, and strike out with wagons to Milledgeville, Millen and Savannah. Until we can repopulate Georgia, it is useless to occupy it, but the utter destruction of its roads, houses, and people will cripple their military resources. By attempting to hold the roads we will lose 1,000 men monthly, and will gain no result. I can make the march, and make Georgia howl."

Grant had given no answer to his previous suggestion, although a letter from Grant on the 4th, to Halleck, shows that he was inclined to favour the project. But it would seem that the objections of Halleck, "from a military point of view," and the still stronger protests of Grant's own Chief of staff, Rawlins, acted as a brake on his decision. Rawlins, indeed, even went behind Grant's back and begged the President to intervene.

Next day, the 10th, Sherman heard that Hood was crossing the

Coosa twelve miles below Rome, apparently bound west. Instantly he made a fresh step backwards to Kingston so as to cover the river-formed triangle of country of which Rome was the western apex, but despatched another telegram to accelerate Grant's decision. The following morning there was still no answer and he wired afresh to point out the drawbacks of surrendering the initiative to the enemy —"I would infinitely prefer to make a wreck of the road and of the country from Chattanooga to Atlanta . . . and, with my effective army, move through Georgia, smashing things to the sea. Hood may turn into Tennessee and Kentucky, but I believe he will be forced to follow me. Instead of being on the defensive, I would be on the offensive; instead of guessing at what he means to do, he would have to guess at my plans. The difference in war is full 25 per cent. I can make Savannah, Charleston, or the mouth of the Chattahooche. Answer quick, as I know we will not have the telegraph long."

Soon after despatching this telegram, he had the following dubious answer to his previous—"If you were to cut loose, I do not believe you would meet Hood's army, but would be bushwhacked by all the old men, little boys, and such railroad guards as are still left at home. . . . If there is any way of getting at Hood's army, I would prefer that, but I must trust to your own judgment. I find I shall not be able to send a force from here to act with you at Savannah. Your movements, therefore, will be independent of mine, at least until the fall of Richmond takes place. . . ."

After sending this, Grant's mind began to veer round and, next afternoon, the 12th, he wired afresh, "On reflection, I think better of your proposition. It would be much better to go South than to be forced to come North." A cipher message informed Sherman that supplies would be sent to any point on the coast to meet him. But a fresh change of wind at City Point—Grant's headquarters in Virginia—came with a message sent from Washington that evening— "The President feels much solicitude in respect to General Sherman's proposed movement and hopes that it will be maturely considered. The objections stated in your telegram of last night impressed him with much force, and a misstep by General Sherman might be fatal to his army."

Meantime, the enemy was augmenting both the immediate and

eventual handicaps of this mature consideration. Hood had originally intended to strike at Kingston, where he would have come within Sherman's reach, but fortunately for himself decided to move north of the Coosa and Oostenaula against the railroad between Resaca and Dalton. On the 12th his troops appeared before Resaca and summoned its garrison, a brigade, to surrender with the brutally menacing words—"If the place is carried by assault no prisoners will be taken." The commander replied, "I am somewhat surprised at the concluding paragraph. . . . In my opinion I can hold this post; if you want it come and take it." This, Hood made little attempt to do, but instead pressed up the valley to Dalton, whose negro garrison was more prompt to surrender.

Sherman had moved his army to Rome on the 12th, whence he pushed his cavalry, supported by Cox's corps, down river to feel for Hood. Next morning he had word of the threat to Resaca and swung his army round thither. Leaving Cox to follow, he was on the way with the rest of the army by afternoon and reached Resaca next day. Finding that Hood had gone north to Dalton, and perhaps beyond, Sherman directed his army north-west through Snake Creek Gap towards Villanow with the idea of cutting Hood's line of retreat. But Hood was only raiding, not striking, and had already left the railroad to retire west to Villanow. And when Sherman reached Villanow Hood was at Lafayette, another step to the west amid the mountains.

Sherman was as eager as Grant to "get at" Hood if the latter would give him the chance, and to this end sent a message to Schofield, now in charge at Chattanooga—"I want the first positive fact that Hood contemplates an invasion of Tennessee; invite him to do so. Send him a free pass in." Unfortunately even the subtlest of traps was of no avail unless the Confederates felt an appetite for the cheese. Hood, indeed, wished to fight but was bluntly told by his subordinates that the morale of the troops—which he had damaged —had not yet recovered sufficiently to justify the risk. So, instead, he retreated south-west to Gadsden in Alabama, fifty miles below Rome on the Coosa. Thither he had previously sent his trains and reserve artillery and, moving light through easily obstructed country, he had no difficulty in slipping away from Sherman's longing arms.

Sherman followed him as far as Gaylesville, on the Coosa, far enough to shepherd him out of the mountainous belt which might cloak his movements and designs, and far enough to be convinced that he had no immediate intention of invading Tennessee. As early as the 17th Sherman notified his subordinates of his intention to resume the Georgia project, meeting a mild protest from Thomas, who preferred the more cautious suggestion, made by Grant on the 11th, of "turning loose" the cavalry to throw Hood on the defensive. Sherman had no faith in such a palliative with cavalry who, he had already complained, only moved ten miles to the Confederates' hundred.

Two days later he wrote to Halleck, "I now consider myself authorised to execute my plan . . . strike out into the heart of Georgia, and make for Charleston, Savannah, or the mouth of the Appalachicola [on the Gulf] . . . I must have alternates, else, being confined to one route, the enemy might so oppose that delay and want would trouble me, but, having alternates, I can take so eccentric a course that no general can guess my objective. Therefore when you hear I am off have look-outs at Morris Island, S. C., Ossahaw Sound, Ga., Pensacola and Mobile Bays. I will turn up somewhere, and believe I can take Macon and Milledgeville, Augusta and Savannah, Ga., and wind up with closing the neck back of Charleston so that they will starve out. This movement is not purely military or strategic but will illustrate the vulnerability of the South. . . . It will take ten days to finish up our road, during which I shall eat out this flank and along down the Coosa and then will rapidly put into execution the plan. In the meantime I ask that you give to General Thomas all the troops that you can spare of the new levies, that he may hold the line of the Tennessee during my absence of, say, ninety days." The last two sentences show: first, that his idea was to simplify Thomas's task by confining the Confederates, for want of supplies on the Chattanooga flank, to a straightforward line of operation against Tennessee; and, second, that he contemplated a possible return west after he had carried his starvation campaign "into the very bowels of the Confederacy."

His object was still more clearly put in a letter of the 20th to Thomas—"I propose to demonstrate the vulnerability of the South and make its inhabitants feel that war and individual ruin are synonymous terms." And he added—"To pursue Hood is folly, for he can twist and turn like a fox, and wear out any army in pursuit; to continue to occupy long lines of railroads simply exposes our small detachments to be picked up in detail and forces me to make counter-marches to protect lines of communication. I know I am right in this and shall proceed to its maturity." Sherman had told Thomas the previous day that he proposed to start "about November 1" and that "Hood's army may be set down at 40,000 of all arms fit for duty"—a remarkably close estimate—"He may follow me or turn against you. If you can defend the line of the Tennessee . . . it is all I ask." "He cannot invade Tennessee except to the west of Huntsville."

In view of the common criticism that Sherman left Thomas an inadequate force for his task, and thereby gambled too heavily, it is significant that on the 25th Thomas, after enumerating the strength of his chain of garrisons, declared "With Fourth Corps [Stanley's, already promised by Sherman], and enough of the new regiments to make up an active force of 25,000 infantry, I will undertake to clear the rebels out of West Tennessee [i.e., Forrest] and draw off enough of Hood's army from you to enable you to move anywhere in Georgia. . . ."

But Hood and Grant combined to threaten a further delay. While his preparations were being made in rear, Sherman had waited at Gaylesville to see if the Confederate army attempted to move directly north in an attempt to cross the Tennessee near Guntersville, in which case he was ready to postpone his Georgia move for the excellent chance of moving across behind Hood to cut off his line of retreat. By strange coincidence that was the very line of invasion upon which Hood had decided in conference with Beauregard, just appointed to co-ordinate the various Confederate forces in the West. But Sherman was deprived of the opportunity, and the Confederate army temporarily preserved, by Hood's sudden change of mind on his march north, in consequence of which he swerved away to the west and attempted a crossing of the Tennessee at Decatur. There repulsed, he moved still further west to Tuscumbia, opposite Florence and 150 miles west of Chattanooga. Wise, for his own safety, as was this move, ostensibly made in order to bring him closer to Forrest's cavalry, it seems to have been prompted even more by a desire to show his independence of Beauregard's authority. If so, we can understand Sherman's irritated complaint earlier that Hood "is eccentric and I cannot guess his movements as I could those of Johnston, who was a sensible man and only did sensible things."

If the change of direction nullified Sherman's hope, it did not upset his expectation, which had never been that Hood would be so foolish as to attempt the Guntersville line. And now, on the 27th, with accurate insight he wired to Thomas, "I have no doubt Hood has gone over about Florence."

The effect of Hood's move west was to clinch Sherman's decision to move east. In deference to Grant's wish that he should "get at" Hood, and in consequence of Grant's slowness of decision, if also of Hood's quickness of movement, Sherman had trailed in his enemy's wake until he had been drawn over a hundred miles back from Atlanta. On the other hand, he had foiled the real object of the Confederate plan—that of forcing him to relax his hold on Georgia. And dispelled their dream of a second "Retreat from Moscow." But to continue the counter-march would make his hold precarious, hearten Southern morale, and depress Northern morale, without promising any result. For the area was so vast, so devoid of natural barricades and valuable objectives, as to offer little chance of cornering a mobile opponent whose only heavy baggage was a pontoon train—a strategic "fire-escape."

Where the ordinary general rigidly pursues the main armed forces of the enemy because such a course is the orthodox principle, Sherman was too wise to waste his strength in pursuit of any goal which was unattainable. Canons must be reconciled with common-sense. Instead of following the enemy's lead his own plan would compel the enemy either to follow him or to sacrifice the heart of their country—the essential duality of objective once more. He hoped that they might do both, for he calculated on moving too fast to be caught up, and his hope was founded on an intimate knowledge of Beauregard's mind. If the event was to dispel it, a study in the records of Beauregard's reactions suggests that the Confederate army might have followed Sherman's trailing coat-tails if Beauregard had possessed the authority to control Hood's actions. The possibility would have been probability if Sherman's move east had begun before Hood had gone so far west—and for this delay the strategy of "getting at" Hood was responsible.

To test the possibility, and also as a step on his eastward way, Sherman on the 28th began to move his army back from Gaylesville to Rome and Kingston. At the same time he wired to Thomas —"I have already sent the Fourth Corps. Use it freely, and if I see that Hood crosses the Tennessee River, I will also send General Schofield. On these two corps you can engraft all the new troops. . . . Hood has but little ammunition and cannot afford to attack fortified places."

In his care for Thomas's security, Sherman had already begun to move Schofield's corps towards Chattanooga, placing it at Thomas's disposal, before news came on the 31st that Hood had obtained a foothold across the Tennessee at Florence. Thereby he left himself with only four corps instead of five, and in addition, to meet Thomas's wishes, denuded himself of all the cavalry except one composite division of 5,000 under Kilpatrick. From experience of Thomas, Sherman felt that he was ideally suited to such a defensive rôle, but nevertheless warned him, "You must unite all your men into one army and abandon all minor points if you expect to defeat Hood." His requests thus more than met, Thomas wrote that same day to Halleck—"With Schofield and Stanley I feel confident I can drive Hood back.

But November 2 brought signs of another ominous change in the higher atmosphere—a telegram from Grant, despatched the previous evening, which said: "Do you not think it advisable now that Hood has gone so far north to entirely settle with him before starting on your proposed campaign. . . . I believed, and still believe, that if you had started south whilst Hood was in the neighbourhood of you he would have been forced to go after you. Now that he is so far away, he might look upon the chase as useless. . . . If you can see the chance for destroying Hood's army, attend to that first and make your other move secondary." Oh, the eternal optimism of these orthodox strategists, based on dogma and not on reality! Surely Grant might have profited by his own vain effort to destroy Lee's army under conditions infinitely more propitious—a circumscribed area and a point, Richmond, which the enemy must safeguard. Yet he was now desirous to see Sherman chase an even more delusive will-o'-the-wisp, and would even seem to have forgotten that Hood was "so far away" because he himself had spurred Sherman in direct pursuit. These reported fluctuations of opinion are hardly in accord with the normal picture of Grant, or, indeed, with the normal habit. The explanation may be that Grant, like many men of strong commonsense but limited education, felt a certain awe for those who were intellectually better equipped. And that, as he had not himself to tackle the problem, he was more than normally sensitive to the protests of the mouthpieces of orthodoxy who surrounded him.

With inexhaustible patience Sherman wired back: "If I could hope to overhaul Hood I would turn against him with my whole. Then he retreats [i.e., would retreat] to the south-west, drawing me as a decoy from Georgia, which is his chief object. . . . No single army can catch him, and I am convinced the best results will result from defeating Jeff. Davis' cherished plan of making me leave Georgia by manœuvering. Thus far I have confined my efforts to thwart his plan. . . ." Nevertheless, submissive as ever to authority, he declares that if Hood ventures north from the Tennessee he is willing to move west across his line of retreat, but with the warning that to strike effectively he will have to let go of Atlanta.

Happily the wind had already changed again at City Point. After reflection upon the details previously given of the measures taken for the security of Tennessee, Grant had sent a further telegram, on the 2nd, saying—"With the force . . . you have left with Thomas, he must be able to take care of Hood and destroy him. I do not really see that you can withdraw from where you are to follow Hood, without giving up all we have gained in territory. I say, then, go on as you propose."

As a safeguard against any fresh change of wind, Sherman on the 6th set forth in a telegram of great length the reasoned arguments for abstaining from a chase of Hood, epitomizing them in the words, "It is a well-settled principle that if we can prevent his succeeding in his threat we defeat him and derive all the moral advantage of a victory." He then turned from the indirect to the direct aspect of his plan—"I have employed the last ten days in running to the rear the sick and wounded and worthless, and all the vast amount of stores accumulated by our army in the advance, aiming to organise this branch of my army into four well-commanded corps, encumbered by only one gun to 1,000 men, and provisions and ammunition which can be loaded up in our mule-teams. . . . I propose to act in such a manner against the material resources of the South as utterly to negative Davis's boasted threat and promises of protection. If we can march a well-appointed army right through his territory, it is a demonstration to the world, foreign and domestic, that we have a power which Davis cannot resist. This may not be war, but rather statesmanship. . . . Now, Mr. Lincoln's election, which is assured, coupled with the conclusion thus reached, makes a complete, logical whole. Even without a battle, the result operating upon the minds of sensible men would produce fruits more than compensating for the expense, trouble and risk. Admitting this reasoning to be good, that such a movement per se is right, still there may be reasons why one route would be better than another. There are three from Atlanta, south-east, south, and south-west, all open, with no serious enemy to oppose at present. The first would carry me across the only east and west railroad remaining in the Confederacy . . . and thereby sever . . . Lee and Beauregard . . . and reach the seashore at Charleston or Savannah, from either of which points I could reinforce our armies in Virginia. The second and easiest route would be due south . . . [to] the Appalachicola. This, however, would leave the army in a bad position for future movements. The third, down the Chattahoochee . . . to Pensacola . . . would enable me at once to co-operate with General Canby in the reduction of Mobile and occupation of the line of the Alabama." With acute judgment, if also with irony, he added: "I will not attempt to send couriers back, but trust to the Richmond papers to keep you well advised." This telegram shows that he still wished to preserve his freedom to vary his direction. But it shows also that he clearly inclined to the first which "would have a material effect upon your campaign in Virginia."

The predominant trend of his mind, as well as his prevision, is still more clearly established by the evidence of a conference just previously with his chief subordinates. Sitting on a camp-stool, with map outstretched on his knees, he pointed out the routes to be followed as far as Milledgeville. "From here, we have several alternatives; I am sure we can go to Savannah, or open communication with the sea somewhere in that direction." Then, pausing to trace routes from Savannah to Columbia, he remarked: "Howard, I believe we can go there without any serious difficulty." His finger moved on north-east to Goldsboro in North Carolina, "When we reach that important railroad junction—Lee must leave Virginia, and he will be defeated beyond hope of recovery." In his faith in the moral and economic effect of his project he had not overlooked the military effect.

Grant replied on the night of the 7th—"I see no present reason for changing your plan. Should any arise you will see it, or if I do I will inform you." On the morning of the 12th Sherman quitted Kingston for Atlanta, breaking his bridges across the Etowah and also his telegraph. His troops had begun their march towards Atlanta on the 1st, and now were assembled between Marietta and Atlanta, save for the rearguard which, after burning Rome, accompanied Sherman. The last message from Thomas was cheerful —"I have no fear that Beauregard can do us any harm now . . . and I believe I shall have men enough to ruin him unless he gets out of the way very rapidly."

His confidence—at the moment—was justified by facts, for the War Records show that he had 71,473 present for duty under his command, including the striking force of two corps with which Sherman had endowed him. Whereas Hood had only 35,662, excluding Forrest's cavalry—a shrinkage which significantly shows the result of the Atlanta campaign. Hood's actual effectives were 30,559 and Forrest's probably 7,700.

Another corps of three divisions was also on its way to Thomas, and had reached St. Louis on November 2. His one serious handicap was in cavalry. General Wilson, who had just been sent by Grant to organize the cavalry as a whole, estimated that 12,000 would be ready by the 12th, but delays in the supply of remounts intervened. But for his defensive rôle Thomas had an ample margin of strength if he fulfilled Sherman's instructions to concentrate his forces, with strong garrisons only at Nashville and Chattanooga. He had also an ample margin of time, for after reaching Florence Hood's further advance was paralyzed for three weeks by lack of supplies—it is noteworthy that Sherman calculated upon this, from knowledge of the already devastated neighbourhood and the hunger of prisoners taken. Cox, who took a leading part in the campaign, considers that even before the corps from Missouri arrived Thomas could easily have concentrated a force of 47,000, with 6,000 cavalry to oppose the Confederate advance.

Hence it was with a just assurance of Thomas's security that Sherman turned his face to the east. None the less it was a supreme act of moral courage. To leave the enemy in his rear, to divide his army, to cut himself adrift from railroad and telegraph, from supplies and reinforcements, and launch not a mere raiding force of cavalry but a great army into the heart of a hostile country —pinning his faith and his fortune on a principle which he had deduced by reasoning contrary to orthodoxy. And with nothing to fortify his spirit beyond that reasoning, for his venture was to be made under the cloud of the dubious permission of his military superior, the anxious fears of his President, and the positive objections of their advisers. If it requires great moral courage under such gloomy conditions to launch an army to an attack from a secure base, how much greater the effort and strength of will required to launch an army "into the blue"—knowing that the nearest point, Savannah, where he could hope to renew touch with his own side, was three hundred miles distant.

The act certainly fulfilled Napoleon's dictum that in war the moral is to the physical as three to one. So did the principle, but in a deeper sense than Napoleon's. For as conceived and applied by Sherman, it was designed to show not merely that the strength of an army depends on its moral foundation more than its numbers, but that the strength of an armed nation depends on the morale of its citizens—that if this crumbles the resistance of their armies will also crumble, as an inevitable sequel.

CHAPTER XX

MARCHING THROUGH GEORGIA

THE army which marched with Sherman from Atlanta to the Atlantic was probably the finest army of military "workmen" the modern world has seen. An army of individuals trained in the school of experience to look after their own food and health, to march far and fast with the least fatigue, to fight with the least exposure; above all, to act swiftly and to work thoroughly. Each individual fitted into his place in a little group which, messing, marching and fighting together, by its instinctive yet intelligent teamship reduced alike the risks and the toil of the campaign. The sum of these teams formed an army of athletes stripped of all impediments, whether weight of kit or weaklings, and impelled by a sublime faith in their captain, "Uncle Billy," a faith which found vent in such slogans as "There goes the old man. All's right."

Sherman's supreme aim in his preparations had been to develop the mobility of his army to such a pitch that it should be a huge "flying column" of light infantry. The twenty-four miles of railroad which the Confederates had destroyed between Marietta and Dalton were repaired by October 28, and then what Sherman called the "accumulation of trash," which the army had carried to Atlanta or collected, was sent back while supplies came forward over the railroad—again destroyed, but by Sherman, as far back as Allatoona and the Etowah bridge before he quitted Atlanta.

The army, which finally totalled just over 60,000, was divided into a right wing under Howard, composed of Logan's 15th corps and Blair's 17th corps, and a left wing under Slocum, composed of Davis's 14th corps and Williams' 20th corps, while Kilpatrick's cavalry were directly under Sherman. Each corps was to be independent for supplies, to move on a separate road, and had a 900 feet section of the "wing" pontoon train given it. There was no general supply train and the corps supply trains were distributed among brigades, which in turn allotted one wagon only, for kit, and one ambulance to each regiment. In all there were about 2,500 wagons, each drawn by six mules, and 600 light ambulances. For mobility also each gun and caisson was drawn by an eight-horse team. Rations for twenty days and forage for five were carried, as well as two hundred rounds of ammunition per man and per gun, while each soldier marched out with forty rounds on his person and three days' rations in his haversack. Droves of beef-cattle accompanied the marching army. But while full precautions were taken to ensure comfortably filled stomachs, external comforts were pared down to little more than a blanket for each man, a coffee-pot and stewing pan for each group of messmates.

On this expedition Sherman fulfilled his ideal of mobility; setting a standard of fifteen miles for the daily march and allowing no comfort-loving subordinate to baulk him by laxness or lax example. The rations with which the army set out were to be treated as far as possible as a reserve, for the army was to live on the country. To this end each brigade organized a foraging party of thirty to fifty men under a picked officer. Every morning before daylight these would be off to scour the plantations several miles ahead, and out to the flanks, for livestock, corn and eatables of every kind. They would usually keep ahead of the column throughout the day, carrying each successive harvest, often on captured horses or carts, to the road along which the column was coming where it would be picked up by the supply trains. These foragers—Sherman's famous "bummers"—were commonly mounted on horses or mules taken from the plantations, and often ridden with a rope for rein and a strip of carpet for saddle.

Their utility did not end with their provisioning duties, for they automatically formed and intelligently acted as a wide screen of scouts covering the front and flanks of the marching column. Thereby they not only protected it from surprise, but saved it time-wasting deployments. If enemy cavalry appeared on the scene, the laden foragers would pour out of barns and kitchen gardens like a swarm of angry bees, each party rallying to form a well concealed and extended firing line, while some of their number drove the laden mules to the rear. If still pressed, they would make a fighting withdrawal while other parties converged to their support, and, being skilled in shooting and cover, constantly gave their opponents

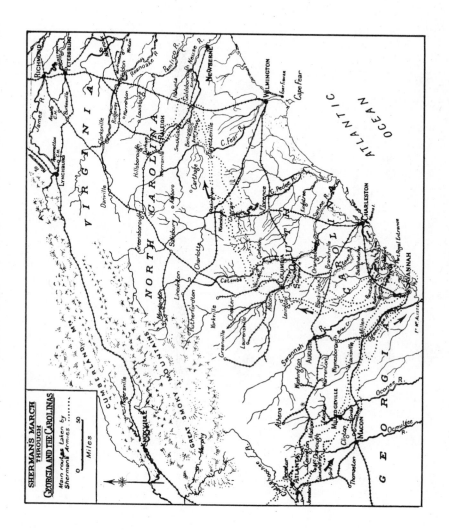

the impression that they were the main line of skirmishers. However careless of the forms of discipline, they were imbued with the essential fighting discipline, and developed such dashing team-work that they would clear the front of enemy cavalry quicker and better than the proper cavalry had done in the previous campaigns.

That team-work was all the better because it was treated as an exhilarating game rather than an enforced task—a game in which to score points and a "rag" in which to indulge humour. Into it they threw themselves with all the mingled enthusiasm and thoroughness of preparation which marks an undergraduate rag. And like all rags this, the greatest of all in scale and duration, was most exciting and amusing except for those who suffered by it.

To the actual foraging no real limit was set, for, apart from the foraging parties, the orders liberally said that "soldiers . . . may be permitted to gather turnips, potatoes and other vegetables, and to drive in stock in sight of their camp." "As for horses, mules, wagons, etc., belonging to the inhabitants, the cavalry and artillery may appropriate freely and without limit, discriminating, however, between the rich, who are usually hostile, and the poor or industrious, usually neutral or friendly." A Robin Hood touch! The only restriction set was that "soldiers must not enter the dwellings of the inhabitants, or commit any trespass"—this clause kindles the vision of a forager using endearing blandishments to attract a reluctant pig from its sty to become pork. As to destruction, however, the limit was more strictly drawn—"To army corps commanders alone is intrusted the power to destroy mills, houses, cotton-gins, etc., and for them this general principle is laid down: In districts . . . where the army is unmolested no destruction of such property should be permitted, but should guerrillas or bushwhackers molest our march, or should the inhabitants burn bridges, obstruct roads, or otherwise manifest local hostility, then army commanders should order and enforce a devastation more or less relentless according to the measure of such hostility."

The elasticity of these limits in practice varied with the corps commander, and when a commander of Kilpatrick's wild temper and rapacious character had the deciding voice principles were often submerged in sheer lust of plunder and destruction. But power can be assumed, as well as intrusted, and in men trained to forage without limit the distinction between forage and pillage is easily obscured. And the pillager disappointed of detachable loot easily finds vent for his feelings in the destruction of fixtures, when the simple conjunction of a barn and a match can relieve them "brilliantly" at little risk of discovery.

That Sherman and many of his officers tried to check excesses and enforce limits is unquestionable. But the very width of front covered by the army on its march made supervision impossible, and even when culprits were detected the only punishment which could be an effective deterrent—death—could not be applied without specific sanction from Washington. All the men knew that Lincoln's mercy dropped ceaselessly like the gentle dew from heaven, and on this expedition had the further assurance that they were safely isolated from even the remote chance of a drought at Washington. Sherman, too, was handicapped by a conflict of principles in his own mind. On the one hand, filled with the idea that the war was at bedrock "a war *against anarchy*" he hated any and every act which savoured of illegality. On the other hand, this man, so kind and considerate as an individual, conceived himself as the angel of wrath, armed with a flaming sword, to punish a people guilty of a mortal sin—that of bringing division into the Union and hence of bringing war into the land.

He himself, with some success, might reconcile the two principles in his actions, and intervene to check or frustrate many an abuse, but his words of violence carried further than his deeds. Among his staff were some whose attitude to the South was as passionate in its hatred as his attitude was dispassionate. Dayton, his inseparable aide-de-camp, and now his acting adjutant-general, was one. Some of them also had a genius for indiscretion, even if he himself had not been so carelessly generous in broadcasting his opinions and ebullitions. Thus it was natural that the idea should spread that Sherman himself favoured indiscriminate destruction, and that men as they ransacked a house of its edible property should laughingly quote to each other the words of his order—"Forage liberally on the country." The permanent damage wrought by the foraging parties or halted columns was comparatively slight however; the burning of barns and dwellings was usually the work of unauthorized foragers who, as the campaign progressed, extended both in space and time the radius of their light-hearted and light-fingered operations. Many of these were stragglers who followed in the wake or on the skirts of the army. That Sherman should be blamed for their crimes was an odd recoil from the vigour of his efforts, during three years of war, to suppress them and to induce the authorities to take drastic measures against this universal blot.

Yet, when the full reckoning is made, the most remarkable feature of the campaign is perhaps that violence to property was accompanied by so little personal violence, and that homicide and rape were almost unknown. In person, indeed, the citizens and women of the South suffered less than from their own defenders. Even Kilpatrick's cavalry were outrivalled by Wheeler's, and the ruffianly behaviour of the latter caused many a cry to rise "save us from our friends." Nor were these outrages limited to the last hungry and desperate months of the campaign, for even during the first retreat to Atlanta Southern papers were complaining that "our own army, while falling back from Dalton, was even more dreaded by the inhabitants than was the army of Sherman." That Wheeler's wild troopers treated their own people so badly is strong indirect evidence for the frequent charge against them of atrocious acts against Union prisoners. And the discovery of mutilated bodies by the advancing Union forces was naturally regarded as proof that the Confederates were fulfilling the Resaca threat of "no quarter"—which had borne the authoritative signature of the supreme commander. It was the inevitable sequel that exasperated men should find balm for their feelings in the sight of blazing buildings.

But the fate of Atlanta as compared with that of Columbia later is proof of the discrimination in destruction intended and practised when Sherman had direct power of control. For at Atlanta the task was placed under Poe, the chief engineer, and although there was only a day in which to accomplish the destruction of all buildings which could be of use to the enemy—machine-shops, mills, warehouses, stores of every kind—the gigantic bonfire was confined to the business part of the town with a degree of success remarkable under the conditions. And sentries stood guard over churches and civic buildings with orders so strict that even high officers were compelled to leave the sidewalk and pass down the middle of the street—lest they might indulge an unauthorized taste for arson.

That day, November 15, the greater part of the army had marched out from Atlanta, Sherman and his staff following next morning with the last corps of the left wing. The great march began—with bands appropriately playing "John Brown's soul goes marching on."

The earlier departure of the right wing was a part of Sherman's strategical plan. For it first moved south by roads near the Macon railroad, then swerved to the south-east at an angle which shortened its march while still giving the impression that Macon was the goal —Logan's corps (temporarily under Osterhaus, a former Prussian officer) and Blair's corps marching along closely parallel routes with Kilpatrick's cavalry on the outer flank. The move successfully deceived the Confederates, who had assembled Wheeler's cavalry, and 3,000 of the Georgia militia at Lovejoy's station, and the prompt retreat of these forces towards Macon was accelerated by Kilpatrick. In all, Wheeler had thirteen brigades, and a strength of about 7,000 men.

Besides these forces there were about 12,000 men stationed in the various garrisons comprised in the "Department of South Carolina, Georgia and Florida" of which Hardee was now in command. Spurred by feverish telegrams from Richmond he hurried from Charleston to Macon while Beauregard came thither from the west, issuing an impassioned appeal—"To the People of Georgia. Arise for the defense of your native soil. Rally round your patriotic Governor and gallant soldiers. Obstruct and destroy all roads in Sherman's front, flank, and rear, and his army will soon starve in your midst. . . ." Simultaneously, Beauregard urged Hood either to send troops for the defence of Georgia or to take the offensive at once against Nashville—Hood preferring of two evils to take the last, the simplest and, as it proved, the worst.

Reading these fevered telegrams we are reminded of Sherman's earlier jest about "Beauregard bursting with French despair." Even so, Sherman did not underrate the dangers of such a *levée en masse*—which was belatedly proclaimed at Milledgeville, the State Capital, just as he was approaching it. In July, on approaching Atlanta, he had told his wife that "if Beauregard can induce Davis to adopt the Indian policy of ambuscade which he urged two years ago, but which Jeff thought rather derogatory to the high pretences of his cause to courage and manliness, every officer will be killed . . . for an enemy can waylay every path and road, and could not be found."

Studying the conditions of the campaign in Georgia it seems clear that the Confederates' best chance of obstructing and imperilling Sherman's progress lay in dispersing instead of concentrating their slender forces, in using them guerrilla-wise as a network on which to support a widespread popular rising. But the possibility was nullified by the speed and deceptiveness of Sherman's approach.

As his right wing appeared to be aiming for Macon, while actually passing north of it, so his left wing created a similar but secondary impression of an advance due east on Augusta. Williams's corps, which also left Atlanta on the 15th, took a short cut across the Covington bend of the Augusta railroad, rejoined it at Social Circle, and continued eastward along it, destroying it, through Madison to the Oconee bridge. At that point the two horns of Sherman's dilemma—for the Confederates—were fifty miles apart. But now Williams's corps suddenly swerved almost due south to Milledgeville, which it occupied on the 22nd. Here it was joined early next day by the other corps of the left wing which, starting a day after, had been directed along an interior line. Simultaneously the right wing reached and encamped at Gordon, ten miles south of Milledgeville.

The effect of these deceptively moving columns had been that until the 21st Hardee believed that Macon was Sherman's initial objective, and then, as rapidly changing to the belief that Augusta was the objective, tried to shift his forces across, only to find that the railroad and telegraph were cut, and that Sherman had interposed between the two places. The Georgia militia marched off in obedience to his order, bumped into the rear guard of Sherman's right wing at Griswoldville, about eight miles out, and fell back to Macon badly bruised. They were then entrained to the south and by a long circuit, including a sixty-mile march, reached Savannah on the 29th. Wheeler's cavalry, by swimming the Oconee River just ahead of the Union columns, succeeded in getting away from their now useless position at Macon and round once more to Sherman's front. Meantime, Bragg, sent posthaste from Wilmington with a

handful of reinforcements, had arrived at Augusta to take supreme
charge of the campaign, only to find himself cut off from the rest
of the Confederate forces and for some days completely in the dark
as to what was happening. He and his force of about 10,000 were
to remain idle and ineffective at Augusta while Sherman tranquilly
pursued his path to the sea.

For, leaving Milledgeville on the 24th, Sherman swung Kilpatrick over from the right to the left flank to convey the impression
that he was the spearhead of an advance on Augusta. Kilpatrick's
north-easterly advance by one of the roads leading to Augusta
caused Wheeler to concentrate to oppose him where the road crossed
the swamps of Briar Creek. Whereupon Kilpatrick, according to
plan, swerved south-east past him, and raced to cut the Savannah-
Augusta railroad at the bridge just north of Waynesboro. Despite
the lead which Kilpatrick had thus gained Wheeler chased him so
hard as to foil his intention—and nearly captured Kilpatrick
himself in the folly of a misspent night. But when Kilpatrick
regained touch with his own infantry he turned on Wheeler and
sharply drove him back, leaving him to follow discreetly in the wake
of Sherman's army during the rest of the march.

Kilpatrick's swerving distraction, moreover, had procured an
almost free passage for the main columns during the second stage
of their march—from Milledgeville to Millen. During this, the
front was once more expanded, but only to a breadth of about fifteen miles, the two corps of the right wing taking up alternately the
job of destroying the Central Georgia railroad along the whole hundred miles from Griswoldville to Millen. Despite this laborious
task, Millen was reached by Blair's corps, which Sherman accompanied, on December 3, with the other corps in line to north and
south.

Two-thirds of the great march had been accomplished without a
hitch despite frequent streams and rivers which intersected the
route. A swathe of desolation two hundred miles long and as
much as sixty wide had been cut through the centre of fertile
Georgia. Save for the exhilaration of the adventure and the variety
of rations, the army might have been engaged in a peaceful route
march. During most of the time the weather had been fine, the air
crisp, and the roads good, with only two or three days of rain just

before reaching Milledgeville to liquefy them temporarily. The comfort of the marching columns in mud and dust was increased by the considerate example set by Sherman, who usually rode over the fields alongside and always sought to avoid passing troops on the road, saying that they, and not he, had the right to it. Food had been abundant, the droves of cattle increasing rather than shrinking, and the trial of hard tack on tender teeth had been infrequent, to the relief of all except Sherman, who ever praised its virtues— but did not disdain soft bread when it was on the table. Even so, his mess was more frugal, his baggage more sparse than any subordinate commander's. And to attest his faith in hard tack he kept his haversack filled with it. A pose, one may say, yet a pose to impress a principle.

But if by his mobility he had outstripped the enemy's power to obstruct or imperil, he was not free from other trials. Repeatedly when he passed or paused at a house the women would seize the opportunity to beg from him the favour of leaving a guard over *theirs*, always with a special reason why their pigs, chickens, or potatoes should be preserved from his "bummers." A Lincoln-like tenderness would soon have reduced the Grand Army of the West to a cordon of unpaid Georgian policemen. Yet, despite his principles, and the firmness with which he outwardly upheld them, Sherman felt the burden of individual misery, and sometimes sitting by the camp-fire at night would musingly say—"I'll have to harden my heart to these things. That poor woman to-day—how could I help her. There's no help for it. The soldiers will take all she has."—and then finish with his logical self-excusing, South-accusing moral soliloquy—"Jeff Davis is responsible for all this." But in the morning before starting, he would sometimes see that a supply of provisions was left at the house.

Another trial came from the flocks of negroes who, often in a semi-religious ecstasy, not only gathered to gaze on and greet him as their deliverer, but craved to accompany him—from fear of retribution. These were usually plantation slaves, for with the household slaves it was as often their mistresses who urged them to accompany the army, in order to save them from want or to economize such provisions as the "bummers" left unforaged. To the more intelligent individuals among them he would often talk, both to explain his policy and to acquire reliable information of the country and its routes. Ending with a pleasant homily that they were now free if they chose, but that this meant freedom to work for themselves, not to idle.

To those who were strong and unmarried he offered employment as pioneers and road-makers, but the rest he advised to stay, at least until peace came—"but don't hurt your masters or their families—we don't want that." For he was more intent on the rôle of Joshua than on that of Moses, and had no wish to hamper his own march round the walls of the Confederate Jericho by conducting an exodus of the children of Ham from the land of bondage. The tepidity of his enthusiasm for mass deliverance, however, was not shared by all his subordinates and men, with the result that the trailing swarms of negroes became an increasing clog. This ended in a tragedy during the last stage of the march to Savannah. Davis, on the extreme left, was still being mildly harassed by Wheeler's cavalry, and also losing patience with the negro refugees' patient disregard of all orders to stay at home. To remedy both ills at one stroke he removed his pontoon bridge immediately the rear of his column had crossed Ebenezer Creek. But either from fear of foregoing their freedom or from fear of the Confederate cavalry, the refugees rushed like the Gadarene swine in a wild stampede down to the bank and into the Creek, where many drowned before the Union troops, turning back, could rescue them.

If the march had revealed an embarrassing enthusiasm on the part of the negroes it had also revealed an encouraging lack of enthusiasm for the war among the greater part of the white population. Most of the richer planters and their families had removed in time to more salubrious districts, and although some of the women who remained were proudly defiant, the more usual assertion was that their men-folk had been forced into the ranks. Least defiant of all were the men who were left at home, and the general tone of hopeless apathy led Sherman to say, with renewed conviction— "Pierce the shell of the C.S.A. and it's all hollow inside." The levée en masse had been a fiasco, although in their desperation the Confederate authorities had even released and armed the convicts from the penitentiary. Most of them were taken prisoners by the Union forces while still dressed in prison garb, and as an apt reprisal Sherman promptly released them again, "believing," as his aide-de-camp Nichols tells us, "that Governor Brown had not got the full benefit of his liberality."

Thereby he also saved food, a factor which now became more pressing with a change of scene. For as the army neared Millen it entered the "Pine Barrens," or savannas of the South—a sandy region with vast forests of pines, towering eighty or more feet above the wide roads which traversed these forests. Even here, however, the necessity of falling back on hard tack was saved by the fact that the cotton-fields were now growing corn to feed the Confederate army—and fed the Union army instead.

From Millen the advance entered the corridor between the Savannah and Ogeechee Rivers, although Sherman kept Logan's corps on the south bank of the Ogeechee ready to turn the enemy's flank if they tried to bar the way down the corridor. So in the first stage of the march, to Milledgeville, his advance had taken advantage of the flank protection afforded by the corridor between the Oconee and Ocmulgee Rivers. And his equal success in circumventing the enemy's attempts to turn the rivers to his disadvantage was renewed in the last difficult stage as he approached the Creek and swamp-intersected outskirts of Savannah.

Here the roads ran along narrow causeways raised above the waterlogged rice-fields, and the whole district was covered with a network of canals, dams, and flood-gates by which it could be inundated, normally to assist the growth of rice, but now available to resist the approach of Sherman. To guard this easily barred gateway, Hardee had gathered about 15,000 men. His orders from Beauregard were that, if forced to choose, he should preserve his army rather than preserve Savannah from the enemy—a wise latitude—and retire northward to cover Charleston. In fulfilment of this purpose Hardee selected and fortified a line, across the narrow part of the corridor, some distance outside Savannah and covering the railroad north to Charleston, and south to the Gulf.

The Confederate outlook was at least better than it had been in the last week of November. While Sherman was advancing through Georgia, a small Union expeditionary force, under Foster, had been landed from the fleet, which was waiting off the coast for his arrival, and had formed a depot of supplies on Port Royal Island—originally occupied in 1861. On November 29 a division (Hatch) had crossed to the mainland with the aim of cutting the Savannah-Charleston railroad near Grahamville, in anticipation of Sherman's approach. It had only ten miles to traverse and only a few cavalry pickets to sweep aside, but Hatch sat down and spent the day entrenching his landing place. At the moment the only Confederate force within reach was the Georgia militia which, providentially, was just reaching Savannah from Macon. But Grahamville lay in South Carolina and the Georgia militia were only enlisted for service in their own State. A general with an acute sense of humour overcame their probable objection to "foreign" service by switching their trains in the dark on to the Charleston line, and when daylight came they woke up near Grahamville "unconscious patriots." And they had time to entrench themselves and repulse the belated assault of Hatch, who then retired to his landing place, before their sense of location was sufficiently aroused to make them demand a return ticket to Savannah. As they had saved the military situation, and gained time for reinforcements to arrive from the north, their belated demand was now gratified.

Retaining a force of about 6,000 near Grahamville to keep open his line of retreat to Charleston, Hardee then prepared to resist Sherman's direct advance. But the flank march of Logan's corps down the south bank of the Ogeechee nullified the prospect of holding his outer line of defence, and he took up his position on an inner line covering the city, with an isolated detachment at Fort McAlister to hold the mouth of the Ogeechee, flooding the country in his front so as to confine Sherman to five narrow causeways which could easily be swept by artillery.

Sherman had no intention of giving them a target, and on December 10 his march came temporarily to a halt about five miles from Savannah, the wings extending outwards to invest the defences. His first desire was to get in touch with the fleet and his destined supplies. Several nights before, one of Howard's scouts, Captain Duncan, had gone ahead in an attempt to drift past Fort McAlister and reach the fleet which was expected to be watching Ossahaw Sound. Kilpatrick's cavalry were also swung across from the left to the right wing and directed to the coast below Fort McAlister. But two days passed without news and Sherman, reluctant to wait longer, despatched Hazen's division (of Logan's corps) on a rapid march down the south bank of the Ogeechee against Fort McAlister, calculating that while strong on the sea side its defences would be weak on the land side. He himself rode down the north bank with Howard to watch the operation and, as the sun began to sink without sign of an assault, signalled impatiently to Hazen to hasten its launching. Hazen replied that he was almost ready.

During the hour's waiting, a cloud of smoke had been seen on the sea-ward horizon, which gradually drew nearer until the funnel of a little steamer could be seen above the undergrowth along the river bank. Then the bridge came into view, and although several miles distant a message from it was signalled—"Who are you?" Back came the reply, "McClintock, General Howard's signal officer." Then the officers on the tug saw the message being signalled across the river—"It is absolutely necessary that the fort be taken immediately. The stars and stripes must wave over the battery at 'sundown'." Almost simultaneously Hazen's troops moved out from the woods on the far bank, bore down on the fort, and swept over the parapets. The way to the sea was cleared, the "cracker line" was joined again after a month's break.

In his exhilaration Sherman, lapsing into "coon song," exclaimed, "Dis chile don't sleep dis night"—a remark that proved completely accurate. The two generals promptly got in a skiff and rowed down river to the captured fort. After supping there, Sherman, too restless to wait for morning, embarked again with Howard despite warnings that torpedoes were laid in the river, and went in search of the steamer which he eventually found at anchor six miles below the fort. From the captain he learnt that Duncan had safely fulfilled his dangerous mission, and that, in consequence, for several days past the fleet had been expecting Sherman at Ossahaw Sound. He learnt also that little had happened in Virginia during the month since he himself had plunged into the depths of the South.

Before returning to Fort McAlister he wrote a hasty message for transmission to Washington, in which he said—"I hope by Christmas to be in possession of Savannah, and by the new year to be ready to resume our journey to Raleigh." A message which was to lead Grant to remark to the Secretary of War, "It is refreshing to see a commander after a campaign of more than seven months' duration ready for still further operations, and without wanting any outfit or rest."

Sherman had only just got back to McAlister and lain down to sleep on the floor when he was awakened with news that a steamer with General Foster had arrived in the river, but had anchored at a safe distance down river. Once more he rose and rowed over the submerged torpedo-field, and then, on Foster's steamer, was taken to the Admiral's flagship. Here he arranged for the river to be cleared and for supplies of bread, sugar and coffee as well as ammunition and heavy guns to be shipped from Port Royal. He also ordered Foster to renew his operations against the Charleston railroad, to prevent the escape of the Savannah garrison.

The next few days were spent in reconnoitring and feeling Hardee's position, and in preliminary steps to drain off the flood water so that an attack could be made on a broader front than the causeways allowed. The left wing had reached the Charleston railroad on the south side of the Savannah River, but Hardee still kept open his communications by means of a bridge of boats further down river, and thence along the Union causeway to a station on the north side of the river. To supplement Foster's efforts Sherman, on the 15th, ordered his left wing to send a force across the Savannah River to close this causeway.

Slocum at once proposed to use the whole of Williams's corps for this purpose, but in the interval Sherman had received a despatch, sent by Grant in anticipation of his arrival on the coast, which instructed him to fortify a base on the coast, leave his artillery and cavalry there, and transport the bulk of his infantry to Virginia by sea as soon as possible. This order, most unwelcome to Sherman, compelled him to revise his plans and acted as a brake on his operations. When a further letter came to cancel it, he was in Savannah but had forfeited the chance of capturing the garrison.

.   .   .   .   .   .

To fulfil Grant's order he had to wait for sufficient transports, and he still hoped to secure Savannah in the interval. But the need of being ready to draw off his forces and embark at short notice inevitably restricted the breadth of his operations. As a defensive base Fort McAlister was obviously the most suitable place. Hence he gave orders to lay out an entrenched camp there and abandoned the too distant move of Williams's corps on to the other flank of Savannah. But he also tried to bluff Hardee into a quick surrender by a note on the 17th which suggested that he controlled all the avenues of escape, and that he was only waiting for heavy artillery to arrive by sea. "I am prepared to grant liberal terms . . . but should I be forced to resort to assault, or the slower and surer process of starvation, I shall then feel justified in resorting to the harshest measures, and shall make little effort to restrain my army. . . . I enclose you a copy of General Hood's demand for the surrender of the town of Resaca, to be used by you for what it is worth."

The threat, even if merely intended as a bluff, was not in good taste, despite the subtle humour of converting Hood's Resaca note into a boomerang. It drew a dignified protest and rejection from Hardee who gauged the situation too well to be bluffed.

Sherman thereupon ordered preparations for an assault rather than forego the prize, but as a means to reduce the cost and seal up Hardee's exit he sailed next day on the flagship for Foster's headquarters with the idea of giving a vigorous impulse to the dilatory operations of the Port Royal force. There, on the 20th, finding that it did not yet command the Union causeway, as Foster had assured him, he gave directions for Hatch to move south and place his division astride this remaining bolt-hole.

On his voyage back the ship ran aground, and after vain efforts had been made to refloat it he continued his journey as best he could in the admiral's barge—to be met late on the 21st by a tug bearing the news that Savannah had been occupied by the Union forces in the morning. Sherman's pleasure, however, was marred by the fact that Hardee had safely escaped to Charleston with the garrison, after blowing up the gunboats and the navy-yard.

Hatch's move, however, could not have succeeded, for Hardee had decided to evacuate Savannah almost immediately after his refusal to surrender it, and after postponing the evacuation for twenty-four hours, he actually moved out on the 20th as soon as darkness fell. Whether the garrison could have been captured even if Grant's order had not hampered the investment, is doubtful. For Hardee, in view of his instructions, would have evacuated Savannah at the first sign of danger to his retreat, and was too competent and too well acquainted with the country to misjudge the situation. It was, indeed, the initial landing of a Union brigade on the north bank of the Savannah River which led him to give the order for evacuation. And the chance of any rapid move across his line of retreat was nullified by a fact aptly expressed in the words of Colonel Poe, who knew both: "These swamps are ten-fold worse than the Chickahominy swamps"—where McClellan had floundered in his 1862 advance on Richmond.

With the capture of Savannah the swathe through Georgia was complete. The "granary of the South" had been ransacked, the Confederacy deprived of its essential resources—not only corn, but cotton, cattle, horses and mules; and 265 miles of railroad had been destroyed. Sherman calculated—if probably overcalculated—the damage in dollar values at $100,000,000, but the moral damage of having pierced the heart of the South, and of having demonstrated the inability of the Confederate armies to guard it, was incalculably greater. In the time-matured verdict of the Confederate general and historian, Alexander—"There is no question that the moral effect of this march upon the country at large . . . was greater than would have been the most decided victory." No longer would the people of Georgia or of any neighbouring State credit the confident assurances of their leaders and press. To loss of faith the sequel is loss of hope and then, in turn, lack of "fight." It only remained to carry that impression into South Carolina and the fate of the Confederacy would be sealed. And this was the next stage of the great plan which had evolved in Sherman's mind.

.   .   .   .

Its fulfilment was facilitated by what had happened before Nashville while Sherman was before Savannah. For in the battle of Nashville, December 15 and 16, Thomas had severely defeated Hood and thrown back his army in disorder. No event of the war has, however, been more misunderstood, more mispraised, or produced more superficial criticism. It can only be understood by placing it in due relation to the autumn campaign as a whole.

In the Atlanta campaign Sherman had not fulfilled his alternative aim of physically destroying Hood's army—an aim which, despite the optimism of peace-time text-books, is very rarely fulfilled in practice. But he had seriously reduced Hood's army and, better still, had lamed its will to fight. The Villanow episode had proved this, and proved also that so long as Sherman sought battle he would never attain it, because the Confederate desire to avoid battle dominated their strategy so long as they could keep him away from Georgia by any other means.

By turning away eastward through Georgia he had nullified the essential purpose of their evasive strategy, and left them only a choice between the unpalatable and unpromising alternatives of trailing in his wake or of risking battle in Tennessee—the "horns of a dilemma." For nothing less than the speedy defeat of Thomas or the capture of such an important point as Nashville would give hope of pulling Sherman back from Georgia, and as Thomas's army covered Nashville this meant accepting battle in either case.

A study of the mind-revealing correspondence between the higher Confederate authorities is sufficient to show that Hood's late November advance on Nashville was inspired less by objective strategy than by desperation. And desperation is a poor lead.

Hood initially, however, scored a point because Thomas neglected to follow Sherman's instructions to "unite all your men into one army, and abandon all minor points." On the offensive, and some-times on the defensive, a wide distribution is more effective than a close concentration, but both its value and its safety lie in the mobility of the distributed parts. In contrast, a wide distribution in a number of static posts means risk without profit.

When on November 20 Hood, propelled by Beauregard's urgency, began his advance northward Thomas was caught with only the two corps which Sherman had sent, assembled at Pulaski to meet Hood. And of these one division had been drawn off to the Tennessee west of Nashville by a feint on the part of Forrest against Johnsonville.

In face of this imminent threat Thomas ordered Schofield, who was in immediate command of the force at Pulaski, to withdraw upon Nashville as slowly as possible in order to gain time, so that when the expected but belated corps from the Missouri arrived he could take the offensive with these three corps. This plan placed a difficult responsibility on Schofield—in timing his successive withdrawals—and in trying to hold the Confederates south of Duck River as long as possible, and longer than was safe, he gave them the opportunity to cross the river a few miles beyond his flank, and move against the Nashville road in his rear.

But, having thus skilfully brought two of his three corps close to Schofield's line of retreat, Hood forfeited the opportunity and allowed himself to be held in check by a single Union division which was guarding it. During the night Schofield's whole force retired along the road past Hood and took up a fresh position at Franklin. Hood did not come up to that until late in the afternoon, of November 30, and then threw his men in repeated frontal assaults on the Union entrenchments, suffering a vain loss which even by his own minimum estimate of 4,500 was double that of the defenders, and probably triple; it included no less than twelve generals. This piece of folly, inspired by mortification over the lost opportunity, completed the ruin of the offensive spirit of his troops. But he was now to follow it by another, which sealed the physical doom of his depleted army.

The Union corps from Missouri, 12,000 strong, had now reached Nashville, and the battle of Franklin had invigorated the morale of Schofield's force, but Schofield himself seems to have been somewhat shaken and Thomas, always anxious to make assurance trebly sure, gave him permission to withdraw to Nashville, where Thomas was now at last concentrating some of his scattered garrisons.

Lacking the moral courage to draw back, Hood thereupon took the worst possible alternative of following Schofield to Nashville, and sitting down in front of defences held by an army considerably larger than his own—and capable of further growth. His weak excuse was that he hoped the Union army would commit the folly of a frontal assault similar to his own. A more feasible reason was the desire to use Forrest's cavalry to collect supplies and recruits from Tennessee before retreating. But this might have been done without pushing his crippled army into the lion's jaws.

The arrival of Hood's army before Nashville naturally produced a bad impression in the North, and Thomas's military desire to withhold his own stroke until his blade was sharpened and polished to perfection began to cause serious alarm among the public whose ideas, inevitably, were based on outward appearances. Even from a military viewpoint it gave Hood the opportunity, if his army had been fit, to slip past Nashville and menace the Ohio itself.

Grant, realizing both dangers as well as Thomas's adequate strength, on December 2 sent a telegram that was virtually an order for an immediate stroke. But Thomas, with invincibly stubborn adherence to his own convictions, refused to be hurried until more remounts had arrived for his cavalry—although this telegram was followed by a series of ever more urgent ones. Then on the 8th the weather intervened, and by covering the roads and slopes with ice caused a fresh postponement of Thomas's move, if it also prevented Hood fulfilling his belated decision to retire.

Grant, his patience now exhausted, regarded this as another of Thomas's excuses and despatched Logan, who was on leave in Washington, to relieve Thomas of the command. But before he arrived, Thomas struck on the morning of the 15th, throwing the bulk of his army against the left flank of the entrenched Confederate line, and slightly overlapping it. This was an able but narrow, and essentially orthodox, manœuvre; the result at the end of the day was that Hood had been forced back to a shorter line two miles to the south. The lightness of the Union loss, less than a thousand men, reveals either the discretion of the advance or the demoralized state of the Confederates—the roads in their rear were filled with stragglers taking an early cue.

Thomas does not seem to have issued any orders for next day, and it was not until late in the afternoon of the 16th that his several corps resumed a gentle parallel pressure on the new Confederate position. Meanwhile, however, Wilson's cavalry had swung out again to the flank and were working round to get astride Hood's line of retreat. Moving by bounds, dismounted, these caused Hood to stretch his left to check them, and a sudden infantry attack on the weakened part was the signal for a general collapse of the Confederates, who streamed away in flight. About 4,500 were taken prisoners, but the bulk managed to get safely away down the Franklin road, owing partly to the firm resistance of a couple of brigades which still retained their unity, and partly to the fact that Wilson's cavalry had not yet reached this road. When the Confederate army broke, the Union cavalry had to send back for their horses, and thus lost the chance of heading off the fugitives. A somewhat ironical comment on Thomas's insistence on postponing his attack until he had enough horses to mount all his cavalry.

When the pursuit was resumed next day the necessity for rebuilding bridges across Duck River—because the pontoon train had been sent off by an extraordinary mistake on Thomas's part towards Murfreesboro—enabled Hood to gain a long lead in his retreat to Tupelo, where his bankrupt forces were reconstituted under new leadership, and in part transferred to meet Sherman's advance through the Carolinas.

The story of the pontoon train mistake is a curious example of what Clausewitz termed the "friction" of war. On the day of battle Captain Jenny, the officer in charge, was met on the way to Murfreesboro' by a comrade, and in reply to the question where was he going replied—"God knows, where a pontoon train can do the least possible good." In subsequent explanation he related how Thomas had given him the order to take the train out on the Murfreesboro' pike, a route both divergent and devoid of river obstacles. In surprise Jenny replied, "General, do you mean the Murfreesboro' pike?", only to receive a curt "yes." Uneasy, and feeling that it must have been a slip of the tongue, Jenny went back again and queried the order. Thereupon Thomas, his normal patience sapped by the several sleepless nights, checked all chance of further explanation by saying with angry conclusiveness, "Yes, the Murfreesboro' pike"—when he really meant the Granny White pike. By that sleepy slip he let Hood slip away.

A psychological, as distinct from a superficial, analysis shows that the victory of Nashville was virtually won at Franklin, at least in so far as it was not already pre-determined at Atlanta. And while we may admire Thomas's constancy of purpose, his willingness to forfeit his command rather than strike before the conditions satisfied him, we may feel that he carried it to the point of sacrificing the interests of the whole to that of a part. That in his anxiety to ensure that his task was executed with complete success, he caused his superior unnecessary anxiety. A loyal subordinate in thought, his thought did not rise like Sherman's to the higher conception of loyalty which tells a subordinate that half a loaf at the desired time is better than a whole loaf later. If Thomas's delay was happily without serious consequences, and his ultimate success most happy, it at least caused Grant to contemplate sending troops from the East to safeguard the Ohio, and seemingly inspired his unfortunate order to bring Sherman's army by sea to Virginia. The echoes of Thomas's victory could not catch the echoes of his previous delay. But the victory itself had quenched all danger to Tennessee, and Sherman himself had disproved the fears which had overhung the inception of such a novel plan. The way was cleared for its further development.

.   .   .   .

On the morning of December 22, Sherman rode into the captured city of Savannah, and after a tour of it returned to the Pulaski House—a hotel named after the Count Pulaski who fell in the 1779 attack on the city, then held by the English forces. Here "Lieutenant" Sherman had stayed on earlier visits and was at least a more profitable customer than the general. For when the manager urged Sherman to be a boarder again, he was told that his prospective boarder was no longer in the habit of paying for board. The manager's pocket was saved, however, if his hotel's distinction suffered, by the appearance of an English resident of Savannah, named Charles Green, who offered Sherman the use of his house. There Sherman spent Christmas, and the season inspired him to a pleasantry—a message to Lincoln on first arrival, "I beg to present you as a Christmas gift the city of Savannah, with one hundred and fifty heavy guns and plenty of ammunition, also about twenty-five thousand bales of cotton." Both of guns and cotton this was an underestimate.

Cotton was the cause of Sherman's relations with other Englishmen being less pleasant than with Mr. Green. For, in pursuance of his idea of economic war and the destruction of war resources, he took the unyielding attitude that "all the cotton in Savannah was prize of war" and arranged for its shipment to New York, there to be disposed of as the Government wished. This drew a consular protest on behalf of cotton claimed by English subjects. But it came at an inauspicious time, for soon after the occupation one of the many English blockade-runners from Nassau—ancestors of the rum-runners of to-day—had actually come into the harbour to collect its load of cotton in blithe ignorance of the change of ownership. So the Consul retired "hurt" from the interview, followed by the parting shot from Sherman that "it would afford me great satisfaction to conduct my army to Nassau, and wipe out that nest of pirates."

Cotton was also in part the ostensible cause of a visit from Stanton, the Secretary of War, which sowed the seeds of future trouble. For Stanton showed an inquisitive interest into the relations between Sherman's army and the negroes during the march through Georgia. To gratify his curiosity Sherman arranged an interview with a score of the leaders, mostly Baptist and Methodist preachers. After Stanton had questioned them on various general points he asked them, after Sherman had withdrawn, how far they regarded the General's "sentiments and actions as friendly to their rights and interests, or otherwise." Although the answer was highly favourable, and biblical, Sherman felt a somewhat natural annoyance that his camp-followers should be asked to pass judgment on his behaviour, and was the less inclined to forget it because of his innate suspicion of politicians.

The explanation came in a letter from Halleck—"There is a certain class now having great influence with the President . . . who are decidedly disposed to make a point against you. I mean in regard to 'inevitable Sambo.' They say that you have manifested an almost *criminal* dislike to the negro, and that you are not willing to carry out the wishes of the Government in regard to him, but repulse him with contempt." Then followed a hint that, while at Savannah, he should employ his forces to go back into Georgia and bring away the slaves.

Sherman's reply is in his wittiest and wisest vein—"I deeply regret that I am threatened with that curse to all peace and comfort —popularity; but I trust to bad luck enough in the future to cure that, for I know enough of 'the people' to feel that a single mistake made by some of my subordinates will tumble down my fame into infamy. But the nigger? Why, in God's name, can't sensible men let him alone . . . Neither cotton, the negro, nor any single interest or class should govern us. But I fear, if you be right that that power behind the throne is growing, somebody must meet it or we are again involved in war with another class of fanatics. Mr. Lincoln has boldly and well met the one attack, now let him meet the other. If it be insisted that I should so conduct my operations that the negro alone is consulted, of course I will be defeated and then where will be Sambo? . . . I know the fact that all natural emotions swing as the pendulum. These Southrons pulled Sambo's pendulum so far that the danger is it will on its return jump off the pivot. . . . I profess to be the best kind of a friend to Sambo. . . . They gather round me in crowds, and I can't find out whether I am Moses or Aaron, or which of the prophets; but surely I am rated as one of the congregation, and it is hard to tell in what sense I am most appreciated by Sambo—in saving him from his master, or the new master that threatens him with a new species of slavery. I mean State recruiting agents. Poor negro—Lo, the poor Indian! Of course sensible men understand such humbug, but some power must be invested in our Government to check these wild oscillations of public opinion."

That Sherman had a deep dislike for the idea of using negro troops to fight white men is unquestionable. Moreover, he had just written to Halleck urging him "so far to respect the prejudices of the people of Savannah, as not to garrison the place with negro troops. It seems a perfect bug-bear to them, and I know that all people are more influenced by prejudice than by reason." But the evidence of many witnesses testifies to his courtesy, kindness and naturalness of manner in dealing with the negroes. It was peculiarly ironical that now, at Savannah, State recruiting agents should descend upon his army and forcibly enlist his valuable pioneers against their wishes for "fighting service"—even shutting them up, prior to shipment north, until Sherman still more forcibly intervened to quench this excessive thirst for recruiting bounties.

Sherman contrived to make himself equally unpopular with another class, the horde of speculators who had hurried down from New York only to re-embark as hurriedly under threat of arrest. With such a gift for making so many enemies in so short a time it was perhaps fortunate for Sherman that military success had armoured him against their darts. For his march through Georgia, following on his Atlantic campaign, had fired the popular imagination and made him, by strange reversal of fortune, the idol of the Northern press and public. His unchecked progress was contrasted with the stagnant disappointment of Grant's campaign in Virginia, and while it strengthened the popular will to victory it also formed a lever for the many who were discontented with Grant.

Had Sherman been ambitious for supremacy he might have unseated his chief and taken his place with small expenditure of effort in the political quarters where he commanded influence. For at this time his promotion was widely suggested, not only in recognition of his success but as a step to his advancement to the supreme command. Indeed, Congress had even gone so far as to propose a bill providing for a second lieutenant-general, with this purpose in view.

Nothing is finer in Sherman's career or character than his attitude to these suggestions, which he quelled by a letter to his brother on January 22—"I wrote you that I deem it unwise to make another Lieutenant-General, or to create the rank of general. Let the law stand as now. I will accept no commission that would tend to create a rivalry with Grant. I want him to hold what he has earned and got. I have all the rank I want . . . and it makes no difference to me whether that be Major-General or Marshal . . . I have commanded one hundred thousand men in battle, and on the march, successfully and without confusion, and that is enough for reputation. Now, I want rest and peace . . ."

With equal consideration for Grant's peace of mind, as well as position, he sent him a personal reassurance—"I have been told that Congress meditates a bill to make another lieutenant-general for me. I have written to John Sherman to stop it. . . . It would be mischievous, for there are enough rascals who would try to sow differences between us, whereas you and I now are in perfect understanding. . . . I should emphatically decline any commission calculated to bring us into rivalry. . . . I doubt if men in Congress fully realize that you and I are honest in our professions of want of ambition. I know I feel none, and to-day will gladly surrender my position and influence to any other who is better able to wield the power. The flurry attending my recent success will soon blow over, and give place to new developments."

If loyalty to Grant was one check on his ambition, another form of loyalty was perhaps an equally strong check. For his love of and trust in his own troops made him dislike even the idea of taking over a command where he would be a stranger and among strangers.

To breathe the atmosphere of mutual trust was essential for the full development of his powers. The storm of Fort McAlister had meant all the more to him because it was carried out by his old Shiloh division, and its inspiration to him is illustrated in his reflection, to his wife, "I never saw a more confident army. The soldiers think I know everything and that they can do anything."

Among men who rise to fame and leadership two types are recognizable—those who are born with a belief in themselves and those in whom it is a slow growth dependent on actual achievement. To men of the last type their own success is a constant surprise, and its fruits the more delicious, yet to be tested cautiously with a haunting sense of doubt whether it is not all a dream. In that doubt lies true modesty, not the sham of insincere self-depreciation but the modesty of "moderation," in the Greek sense. It is poise, not pose. And at this moment, when the world was ringing with acclaim of Sherman's "march through Georgia," no better proof of his balance, no better augury for the greater feat to follow, could be desired than the feeling which underlay his musing comment—"Like one who has walked a narrow plank, I look back and wonder if I really did it."

CHAPTER XXI

THROUGH THE CAROLINAS—CUTTING THE ROOTS OF THE CONFEDERACY

DEEP as was Sherman's disappointment when on December 15 he had received Grant's order to take his force by sea to Virginia, with his strategic task uncompleted, he had sent an instant reply by Colonel Babcock that he would come directly sufficient sea-transport arrived. And he made no protest beyond the incidental remark that he "had expected, after reducing Savannah, instantly to march to Columbia, South Carolina; thence to Raleigh, and thence to report to you."

In a further letter two days later he concluded with the remark, "I have a faint belief that, when Colonel Babcock reaches you, you will delay operations long enough to enable me to succeed here. With Savannah in our possession, at some future time if not now, we can punish South Carolina as she deserves. . . . I do sincerely believe that the whole United States, North and South, would rejoice to have this army turned loose on South Carolina, to devastate that State in the manner we have done in Georgia, and it would have a direct and immediate bearing on your campaign in Virginia."

Sherman's hope was already gratified, for on its way to him was a despatch from Halleck conveying word of Grant's change of mind and his decision to let Sherman stay in the South and operate in any way that he wished. In a personal note Halleck dropped the pleasant sentiment and hint—"Should you capture Charleston, I hope that by *some accident* the place may be destroyed, and, if a little salt should be sown upon its site, it may prevent the growth of future crops of nullification and secession."

On December 18 also, Grant wrote himself. First, in congratulation. "When apprehensions of your safety were expressed by the President, I assured him with the army you had, and you in command of it, there was no danger but you would *strike* bottom on salt water some place; that I would not feel the same security—in fact, would not have intrusted the expedition to any other living commander." Second, as to the future. "I did think the best thing to do was to bring the greater part of your army here, and wipe out Lee. The turn affairs now seem to be taking has shaken me in that opinion. I doubt whether you may not accomplish more toward that result where you are than if brought here,—especially as I am informed . . . that it would take about two months to get you here with all the other calls there are for ocean transportation. I want to get your views about what ought to be done, and what can be done. . . . My own opinion is that Lee is averse to going out of Virginia, and if the cause of the South is lost he wants Richmond to be the last place to surrender." Was this shrewd insight into the last infirmity of a noble Virginian's mind? "If he has such views, it may be well to indulge him until we get everything else in our hands." Grant, under Sherman's inspiration, appears to be slipping away from his old obsession with the goal of destroying the enemy's main army.

On Christmas Eve, Sherman supplied the views for which Grant had asked. "I feel no doubt whatever as to our future plans. I have thought them over so long and well that they appear as clear as daylight. I left Augusta untouched on purpose, because the enemy will be in doubt as to my objective point, after we cross the Savannah River, whether it be Augusta or Charleston, and will naturally divide his forces. I will then move either on Branchville or on Columbia, by any curved line that gives us the best supplies, breaking up in our course as much railroad as possible; then, ignoring Charleston and Augusta both, I would occupy Columbia and Camden, pausing there long enough to observe the effect. I would then strike for the Charleston and Wilmington railroad . . . and, if possible, communicate with the fleet. . . . Then I would favor an attack on Wilmington, in the belief that Porter and Butler will fail in their present undertaking. Charleston is . . . a point of little importance, after all its railroads leading into the interior have been destroyed or occupied by us . . . I would then favor a movement direct on Raleigh. The game is then up with Lee, unless he comes out of Richmond, avoids you and fights me; in which case I would reckon on you being on his heels. Now that Hood is used up by Thomas, I feel disposed to bring the matter to an issue as quick as possible. . . . I have ordered him [Thomas] to pursue Hood down into Alabama, trusting to the country for supplies. . . . I wish you could run down and see us; it would . . . show to both armies that they are acting on a common plan."

The full growth of Sherman's conception of war is even more clearly shown in his coincident reply to Halleck—"I think the time has come now when we should attempt the boldest moves, and my experience is, that they are easier of execution than more timid ones, because the enemy is disconcerted by them—as, for instance, my recent campaign. I also doubt the wisdom of concentration beyond a certain extent, for the roads of this country limit the amount of men that can be brought to bear in any one battle, and I do not believe that any general can handle more than sixty thousand men in battle." It is significant that Sherman's deep reflection and experience had brought him to the view expressed by that oft-neglected genius Marshal Saxe a century earlier. "I think our campaign of the last month, as well as every step I take from this point northward, is as much a direct attack upon Lee's army as though we were operating within the sound of his artillery. . . . I attach more importance to these deep incisions into the enemy's country, because this war differs from European wars [of the old style] in this particular: we are not only fighting hostile armies but a hostile people, and must make old and young, rich and poor, feel the hard hand of war as well as their organised armies. I know that this recent movement of mine through Georgia has had a wonderful effect in this respect. Thousands who had been deceived by their lying newspapers to believe that we were being whipped all the time now realise the truth, and have no appetite for a repetition. . . ."

Finally, Sherman replied to Halleck's "hint as to Charleston," saying "the whole army is burning with an insatiable desire to wreak vengeance upon South Carolina. I almost tremble at her fate, but feel that she deserves all that seems in store for her. Many and many a person in Georgia asked me why we did not go to South Carolina; and, when I answered that we were *en route* for that State, the invariable reply was, 'Well, if you will make those people feel the utmost severities of war, we will pardon you for your desolation of Georgia.' I look upon Columbia as quite as bad as Charleston, and I doubt if we will spare the public buildings there as we did at Milledgeville."

For, after leaving Atlanta, the towns of Georgia had been treated leniently by Sherman, and at Savannah there had been such an avoidance of destruction and so little interference that the life of the town rather revived than decayed under the occupation, helped by Sherman's action in issuing supplies to relieve immediate wants. And the behaviour of the troops was remarkably good. This clemency was dictated by statecraft, for at Savannah the desire for peace was manifest among a large and influential section of the people, and Sherman nourished it with the aim of developing schism within the Secession.

But in the eyes of the North, South Carolina had been the symbol of secession ever since Sumter, and to scourge her as the scapegoat would be a satisfaction to the instinct of vengeance. An appropriate vengeance in that it ironically recognized the very principle of separate State sovereignty for which the South had seceded. Woe unto South Carolina.

For the fate that was now in store for her there were, however, two military justifications, one good, one bad. The first, that Lee's army now depended mainly for its supplies on the area around Columbia. The second, expressed in Sherman's memoirs—"Personally I had many friends in Charleston, to whom I would gladly have extended protection and mercy, but they were beyond my personal reach, and I would not restrain the army lest its vigor and energy should be impaired. . . ." Here Sherman's war-creed almost passed beyond the logical to the diabolical, and no utterance does his reputation a worse disservice.

On January 2 he received from Grant a definite approval of his proposals and entire freedom to change his route as he might wish. Sherman planned to begin his northward march about the middle of January, and to that end promptly began the transfer of his right wing by sea to Port Royal and thence to Pocotaligo on the Charleston railroad—an experience which amply reconciled the men to the prospect of marching the rest of the way to Virginia over land. The left wing also began moving across and up the Savannah River with the aim of making Robertsville, some thirty miles north-west of Savannah, its assembly point. The army would thus form two horns, twenty miles apart and over forty in front of Savannah, one pointing to Charleston and the other to Augusta. This disposition had a dual advantage, for it not only kept the Confederates in doubt as to the ultimate direction of advance, but enabled the supplies for both horns to be brought to the starting points by water.

But the necessary supplies for the new move were slow to arrive by sea from the North, delayed by storms, and a further cause of delay was the torrential onset of the winter rains, which flooded the country and the roads and even swept away the pontoon bridge across the Savannah River, imperilling a division which was in the act of crossing. In front of the right wing the Salkiehatchie swelled to a breadth of a mile, and at Sister's Ferry, where the bulk of the left wing was aiming to cross the Savannah, this river became nearly three miles wide.

About January 24 the weather began to clear and Sherman, remembering from his South Carolina experience that February was usually a good month, fixed his start for the 1st. His calculation was that he would thus complete his inland curve and be approaching the sea again before the March storms arrived. He had provisionally decided that from Columbia he would move outward and north-eastward on a curving path through Fayetteville to Goldsboro. By this course he would not only sever the roots of all the railroads running in from the coast but bring himself within reach of helping hands on the North Carolina coast.

For important changes had begun to mature there. At the end of December, Butler's attempt on Fort Fisher, the key to Wilmington, had failed ignominiously, in accordance with Sherman's expectation, based on his judgment of Butler. Admiral Porter, whose relations with Butler had been as bad as with McClernand, then appealed to Sherman for the loan of a division. Sherman declined, preferring that the Confederate garrisons along the coast should stay there rather than be set free, for want of anything to guard, to concentrate inland and block his own advance. A strategic calculation both wise and subtle. Moreover, he was certain that as he cut their communications with the interior each of these ports would, in turn, fall like ripe plums.

But in the meantime Grant had taken the more obvious course of sending back the force for a fresh attempt under a new commander, Terry, who successfully stormed the fort on January 15. A smaller force was also at New Berne, higher up the coast, which had been first occupied in 1861. Further, Grant had ordered Schofield's corps (21,000 strong) to be brought thither from Tennessee, in order to co-operate with Sherman's approach, and to come under his command.

So eager was Grant to help his lieutenant that he even told him "should you be brought to a halt anywhere, I can send two corps . . . to your support, from the troops about Richmond." But Sherman replied: "My army is large enough for the purpose and I ask no re-enforcement, but simply wish the utmost activity to be kept up at all other points, so that concentration against me may not be universal."

Sherman appreciated that weight of numbers meant loss of mobility and that indirect aid was more effective than direct. Apart from his request that supplies should be despatched to New Berne to await him, and that Schofield should move inland and seize Goldsboro' in anticipation of his approach, he arranged with Admiral Dahlgren to keep step with him along the coast, ready to communicate and co-operate at the mouths of the successive rivers which ran out from the interior. Sherman had established his usual happy relations with the navy, and he and Dahlgren were now working as intimately as previously on the Mississippi he had worked with Porter. Finally, Sherman arranged with General Foster to hold Savannah, where new and shorter defences had been built, as well as the fortified camp at Pocotaligo; and to demonstrate against Charleston, occupying it if and when Sherman's advance past its rear led the Confederates to evacuate the port.

By the last day of January the right wing, all but one division, was assembled at Pocotaligo, with its trains loaded afresh with twenty days' rations and ample ammunition. And having proved in the march through Georgia how light an army could move, Sherman now proved that it could move lighter still. Although it was winter, even the officers were now made to abandon tents and bivouac in pairs under a strip of tenting stretched over sticks or boughs, while all camp furniture was relentlessly discarded. On the left wing Williams's corps was also ready, but the floods had not yet subsided sufficiently for Davis's corps and the cavalry to reach their assembly point north of the Savannah. Rather than lose time and the fine weather, Sherman decided to lead off with the right wing, which had worse obstacles to cross on its actual march-route, while the left wing followed on—so that his formation was like a man pushing with his right shoulder forward.

On the morning of February 1 the troops, advancing inland, began their four-hundred-mile march. Compared to it the march through Georgia was a simple problem—"child's play" in Sherman's words—for the way north was barred by a many-layered series of deep and wide rivers with swamp-bordered banks. Sherman, indeed, was always vexed at the disproportionate praise lavished on the first and in retrospect rated the relative difficulty and importance of the second as ten to one.

Covering twenty miles on the first day, the advance continued for two days up the corridor or watershed between the Salkiehatchie and Savannah Rivers, as if moving direct on Augusta; then on the 3rd, suddenly wheeled to the right and forced its way across the upper reaches of the Salkiehatchie.

This was a brilliant feat, Mower's division wading through the swamps and propelling themselves across the river on floats and rafts under a heavy fire, while G. A. Smith's division outflanked the defenders by wading or swimming across at another point. But the feat did not end with the capture of the far bank, for the wide-skirted river had then to be bridged, and the roads through the swamps on either side paved with logs, for the passage of the main columns and the trains. Where Logan's corps, for example, crossed there were no less than fifteen separate channels to be bridged.

This laborious process had to be repeated not only at the main rivers, but at each of the multitudinous streams which intersected the route—along which sixty thousand men, forty thousand animals, and three thousand wagons and ambulances were advancing by several parallel roads. Little wonder that Sherman's army of expert woodsmen from the West came to be regarded with almost superstitious awe and, by their irresistible conquest of natural obstacles, acquired a moral dominance which was worth more than numbers.

Meantime, Beauregard, Hardee, and D. H. Hill (who had taken over the immediate command at Augusta) had met in conference on February 2, to decide upon a plan. If the consultation was somewhat belated, the Confederate commanders probably imagined that the floods would prevent Sherman moving and give them an adequate interval of grace. It was estimated that, including the shrunken corps of Hood's late army, they could concentrate a force of 33,450 effectives to resist Sherman. But of these Stewart's corps, reckoned as 3,000, was not expected until the 10th or 11th. Should they concentrate at Augusta, Charleston, or Branchville, the midway junction for Columbia and the North? They considered that it was essential to hold Augusta and Charleston as long as possible, and in consequence decided that Hardee should resist Sherman on the line of the Salkiehatchie, falling back to cover Charleston if this line was pierced. The rest of the forces would guard Augusta, except that part of Wheeler's cavalry were left to cover Branchville and Columbia. But "it was held in contemplation" that one of the corps from Tennessee might also be sent to Branchville. The plan was certainly a military mixed grill, flavoured by the Confederate government's natural reluctance to abandon so important a city and port as Charleston.

In country which afforded so many and strong natural barriers a force of 33,000 should be able to resist one of barely double its strength, and Jefferson Davis, on receiving the report, was unpleasantly surprised at its gloomy tone. All the more because he felt that a stronger force might well be concentrated—Hardee alone had 25,000 men reported present for duty whereas the conference estimate only counted him as having 14,500 effectives. And it is just to this much-maligned "amateur strategist" to note that in reply he urged Beauregard to concentrate all his forces south of Branchville.

Unfortunately Sherman now gave the Confederate command no time either for "contemplation" or concentration. By February 5 his whole right wing was across the Salkiehatchie and, as his left wing was now coming up, he gave the order to advance next morning on the Augusta-Charleston railroad—not at Branchville, the natural point where the enemy would expect him, but west of it. Despite heavy rainstorms and flooded streams the Union columns came within five miles of it by nightfall. Early on the 7th they were advancing, with the leading divisions deployed in anticipation of battle, when Howard sighted one of the foragers galloping back to meet the column and shouting, as he neared it, "Hurry up, General, we've got the railroad."

For the Confederate forces, surprised and dazed by the way Sherman's men had come through the swamps, had folded back like a double door on its hinges towards Branchville on the east and Augusta on the west. Even burning the bridges, which suited Sherman admirably, for they thus protected his flanks while he was going on through the open doorway to Columbia.

To keep up the delusion, Kilpatrick was sent to within a few miles of Augusta, while the infantry "expanded" along the railroad, breaking it up over a front of nearly fifty miles. On the 11th the right wing again advanced, swinging outwards to cut the Columbia railroad behind Branchville before closing in on Columbia. As a preliminary, the swamps of the South Edisto had been crossed by a moonlight passage, the men wading up to their armpits in the slimy ooze, and the railroad was reached at Orangeburg on the 12th. This effectually separated the Confederate forces and prevented any chance of the two halves re-uniting. The left wing, which had reached the railroad later, quitted it later and then moved, by corps successively, direct on Columbia across the two forks of the Edisto River.

This phase of the march was punctuated by an interchange of letters between Wheeler and Sherman. Wheeler offered to cease burning cotton—leaving it as prize of war—if Sherman would cease burning other property. Sherman, who had no spare transport to carry it off, replied, "I hope you will burn all cotton and save us the trouble. We don't want it, and it has proven a curse to our country. All you don't burn I will. As to private houses occupied by peaceful families, my orders are not to molest or disturb them, and I think my orders are obeyed. Vacant houses being of no use to anybody, I care little about, as the owners have thought them of no use to themselves. . . ." But, evidently with a shrewd idea where the trouble lay, he wrote to Kilpatrick: "You may burn all cotton; spare dwelling houses that are occupied, and teach your men to be courteous to women; it goes a great way. . . ." And a casual entry in the diary of his judge-advocate and secretary, Henry Hitchcock, on February 11, suggests that Wheeler's complaint had made an impression—"Audenried brought word house burned. General mad." Curiously, the week when there is most clear evidence of Sherman being aroused to a real effort to check such abuses is the very week in which occurred the "crime" for which he has been most stigmatized—the burning of Columbia.

For, on the 16th, Sherman's converging columns came within sight of the capital of South Carolina—and entered the heart of the most fertile agricultural area in the South. Too late, Beauregard on the 13th had ordered his three small infantry corps from Augusta to march for Columbia, whither Lee had despatched Wade Hampton, a famous South Carolinian general, to take charge of the defence—in compensation for lack of an army he was given a step in rank. Meantime Hardee was still expecting Sherman to attack Charleston.

During the next few days the telegraph wires between Columbia, Charleston and Richmond buzzed with frantic messages. The first decision was the abandonment of Charleston, which in Northern eyes was the soul and spring of the Secession, under strategic pressure exerted a hundred miles distant in its rear—an effect foretold by Sherman. Indeed, when the rumour reached him now his only comment was, "I have but little doubt of the truth of the story; I have already cut two of the great arteries which give them life; in a few days I will strike the Florence railroad, and they must leave then."

On the 15th Beauregard gave orders for the prompt evacuation of Charleston and for Hardee to join him. But Charleston had been held too long for Columbia to be saved and Beauregard, finding reinforcements could not reach Columbia in time, directed all forces to concentrate in rear of it, at Chester on the railroad which ran through Charlotte and Danville to Richmond. Simultaneously Sherman was issuing orders that after Columbia his columns, instead of continuing north, were to swerve to the north-east through Cheraw and Fayetteville.

On the morning of the 17th the Confederates gave up the crossings of the Congaree, and Columbia itself, falling back to Chester, just as Sherman's left wing columns were moving to gain crossings fifteen miles above the city. The evacuation was too hurried for the bulk of the ordnance stores to be destroyed, but in the early morning, by the witness of the Confederate ordnance officer, "the straggling cavalry and rabble were stripping the warehouses and railroad depots, and the city was illumined with burning cotton." Another witness, Colonel Portlock, relates how men engaged in looting a store "drew their pistols" on Wade Hampton himself, and adds, "These men were cut off from their brigade, and were under the influence of liquor given them by the citizens of Columbia. It is beyond question that many disgraceful acts were committed during the evacuation. . . ."

Thus, when the Union troops marched in, hundreds of cotton bales littered the streets, some still ablaze and others smouldering, while a high wind was blowing the flakes far and wide, so that the trees and roofs were coated in white as by a snowstorm. Only Logan's corps entered the city, passing through to the far side but leaving a brigade to furnish guards. From a foolish desire to propitiate the invaders, many of the citizens offered them drink, bringing out pailfuls of neat whiskey, and soon numbers of tipsy soldiers were reeling about the streets. So many, indeed, that Howard brought in a fresh brigade to relieve the first and gather into arrest its drunk and disorderly members.

Nevertheless, at sundown the city was still fairly quiet, while extra guards had been brought in by Howard to check trouble and to arrest the drunken stragglers. Sherman himself, in company with the mayor, visited several old acquaintances who had hastened to bring their presence to his notice and then retired to rest at the house where he had taken up his quarters. But about 8 P.M. fires broke out in the heart of the city and the sparks, carried by a wind that had now risen to gale strength, spread the conflagration from building to building. As most of them were of wood, and cotton warehouses were intermixed, the flaming inferno was beyond all power of man to curtail, although fresh brigades were hurried in to fight the fire, and the whole city would probably have been gutted but for a providential change of wind in the early hours of the 18th. The fact that Howard, most truly Christian of soldiers, was in personal charge of these efforts throughout the night is good testimony to their genuine vigour. And Sherman himself came down to rescue his old acquaintances, giving up his own quarters to them.

Whilst the majority of the Union soldiers struggled hard and at risk to themselves to check the fire and bring away the homeless inhabitants, a considerable number ran riot in a drunken frenzy of loot and destruction. Drunken ruffians were arrested by the score or even shot down, but to restrain the orgy was all the more difficult because to them were added not only the rabble of the city but released Union prisoners bent on revenge for their sufferings in the dismal prison pens of the neighbourhood.

The sun rose on a ruined city, half of it a gigantic ash-heap. Fortunately the chief residential part had escaped, but, even so, thousands were homeless and those who had not found refuge with friends were now gathered in despairing and nerve-stricken groups along the streets or in the open spaces of the unburnt area, hugging to them such scanty chattels and furniture as they had saved from the devouring furnace. Howard, greatly distressed at the misery of the people, busied himself in finding accommodation for the refugees and, with Sherman's approval, handed over to the mayor five hundred beef cattle and a hundred muskets with which to arm a citizen guard to preserve order and quell the rabble.

The real origin of the first outbreaks of fire in the evening of the 17th will never be known. It may well have come from the smouldering cotton so foolishly set alight by the retiring Confederates. But once these outbreaks had occurred, there is no doubt that the sight kindled the fuddled imagination and passion of the many drunken soldiers and that these not only made the fire more difficult to control but spread it with their own hands. Once the wooden buildings of the city were well alight, the wind completed the tragedy, and stultified any hope of restricting it. Without the wind the drunkards would have lost their most powerful accomplice; without the drink, the fire would probably have failed to gain a wide grip. In support of the common Confederate accusation that the disaster was deliberately and officially instigated, no tittle of reasonable evidence has ever been adduced. And generals who plan to burn a city are unlikely to take up their quarters in the middle of it.

That suspicions lingered in Confederate minds, even years after, was natural in view of Sherman's intemperate language at Savannah. But as he marched through the Carolinas even his language tended to moderate as the conviction grew upon him that the end of the war was drawing near, and with it the need for the reconstruction of peace. He was still on occasion relentless, as, for example, when a number of murdered foragers were found with the label "Death to all foragers" pinned on their mutilated bodies, and he ordered an equal number of prisoners "to be disposed of in like manner." But drastic as this reprisal, his temperate and dignified remonstrance to Wade Hampton contrasts favourably with the latter's lurid abuse and foolish threats to kill two for one, singling out officers—foolish, because he held few prisoners and Sherman many.

But it was also an anachronism that the Confederate cavalry should constitute themselves judges, for the complaints against them from their suffering fellow-countrymen were now even more numerous than during the Georgian campaign. With both armies the practice of living on the country led to an increasing laxness of discipline, so that foragers searched not only for food but for clothes and jewels.

Yet, even at its blackest, when viewed against the background of history the conduct of the armies was white compared with that of other troops, before and since, who have practised the same methods of subsistence. And the historian who examines the crimes they committed when drunk can only marvel at the way in which they avoided the worse crimes common in a drink- or passion-intoxicated soldiery. Did the very fact that they were held on a light rein develop in them a fundamental self-control that restrained them from the mass outrages which other armies have committed in ungovernable reaction from the more rigid bonds of discipline?

This was certainly in accord with the fundamental nature of Sherman's army—whose strength lay in its suppleness not in its rigidity. It was as characteristic that the foragers should, with few exceptions, restrain themselves from the more brutal abuses of war as that they should drop their loot to seize a railroad or other strategic point. The distinction, both subtle and supple, is akin to that between a privateer and a pirate, on the seas. A distinction easily missed, yet one that is vital in the sphere of war.

This strength in suppleness which Sherman's army developed had a far-reaching influence—not least on the purely military operations. For in its physical and moral effect lies the only reasonable explanation of Sherman's unchecked progress for several hundred miles through a country strewn with obstacles and in face of an enemy whose numerical strength was now ample for an effective resistance. To the irresistibility of this progress Sherman's flexibility contributed as much as his variability of direction. Moving on a wide and irregular front—with four, five or six columns, each covered by a cloud of foragers—if one was blocked, others would be pushing on. And the opposing forces in consequence became so "jumpy" that they repeatedly gave way to this moral pressure, and fell back before they felt any serious physical pressure, their minds so saturated with the impression of the uncanny manœuvring power of Sherman and his men, that whenever they took up a position of resistance they were thinking about their way of retreat. It was even recorded that the shout "We're Bill Sherman's raiders—you'd better git" sufficed as a hint on occasions. If confidence be indeed half the battle, then to undermine the opponent's confidence is more than the other half—because it gains the fruits without a fight.

The "long-range" effect is vividly and ominously shown in a letter from Lee to the Governor of North Carolina on February 24— "The state of despondency that now prevails among our people is producing a bad effect upon the troops. Desertions are becoming very frequent and there is good reason to believe that they are occasioned to a considerable extent by letters written to the soldiers by their friends at home . . . that our cause is hopeless, and that they had better provide for themselves." Sherman's rays were melting the rear of the military ice-barrier which had so long blocked Grant's advance.

On February 20 Sherman had resumed his march from Columbia, after two days spent in destroying the railroads round it as well as the State arsenal, mint, and foundries. The initial direction was due north and both wings converged on Winnsboro. From there, the cavalry and Davis's corps continued towards Chester, as a deception, but the rest suddenly wheeled to the right on the 22nd, and next day crossed the broad Catawba River unopposed in an easterly direction. Beauregard, having now fallen back from Chester, was concentrating his troops at Charlotte, still further north.

But tremendous rains caused so rapid a rise in the Catawba River that the pontoon bridge was swept away before Davis's corps, which had now wheeled round in turn, could follow the other corps across. Not until the 28th was Davis able to cross, on a bridge securely laid at a fresh point. Meantime, the right wing was allowed to go slowly forward across the fifty-mile stretch between the Catawba and the Pedee Rivers; the other corps of the left wing being held back to safeguard the crossing for Davis, and the cavalry pushed up the east bank to maintain the impression that Charlotte was still the objective. Once Davis had safely started eastward on March 1, the right wing was released and bounded forward so rapidly over a series of swamp-bordered creeks that Cheraw was reached early on the 3rd.

A few days before, Hardee had arrived at Cheraw on his cross-country journey from Charleston to Charlotte, and had been halted there on the discovery of Sherman's eastward move from the Catawba. But both he and Beauregard were still confused as to Sherman's real direction, and although Beauregard guessed the truth first, it was too late to reinforce Hardee. And Sherman's right wing came upon Hardee so quickly that his only thought was to get away. Abandoning the line of the Pedee, he fell back north of Rockingham, barely able to destroy the bridges and unable to prevent the Union troops laying and crossing on a pontoon bridge.

Hardee's intention to continue his retreat northwards to Greensboro was, however, interrupted by an urgent message from Beauregard to turn north-eastwards to Fayetteville. For it was now Beauregard's hope and idea to concentrate all his forces there and block Sherman's advance across the Cape Fear River, the last big river which separated Sherman from Schofield's friendly aid. To this end Beauregard sought to arrange that the force under Bragg which was facing Schofield should withdraw unseen and join the concentration against Sherman. As Bragg had already, on February 24, evacuated Wilmington, the last Confederate port on the Atlantic coast, he had nothing to detain him if he could slip away from Schofield.

But this plan in turn was to be frustrated by the effect of Sherman's progress and Schofield's intervention—on the mind of a fresh opponent. For at this crisis Joseph Johnston was summoned from his North Carolina home to take supreme command of the forces opposing Sherman. Jefferson Davis's reluctance had been overcome and his hand forced by the overwhelming military and public demand for "Old Joe" who alone, it was held, could rekindle the flagging confidence of the Confederate forces for a final effort.

Johnston's task was complicated not only by the existing dispersion of his forces but by the fact that he had to operate in what were virtually Lee's back areas. For in North Carolina were Lee's supply depots, and with South Carolina lost Lee insisted that these remaining supplies must be kept for his army, leaving Johnston to forage on the country—and so hampering his mobility. Even stronger than Johnston's impression of his own handicaps was that of Sherman's superiority for—as he related subsequently, when he heard of Sherman's unchecked progress through South Carolina, surmounting so many obstacles—"he made up his mind that there had been no such army since the days of Julius Cæsar." The conviction that his task is a forlorn hope is an unpromising foundation for a commander's success in executing it.

Indeed, like Beauregard earlier, he felt that the only chance lay in prompt aid from Lee, and almost his first step was to telegraph Lee on March 1—"Would it be possible to hold Richmond itself with half your army, while the other half joined us near Roanoke to crush Sherman? We might then turn on Grant."

The suggestion was undoubtedly wise. During his march through South Carolina, Sherman had remarked—"If Lee is a soldier of genius, he will seek to transfer his army from Richmond to Raleigh or Columbia; if he is a man simply of detail, he will remain where he is, and his speedy defeat is sure." The longer it was postponed the better for Sherman because the nearer would he be to supplies, to Schofield and to Grant, and the more time for the demoralizing and supply-denuding effect of his progress to weaken the Confederate troops and people.

But Lee was unwilling to turn against Sherman unless and until he reached the Roanoke, and Johnston was left to devise a counter to Sherman's advance from his own resources. His doubt whether Hardee could reach Fayetteville before Sherman, and his uncertainty whether Goldsboro' or Raleigh was Sherman's objective, led him to fix Smithfield, in rear midway between these two places, as his concentration point. Accordingly, the troops from Charlotte were sent thither by rail.

Then, on the 6th, the appearance of some of Schofield's troops, who were beginning to repair the railroad from New Berne towards Goldsboro, gave Bragg the impression that a serious attack on Goldsboro was intended. He obtained Johnston's permission to take such troops as had already reached Smithfield, add them to his own, and strike a crippling blow at Schofield. But after overrunning the outposts Bragg was brought to a halt in front of the Union entrenchments and there wasted three days. When, on the 11th, he marched back through Goldsboro, Hardee had already yielded Fayetteville and the Cape Fear River to Sherman's advancing troops.

There would, actually, have been adequate time for a concentration at Fayetteville, for not until early on the 7th had Sherman's left wing, delayed by roads which were becoming worse with the incessant rain, come up across the Pedee. In anticipation of battle, he now wished to group his forces more closely and with the left wing ahead, as this was the flank of danger. But, once started, the march across the seventy-mile stretch between the Pedee and Cape Fear Rivers, a wild and dense forest region, was perhaps the most remarkable of all the feats of his army. Following two days of good weather, storm after storm swept over his marching columns as they ploughed through quagmires that had once been roads, and now had to be corduroyed almost every foot of the way to enable the artillery and trains to follow on. Yet, in accord with Sherman's design, Davis's corps, the last to start, was the first to reach Fayetteville on the 11th.

Thither all the columns had converged, the two "horns" leading, and the news of the enemy's advance from so many directions simultaneously seems to have stampeded Hardee into an unduly precipitate retreat across the Cape Fear River, whence he again retired divergently from Sherman's line of advance and took up, near Averysboro, a position covering the road to Raleigh, the capital of North Carolina.

In view of the shrinkage of his supplies, Sherman had contemplated a possible wheel to the right if his way across the Cape Fear was barred, and a move down to the sea at Wilmington. But the ease with which he had gained the last barrier in his path led him at once to decide to make Goldsboro' his next bound. While the pontoon bridges were being laid across the Cape Fear River on the 12th, a shrill whistle was heard down river, and soon a small tug appeared bringing despatches from the Union force at Wilmington.

Once more Sherman and his men felt the glorious sensation of coming to the surface after a deep dive—into the Confederacy. By this boat, Sherman sent off a report to Grant and an urgent request for shoes and underclothes to be forwarded at once from Wilmington. In the meantime he destroyed the arsenal at Fayetteville, but otherwise left the town untouched, impressing strongly on the troops that now they were in North Carolina foraging must be strictly regulated and a conciliatory attitude adopted. By the morning of the 14th the whole army had crossed the river, and that afternoon the tug returned, with a couple of gunboats, bringing supplies of sugar and coffee but the unpleasant news that no supplies of clothing were at Wilmington.

So, rather than wait, Sherman ordered his ragged army to advance once more, on the 15th. As a means to additional security by mobility in this final bound, he formed four "light" divisions out of each wing, unencumbered by trains. The trains were to march on the less exposed flank. Then, to persuade Johnston that Raleigh, and not Goldsboro', was his objective—that he was still "collecting" State capitals—he moved the cavalry and the four "light" divisions of the left wing northward up the Raleigh road, with orders to swerve eastward on the second day and converge to meet the right wing at Bentonville, ten miles short of Goldsboro'. Thus they would form a shield behind which the rest of the army could pursue its way safely to Goldsboro'. "I want the three first marches [to Bentonville] to be made with prudence and deliberation. I am willing to accept battle with Johnston's concentrated force, but would not attack him in position until I make junction with General Schofield."

The four "light" divisions of the right wing were to move centrally, within supporting distance of the "shield," but about five or six miles ahead so that, if it was attacked, they could come up on its flank by a simple wheel to the left.

On the second day, the "shield" came in contact with Hardee's entrenched position on a narrow ridge between the river and a swamp south of Averysboro'. Sherman, coming up in person, directed a flank manœuvre which caused Hardee's troops to fall back to a fresh position. During the night they retired from this towards Raleigh—and Sherman, according to plan, swung his "shield" eastward on its way towards Bentonville.

During the past few days vital messages had been travelling between Raleigh, Petersburg and Richmond. In a gloomy despatch to Lee on the 11th Johnston had said, "I will not give battle to Sherman's united army, unless your situation may require such a course; but will if I can find it divided. Of this please advise me. . . ." On the 13th, Jefferson Davis wrote urgently to Lee saying that Johnston was reported to have ordered the removal of supplies from Raleigh, and that, "If this indicates a purpose to retire behind the railroad line from Goldsboro' to Raleigh . . . the region of supplies will be lost, and we cannot maintain our position in Virginia and North Carolina. I hope you will be able, by specific instructions, to avert so great a calamity."

Next day Lee replied to Johnston—"If you are forced back from Raleigh, and we be deprived of the supplies from East North Carolina, I do not know how this army can be supported. . . . That you may understand my situation I will state that the supplies in Virginia are exhausted." He urged Johnston to seek an opportunity of striking a prompt blow, provided that he could do it without risking actual disaster. "But should that not be possible, you will also see that I cannot remain here."

Thus Johnston was spurred to a battle which he feared unless he could find and catch one part of Sherman's army out of reach of support from the rest. This hope seemed to be fading, for even up to the night of the 17th he was still puzzled and uncertain of Sherman's direction. But soon after dawn next morning he received a report from Wade Hampton which showed beyond doubt that Sherman was aiming for Goldsboro. Johnston at once set his forces in motion for Bentonville. Knowing that Sherman's left wing only had been identified at Averysboro', his hope was to intercept its march on Goldsboro, in the belief that the right wing was moving by routes well away to the east. Faulty maps gave him an exaggerated idea of the distance separating Sherman's two wings. But his concentration at least was helped by the fact of being in telegraphic touch with his subordinates and by the knowledge that Schofield was still repairing the railroad from New Berne, with no sign of pressing towards Goldsboro'. In contrast, Sherman since he left Fayetteville, was once more cut off even from tugboat communication with Schofield.

In choosing to give battle at Bentonville, Johnston had unwittingly chosen a site which threatened disaster in view of Sherman's choice of the same spot, and an earlier time, for the convergence of his columns. But he was favoured by the weather, so vile that Sherman's columns, floundering through the mud, became not only delayed but strung out. Instead of reaching Bentonville on the night of the 17th, Davis's two "light" divisions were still eight miles short of it on the night of the 18th, with Williams's divisions eight miles further in rear, while the right wing, marching on more or less parallel roads to the east, was behind instead of ahead of the left wing.

Johnston was helped, too, by a misleading but natural inference which Sherman, ignorant of Bragg's recent thrust towards New Berne, drew from the action at Averysboro'—that Hardee was merely fighting to gain time for Johnston's forces to concentrate at and cover Raleigh. The direction of Hardee's retreat strengthened this deduction, as also did Sherman's knowledge of Johnston's character—he had not been able to see the messages from Jefferson Davis and Lee!

Even so, Sherman stayed with the left wing, the flank of danger until the early hours of the 19th. Then, feeling that his surmise was correct, he rode over to the right wing in order to hasten its march and be nearer Schofield's line of advance on Goldsboro—the earlier he could get in touch with Schofield the earlier would his security and his concentration be ensured. The mud and the mistaken inference had now combined to cause a change in Sherman's original march orders. Instead of converging northwards towards Bentonville, the columns of the right wing were directed to keep apart and continue north-eastwards in order to reach Goldsboro and its potential supplies as early as possible. Unless the enemy gave battle south of Bentonville and the Neuse River the convergence might merely produce a traffic jam and a shortage of provisions; Sherman had to keep moving in order to live and every day's delay placed a strain on his supplies.

He had further reassurance to his decision when, about noon on the 19th, he was overtaken on his ride by a messenger from Slocum with the news that the left wing had still met no opposition stronger than cavalry and needed no help. But when the message overtook him the left wing was being overtaken by a less pleasant discovery.

For the leading division had bumped into a partly concealed line of breastworks astride the Bentonville road, and an attempt to carry them revealed that they were held in strength and extended ominously wide—like an iron maiden with arms outstretched to enfold a reluctant lover. Scenting danger, Davis's two divisions deployed and hurriedly entrenched, while Williams's were hurried forward. Before these could arrive, Johnston's right arm (Hardee) had begun an enfolding movement and pressed so hard on Davis's left flank (Carlin's division) that it was rolled back and inwards, leaving four guns mired in the swamp.

Fortunately, the left arm (Bragg) had so reacted to the strain of Davis's early attack that Bragg called for reinforcements and Johnston strengthened him by a division which might otherwise have given a deadly power to the right arm's embrace.

The Confederate chances, however, were increased by the compensating fact that Slocum had deployed both Davis's divisions in line with the advanced brigade, keeping no reserve, and this condition helped them to break the connection between the two divisions, and even between brigades. But the Union troops had become so cool and skilled in independent manœuvre that the menace of being taken in rear and isolated had much less than the normal effect, and although forced to give way they did not dissolve. Thus, helped by the thickets and swamps, they gained time for the arrival of part of Williams' corps to strengthen the left flank and cement the joints, each assault finding the Union forces better prepared to withstand it, and by nightfall the Confederate onslaught had so definitely failed that Johnston drew back his "arms" to a semi-circular position defensively convex instead of offensively concave. Now anticipating Sherman's early arrival, he only sought time to evacuate his wounded and prepare his retreat across Mill Creek to Smithfield.

At two o'clock in the morning of the 20th Sherman was aroused by a messenger from Slocum with news of the fighting. Thereupon Sherman sent orders for the nearest division (Hazen), which was with the trains in the centre, to go at once to Slocum's support, and for the rest of Logan's corps to march at daybreak. Blair's corps, the easternmost column, was also turned north-westwards. Hazen's division reached Slocum by dawn, finding the whole left wing now in position facing north. Sherman himself came up by noon and deployed Logan's corps facing west, feeling his way through the woods and swamps which covered Johnston's flank.

His object, however, was defensive rather than offensive; not to bring on a battle in this blind and sodden country but to frighten Johnston back, so that he could slip safely into Goldsboro and re-provision himself as a preliminary to a fresh spring upon Johnston from that secure base. To this end he had already sent a messenger with orders to Schofield to march at once from Kinston and occupy Goldsboro while he was "occupying" Johnston's army.

But next day, the 21st, blind fortune and blind country turned dramatically in his favour and offered a possible chance of disrupting Johnston's army. Blair's corps had come up on Logan's right and, like it, was progressing westwards despite the desperately tenacious efforts of the Confederate skirmishers to delay his approach to their hasty flank entrenchments; Mower's division on the extreme right threaded a way through the swamp, rushed two lightly held lines of breastworks, and then, finding an open path, swept forward rapidly on its own until it came within musket range of the bridges across Mill Creek—Johnston's line of retreat. Johnston belatedly switched such reserves as he had at hand to check this thin end of a dangerous wedge.

But Mower's rapid advance beyond the swamp and past the Confederate flank had been upon his own initiative and only became known when firing was heard far to the west of the remainder of the Union line. When the news travelled back to Sherman, he had to make an emergency decision as to whether the prospect justified him throwing his whole army into a blind attack to develop Mower's success. Still uncertain of the topography and of the enemy's strength, he decided to adhere to his original plan, and sent orders for Mower to be withdrawn under cover of a demonstration by the rest of the right wing. That his ambulances were already full was a further restraining factor, for if wounded have to be left untended the morale of an army soon suffers.

In later years he was inclined to blame himself for this decision, feeling that he had thereby lost the chance of a decisive tactical victory. But from the wider viewpoint of strategy he was probably wise to abstain from a leap in the dark when he had only to wait until "daylight" to be certain of a successful leap. Once in Goldsboro', with Schofield's force added to his own and a secure sea-base behind, the fall of Raleigh and the futility of Johnston's army would be assured. By his restraint, Sherman forfeited a tactical crown but gained a strategic base. And, in the issue, the difference proved to be that Johnston's army was extinguished by a bloodless surrender instead of being extinguished on the battlefield. Thereby Sherman lost an additional laurel, but several thousand of his men preserved their lives.

As Sherman calculated, his rear threat, accentuated by Mower's unexpected penetration, was followed by Johnston's prompt retreat that night. And on the 22nd Sherman's army resumed its interrupted march to Goldsboro, which it entered next day, already preceded by Schofield's force.

The greatest march in modern history was complete. Four hundred and twenty-five miles of intensely difficult country had been traversed in seven and a half weeks—in face of a galaxy of Confederate generals and their great allies, Generals Winter and Mud. All alike had failed to endanger or even obstruct Sherman's advance, which despite the passage of five large rivers and innumerable creeks had averaged nearly ten miles a day—deducting the several brief halts. And with the completion of this "March of the Sixty Thousand" Sherman's strength was raised to nearly 90,000 men. Even at Bentonville he had lost only 1,604, a total exceeded by Johnston's casualties, apart from 1,625 prisoners who fell into Sherman's hands. And the toll of sickness had been almost negligible despite the rigours of the march, and in extreme contrast to the more static and "civilized" campaigns of the war—an apparent phenomenon which Sherman thus explained in a letter to his wife: "It is a general truth that men exposed to the elements don't 'catch cold' and I have not heard a man cough or sneeze for three months, but were these same men to go into houses in a month the doctor would have half of them." To her also he acutely remarked, anticipating the verdict of history, "I regard my two moves from Atlanta to Savannah, and Savannah to Goldsboro' as great blows as if we had fought a dozen successful battles," and "the last march . . . is by far the most important in conception and execution of any act of my life."

By the junction of Sherman and Schofield, and of Sherman with the coast, the strategical possibilities of a Lee and Johnston combination were practically nullified—less hopeful even than Johnston's isolated efforts to checkmate Sherman's move before the junction at Goldsboro'. Sherman, however, had to refit before he could begin his post-junction advance. Numbers of his men had been marching barefoot, while thousands had split boots and tattered clothing. Twenty thousand pairs of shoes were needed, as well as fresh clothing and provisions for the whole army.

Unfortunately these were not immediately at hand, for despite Grant's instructions and the long interval since the capture of Wilmington the repair of the railroads from the coast to Goldsboro' had been tardy, as likewise the shipment of fresh locomotives and freight cars to augment the scanty rolling stock left by the Confederates. In consequence, Sherman's men had still to wait longingly for the provisions and other stores amassed in readiness for them on the coast, so near and yet so far. Characteristically, Sherman's first action on reaching Goldsboro was to telegraph to the Chief Quartermaster at the coastal base. "There should always be three details of workers, of eight hours each, making twenty-four hours per day of work on every job, whether building a bridge, unloading a vessel, loading cars or what not. . . . Remember that we want stores and nothing else. We don't want a permanent establishment. Our wagons are our storehouses. I must be off again in twenty days with wagons full, men reclad. . . ." For, after a prompt reckoning of the present state and conditions of supply, and of the acceleration possible, he calculated that he would be ready for "diving again into the bowels of the country" by April 10, and fulfilled his calculation to the day. A sidelight on his insight into the "Q" side of strategy.

CHAPTER XXII

THE COLLAPSE OF THE CONFEDERACY

On arrival at Goldsboro Sherman found two letters from Grant. The first, written as far back as February 7, had an unintentional irony in view of the conditions which Sherman actually met at Goldsboro, for it said that every precaution had been taken "to have supplies ready for you" and to send rolling stock from the "abundance of it idle" in Virginia. This letter concluded with a comment which does as much honour to Grant as was due to Sherman for his rejection of the possibility—"No one would be more pleased at your advancement than I, and if you should be placed in my position, and I put subordinate, it would not change our personal relations in the least. I would make the same exertions to support you that you have ever done to support me, and would do all in my power to make our cause win."

The near approach of that victory was due far less to formal unity of command than to such practical and perfect unity of spirit between these two men. And when that abnegatory letter from the supreme commander was received, the success of his coadjutor had been so decisive that the supersession of the one and the succession of the other was no longer in question.

Indeed, the measure of the success was graphically indicated in Grant's second letter, of March 16. For although Grant's army had not yet attempted to move from the trench lines round Petersburg where it had been "stalemated" eight months previously, and had since lain almost passive, Grant was able to tell Sherman that Lee's "army is now demoralised and deserting very fast, both to us and to their homes."

To that demoralization and desertion, the weary strain of trench life was a contributory cause. Hunger, due to the contraction of the Confederate supply areas, was a still greater cause. Letters from home, the greatest. It was not merely that Sherman's unchecked progress through the heart of the Confederacy had been a visual proof to the people of their helplessness and a physical blow at the stomachs of people and army alike. But by making the non-combatants suffer it had sent a wave of pacifism and despair through the land, and the echoes unnerved the combatants.

Man has two supreme loyalties—to country and to family. And with most men the second, being more personal is the stronger. So long as their families are safe they will defend their country, believing that by their sacrifice they are safeguarding their families also. But even the bonds of patriotism, discipline, and comradeship are loosened when the family is itself threatened. The soldier feels instinctively that if he was at home he could at least fight for the immediate protection of his family, work to gain food for it, and at the worst die with it. But when the enemy is closer than he is, the danger and his fears are magnified by his remoteness. Every letter, every rumour is a strain on his nerves and on his sense of duty.

It is the supreme deadliness of the rear attack as conceived and executed by Sherman—against the rear of a people, not merely of an army—that it sets the two loyalties in opposition and so imposes a breaking strain on the will of the soldier. The "horns of a dilemma" once more.

The day after Sherman's arrival at Goldsboro he received a third letter from Grant with an outline of the final plan. Now that the great gash made by Sherman in Lee's supply areas was being followed by his imminent approach to the immediate rear of Lee's army it was obvious that Lee must let go of Richmond. He had stayed until all hope of checking Sherman or of turning the tables had passed, and the question now was whether he had tarried too long even for a safe exit.

Grant's object now was to answer this question with an emphatic "yes," and to this end his first aim was to close Lee's remaining boltholes. On February 27 Sheridan, picking up the scent of his autumn successes in the Shenandoah Valley, had advanced up it with 10,000 cavalry as far as Staunton and cut the Virginia Central Railroad. Then, however, he had left his strategic mission incomplete although, in contrast to Sherman's experience, there were no forces to oppose him save those of Generals Winter and Mud. Instead of pushing on to Lynchburg—to cut the railroad from Virginia to East Tennessee—and thence south-east to join Sherman in North Carolina, he had turned aside to join Grant, reaching White House on March 19.

It was a curiously significant feature of the campaign of 1865 that all the efforts intended by Grant to ease Sherman's path through the Carolinas miscarried or were delayed too long to be of service. Canby, from Mobile Bay, had been ordered to move northward into Alabama, in order to prevent Hood's former troops being sent to oppose Sherman, but was as unconscious of the value of time as Thomas who, having already failed to follow up his Nashville success, was now slower than ever in beginning the cavalry moves from Tennessee which Grant ordered. Wilson was as late in moving south into Alabama as Canby northwards. Stoneman, whose cavalry expedition should have entered South Carolina and approached Columbia simultaneously with Sherman, was found to be still in Kentucky when Sherman was on his way to Goldsboro! And, as we have already seen, Schofield neither prevented Johnston concentrating against Sherman nor brought forward supplies in readiness for Sherman's arrival.

In default of any effective distraction from outside, the march through the Carolinas was achieved and secured by the internal distraction which Sherman himself supplied through the elasticity of his direction and formation—which generated uncertainty in the mind of his opponents, while his capacity to conquer natural obstacles surprised them. Even after Sherman had reached Columbia, Lee himself had told the Confederate Government, "I do not see how Sherman can make the march anticipated by General Beauregard" —either to Greensboro and Danville or to Raleigh and Weldon. As Sherman's immediate opponent was surprised because of uncertainty as to which direction he would take, so his ultimate opponent was surprised by the realization of the march itself. And, in consequence, the line of least expectation proved the line of least resistance—with fatal results to the resisting power of the Confederacy.

Whilst the several distractions planned by Grant to help Sherman's progress failed of their purpose, Grant was able to convert them to a fresh purpose in the last phase—for which they were just in time! Canby and Wilson began moving into Alabama just as Sherman reached Goldsboro'; Stoneman also from East Tennessee towards Lynchburg, while Thomas sent the Fourth Corps from Knoxville to Bull's Gap to seal this possible mountain exit westwards out of Virginia.   Sheridan, reinforced by another 5,500 cavalry, was to pass down the east side of Petersburg and then make a wide circuit to the south, cutting Lee's two remaining railroads, through Weldon and Danville respectively.   Grant's own rôle was thus indicated to Sherman—"When this movement commences, I shall move out by my left, with all the force I can, holding present intrenched lines.   I shall start with no distinct view, further than holding Lee's forces from following Sheridan.   But I shall be along myself and will take advantage of anything that turns up."

This letter yields a significant sidelight on the trend and development of Grant's strategical thought during these years of practical experience.   Like Sherman he had come to realize that opportunism is essential in war; that fixed purposes and objectives are contrary to its nature and, if rigidly maintained, lead usually to a blank wall.   But Grant would seem to have come to a belief in pure opportunism—to take an obvious course and exploit any chance that occurred; whereas Sherman had sought and found a solution in variability, or elasticity—the choice of a line leading to alternative objectives with the power to vary his course to gain whichever the enemy left open.

Perhaps Grant's thought was influenced by a sense of his relatively inferior mobility.   For he confesses in his memoirs that Lee was "held" only by the political and moral value of Richmond, and not by the pressing embrace of the Union army—"I was afraid, every morning, that I would awake from my sleep to hear that Lee had gone. . . . I knew he could move much more lightly and more rapidly than I, and that, if he got the start, he would leave me behind. . . ."   As week succeeded week, with Lee still in Richmond and the strategic encircling forces of the Union closing in, Grant's anxieties declined.   For even if Lee slipped away, he would have less room to manœuvre and Grant a shorter distance to cover—before he could come up to the aid of any of his detachments which Lee might meet.   This increased confidence had an influence on Grant's final plan.

On March 25, as soon as the flow of supplies into Goldsboro' had begun to swell, Sherman quitted his army for a flying visit to Grant, in order to settle the details of his share in the final combination. Travelling by sea from Morehead City he steamed up the James River and reached City Point on the 27th. It would seem that Sherman's personal visit was dictated partly by a desire to persuade Grant to hold the Armies of the Potomac and of the James in leash until the Grand Army of the West could arrive within striking distance of Lee. This was wise strategy, but strategy was now subsidiary to another motive and Grant was unwilling to wait.

For Grant candidly says in his memoirs that he was "very anxious to have the Eastern armies vanquish their old enemy who had so long resisted all their repeated and gallant attempts. . . . The Western armies had . . . conquered all the territory from the Mississippi River to the State of North Carolina, and were now almost ready to knock at the back door of Richmond, asking admittance. I said to him [Lincoln] that if the Western armies should be even upon the field, operating against Richmond and Lee, the credit would be given to them for the capture. . . . It might lead to disagreeable bickerings between members of Congress of the East and those of the West in some of their debates. Western members might be throwing it up to the members of the East that in the suppression of the rebellion they were not able to capture an army, or to accomplish much in the way of contributing toward that end, but had to wait until the Western armies had conquered all the territory south and west of them, and then come on to help them capture the only army they had been engaged with."

For the sake of his men, rather than for himself, Grant was anxious to avoid calling on Sherman's aid in the epilogue of the campaign. Sherman had been the reaper in the cornfields of the South—cornfields both actual and metaphorical—but there was now a chance for the gleaners among the cut swathes, and Grant desired that they should enjoy it. And the growing demoralization of Lee's army was now so clear that Grant had few qualms. On March 25 Lee had made a surprise sortie from Petersburg in the hope of inducing Grant to draw in his enfolding left arm and so allow Lee more room for a secure retreat. But the sortie was repulsed and its recoil tightened rather than loosened the uncomfortably close embrace which Grant was now about to make dangerously tight. With some of the Confederates desperation might still triumph over despair, indomitable will over an empty stomach, but as a whole Lee's army was but a long-buried skeleton ready to crumble into dust at a touch when exposed in the open.

But if Sherman's visit to Grant was strategically vain, it had far-reaching political consequences. For while at City Point he had two talks with Lincoln on board the steamer *River Queen*. According to the evidence of Admiral Porter, who was present, Lincoln seemed anxious lest Johnston might take advantage both of Sherman's absence and of the enforced delay for refitting in order to slip back southwards. To these fears Sherman replied: "I have him where he cannot move without breaking up his army, which, once disbanded, can never again be got together; and I have destroyed the Southern railroads so that they cannot be used again for a long time." Sherman then asked for the President's wishes as to the terms of surrender and the treatment of the Confederate troops, and was pleased to find that Lincoln shared his own liberal views and desire for absolution of sins after surrender. Lincoln's consuming desire was to curtail the bloodshed and to get the Confederate troops back to their homes as peaceful citizens of a restored Union, without penalty or even change in their status beyond the abolition of their right to own slaves. He left no doubt on Sherman's mind that his peace would be a peace of "malice toward none; with charity for all"—truly fulfilling the words of his second inaugural address. Indeed, his charity extended even to the military terms of surrender and not merely to the political. In Porter's account—"Sherman energetically insisted that he could command his own terms, and that Johnston would have to yield to his demands; but the President was very decided about the matter, and insisted that the surrender must be obtained on any terms." Here Lincoln's extreme moderation seems to have been due to a desire to avoid any chance of Johnston's army continuing its resistance, perhaps prolonging the defence of Richmond, while Sherman's attitude was inspired by the longer-sighted desire to nullify any chance that Johnston's men might take up their arms as guerrillas.

Another question on which Sherman sought guidance was in regard to Jefferson Davis and the other political leaders of the Confederacy. Lincoln hoped that they might "escape the country," and characteristically hinted the desire that he could not express formally by telling a story—"A man once had taken a total-abstinence pledge. When visiting a friend, he was invited to take a drink, but declined, on the score of his pledge; when his friend suggested lemonade, which was accepted. In preparing the lemonade, the friend pointed to the brandy-bottle, and said the lemonade would be more palatable if he were to pour in a little brandy; when the guest said, if he could do so 'unbeknown' to him, he would not object."

This was the first meeting between Lincoln and Sherman since the black morrow of Bull Run. Not merely the situation but the outlook of both men had vastly changed in the four years' interval, and Sherman was impressed above all by the statesmanship which now governed Lincoln's humanity, the political wisdom which guided his sympathetic desire for reconciliation and reconstruction. In Lincoln, Sherman joyfully recognized a politician whose harmonious conception of the supreme issues was attuned to his own. This second meeting was also to be their last and Sherman left it with the feeling that "of all the men I ever met he seemed to possess more of the elements of greatness, combined with goodness, than any other."

Returning at once to North Carolina, with a clear idea of Lincoln's policy, Sherman reorganized his forces for the final advance. Maintaining the forces of Howard and Slocum—the last rechristened the Army of Georgia—as his right and left wings, Sherman reverted to his Atlanta formation by inserting between them, as a central pivot, a mobile force of some 27,000 men which was created from Schofield's troops.

His plan was once more based on the governing idea of placing his opponents upon the horns of a dilemma, leaving them uncertain both as to his direction and as to whether he was aiming at Johnston or Lee. In brief, his idea was to feign on Raleigh and actually interpose between Johnston and Lee. His left horn was to aim west towards Raleigh and then, when just short of it, swerve northwards, using the Neuse River as a flank protection. His right horn was first to aim northwards up the Weldon railroad as far as Nahunta, and then swing north-westwards. The delusion of an advance on Weldon would, however, be kept up by Kilpatrick's cavalry. The centre was to take a central path, and the three "armies" were to reunite at Warrenton, just south of the Roanoke, as a preliminary to placing the whole army north of this river. For if Johnston ventured within reach, in an attempt to fulfil his strategic mission of obstruction, Sherman was ready at any moment to cast his columns like a net around him. The march was to be kept up at the rate of "about twelve miles a day, or according to the amount of resistance. All the columns will dress to the left (which is the exposed flank), and commanders will study always to find roads by which they can, if necessary, perform a general left wheel. . . ."

Meantime the base was to be shifted northwards up the coast so that as soon as Sherman was across the Roanoke he could re-open his communications and draw supplies from new depots at Winton and Murfreesboro' on the Chowan River. Then, if Lee had not yet quitted Richmond in an attempt to join Johnston, Sherman would turn west and pounce on Burkesville Junction, where he would have a strangling grip on Lee's remaining arteries of supply. This plan deserves study as an example of Sherman's matured method, although it was to be unfulfilled.

For on March 29 Sheridan had moved out to Dinwiddie Court House to threaten Lee's right as a preliminary to his railroad raid. Sheridan's movement caused an immediate stretching of the Confederate front and next day Grant converted this cavalry threat into a definite stroke against the Confederate flank, in co-operation with his infantry left arm. Although Sheridan was temporarily isolated and in danger until Warren's corps came up, a combined attack by Sheridan and Warren just before dusk on Saturday April 1 overthrew the equally isolated Confederate detachment opposing them. And at dawn on Sunday a general assault, ordered by Grant, broke into the outer defenses of Petersburg.

Jefferson Davis was in church at morning service when a telegram from Lee was brought to him, telling him that Richmond as well as Petersburg must be abandoned at once. The Government hastily packed up and took train for Danville, whither Lee hoped to follow. After dark the military evacuation began and the troops turned their backs on the two deserted cities. Tired and hungry, shedding stragglers continually, they moved slowly and were late in reaching their assembly position at Amelia Court House, where they were disappointed to find no supplies awaiting them; a day was lost in collecting food and forage from the countryside. The delay was fatal. After the discovery, early on the 3rd, of Lee's retreat the Union pursuit had been vigorously pressed and Sheridan, with the advantage of a flanking position, was able to reach the Danville railroad south of Amelia Court House and head off the Confederates. Disintegration spread rapidly under the pressure of hunger and Grant, and on the 9th Lee surrendered the remains of his army at Appomattox Court House.

News of the fall of Richmond and Petersburg reached Sherman on the 6th, and he at once altered his plan to one of an advance westwards through Raleigh on Greensboro', with the intention of netting Johnston and then, if necessary, intercepting Lee's retreat. For this direct advance on Johnston he reverted to his favourite concave or "Y" formation, with two arms outstretched from a central body, or pivot, to threaten the enemy's flanks and rear. In contrast, when he was swerving past an opponent he utilized a "stepped" or echelon formation which, by a simple left wheel of its columns, could be swung into line to outflank in turn and menace the retreat of any enemy who fastened on to his own flank. It is interesting, also, to note the elasticity of his dispositions, which had been framed for an advance northwards. In order to save reshuffling of camps and extra marching, the original left wing became the centre in the advance on Raleigh; the "refused" (drawn back) centre became the left wing on facing west and moved with the cavalry along the south bank of the Neuse, aiming to reach the enemy's rear; the right wing swung round in a circuit on the other flank to deceive the enemy as to Sherman's real direction.

On the 10th the move on Raleigh, fifty miles distant, began to the accompaniment of the usual heavy rain. Brushing aside the Confederate cavalry, Smithfield was reached next morning, but Johnston had retreated in time on Raleigh, burning the bridges over the Neuse. The day was spent in repairing them and that night Sherman received news of Lee's surrender. Next day, dropping his supply trains, he pushed on so rapidly over the mired roads that Raleigh, the beautiful "City of Oaks," was entered twenty-four hours later. Johnston, however, had not tarried in his retreat and had already gone back, ahead of his troops, to Greensboro' for a conference with Jefferson Davis and the Confederate cabinet. There he declared the hopelessness of resistance and urged Jefferson Davis to sue for peace. The suggestion annoyed the President, who still talked of raising a fresh large army in a few weeks; but at a second conference he reluctantly accepted the necessity, and also Johnston's suggestion to propose an armistice to Sherman as a preliminary to peace negotiations.

The implied tribute to Sherman's almighty power had a more humorous corollary at Raleigh, where Sherman visited the asylum for the insane. One of the more rational among the inmates begged Sherman to release him, and as a sedative Sherman replied, "When the papers come up to me in regular shape I will attend to them. Meanwhile you must be quiet, and put your trust in God." To which the man rejoined—"In God? Well, I think I do believe in a sort of divine providence; but when it comes to the question of power, it strikes me that for a man who has been walking about over the country whipping these cursed rebels, you have a damned sight more power than anybody I know of." One feels that at that moment there was rather more sanity in the asylum at Raleigh than in the cabinet at Greensboro'.

Lee's surrender had changed Sherman's problem, again, as well as Davis's. It was no longer urgent to catch Johnston before he could join Lee, but instead to head him off from a retreat southwards. Accordingly Sherman made a short pause at Raleigh in order not to alarm Johnston into a fresh retirement before his own railroad to Raleigh was repaired, and with the expectation that the cavalry of Sheridan and Stoneman would be closing in on Johnston's rear. His supreme concern was lest pressure should dissolve Johnston's army into guerrillas before it could be rounded up as a whole. Meantime he redistributed his columns for a swift swerve to the south-west, through Ashboro', by which he hoped to get astride the line from Greensboro' southward, while Johnston was falling back westward on Greensboro' itself, eighty miles from Raleigh. To cloak this move Kilpatrick's cavalry, switched across from the other flank, was to advance directly down the railroad from Raleigh to Greensboro'. In his orders for this move, Sherman added that "No further destruction of railroads, mills, cotton, and produce, will be made without the specific orders of an army commander, and the inhabitants will be dealt with kindly, looking to an early reconciliation."

But on the 14th he received from Johnston a request for "a temporary suspension of active operations . . . to permit the civil authorities to enter into the needful arrangements to terminate the existing war." Not only Lincoln's instructions but Sherman's own "guerrilla" fears impelled him to grasp the opportunity thus offered. He replied at once that he was fully empowered to arrange any terms "between the armies," and suggested a meeting. "I will limit the advance of my main column, tomorrow, to Morrisville"— thereby conveying subtly the impression that Greensboro was still his objective—" . . . and expect that you will also maintain the present position of your forces. . . . That a basis of action may be had I undertake to abide by the same terms and conditions as were made by Generals Grant and Lee . . . and, furthermore, to obtain from General Grant an order to suspend the movements of any troops from the direction of Virginia. General Stoneman is under my command, and my order will suspend any devastation or destruction contemplated by him. I will add that I really desire to save the people of North Carolina the damage they would sustain by the march of this army through the central or western parts of the State."

A meeting was arranged for the 17th at a station midway between the two armies. As Sherman was about to leave Raleigh he was stopped by the receipt of a ciphered despatch from Stanton which brought the news of Lincoln's assassination at Washington, and a warning that a like fate might be designed for Sherman himself. If there was any doubt of Sherman's dispassionate outlook and absence of vindictiveness, his action at this critical moment would dispel it. Fearing that if the murder was known an outburst of indignation among the troops might wreck not only Raleigh but his purpose of peace, he bade the telegraph operator not to reveal by word or look the contents of the message. Then he went forward on his mission, met Johnston, and only when he was alone with him did he show the despatch. The news and the deed shocked Johnston, and the beads of perspiration which stood out on his forehead revealed as much as his words the distress which he felt at the consequences to the South. But his evident fears of an immediate ill were soon dispelled by Sherman's reassuring and forbearing attitude.

Sherman explained that negotiations between the civil authorities were impossible, as the United States Government had never recognized the existence of a Southern Confederacy, and suggested instead that Johnston should capitulate on the same terms as Lee —the officers and men to be paroled, retaining their side-arms, personally owned horses, and baggage, and to return to their homes "not to be disturbed by United States authority so long as they observe their paroles and the laws in force where they may reside."

While declaring that further fighting would be "murder," Johnston argued that he was not cut off like Lee nor his situation so hopeless as to justify a similar capitulation. He suggested, instead, that they might draft terms which would cover all the Confederate armies and form the basis of general peace.

Sherman's quick brain perceived the deeper value of the proposal and seized upon the idea that at a stroke—of the pen—he might lift the danger of guerrilla warfare from the land and avoid the cost and trouble of a long military occupation. So also his broad political vision impelled him to secure the fulfilment of Lincoln's policy before the lust for vengeance had time to sweep more petty politicians off their feet. Here his remoteness from Washington led him to miscalculate the political and public strength of the flood. For him, or any other soldier, to withstand it was all the more difficult because Stanton, the Secretary of War, was instigating the campaign of vengeance, while the Southern-born Vice-President, Andrew Johnson, who now succeeded Lincoln, for a time lent his support to it— seemingly because he suffered from the inferiority complex of a poor white. Grant had difficulty, despite his pledged word, in preventing the imprisonment of Lee and his chief subordinates, while the wolf-pack cry of "Hang Jeff Davis!" was as ferociously insistent as that of "Hang the Kaiser!" in 1919.

Taking up Johnston's suggestion, Sherman demanded to know if he had power to control the other Confederate forces, and received the reply that, although Davis was not at hand, authority could probably be obtained from Breckenridge, the Confederate Secretary of War. The talk then merged into a discussion as to the restoration of the political rights of the Southern States after submission, and Sherman, basing himself on Lincoln's simple principles of the restoration of the Union and the emancipation of slaves, sought to interpret Lincoln's views. The one stumbling block in the discussion came over the question whether Davis and his cabinet would be included in the general amnesty, Johnston seeking a guarantee and Sherman a way out—such as had been suggested by Lincoln's lemonade-and-brandy story. No solution had been reached when at sunset they parted temporarily, Johnston to consult with Breckenridge and Sherman with his generals, who were strongly in favour of a peaceful solution. Now that it was at last in sight, officers and men alike felt the reaction of their great ordeal and were anxious to avoid its renewal, in the perhaps endless chase of a fugitive remnant.

Next morning the conference was resumed, and Sherman's desire for a simple settlement was baulked both by Johnston's anxiety to give his men some definite guarantee of their rights of citizenship and by the amnesty question. Unlike Lee, Johnston was fettered by the presence of political chiefs and could not, even if he had wished, disregard their interests. At his request Breckenridge was introduced into the conference, although ostensibly in his capacity as a general in the Confederate Army and not as a member of Davis's cabinet. Inevitably, however, with his entry the discussion drifted into deeper waters—waters in which Sherman was out of his depth. His broad political vision was greater than any man's save possibly one, and he was dead, but to apply it Sherman had only the help of a self-education in constitutional law, and was handicapped by deliberate abstention from the political arena. Handicapped also by a deep-seated contempt for the shortsightedness and pettiness of politicians which perhaps created in him a feeling of his own superior fitness to interpret Lincoln's scheme of laying the foundations of a peace of reconciliation. Rather than see this prospect wrecked on a quibble, he struck out boldly, although careful to keep firm hold of a life-line. Sitting down at a table he rapidly wrote out his own "memorandum, or basis of agreement."

It provided, first, for an armistice terminable at forty-eight hours' notice. Second, that the scattered Confederate armies should be disbanded and conducted to deposit their arms in the various State arsenals. Now convinced that the men of the South were utterly sick of war, he realized the value of trust and the folly of needless humiliation, and by this last clause also sought to ensure that the State governments should be able to control their own "die-hards" and bandits. Next, the recognition of the several State governments on taking the prescribed oaths of allegiance, the re-establishment of the Federal courts, the restoration to the people of their political rights and franchises, as well as their rights of person and property, and the promise of a general amnesty.

As a peace treaty its blended wisdom and mercy made it a model for history and humanity, and if Lincoln had lived it might have been accepted, as eventually it came piecemeal to be, the framework of the reconstruction of the United States. But common humanity was not ready for it.

In the clause which provided for the recognition of the State governments Sherman was guided by his conversation with Lincoln; by past encouragement from Lincoln, while in Georgia and South Carolina, to negotiate with the civil authorities; and by the report that Lincoln had allowed the legislature of Virginia to assemble, in order to recall its troops from the Confederate service. And in conceding the point of a general amnesty, he gave Breckenridge the hint to make his escape before the inclusion of Davis and his cabinet was called in question.

If in drawing up this basis of agreement Sherman followed his principle of elasticity by stretching his powers as a military servant of his government beyond constitutional practice, he did not actu-ally break it. For both in the wording of the memorandum and in his words to Johnston he made it clear that the document was merely a draft for submission to his government, and, in addition, all the political clauses were qualified by references "to the future action" of Congress, to the Supreme Court, or to the Constitution of the United States.

Moreover, while it is clear that Sherman believed in the rightness of his provisional peace terms and had an excessive hope in their ratification, the armistice was militarily to his advantage, and the advantage of the Union Government. For it gave him time to bring his railhead forward to Raleigh in readiness for his next spring if negotiations broke down.

After the draft had been signed, Sherman despatched it by Major

Hitchcock to Washington, with a covering letter which explained his motives—"You will observe that it is an absolute submission of the enemy to the lawful authority of the United States, and disperses his armies absolutely; and the point to which I attach most importance is, that the dispersion and disbandment of these armies is done in such a manner as to prevent their breaking up into guerrilla bands. . . . I agreed to the mode and manner of the surrender of arms set forth, as it gives the States the means of repressing guerrillas, which we could not expect them to do if we stripped them of all arms. Both Generals Johnston and Breckenridge admitted that slavery was dead, and I could not insist on embracing it in such a paper, because it can be made with the States in detail. I know that all the men of substance in the South sincerely want peace, and I do not believe they will resort to war again during this century. . . . The question of finance is now the chief one, and every soldier and officer not needed should be got home to work. . . ."

In an accompanying personal note to Halleck, he said: "I received your despatch describing the man Clark, detailed to assassinate me. He had better be in a hurry, or he will be too late. The news of Mr. Lincoln's death produced a most intense effect on our troops. . . . I cannot believe that even Mr. Davis was privy to the diabolical plot, but think it the emanation of a set of young men of the South, who are very devils. I want to throw upon the South the care of this class of men. . . . Had I pushed Johnston's army to an extremity, it would have dispersed, and done infinite mischief . . . if the President sanctions my agreement with Johnston our interest is to cease all destruction . . . influence him, if possible, not to vary the terms at all, for I have considered everything, and believe that, the Confederate armies once dispersed, we can adjust all else fairly and well."

On the 21st, while awaiting the answer, he wrote Johnston further —"I send you a letter for General Wilson, which, if sent by telegraph or courier, will check his career (through Georgia). . . . He seems to have his blood up and will be hard to hold. . . . By the action of General Weitzel in relation to the Virginia Legislature, I feel certain we will have no trouble on the score of recognizing existing State governments. It may be that the lawyers will want us to define more minutely what is meant by the guaranty of rights of person and property. . . . I believe if the South would simply and publicly declare what we feel, that slavery is dead, that you would inaugurate an era of peace and prosperity that would soon efface the ravages of the past four years of war. Negroes would remain in the South, and afford you abundance of cheap labour which otherwise will be driven away ; and it will save the country the senseless discussions which have kept us all in hot water for fifty years."

The draft agreement left Raleigh as a dove of peace but arrived as a bombshell in Washington, where, detonated by Stanton, it caused an explosion of wrath in the cabinet. Not only were orders sent that the draft was "disapproved" and hostilities to be resumed "immediately," but Grant was directed to go at once to North Carolina and take personal charge of operations over Sherman's head. But this was the least consequence. For Stanton lost not only his temper but his head, and to his fanatical mind, still nursing a grievance over Sherman's reluctance to use negro troops, the peace terms appeared to imply the continuance of slavery and conclusive evidence that Sherman was really a disguised Confederate. The epithet "traitor" was freely bandied, and to increase its circulation Stanton promptly issued a denunciatory bulletin to the press. This not merely violated the secrecy under which the proposals had been submitted, but in publishing them to the accompaniment of fiery criticisms left unpublished Sherman's covering letter. In conclusion it suggested that Sherman's action would "probably open the way to Jefferson Davis to escape to Mexico or Europe with his plunder, which is reported to be very large. . . ."

A press thirsting in security for Confederate blood burst into flaming indignation at Sherman's clemency, and in slinging ink at the man who had so rapidly changed from their target to their idol and back again was only divided in opinion as to whether he was a Cromwell, an Arnold, or a Judas—bribed by Jefferson Davis's gold. Indeed, the very height of his fame led many politicians, especially those who were opposed to his brother, to conjure up visions of a military dictatorship and to forestall the possibility by exciting the fickle public against him. The tempest blew itself out as quickly as it had arisen, but for some weeks it looked as if yet another of Sherman's prophecies would be fulfilled—one regarding himself, made in a letter to his wife after Atlanta—"Read history, read Coriolanus, and you will see the true measure of popular applause. Grant, Sheridan, and I are now the popular favourites but neither of us will survive the war."

The real treachery—to the laws of war—was on the part of Stanton and it leaves a dark stain on American history. For, repudiating both Sherman and the truce, he sent orders to the other commanders in the South to press forward against Johnston and the other Confederates, disregarding any orders from Sherman. If passion blinded Stanton to decency, it was probably jealousy which prompted Halleck to extend his outrage. On Grant's return to Washington, Halleck had gone South to take charge of the Armies of the Potomac and the James—coincidently with the arrival of Sherman's letter and draft. Here he not only ordered his subordinates to advance upon Johnston in disregard of the truce, but when they informed him that Sherman had made fresh terms with Johnston, he reported gleefully to Stanton, "I have telegraphed back to obey no orders of Sherman, but to push forward as rapidly as possible." And Stanton promptly published the message in a fresh bulletin.

In this crisis the good sense and tact of one man saved the "face" of Sherman, the honour of the Union, and the prospect of peace. The one man who had both the power and the inclination for such a healing mission—Grant. Sherman had no hint of the crisis or of Grant's coming until he appeared at Raleigh on the 24th in company with Hitchcock. Grant had taken this precaution in order to prevent either Sherman's army or the enemy learning of his intervention. And, on arrival, instead of superseding Sherman, he informed him of the President's instructions and instructed him to negotiate afresh on the basis of the same terms as had been granted to Lee. Indeed, he not only left Sherman a free hand, but spared his feelings by conveying no hint that the Cabinet had "disapproved" not only of the draft but of Sherman himself.

Sherman at once gave forty-eight hours' notice to Johnston of the renewal of hostilities, and at the same time sent a formal demand for his surrender on the same, purely military, terms as Lee. Johnston's position had been weakened during the five days' truce by nearly eight thousand desertions and in telegraphing to his government he advised acceptance of Sherman's demand. Back came the contrary suggestion that the infantry should be dispersed to rally again at a rendezvous—the very danger Sherman feared— and that Johnston should get away with all the mounted troops.

In Johnston's view this suggestion merely ensured a strong escort for the flight of the Confederate Cabinet, and handed over the country to further devastation. Refusing to prolong the misery of his countrymen, he decided to act on his own responsibility, for his own army, and on the 26th signed a convention with Sherman whereby his arms were stacked at Greensboro and his men allowed to go to their homes, with a promise of immunity from disturbance by the Union authorities, after giving individually a written promise not to take up arms again. Under this convention 37,047 officers and men surrendered and were paroled—compared with 28,356 in Lee's army—so that, counting the desertions during the truce, Johnston must have had fully 45,000 to oppose Sherman's march through North Carolina. His inability to check Sherman is a testimony to Sherman's local generalship if perhaps still more to the moral effect which Sherman's strategy had produced.

As regards the terms, the Union government's intervention had the ironical effect that it cost them a quarter of a million rations. For in default of any civil authority in the Confederate States and of any power to enforce the laws, the remaining supply depots were plundered by the inhabitants and by deserters, so that the homeward movement of Johnston's army was paralyzed until Sherman came to the rescue with that number of rations. Even then the original convention had to be supplemented by additional terms under which field-transport was loaned to the Confederates and a proportion of one-seventh of their arms retained as a safeguard against the wide- spread anarchy. And the actual cost of that prolonged anarchy was to be far greater. Political sense is not necessarily synonymous with a political seat. Nor is common-sense acquired by democratic election.

Sherman's view, the truth of which the years were to prove, was expressed in a letter to his wife after signing the convention—"The mass of the people south will never trouble us again. They have suffered terrifically and I now feel disposed to befriend them. . . . I perceive the politicians are determined to drive the Confederates into guerrilla bands, a thing more to be feared than open organised war. They may fight it out. I won't. We could settle the war in three weeks by giving shape to the present disordered elements."

Only on the 28th, after Grant's departure, did Sherman learn from the papers of Stanton's outrageous behaviour. Then he in turn exploded. But his official protest, to Grant, was couched in temperate and dignified language—"Since you left me yesterday, I have seen the *New York Times* of the 28th, containing a budget of military news, authenticated by the signature of the Secretary of War, Hon. E. M. Stanton, which is grouped in such a way as to give the public very erroneous impressions. . . ." As regards the original agreement itself the time to discuss it would be "two or three years hence, after the Government has experimented a little more in the machinery by which power reaches the scattered people of the vast country known as the 'South.' " Then, after a protest at the publication of matter which was "communicated for the use of none but the cabinet," he emphasized that the authorities had failed to send him any hint or copy of the order, sent to Grant, restricting communication with the enemy to purely military matters, and had failed also to give any hint "of a plan of reconstruction, or any idea calculated to allay the fears of the people of the South, after the destruction of their armies and civil authorities would leave them without any government whatever." Here we see the one motive underlying Sherman's peace terms—that maintenance of law which had been his bedrock principle when all his world was crumbling around him. Hence also his strongest protest was directed against the implied charge of insubordination. "As you did not undertake to assume the management of the affairs of this army, I infer that, on personal instruction, your mind arrived at a different conclusion from that of the Secretary of War. I will therefore go on to execute your orders to the conclusion, and, when done, will with intense satisfaction leave to the civil authorities the execution of the task of which they seem so jealous. But, as an honest man and soldier, I invite them to go back to Nashville and follow my path, for they will see some things and hear some things that will disturb their philosophy."

Nevertheless it was mainly with the idea of curtailing the damage done to a country which "it was now our solemn duty to protect,

instead of plunder" that on the 29th he left Raleigh to take ship
for Savannah, and there get in touch with and send supplies to
Wilson, nominally his subordinate, whose cavalry sweep through
Georgia was too late for military value but needlessly destructive
of property. Having taken steps to remove the need for Wilson to
live on the country any longer, Sherman sailed back on May 2, just
before the last Confederate forces east of the Mississippi surrendered.

There was, however, one piece of destruction even in North Carolina after hostilities had ceased. General Slocum tells the story of
"the last property that I saw destroyed by the men of Sherman's
army." Near Raleigh he noticed a group of soldiers standing
around a burning cart, and at once sent a staff officer to intervene.
The officer returned with the message—"Tell General Slocum that
cart is loaded with New York papers for sale to the soldiers. These
papers are filled with the vilest abuse of General Sherman. We have
followed Sherman through a score of battles and nearly two thousand miles of the enemy's country, and we don't intend to allow
these slanders against him to be circulated among his men."

Owing to his journey south Sherman himself only heard on his
return of the full extent of Stanton's and Halleck's efforts to undermine his authority. With the surrender of the Confederate forces
popular feeling had once more veered round in Sherman's favour,
but for him the sweet joy of achievement was turned to bitterness.
And, his task complete, he allowed himself the luxury of a human
reaction. On reaching Fort Monroe, on his way to meet his homeward marching army, he found a message from Halleck, the false
friend, offering him hospitality at Richmond. This he refused in
a pungent cipher-despatch, telling him that he had seen Halleck's
message to Stanton, that he preferred not to meet him after such
an insult, and that it might be unwise for Halleck to show himself
to Sherman's indignant troops. On reaching Richmond he found
that Halleck had ordered a review of one of Sherman's corps on its
way through, and promptly cancelled this, telling his wife—"I dare
him [Halleck] to oppose my march. . . . Unless Grant intervenes
from his yielding and good nature I shall get some equally good
opportunity to insult Stanton. . . ." To his credit, he gave her a
further and chivalrous reason—"We cannot kill disarmed men. All

this clamor after Jeff Davis . . . and others is all bosh. Any young man with a musket is now a more dangerous object than Jeff Davis. He is old, infirm, a fugitive hunted by his own people, and none so poor as do him reverence." To suffer from the fickleness of the crowd was a sure passport to Sherman's sympathy. Perhaps he would have been more restrained if he had realized that his own action was to tickle the sensation-loving palate of the "crowd" that he so despised. For, by his intention, his letter to a friend, Colonel Bowman, was published in the press coincidently with his arrival in Washington—"I am just arrived. All the army will be in to-day. I have been lost to the world in the woods for some time. Yet, on arriving at the 'settlements,' found I had made quite a stir among the people at home, and that the most sinister motives have been ascribed to me. . . . I have been too long fighting with real rebels, with muskets in their hands, to be scared by mere non-combatants, no matter how high their civil rank or station."

"It is amusing to observe how brave and firm some men become when all danger is past. I have noticed on fields of battle brave men never insult the captured or mutilate the dead; but cowards and laggards always do. I cannot recall the act, but Shakespeare records how poor Falstaff, the prince of cowards and wits, rising from a figured death, stabbed again the dead Percy, and carried the carcase aloft in triumph to prove his valor. So now, when the rebellion in our land is dead, many Falstaffs appear to brandish the evidence of their valor, and seek to win applause, and to appropriate honors for deeds that never were done. . . . I do want peace and security, and the return to law and justice from Maine to the Rio Grande; and if it does not exist now, substantially, it is for state reasons beyond my comprehension. It may be thought strange that one who has no fame but as a soldier, should have been so careful to try to restore the civil power of the Government, and the peaceful jurisdiction of the Federal courts; but it is difficult to discover in that fact any just cause of offence to an enlightened and free people."

That all the world knew Halleck to have been an office-soldier added sting to the Falstaff joke. Sherman was able to score a subtler point when Grant officially asked him to delete from his report his condemnation of Halleck's intended breach of the truce and his candid assertion that, if necessary, "he would have protected Johnston's army and defended his own pledge of faith, even at the cost of many lives." For in declining to delete these remarks he quoted Halleck's own text book on military law as to the necessity of maintaining good faith, the "higher law," and the penalty for violating a safeguard.

The opportunity to repay Stanton's insult came quickly. On May 19 Sherman and his army reached Alexandria on the outskirts of Washington, thereby completing the last three-hundred-and-fifty-mile lap of their great circular march. Indeed, for him and for some of his comrades it was the exact completion of a circle which had begun from the same spot nearly four years earlier—on the march out to Bull Run. The greatest strategic circle in military history. On the 23rd, the Eastern armies marched in review through Washington, an endless column of troops well-clad and well-drilled, their ranks trim and spotless. Returning from the pageant Sherman, with his customary candour, declared, "It was magnificent. In dress, in soldierly appearance, in precision of alignment and marching we cannot beat those fellows." Then some one suggested that they should not attempt it but instead should be workmanlike and pass in review "as we went marching through Georgia."

Sherman caught up the suggestion and next morning as the people of Washington watched the Grand Army of the West defile before their eyes they saw no glittering pageant, but instead an exhibition of virility. With uniforms travel-stained and patched, colours tattered and bullet-riven, brigade after brigade passed with the elastic spring and freely swinging stride of athletes, each followed by its famous "bummers" on laden mules ridden with rope bridles. The most practically trained, physically fittest and most actively intelligent army that the world had seen.

Sherman himself was at the head and on passing the Presidential stand dismounted and greeted his wife. Then he shook hands with the President and with each of his cabinet until he came to Stanton, when he withheld his hand and turned away. The rebuff was too obvious to pass unnoticed by the spectators. However severe the provocation, in the cool light of history the incident seems a rather regrettable lapse on the part of a great historical figure. Yet it has a compensating value as a counteractive to his statue which fills the eye in New York, and by which alone too many of his countrymen know him. For when a man suffers memorial elevation in dignified petrification as a statue, still more an equestrian statue, his interest for and influence on future generations is in danger of becoming static. The last fate that Sherman, by heredity and philosophy an iconoclast, would have desired was that of being contemplated by posterity as a flawless graven idol. Perhaps an intuition inspired him to shatter the image already cast, in May, 1865, by the magnitude of his achievement, and to assert his common humanity.

But the trend of his letters at this time shows us that even in this "human" retaliation he was intent to avenge an insult to humanity rather than to his own dignity. Here is one, in that same week, which gives the tenor of his thought—"I confess, without shame, I am sick and tired of fighting—its glory is all moonshine; even success the most brilliant is over dead and mangled bodies, with the anguish and lamentations of distant families, appealing to me for sons, husbands and fathers. You, too, have seen these things, and I know you also are tired of the war, and are willing to let the civil tribunals resume their place. And, so far as I know, all the fighting men of our army want peace; and it is only those who have never heard a shot, never heard the shriek and groans of the wounded and lacerated (friend or foe), that cry aloud for more blood, more vengeance, more desolation. I *know* the rebels are whipped to death, and I declare before God, as a man and a soldier, I will not strike a foe who stands unarmed and submissive before me, but would rather say—'Go, and sin no more.'" And to his subordinate in North Carolina he gave the watch-word—"Maintain peace and good order, and let law and harmony grow up naturally. I would have preferred to leap more directly to the result, but the same end may be attained by the slower process."

CHAPTER XXIII

EPILOGUE

"War's over—occupation's gone." With this brief comment Sherman had announced to his staff the fact of Johnston's original peace parley and his own welcome to it. Perhaps only he realized the deeper truth of his remark. For the last act of war was, in a dramatic sense, the last act of his career, and all that followed merely epilogue.

He was still only forty-five, but there were no worlds left to conquer. He had reached the zenith of his military fame and achievement at the exact age prophetically fixed by Napoleon as the zenith from which the power of generalship declines. But the Civil War had ended war on the North American continent, so that Sherman would be saved any opportunity of testing Napoleon's prediction. And Sherman, the last, was also the least desirous among the Great Captains for martial glory. Napoleon III might pay tribute to him as the modern "genius" of war, but Sherman preferred to leave to his admirer the uncertain pursuit of such glory.

Admirers might find another historical parallel, and suggestion, in the fact that Sherman was almost the same age as Wellington at Waterloo. But Sherman regarded it as a warning rather than an inspiration, and of the two evils would almost have preferred war to politics as an exercise for his remaining, or declining, years. As democratic in manner as "the Duke" was the reverse, he had the same "aristocratic" disdain of mind for the emotional vagaries of the mass. But he had also more balance of mind, sprung on realism and acute self-judgment. Thus, more conscious of the limitations of his own experience as a training for politics, he avoided the bait which the aristocratic Wellington and the democratic Grant alike swallowed—and avoided the fate which swallowed them. His restraint is the more remarkable because of the frequency with which the bait was offered.

The immediate aftermath of the war held out to him a deceptive promise of tranquillity.   For the country was divided into five military divisions and he received command of the second, the "Military Division of the Mississippi."   Although the title was the same as that of his war-time command, the area was different, lying mainly west of the river and stretching towards the Rocky Mountains. His headquarters were at St. Louis, so that he began the peace where he had begun the war.   An ill omen for his own peace.

At first the distance seemed to assure this peace, for he felt that both the President and Stanton were as pleased as himself at his departure from Washington.   Untroubled by the problems of "reconstruction" he could turn his attention to more promising construction—the great Pacific railroad, which would ultimately span the great gap between Omaha and San Francisco.   Essentially a realist, Sherman was a little sceptical of the pæans of premature delight with which the opening of the first 16½ miles westwards from Omaha was hailed.   He recalled that a decade earlier a similar indulgence in words had marked the opening of the first tiny section eastwards.   But, once convinced that the promoters had the necessary staying power and capital, he became an enthusiastic supporter.   Better than enthusiasm, Sherman lent his practical aid, making frequent and far-ranging reconnaissances of the country ahead of the advancing railroad; reconnaissances in which, at personal hazard, he traversed the buffalo regions from south to north and east to west.   Mingling with the Indians whenever possible, he sought to allay their fears of the coming railroad, but when confronted with a blank wall of superstitious conservatism told them bluntly, with remorseless logic, "you cannot stop the locomotive any more than you can stop the sun or moon."   And it was on his suggestion that in March, 1866, a new military department was constituted with headquarters at Omaha, specially to protect and assist the construction of the railroad.   Indeed, it is almost true to say that "Sherman's army" linked the Atlantic with the Pacific.   For the builders of the Union Pacific Railroad were almost entirely ex-soldiers of the Union armies, with one of Sherman's old corps commanders, Dodge, as chief engineer; and the success of their task would have been impossible without the "advanced guard" of regular soldiers who cleared and protected the way.   Time after time Sherman himself intervened to smooth out difficulties and, in

Dodge's verdict, "There is no one who has taken so active a part, and who has accomplished so much for the benefit of the Government, in the building of the trans-continental railroads as General Sherman." As an apt recognition of his share in spanning the Rocky Mountains, the loftiest station on the completed line, over 8,000 feet above sea-level, was named "Sherman." From Dodge also we learn, what Sherman passes over in his memoirs, that the first exploring party which reconnoitred the possible routes across the mountains for a railroad was one sent from San Francisco in 1849 at Lieutenant Sherman's suggestion—almost exactly twenty years before the last spike was driven in to make the dream a reality.

General Sherman's help was guided by his vision towards a dual object, for as, in his opinion, the hostile Indians were the greatest obstacle to the scheme so he also calculated that the extension of the railroads was the surest way to the pacification of the Indians. Transportation is civilization. The truth is being proved again, half a century later, on another "Indian" frontier—the long-vexed north-west frontier of British India.

With similar insight, Sherman had urged the rapid demobilization of the army, and its reduction to a small peacetime establishment. The constant cheese-paring of later years by which Congress atoned for keeping up an army by keeping it inefficient, he regarded as bad national economy, but the original reduction as good. For his hope, fulfilled by the result, was that the demobilized soldiers would flock westward to settle and seek a living, and this virgin territory be peopled by a race of men trained to hardihood and self-reliance in the school of war, so that producers might replace nomads, and cattle ranches, buffaloes.

In the reorganization of the army, provision was made for one full general and one lieutenant-general. Grant, naturally, became the first, and Sherman the second. He accepted this step in rank without exhilaration, but without objection, now that it no longer appeared to bring him into rivalry with Grant. The avoidance of undesired rivalry was, however, not so simple.

From his busy yet tranquil post in the West Sherman had watched, with growing distress, the course of a political "reconstruction" that was more destructive than constructive. At the outset he had sounded several notes of warning. Thus on the subject of negro suffrage he wrote to his brother, in August, 1865—"Negro equality will lead to endless strife, and to remove and separate the races will be a big job . . . it is better to study the case and adapt measures to meet it, than to lay down the theory or force facts to meet it." "We cannot keep the South out long, and it is a physical impossibility for us to guard the entire South by armies; nor can we change opinions by force." Again, in September—"You hardly yet realize how completely this country has been devastated, and how completely humbled the man of the South is. Of course editors and talkers may express opinions we don't like, but they will take good care not to reduce those opinions to acts."

History was to prove him right, but in Washington prevision was as lacking as provision; good sense, as good will. Radical opinion in the North was determined to make the South grovel, and, as a means to this end, to force negro suffrage on the Southern States. This opinion found its chief mouthpiece in Charles Sumner—from an abstract love of the blacks—and its chief manipulator in Thaddeus Stevens—from a concrete hatred of the whites. They fomented the opposition to the President who, soon tiring of vengeance, had reverted to Lincoln's policy and his own party creed. And in Stanton they found an invaluable Cabinet ally, who always gave them intimation of Presidential moves in time for counteraction. Another ally was the folly of human nature in the South, where men, although ready to abandon active service, were loth to abandon lip service to their old idols; thereby they gave an excuse to their eager foes. Congress refused to admit the newly elected representatives from the Southern States and pursued its campaign of humiliation in defiance of the President.

Sherman had rejoiced to see the President coming round to Lincoln's policy and, although Johnson had been no friend to him, he felt a growing friendliness for the man, or any man, who would pursue the path of reconciliation and restoration. This sympathy was to endanger his desire for tranquillity. For as Johnson had drifted towards the policy implicit in Sherman's peace terms to Johnston, he felt that he might now call on Sherman's aid, as a lever to remove the obstruction caused by Stanton in his own Cabinet.

He had first tried to induce Grant to take over the duties of Secretary of War in addition to his own command of the Army. But Grant was averse to such a proposal on constitutional grounds and, in addition, was inclining towards the radical camp, under the influence of Rawlins, his old and often mischievous chief of staff. As painted by Rawlins the prospect of the Presidency looked pleasant in his sight.

The President then had a "happy" thought. Why not get rid of this obstinate general and potential political supplanter by sending him on a convenient mission, to Mexico. Accordingly, he ordered Grant to escort the newly appointed minister to the court of Juarez, the newly elected president in name of a republic that was still in fact the empire of Maximilian—so long as French bayonets protected his imperial dignity.

Sherman, on returning from a trip to the mountains of New Mexico, found a summons to Washington. On arrival there he heard that the President wished him to command the army temporarily in Grant's absence, as an obvious step to placing him in permanent command. Sherman rejected this proposal as emphatically as he did the alternative of making him Secretary of War in place of Stanton. In telling his brother of the proposal he caustically remarked: "Grant was willing that I should be Secretary of War, but I was not." Instead, to relieve a situation now awkward for both Johnson and Grant, he offered to go himself on the ornamental mission to Mexico. And to round off his peace-bringing visit he even made up his own quarrel with Stanton; if neither man could appreciate the other's point of view, each had come to respect the other's fearless strength of will.

On November 11, 1866, Sherman embarked at New York for Vera Cruz, and "as soon as we were outside Sandy Hook I explained to Captain Alden that my mission was ended, because I believed that by substituting myself for General Grant I had prevented a serious quarrel between him and the Administration, which was unnecessary."

Thereafter Sherman settled down to enjoy the voyage, despite a rough passage. On reaching Vera Cruz there were signs of a French evacuation but none of Juarez, and the diplomatic inconvenience that Sherman belonged to a mission accredited to Juarez compelled him to decline Marshal Bazaine's invitation to Mexico

City. After a vain search of the other ports along the coast, Sherman put the minister ashore to continue the chase, without result, and himself returned to New Orleans, saying, "I have not the remotest idea of riding on mule back a thousand miles in Mexico to find its chief magistrate. . . . The truth is these Mexicans were and still are as unable as children to appreciate the value of time." A personal view of Mexico had merely confirmed his previous impressions and he was far more anxious to get home than to try his brother's "suggestion" that, with slight encouragement, the Mexicans might elect him their ruler. Further, "I should deplore anything that would make us assume Mexico in any shape—its territory, its government, or its people." "Mexico does not belong to our system."

He journeyed back to St. Louis through the country he had devastated, and was pleasantly surprised to find that the Southerners showed him no ill-will, but rather looked to him as their champion. On arrival he found that the Indians were causing more trouble than ever, in their despairing effort to resist the tide of white settlement which was sweeping over their hunting grounds. To counteract the raids of so elusive a foe was, militarily, an unfruitful task, and in July, 1867, Sherman remarks that the "clamor for protection everywhere has prevented our being able to collect a large force to go into the country where we believe the Indians have hid their families." He still adhered to his war-proved conception of the grand strategic goal in war. But he had still greater faith in the ultimate effect of the railroads in nullifying the need for war. Meantime his idea was either to induce or to force the Indians to "collect on agreed-on limits far away from the continental roads." In August he was appointed a member of the Indian Peace Commission, which agreed on the policy of removing the Indians from the neighbourhood of these railroads and establishing them on two great reservations, to north and south, where they would receive maintenance for ten years until they could become, it was hoped, self-supporting. Sherman himself went among the Navajos, meeting the chiefs for discussion of their grievances; but, as he complained, the authorities failed "to fulfil any of the promises we held out to them of ploughs, seed, cattle, etc., to begin their new life of peace."

If the Commission was not remarkably successful in helping the Indians, it at least helped the railroads.

Sherman's work on the Commission was punctuated by equally harassing calls to Washington; the first in October, when he temporarily smoothed over the friction between Johnson and Grant. In August, Johnson had definitely broken with Stanton and suspended him from office, officially appointing the reluctant Grant to exercise his functions. But by the "Tenure of Civil Office" bill, passed in March over the President's veto, the consent of the Senate was necessary for any such removal. So in January, 1868, the Senate duly repudiated the President's act, and Stanton resumed occupation of his office.

During that month Sherman was in Washington, as member of a board on army regulations, and inevitably was drawn into the three-cornered tug of war as mediator and intermediary. His own feelings at this uncomfortable tribute were thus forcibly expressed to Grant—"I'm afraid that acting as go-between for three persons, I may share the usual fate of meddlers, and at last get kicks from all. We ought not to be involved in politics, but for the sake of the Army we are justified in trying at least to cut this Gordian Knot, which they do not appear to have any practicable plan to do."

Once more a crisis offered him the opportunity for personal advancement; once more he rejected it. The President proposed to create a new office, making him Brevet General of the Army and bringing him to Washington, in command of a new "Military Division of the Atlantic" but actually to discharge the duties of Secretary of War. He could thus use Sherman's fame as a safety curtain against interference from the Senate.

In formally refusing the offer, Sherman replied: "To bring me to Washington would put three heads to an army—yourself, General Grant, and myself—and we would be more than human if we were not to differ. In my judgment it would ruin the army, and would be fatal to one or two of us. . . . I have been with General Grant in the midst of death and slaughter . . . and yet I never saw him more troubled than since he has been in Washington. . . . If this political atmosphere can disturb the equanimity of one so guarded and so prudent as he is, what will be the result with me so careless, so outspoken as I am. Therefore, with my consent,

Washington never." And he concluded with the advice that Johnson should be patient and allow "the absurdity of holding an empty office" to weaken Stanton's position, rather than provoke a popular reaction in his favour by foolish measures.

The comforting illusion that he had shaken off Johnson was dispelled within a fortnight of Sherman's return to St. Louis. For on February 13 he received a telegram from Grant telling him that he had been appointed to command of the Atlantic Division, and in the papers next morning read the news that he had been nominated as Brevet General. Thereupon he took drastic and instant action. Sending his brother a telegram to oppose, in the Senate, his own nomination, he wrote to the President a conciliatory yet emphatic letter, asking that at the least he should be excused from taking up his headquarters at Washington, and plainly hinting at his own resignation if he was refused this concession to "soften the blow which, right or wrong, I consider one of the hardest I have sustained in a life somewhat checkered with adversity."

His action succeeded and he was allowed to remain at St. Louis although Johnson, in a momentary fit of spite, tried to compromise him politically by publishing extracts from some of his private letters, in which he had advised the President on the Stanton case. Ten years earlier such a trick would have drawn a fiery outburst from Sherman, but now his temper had mellowed, his charity had increased; and his letters show merely compassion for Johnson's plight, and regret that Johnson should jeopardize a good cause by impolitic action.

That regret, and his verdict as a realistic idealist, had already been expressed in a letter to his father-in-law after returning from Washington—"He attempts to govern after he has lost the means to govern. He is like a General fighting without an army—he is like Lear roaring at the storm, bareheaded and helpless. And now he wants me to go with him to the wilderness. I do want peace, and do say that if all hands would stop talking, and writing, and let the sun shine, and the rains fall for two or three years, we would be nearer reconstruction than we are likely to be with the three or hundred statesman trying to legislate round the prejudices begotten of four centuries." For good sense and good prose the passage has few equals.

But Johnson drove on to his doom and, in default of Grant or Sherman, appointed Lorenzo Thomas Secretary of War *ad interim.* This act of defiance to his opponents was answered by his own impeachment and trial before the Senate—one of the most degrading incidents in American history. Although he escaped conviction, by a single vote, and so procured Stanton's resignation, his power for good was paralyzed during the remainder of his presidency.

It was an infective paralysis for, in a different form, it passed on to his successor, and thereby impaired the fame of a greater man. Grant, after initial reluctance, had yielded to the combined pressure of his military and domestic chiefs of staff, Rawlins and his wife, and had accepted the Republican nomination. His election, in November, 1868, left to Sherman the succession as General of the Army—although, at Sherman's suggestion, Grant retained his office until on March 4 he became the tenant of the White House.

Sherman's first task as General of the Army was his now habitual one of acting as mediator. Grant had chosen Sheridan to succeed both to Sherman's grade and command, a choice dictated not only by past services but by the present need of a bold and vigorous commander on the Indian border. But Sheridan's promotion carried him over the head of Halleck and Meade, and also passed over the claims of Thomas. Halleck was not in the running but the others were, and in consolation Meade was given the command in Philadelphia, which increased the over-sensitive Thomas's sense of injury. He complained that he was always left in remote commands, and although Grant would not alter his previous appointment, he allowed Sherman to offer Thomas any other alternative, and Thomas chose to go to San Francisco—not that he wished to go there, but because of his "regulation" feeling that his rank would be degraded if an officer of lower grade was appointed to this higher grade post. But, in Sherman's opinion, the premature death of both Meade and Thomas was accelerated by the ungenerous failure of the Government to recognize their services at the cheap price of allowing for two more lieutenant-generals. That lack of generosity was repeated half a century later.

Sherman himself was the next sufferer from the failure of the new government to rise to the occasion. And this time the damage passed beyond the injury of feelings to the injury of the Army and the national security. For generations the old cleavage and quarrel between "the staff" and "the line," due to separating administration from command, had hampered the efficiency of the war-machine. Grant himself had made formal protest to Stanton soon after the war, but this argument was swallowed in the noisier controversy between Stanton and Johnson. Grant and Sherman, however, had long agreed upon the need for reform and, in fulfilment of this, the day after Grant assumed the reins of power he issued the decree that "the chiefs of the staff corps, departments and bureaus, will report to and act under the immediate command of the general commanding the army," and further, that all orders from the President and Secretary of War would be transmitted through the General.

At a stroke this long-sought reform had been achieved. It was destroyed almost as quickly. For, a few days later, the saturnine and dominating Rawlins became Secretary of War and, jealous of power, brought all the pressure of his influence to bear against the change. Reluctantly, Grant sent for Sherman and broke the news, giving the amazingly weak excuse—"Rawlins feels badly about it; it worries him and he is not well." Sherman, incredulous, protested that a public measure which Grant had advocated for years ought not to be set aside for such a "reason," all the less so that the orders had taken effect. "Yes, it would ordinarily be so, but I don't like to give him pain now; so, Sherman, you'll have to publish the rescinding order." "But, Grant, it's your own order that you revoke, not mine, and think how it will look to the whole world." For lack of a justification Grant seized on a quibble and testily said—"Well, if it's my own order, I can rescind it, can't I?" The first jarring note in a glorious harmony. And in formal tones such as these two had never used Sherman, standing stiffly, replied—"Yes, Mr. President, you have the power to revoke your order; you shall be obeyed. Good morning, sir."

With this order, all his dreams of usefulness, and of laying the foundations of a sound military organization, had dissolved. But if purpose was shattered, loyalty remained, and after suppressing a first impulse to break with Grant he strove to make the best of a bad arrangement for the sake of good friendship.

For a time it was feasible. Rawlins, content with his victory, made his practice more workable than his theory during his short

spell of power and life. In September he died and Sherman temporarily fulfilled his functions, so that real unity of control was
established. It is significant to note that his brief experience of the
functional advantages of this combination, under one head, led him
to advocate a single cabinet minister of defence for the combined
services. The suggestion was at least altruistic, for nothing would
have drawn him into a cabinet office. And the choice of a soldier as
Secretary of War proved as disastrous as that of a soldier-president.

To fill Rawlins's place Grant asked Sherman to suggest a suitable
ex-volunteer officer from the West, and Sherman put forward three
names. Of these, Dodge, unhappily if rightly, considered railroads
more important than politics and General Belknap was appointed.
His love of authority soon proved greater than his gratitude, and
soon he not merely claimed his full theoretical power but infringed
on Sherman's. Orders were repeatedly issued and officers interfered
with unknown to the General of the Army who, apart from his
own aides-de-camp, had no staff through whom he could even carry
out his functions of command. As protests to Belknap produced
no effect, nor answer, Sherman took the question up with Grant
who, however, merely shilly-shallied. Perhaps the explanation is
contained in Sherman's comment—"I do think that because some
newspapers berate Grant about his military surroundings, he feels
disposed to go to the other extreme." And Sherman, ever a realist,
left the Secretary of War to be virtually the General of the Army,
while he himself found a safety valve in travel. If he could not
maintain his own world he could at least enlarge his knowledge of
the world.

This solution, both peaceful and unresting, was not attained without an effort of will, of his will against that of the American public,
which was already growing dissatisfied with an administration which
did not even redeem its mediocrity by honesty. Indeed, it is the
crowning irony of political history that the eight years' tenure of
a man who was a byword for honesty has become a byword for corruption and nepotism—truly a double term. So also the attempt to
rule the South by force merely produced the Ku Klux Klan, fulfilling Sherman's prediction that the policy of military occupation
spelt anarchy. More a man of the world than Grant, Sherman
knew it well enough to shun it, and realized the limitations of per-

sonal honesty, the dangers of loyalty. Hence he was quick to forestall a new danger, which he first discovered, from the papers, on
returning from a trip along the Texas Frontier in the spring of
1871. He sat down and wrote his brother a letter which in its
brevity contrasted with his normal epistles—"I see the *Herald* is in
full blast for me as President. You may say for me and publish it
too, that in no event and under no circumstances will I ever be a
candidate for President or any other political office; and I mean
every word of it."

His steadfastness in refusing the temptation is the more im-
pressive because acceptance would have promised not only a dramatic turning of the tables but a release, by ascension, from a
"tomb" that only his forbearance made bearable. For, as he told
his brother in July, "my office has been by law stript of all the influence and prestige it possessed under Grant, and even in matters
of discipline and army control I am neglected, overlooked, or
snubbed. I have called General Grant's attention to the fact several
times, but got no satisfactory address." The prefix "General" is
perhaps significant, yet still more significant is the absence from
Sherman's letters during these trying years of a single harsh word
or reproach against his old comrade-in-arms. But he was not content to lend his reputation to a régime he distrusted or to fill an
office that was a sinecure. Already he had formed the decision that
if it so continued he would remove to St. Louis, where he could
better perform the duties of inspection minus authority—the sum
of his remaining responsibility.

Meantime he was glad to take advantage of an invitation from
Admiral Alden for a free passage across the Atlantic, as a means
to a long tour abroad—although he scrupulously insisted on paying
for his food on the voyage. Permission was easy to obtain, for although his refusal to consider a presidential nomination from either
party had been published, his feeling of relief was doubtless shared
by the Cabinet.

He embarked on the steam-frigate *Wabash* on November 11—
strange how often this date recurs among the landmarks of Sherman's career—and after landing at Gibraltar travelled through
Spain and Southern France to Rome. Thence after visits to Sicily,
Malta and Egypt, he went to the Black Sea and saw the Crimean

battlefields, before continuing his journey overland to Moscow and St. Petersburg, and back through all the countries of Western Europe in turn to England. And before sailing home he took care to see Scotland and Ireland as well. He was certainly the complete tourist, but not the traditional tabloid dose-taker, for he spent almost a year in Europe, and noted all that he saw with the thoroughness and almost the enthusiasm of his subaltern days. During his stay in England he visited Aldershot, but apparently was not impressed with the equipment and thought of the British Army of the period. Some time later he remarked—"The English cannot discuss any proposition without bringing in the Duke of Wellington. No man, if living, would be quicker to avail himself of improved transportation and communication than the Duke"—a perhaps too generous estimate—"The Science of War like that of natural philosophy, chemistry, must recognise new truths and new inventions as they arise. . . ."

While in Paris he remembered his rejected invitation from Bazaine five years earlier and obtained permission to visit the Marshal, then in arrest and awaiting trial for his surrender of Metz. And he capped this kindly courtesy by a personal tour of the 1870 battlefields so that, when he returned home and the trial came on, he would be qualified to follow the reports intelligently! He also succeeded in annoying the German soldiers by some of his candid criticisms on this campaign.

But his interest in "sight-seeing" far outranged the military sphere, and, as in earlier years, his comments reveal him as that curious combination—a man with an unusual appreciation of natural beauty, and refreshingly free from conventional enthusiasms, yet always preferring the practical to the æsthetic when the two were opposed. The most amusing instance of this trend of thought was when, in his last years, he accompanied his brother on a first visit to the pre-Ohio home of his family, at Woodbury, Connecticut. John was enchanted with the wooded and rugged charm of the neighbourhood, but William, although admiring it as scenery, remarked, "I cannot see how this rocky country can be converted into farming lands that can be made profitable," and then emphatically voiced his thankfulness "that my ancestors moved from this region to Ohio."

In travelling, however, this pursuit of the practical was broad rather than narrow, and to those who were surprised at his love of acquiring out-of-the-way knowledge he had a favourite retort— "You don't know how soon you will have use for the seemingly useless thing that you can pick up by mere habit." His travels in Europe were in extreme contrast to the "comic opera" tour of Grant —or, more truly, the Grant family. For although his fame paved the way for a triumphal progress, he sought quietude as far as possible and avoided receptions unless they promised some new interest, to the grievance of numerous "lion-hunters." The most novel, certainly, was when the Sultan of Turkey entertained him on the Black Sea. As a token of friendship, Sherman had taken Grant's son, newly graduated from West Point, with him as his aide-de-camp. The Sultan was not, apparently, versed in the American constitution and, regarding Fred Grant as the heir to the throne, put him in the place of honour. Sherman quietly enjoyed the joke, but less so its sequel, when a bill for six hundred dollars to defray the hospitality was handed to him, as the assumed comptroller of the royal household. For it not only upset his modest and rigidly kept accounts, but violated that strict financial code which had been manifested in California and Louisiana. He disliked a new tax almost as much as a new uniform, and had even sold land rapidly rising in value rather than pay taxes that seemed unreasonable. So also when his admirers subscribed $65,000 to purchase a house for him in Washington he would only accept it on condition that it was accompanied by bonds sufficient to pay the taxes. Even then, his fear of living beyond his means, and running into debt, led him to divide it, letting one half. Yet another contrast with Grant!

On his return to America, moreover, that house was the means of keeping him at Washington when all other motives urged a speedy departure, for the encroachment on his office continued rather than abated. At last he sold his house and in October, 1874, moved his headquarters—"without charging a cent for transportation"—to St. Louis, beside the great trench through which ran his beloved Mississippi and the narrow trench in which lay his Willy. These two had been his supreme inspirations, and in the everflowing current of the one the life of the other seemed to flow on, their union symbolizing the source and future of the greatness of his Union.

He was all the more pleased to quit Washington because the prospect of his nomination for the presidency was again being bruited. Accordingly, he wrote to his brother before leaving Washington— "Don't ever give any person the least encouragement to think I can be used for political ends. I have seen it poison so many otherwise good characters that I am really more obstinate than ever. I think Grant will be made miserable to the end of his life by his eight years' experience. . . ."

His self-imposed exile was, however, interpreted as a proof of political hostility to the régime, and the Government press hinted that he ought to resign. Such hints he ignored, saying, "By my office I am above party, and am not bound in honor or fact to toady to anybody. Therefore I shall never resign, and shall never court any other office." On the other hand, he suggested that as his office was treated as purely ornamental it might be abolished, and the nation's money saved.

It would seem, however, that another cause, beyond Belknap's lust of power, lay behind these press hints and the curtailment of Sherman's powers. For as General of the Army he had sought so far as possible to protect his officers and men from the distasteful demands of police duty in the occupied South, where "black and tan" State governments composed of the lowest elements were maintained solely by the overawing bayonets of the Northern soldiery, who loathed their task. Although orders were now issued to them direct by the Secretary of War, "short-circuiting" Sherman, the mere presence of his personality was inevitably felt as an obstruction. In a letter of January, 1875, to his brother, referring to the debate on the Louisiana riots, he recognizes this cause of grievance— "I have all along tried to save our officers and soldiers from the dirty work imposed on them by the city authorities of the South; and may, thereby, have incurred the suspicion of the President that I did not cordially sustain his force. My hands and conscience are free of any of the breaches of fundamental principles in that quarter. And I have always thought it wrong to bolster up weak State governments by our troops." Again, in February—"the quicker you allow the people to select their own governors the better. . . ."

Great as his desire for peace, he was born to be a stormy petrel, and even at St. Louis could not keep out of controversy. There, he had little with which to occupy himself, for although he went through the form of command, he realized that it was a farce. And so, in the intervals of touring the frontier, he spent his time in writing his memoirs. Their publication caused a storm of criticism if also a wave of applause, and much of the storm was political in origin. For by revealing the full story of the peace negotiations he inevitably caused a bad reflection on the Radicals who were still trying to crush a rebellion that had ceased ten years before. Naturally, however, such critics preferred to conceal the cause of their wrath by attacking his memoirs on other grounds. They were joined by Thomas's "body-guard," that band of young staff officers who had been to their massive chief in life what the "Young Turks" were later to Joffre, and who, now that he was dead, struck out savagely to avenge the unslaked thirst for recognition which had fretted him into the grave. Several of these critics sought to widen the official breach between Grant and Sherman into a personal breach, and Grant confesses that after reading Boynton's "review" he felt somewhat bitter—until he read the memoirs for himself and discovered Boynton's maliciously distorted use of them. As Grant then appreciated, there was no cause for complaint. His own memoirs, compiled ten years later, are notable for their generosity in giving full credit to Sherman when all causes of estrangement between the two friends had long since disappeared. But Sherman's were written when he was feeling sore, and their generous fairness to Grant is thus more remarkable.

More historically significant is the question of their accuracy, which has been impugned by his critics. On the other hand, all who knew him intimately pay tribute to his wonderful power of memory. In this difference lies the explanation. The impression created on one who, as a biographer and not as a quibbler, has checked his memoirs against the official records, is that in writing them he relied too much on a prodigious memory when minor issues were concerned. Thus in such points as dates, especially, there are occasional careless slips, while at the same time the general impression conveyed in the memoirs coincides closely with that obtained by an analysis of the records, and the only important omissions are some of his own achievements, such as the inspired action which turned the scales on July 22, 1864. The faults of his memoirs are of detail, not of

vain glory or bias. For in his later years he could even be fair to
newspaper correspondents, although calling them "damned reporters" in extenuation of his mildness.

It was the reflection of the peace of spirit which he had at last
attained, a peace which, curiously, was compatible with a restless
activity of mind. His interests and interest in men and matters
were as great, even growing, but his desire to change them had
gone—although conditions now turned to meet him. For in 1876
the War Department shared with several others the exposure of its
scandalous state of corruption and Belknap hastily resigned before
his impeachment for selling sutlerships. The new Secretary of
War, Alphonso Taft, appealed to Sherman to return to Washington, and, although at first reluctant, he yielded when an order was
issued which met his claim that orders to the various departmental
branches should go through him, and that they should report to
him. If it was not his ideal system for war needs, it was at least
workable in peace. And in Taft he found the first of a series of
Secretaries of War with whom his relations were always amicable.

In 1877 a new President, Hayes, was elected, who soon proved
that in addition to an honesty equal to Grant's he had the will and
power to enforce it in others. He purged the Government of its
least reputable officials, included an ex-Confederate in his cabinet,
and recalled the troops from the South. And to John Sherman, as
Secretary of the Treasury, fell the honour of bringing the country
back to financial rectitude.

Meanwhile General Sherman did what he could within the limits
of his power and the army estimates to improve the badly deteriorated state and status of the army, and from his foundation of
the Leavenworth Schools in 1881 is commonly dated its educational
renaissance. No commanding general could have toured the scattered posts of his army more assiduously, for he frequently travelled
two hundred miles a week in a "Dougherty," the familiar rattle-trap
coach, drawn by four mules, of the Western Plains; journeys which
were mingled not only with the shooting that he loved but with the
almost daily writing of the long topographical reports which he
loved even better. One of his now rare protests was caused by the
assertion of a Senator that these tours "really for pleasure" were
made in a "palace-car." Actually Sherman received the same eight

cents a mile travelling allowance as a second lieutenant, and although this would not have paid for a "palace-car," such luxurious transport would have given him less pleasure than a Dougherty. In so far at least the Senator was correct.

In 1882 a bill was passed fixing sixty-four years as the age-limit for retirement, and Sherman strongly supported this measure because of his indignation at the injustice which sundry officers had suffered from the old practice of arbitrary retirement at the will of the President. When this bill became law the offer was made that he should be treated as an exception, but he refused, giving the reason that "no man could know or realize when his own mental or physical powers began to decline—I remembered too well the experience of Gil Blas with the Bishop of Granada." A realist to the end. Another reason, however, was his desire to give Sheridan a chance. "He don't ask it or want it, but there is such a principle as 'turn about fair play.' " But a concession undoubtedly more pleasing to Sherman than any eulogies was that he was allowed to retire on full pay.

His sixty-fourth birthday was not until February 8, 1884, but he anticipated it on the ground that "It is better that the change should occur with the new Congress. The country is now generally prosperous, and the army is in reasonably good condition, considering the fact that peace and politics are always more damaging than war. . . ." But first he took the chance of a final tour in the Far West, and this time travelled further and in more luxury than previously. In September he writes to his wife from Santa Fé— "I have been travelling in three months, in beautiful cars . . . , over an extent of more than ten thousand miles of country, every mile of which is free from the danger of the savage and is being occupied by industrious families. Of course the Army has not done this, but the Army has gone ahead and prepared the way, and year by year I have followed up with words of encouragement. . . . I honestly believe in this way I have done more good for our country and for the human race than I did in the Civil War."

Then on November 1, 1883, he wrote a brief farewell order, rose from his desk, gave Sheridan the chair, shook hands, and made his departure as casually as on any ordinary day. After retirement he first settled at St. Louis, and was as promptly unsettled by the new presidential campaign. Letters poured in urging him to accept nomination, and when it became likely that a deadlock would occur at the Chicago Convention in the early ballots even his brother joined in the appeal. Promptly he retorted—"Why should I at sixty-five years of age, with a reasonable provision of life, not a dollar of debt, and with the universal respect of my neighbours and countrymen, embark in the questionable game of politics? The country is in a state of absolute peace, and it would be a farce to declare that any man should sacrifice himself to a mere party necessity." As for the ground of the appeal—that a great man and name were needed—"I . . . honestly believe that we are approaching that epoch in our history when King Log is about as good as King Stork. Queen Victoria has proven about the best executive a nation has ever had. . . ."

But as a safeguard he empowered a friend to represent him at the Convention, giving him instructions, first, to prevent so far as possible his name being brought up; second, to decline politely if it was put forward after the first ballots; third, if he was nominated despite this, to decline emphatically. Henceforth his tranquillity and independence were assured, and the radiant calm of his life's sunset, atoning for all early misfortunes, proved yet another contrast with Grant—those two friends whose union of spirit had restored the Union and yet who were so utterly diverse in all save personal honesty and loyalty. As in war Sherman had acutely adjusted his end to his means and his means to the resistance in his path, so now in peace he had shown a singular ability to gauge his own capacity and to adjust his ambition accordingly. In war that quality represents true economy of force, in peace it represents the virtue which the Greeks called "moderation."

Soon after the war, when riding one day with Grant, his companion had suddenly fired at him the question, "Sherman, what special hobby do you intend to adopt?" and then humorously explained that as it was a popular custom to label celebrities with a fad of some sort he intended to choose "horses" before he was labelled with a worse, and also as a convenient means of guiding conversation away from awkward subjects. Sherman, for his part, chose "theatres and balls," both because his pleasure in such social amusements grew with age, and because, as he said later, "I was always fond of seeing young people happy." As a dancing partner, indeed, he achieved both reputation and attraction among women old and young, all the more because to fame and charm of manner he now added an increasing courtliness of manners. And perhaps he rather impishly enjoyed putting younger men in the shade. Byers, who saw much of him both at home and abroad during these latter years remarks: "I never saw a man so run after by womankind in my life." But he was as ready to give his arm to an old woman as to kiss a young one, and in his ripened enjoyment of feminine society he found not only safety in numbers but a safety valve from a home atmosphere that was oppressively heavy with the incense of religious devotion. For his wife, always a zealous Catholic, had now almost become lost to the present life in her preparation for the next. And his eldest son had become what he called "some sort of Catholic divine. . . . This is all directly antagonistic to my ideas of right. He ought . . . to take part in the great future of America. I feel as though his life were lost"—more than ever Sherman mourned the boy he had buried beside the Mississippi.

Thus even the ties of family affection could not span the inevitable gulf of spirit, and one is left with the feeling that Sherman was rather a lonely unit in such a devout family circle. In the mornings "Cump"—as his wife still called him, to his pleasure—would come down to breakfast in comfortable old slippers and a shiny morning coat, and then when the others dispersed to busy themselves in household cares, religious exercises, or good works, he would go down to his little basement room, labelled "Office of General Sherman" and filled with the neatly filed docketed records of his career and campaigns. Here he would settle down to answer, in his own hand, a stream of letters which never slackened. Many of them, inevitably were appeals for aid from old soldiers and, despite his strict financial code, he constantly helped them by giving them orders for clothing on one of the several stores where he kept a regular account—a form of charity more practical than giving money.

After finishing his day's correspondence, he would often settle down with Burns and a cigar—two companions of which he never tired. Among prose writers Dickens and Scott were his favourites, but Burns he would read by the hour with never-failing zest. A talk, a walk, or a ride filled in the time until evening when his day commonly culminated in a burst of social exercise. Free evenings were rare, for besides the theatre and opera, private and public dinners filled his engagement book. On the whole, he did not bear these accompaniments of greatness as a cross but, rather, as a milder form of travel—to observe human nature, now that age debarred him from exploring nature. He was asked once how he could attend so many functions without committing gastronomic suicide, and replied, "I don't touch fifteen per cent of the dinners I go to. I go to see the diners and enjoy their enjoyment, which I never could do if I was foolish enough to treat my stomach disrespectfully. You see, it has been too staunch a friend to me." It is pleasant to find this discerning sense of gratitude, for an exceptionally good digestion had truly been the foundation of his most unique achievements.

Moderation was less possible—because of the physical strain—in attending the innumerable war reunions and celebrations throughout the country which besought his presence. Ever since the war he had striven to attend as many as possible, although he had an increasing dislike of the more formal ones where he was merely a public exhibit. At last in a letter of July, 1890, to his brother he broke out in revolt—"I had a letter from General Alger yesterday, asking me to ride in the procession at Boston . . . in full uniform, to which I answered No with emphasis. I will attend as a delegate from Missouri, as a private, and will not form in any procession, horseback or otherwise. It is cruel to march old veterans five miles, like a circus, under a midday sun for the gratification of a Boston audience. . . ."

Four years earlier he had moved from St. Louis to New York, where he took up his residence at the Fifth Avenue Hotel before finally settling down in a house. His untarnished laurels had now given him a unique position in the affections of his countrymen, and the distinction of being the most revered and best beloved man of his time was one that he coveted and enjoyed far more than the empty dignities that he had spurned. In the life of New York he filled the same place that Wellington filled in London, during his last lap of life. Many observers have emphasized the parallel. But they have missed the great difference—that Sherman drew far more pleasure out of it, because he remained young and elastic in mind. John

Russell Young relates how, almost at the end, Sherman attended a supper that was given to Henry Irving and his company before their return to England; how, being persuaded to take the chair, he sat up until after daylight, and then, about six A.M., wound up the party with a sparkling and graceful speech of farewell to Irving.

Such a farewell was all the happier by contrast with those to which he was growing accustomed. Old friends were dying fast. Grant had gone, comforted in his last gloomy yet heroic struggle by the visits of Sherman; between these two all momentary barriers had long disappeared, and each was ever in the other's thoughts, and on the other's lips. Sheridan, despite his youth, followed. Then, in 1888, Sherman's wife began to fail suddenly, and was dead within a few weeks. He found content, as he remarked, in the knowledge that "no mortal was ever better prepared to put on immortality."

Henceforth there was for Sherman all the stronger urge to quaff the cup of life and fellowship before it was removed from his lips, and all the less desire to prolong the draught by sips till the sense of taste had faded. And he paid small heed to the anxious entreaties of his family that he should eke out his remaining energy.

On February 3, 1891, he wrote to his brother—"I am drifting along in the old rut in good strength, attending about four dinners a week at public or private houses, and generally wind up for a gossip at the Union League Club." A few days later, going out to the theatre on a bleak winter night, he caught a chill, which turned to erysipelas of the face and throat, and then to pneumonia. Power of speech failed before consciousness, and the children, with love but without understanding, summoned a priest, who administered to a man just lapsing into unconsciousness the extreme unction of the Roman church. The last of life's little ironies.

But, following in the wake of the spirit, the body was carried in accordance with his wish to St. Louis, there to be buried beside his wife and Willy on the banks of the "dirty old Mississippi"—old and yet ever young. *Tria juncta in uno.*

And although the ranks of the Southern politicians were silent when the Senate gave voice in eulogy of the dead, one greater and nobler than any of these, "Old Joe" Johnston, came to be pall-bearer to the man who in conquering him had conquered war; who in making peace had shown the spirit that alone can maintain peace. By this last act of chivalrous respect he hastened his own end five weeks later. But the union at death, and in death of these two, symbolized the new union in life of the United States.

"The legitimate object of war is a more perfect peace"—this sentence inscribed on the statue of General Sherman at Washington is a paraphrase of the words he used at St. Louis on July 20th, 1865, and the key to his thought and conduct before, during, and after the war. Because of his restless manner, the occasional extravagance of his language, and the ceaseless stream of ideas which he poured out, superficial observers often regarded him as an erratic genius, brilliant but unstable. A close study and analysis of his letters—and no man has stripped his soul more nakedly or more often—yields a different impression. His consistency is seen to be almost unparalleled among the great figures of history, and for the reason that none was more governed by reason or less influenced by instinct. His one strong instinct was the instinct for government, for order, and it guided him—through observation, historical study, and reflection—to a profound distrust of the influence of instinct in "self-government" and to an equally profound conviction that logical reasoning was the only sure guide. Reason had lifted man above the animal, which instinct would never have done, and to it was due not only the national but the moral progress of mankind. Reason was the light of humanity, instinct but the discarded skin of reason in an earlier stage of growth. Hence Sherman had a logical faith in progress, which was the firmer because he realized that the progress of the human mind is infinitely gradual, that it must be measured by æons, not by generations; and that it follows, if so gradually as to be almost imperceptible, in the wake of physical progress. No man of action has more completely attained the point of view of the scientific historian, who observes the movements of mankind with the same detachment as a bacteriologist observes bacilli under a microscope and yet with a sympathy that springs from his own common manhood. In Sherman's attainment of that philosophic pinnacle, soaring above the clouds of ignorance and passion, lies the explanation of much that seems perplexing and contradictory in his character—the dispassionateness of an impulsive man, the restfulness of a restless man, the patience of an impatient man, the sympathy of a relentless man.

It was logical, and due to reasoning that was purely logical, that he should first oppose war; then, conduct it with iron severity; and, finally, seize the first real opportunity to make a peace of complete absolution. He cared little that his name should be execrated by the people of the South if he could only cure them of a taste for war. And to cure them he deliberately aimed at the non-combatant foundation of the hostile war spirit instead of at its combatant roof. He cared as little that this aim might violate a conventional code of war, for so long as war was regarded as a chivalrous pastime, and its baseness obscured by a punctilious code, so long would it be invested with a halo of romance. Such a code and such a halo had helped the duel to survive long after less polite forms of murder had grown offensive to civilized taste and gone out of fashion. In Sherman's view law and war were two opposed states, and war began when law broke down. In other words, war was primarily an anarchical state of mind and only secondarily a matter of physical blows. Here we see the deeper meaning underlying Sherman's phrase "war is only justifiable among civilized nations to produce peace." In logic and in fact, peoples make war, armies merely end it. The corollary of this deduction was expressed in Sherman's declaration, "Therefore, I had to go through Georgia and let them see what war meant."

Law might not be perfect but at least it was the most practical form of expressing right yet devised by the human reason. War, in contrast, was an assertion by a human group that right was merely a question of superior or inferior might. To contradict this assertion Sherman had reluctantly lent himself to the war—not against the South but "*against anarchy*"—his ceaseless refrain. Vigorously rejecting that specious salve of conscience—"my country right or wrong," he would just as readily have lent himself to a war against the North if his reason had told him that there lay the cause of anarchy.

His logic may seem extreme, his implied verdict against the South may seem an inequitable assessment of the responsibility for the war, but the peace and prosperity which have since reigned in the United States, are its practical justification. And if the abolition of anarchy on a national scale has not been completed on the smaller social scale, it is because of the subsequent imperfection of law, because those who have made and multiplied the laws have fallen so far below Sherman's standard of foresight and wisdom. He was too imbued with realism to believe that the legislative and political system of the United States could be reformed from within, and justified his own abstention from the attempt by saying, "It is too much like the case of a girl who marries a drunken lover in the hopes to reform him. It never has succeeded and never will." But he had a boundless faith in the healing and recreative power of time plus prosperity. His creed was summed up in the concluding words of his post-war Saint Louis speech, wherein he had pointed out that the reconstruction and economic improvement of the South meant the benefit of the whole—"Therefore, my friends, now that the war is over, let us all go to work and do what seems honest and just to restore our country to its former prosperity—*to its physical prosperity*. As to its political prosperity, I know nothing of it, and care far less about it."

His hatred of anarchy was not inspired by an abstract motive but by the essentially practical one that only in a state of order are prosperity and progress possible. Order was merely the means to the end—progress. For Sherman's consistency was not a static conservatism but a progress through order to a better order. An advance from a secure base to gain a base for a fresh advance. It may truly be said that he based his life on the principles which governed his generalship, and proved that they were universally applicable.

Moreover, both the generalship and the principles were evolutionary. At the beginning of the war Sherman's military thought ran on the same lines as that of the normal studious soldier. Although his civil experience had widened his intellectual range he had not yet appreciated how profoundly this experience affected the military sphere. Bred on Jomini's teachings, he had a great respect for orthodox doctrine, with its emphasis on geometrical rather than on the psychological, on the bodies rather than on wills, on numerical superiority rather than on surprise. Thus, like the other "educated" soldiers of the day, he was at first handicapped in comparison with a Grant, or a Forrest, who for want of such education applied pure common sense in solving the problems of war. But the Vicksburg campaign, Sherman's "first gleam of daylight," was also his light of revelation, and the road to Vicksburg his road to Damascus. The campaign revealed to him, more clearly than any previous experience, that strategy is not merely the forerunner but the master of tactics, that the purpose of strategy is to minimize fighting and that it fulfils this purpose by playing on the mind of the opponent —so as first to disturb and then to upset his balance of mind. The campaign revealed to him also that in war unexpectedness and mobility are the master-keys of generalship—opening many doors which no physical weight can force—and it demonstrated, in particular, the incalculable value of a deceptive direction and of cutting loose from communications.

Because of his intellectual superiority, the experience made a deeper impression on him than on the simple soldier from whose instinctive practice he had acquired it. It became the foundation of a new conception of strategy which took form in his mind and henceforth he applied it with progressive consistency, developing it more boldly with each successive proof of its efficacy. For his military character as well as his thought underwent evolution. His own past experience had combined with his outlook on the war to give him a natural bias towards the security of caution, and only gradually did this yield to a growing perception that in calculated audacity and unexpectedness lay an even better guarantee of security. Hence, we see his moves becoming progressively bolder during and after the Atlanta campaign—while, on examination, they seem progressively safer. In acquiring boldness, he had learnt to measure both his own capacity and the margin of safety perhaps more acutely than any other great commander. And the reason was that his boldness was itself the product of a closely reasoned theory of war which had evolved from reflection and was supported on unrivalled knowledge of the conditions of topography, transportation, and supply. This was the real security for his progress, the logical base for his logistical moves. More perhaps than any other commander he *knew* what he was aiming at and his capacity to attain it.

He had come to realize also that in war all conditions are more calculable, all obstacles more surmountable, than those of human resistance. And having begun the war with an orthodox belief in the sovereign efficacy of battle as a "cure-all" he had learnt that the theoretical ideal of the destruction of the enemy's armed forces on the battlefield is rarely borne out in practice and that to pursue it singlemindedly is to chase a will-o'-the-wisp. Because of his original orthodoxy it is all the more significant that he reached the conclusion that the way to decide wars and win battles was "more by the movement of troops than by fighting." This was his ultimate theory, constantly expressed. And of its practice he could say, as truly as Napoleon in Austria—"I have destroyed the enemy merely by marches."

To attain such a result he radically recast the customary code of organization and maintenance, and for his superior "manœuvrability" he was dependent on the elasticity of his instrument as well as on the elasticity of his thought, his aim being to convert his army— "into a mobile machine willing and able to start at a minute's notice, and to subsist on the scantiest of food." He was able to demand from his men such sacrifice of comfort because he demanded so comparatively little sacrifice of life. His men had a supreme faith in his ability and will to spare them loss and the consequence was that when he called on them to fight they had both a willingness and a confidence in success that made them irresistible. The ardour of the charge which carrier Fort McAlister was in "striking" contrast with the assaults made in other armies during the last lap of the war.

Sherman's greater distinction in history, however, is that he not only forged new master-keys of generalship to open military locks but fitted them to a new type of lock. Even above his greatness as a strategist is his greatness as a grand strategist. He perceived that the resisting power of a modern democracy depends more on the strength of the popular will than on the strength of its armies, and that this will in turn depends largely upon economic and social security. To interrupt the ordinary life of the people and quench hope of its resumption is more effective than any military result short of the complete destruction of the armies. The last is an ideal rarely attained in the past, and increasingly difficult since the appearance of nations in arms.

As the greater size of armies and the lengthening range of weapons have made it more difficult to defeat a hostile army decisively, so the growth of the press has tended to reduce the effects of any defeat. For, from patriotism or censorship, they disguise the reality of defeat and keep the people under a pleasant opiate. Hence, as Sherman appreciated, rude personal contact with the hostile forces is necessary to awaken the enemy people from these drugged dreams of unreality and to shock them into surrender.

In contrast, however, to the increased difficulty and reduced effect of victory in battle, interference with the enemy people has become both easier and more effective as civilization has become more complex and the distribution of comfort more general. These new conditions of war were first manifest in the American Civil War, although still immature because of the loose agrarian nature of the Southern Confederacy. It is thus the more notable that these conditions should have been appreciated and turned to decisive advantage. As that war was the first modern war, so was Sherman the first modern general. And hitherto the only one. For although the same conditions, now more highly developed and obvious, governed and ultimately decided the World War, no grand strategist exploited and directed them consciously towards the collapse of the hostile will. That war did not produce a second Sherman. Nor did the Armistice.

Indeed, it is only after the dust of that conflict has settled that we can fully appreciate Sherman's outlook on war and peace. And without that war no complete understanding of Sherman would have been possible. For he was not a typical man of his age, but the prototype of the most modern age, of that age upon whose threshold we now seem to be standing. Far better than his own contemporaries we can understand his combination of restless energy with an ironical, almost fatalistic, perception of the limited results of human effort; his insistence on reasoning from facts and distrust of all received opinions; his passionate sincerity and fondness for psychological analysis; his balanced pride in his own constructive achievements—never in his instinctive attributes or nominal dignities—and awareness of his own defects; his democratic simplicity of manner and sardonic distrust of democracy as a political panacea; his loyalty to a cause, not to an emblem—a loyalty all the greater because it sprang from appreciation of its practical necessity and not from blind worship of authority; his lack of any definite religious beliefs, but increased belief in righteousness of life; his contempt for all creeds, as strait-jackets of the reason, yet respect and admiring support for any one who, like Howard, carried his religion into the practice of daily life, even in war.

But to understand Sherman it is also essential to realize the effect of the war upon his character. Momentarily it hardened him, ultimately it mellowed him. Logic had become more toned by generosity, sincerity by tolerance, purpose by sympathy. The trend of his own interests had carried him from the mountain top to the market place; the evolution of his character, from the Old Testament to the New.

SOURCES

FOREWORD

THE absence of footnote references from the pages of this book may aggrieve some readers but will, I hope, please a larger number, who do not care for the untidy and irritating modern fashion of treating any historical study as a card-index rather than a book to be read. Footnote references are an inevitable distraction to the reader's eye and mind. The justification for omitting them is not, however, merely one of narrative smoothness and page cleanliness. Such references are only of value to a small proportion of readers— as a means to personal research or composition. By directing the student's attention to an isolated quotation or piece of evidence, such footnote references are apt to give this a false value; and can also be the means of conveying a false impression. They may enable the student to find out whether the author's use of a quotation is textually correct, but they do not enable him to find out whether it gives a correct impression. For the true worth of any quotation can only be told by comparison with the whole of the evidence on the subject. Further, the practice of littering the pages with references is not even a proof that the author has consulted the sources. It is easy to copy a quotation—complete with footnote reference!—from some previous writer, and a study of books on the Civil War, especially, suggests that this labour-saving device is not uncommon.

Among the sources for the Civil War, the Official Records come first, and form the essential foundation of any study. A foundation more solid than any other war offers, for here are preserved the day to day, even hour by hour, impressions and decisions of both sides. But the student will be wise to draw a sharp distinction between the "correspondence" and the "reports." The last are so often, in all wars, written for history that they are dubious material for the historian. Hence they should only be used as a supplement to the correspondence, and subject to a critical assessment. This should take account of the time that elapsed between action and report, and should give more weight to the reporting officer's evidence on facts which did not concern him personally than on those which might effect his own credit and prospects. In writing this book I have made the same distinction in assessing other and unofficial sources.

Apart from the Official Records, the most valued sources have been the letters, diaries, or narratives of contemporary witnesses, with a preference to those which were written contemporaneously, and with a discount in proportion as they showed signs of bias or where a motive for bias existed. The aftermath of the war produced such a volume of controversial discussion that all narratives, commentaries, and biographies compiled in that heated atmosphere are open to suspicion, while the books of a later and cooler generation have too often been based on these without adequate independent examination of the Records. Almost the only value of the controversial literature of the post-war period is as a marker for the points where the researcher should dig. Hence, many of the sources listed below have been sources for reference rather than sources of guidance.

GENERAL

Memoirs of General W. T. Sherman, by himself (1875, revised edition 1886).

The Sherman Letters, correspondence between General and Senator Sherman from 1837 to 1891, edited by Rachel Sherman Thorndike (1894).

Home Letters of General Sherman, edited by M. A. de Wolfe Howe (1909).

Official Records of the Union and Confederate Armies.

Report of the Joint Committee on the Conduct of the War.

Battles and Leaders of the Civil War (1887).

Marching with Sherman, passages from the letters and campaign diaries of Henry Hitchcock, November, 1864-May, 1865, edited by M. A. de Wolfe Howe (1927).

S. M. Bowman and R. B. Irwin, *Sherman and His Campaigns* (1865).

M. F. Force, *General Sherman* (1899).

Edward Robins, *William T. Sherman* (1905).

G. M. Dodge, *Personal Recollections of President Abraham Lincoln, General Ulysses S. Grant, and General William T. Sherman* (printed for private circulation, 1914).

P. Tecumseh Sherman, *General Sherman in the Last Year of the Civil War* (printed for private circulation, 1908).

W. F. G. Shanks, *Personal Recollections of Distinguished Generals* (1866).

R. M. Johnston, *Leading American Soldiers* (1907).
Critical Sketches of Some of the Federal and Confederate Commanders
(Vol. 10 in Papers of the Military Historical Society of Massa-
chusetts).
Gamaliel Bradford, *Union Portraits* (1916).
J. D. Cox, *Atlanta* (1882).
J. D. Cox, *The March to the Sea—Franklin and Nashville* (1882).
J. D. Cox, *Military Reminiscences of the Civil War* (1900).
G. W. Nichols, *The Great March, from the Diary of a Staff Officer*
(1865).
T. E. Burton, *John Sherman* (1906).
J. B. Hood, *Advance and Retreat: Personal Experiences* (1880).
Jefferson Davis, *The Rise and Fall of the Confederate Government*
(1881).
Joseph E. Johnston, *Narrative of Military Operations* (1874).
E. P. Alexander, *Military Memoirs of a Confederate* (1907).
A. Roman, *Military Operations of General Beauregard in the War
Between the States* (1884).
John B. Gordon, *Reminiscences of the Civil War* (1904).
Richard Taylor, *Destruction and Reconstruction* (1879).
The Autobiography of Oliver Otis Howard.
J. H. Wilson, *Under the Old Flag* (1912).
John A. Logan, *The Great Conspiracy* (1886).
J. M. Schofield, *Forty-six Years in the Army* (1897).
C. A. Dana, *Recollections of the Civil War* (1898).
Memoirs of Henry Villard (1904). [War-correspondent.]
Personal Memoirs of U. S. Grant (1885).
A. Badeau, *The Military History of U. S. Grant* (1868).
Charles King, *The True Ulysses S. Grant* (1914).
J. R. Young, *Round the World with General Grant* (1879).
J. T. Headley, *Grant and Sherman* (1865).
P. C. Headley, *The Life and Campaigns of General Grant* (1866).
M. J. Cramer, *Ulysses S. Grant, Conversations and Unpublished Let-
ters* (1897).
J. C. Cramer, *Letters of Ulysses S. Grant to His Father and Younger
Sister, 1857-78* (1912).
Jesse R. Grant, *In the Days of My Father, General Grant* (1925).
W. E. Woodward, *Meet General Grant* (1928).
Horace Porter, *Campaigning with Grant* (1897).
Personal Memoirs of Philip Henry Sheridan (1902).
Hugh McCulloch, *Men and Measures of Half a Century* (1888).
H. C. Whitney, *Life on the Circuit with Lincoln* (1892).
H. V. Boynton, *Sherman's Historical Raid. The Memoirs in the Light
of the Record* (1875). [Like Henry Stone in *Papers of the M. H.*

S. M., Boynton, the correspondent of the Cincinnati *Gazette*, mars the value of his diligent criticism not merely by an excess of prejudice but by repeated misquotations from the records. Their writings, although of use to the researcher, are thus misleading to the ordinary student.]

C. W. Moulton, *The Review of General Sherman's Memoirs Examined* (1875).

C. P. Spencer, *The Last Ninety Days of the War in North Carolina* (1866).

T. E. Taylor, *Running the Blockade* (1896).

Emory Upton, *Military Policy of the United States.*

J. B. McMaster, *A History of the People of the United States during Lincoln's Administration* (1927).

John Fiske, *The Mississippi Valley in the Civil War* (1900).

F. V. Greene, *The Mississippi* (1882).

J. C. Ropes and W. R. Livermore, *The Story of the Civil War* (1894 *et seq.*)

T. A. Dodge, *A Bird's Eye View of Our Civil War* (1897).

S. E. Morison, *The Oxford History of the United States 1783-1917.* Vol. II (1927).

J. F. Rhodes, *History of the Civil War.*

J. F. Rhodes, *Lectures on the American Civil War* (1913).

Edward Channing, *History of the United States.*

T. R. Livermore, *Numbers and Losses in the Civil War* (1901).

W. G. Shotwell, *The Civil War in America.*

Cambridge Modern History, Vol. VII, Chapters XIV-XX.

W. B. Wood and J. E. Edmonds, *The Civil War in the United States, 1861-1865* (1910).

W. A. Ganoe, *The History of the United States Army* (1924).

E. P. Oberholtzer, *History of the United States Since the Civil War* (1917 *et seq.*)

Papers of the Military Historical Society of Massachusetts, 14 Vols. [The drawback of these is that they were often compiled by "interested parties," and have a bias that needs careful checking from the Records. One cannot expect, for example, that an officer whose regiment has been reported for running away should be a reliable historian on the subject of the higher command.]

SPECIAL

(N.B. In the appended list of sources for special phases of Sherman's career and campaigns, the page references are for those parts, only, of any book which are directly concerned with Sherman's action.)

I. EARLY LIFE TO 1859 (Chapters 1-2)

The Sherman Letters, 1-75.
Home Letters of General Sherman, 3-159.
John Sherman, *Recollections* (1895).
Sherman and the San Francisco Vigilantes—Unpublished Letters (*Century Magazine*, December, 1891).
T. H. Hittell, *History of California*, Vol. III (1897).
H. H. Bancroft, *Popular Tribunals* (1887). [The fact that this is dedicated to the President of the San Francisco Vigilance Committee is a warning of its bias.]
M. F. Williams, *History of the San Francisco Committee of Vigilance of 1851* (1921).
S. E. White, *The Forty-Niners* (1920).
Charles King, *The True Ulysses S. Grant*, 36-79. [West Point conditions.]
J. D. Cox, *Reminiscences*, 176-182. [West Point conditions.]
G. M. Dodge, *Personal Recollections*, 132-134. [Boyhood.]

II. CAREER IN LOUISIANA, 1859-61 (Chapter 3)

The Sherman Letters, 76-108.
Home Letters, 160-195.
General W. T. Sherman as College President (letters and records) edited by W. L. Fleming (1912).
D. F. Boyd, *General W. T. Sherman as College President* (1910).
W. L. Fleming, *W. T. Sherman as a History Teacher* (Univ. Bulletin, Louisiana State Univ., October, 1911).

III. WAR CAREER DURING 1861 (Chapters 4-6)

The Sherman Letters, 108-136.
Home Letters, 197-219.
Official Records:
    Vol. *2*, 303-574, 755.
    Vol. *4*, 259-359 [Kentucky phase].
    Vol. *8*, 374-514, 819-821; Vol. *109*, 198-201; Vol. *111*, 507 [Missouri phase].

E. P. Alexander, *Military Memoirs of a Confederate*, 1-62.
Richard Taylor, *Destruction and Reconstruction*, 1-29.
Edward Anderson, *Missouri in 1861-1862* (in M. H. S. M., Vol. viii).
Henry Villard, *Memoirs*, 176-217.
J. B. Fry, *McDowell's Advance to Bull Run* (in B. & L. i).
G. T. Beauregard, *The First Battle of Bull Run* (in B. & L. i).
J. D. Imboden, *Incidents of the First Bull Run* (in B. & L. i).
J. E. Johnston, *Responsibilities of the First Bull Run* (in B. & L. i).
R. M. Kelly, *Holding Kentucky for the Union* (in B. & L. i).

IV. CAIRO TO CORINTH—THE SHILOH CAMPAIGN, SPRING OF 1862
(Chapters 7-10)

The Sherman Letters, 136-155.
Home Letters, 219-229.
Official Records:
> Vol. *7*, 436-682; Vol. *8*, 555-591; Vol. *109*, 204-217 [Cairo & Columbus].
> Vol. *10*, 8-29, 83-84, 89-627, 639-641; vol. *11*, 3-104, 297-408; Vol. *109*, 16-29, 223-234, 559 [Shiloh].
> Vol. *10*, 644-646 [Bear Creek].
> Vol. *10*, 647-648, 660-874; Vol. *11*, 134-241, 463-467, 484-546, 555-570 [Corinth].

M. F. Force, *From Fort Henry to Corinth* (1882).
G. A. Bruce, *The Donelson Campaign* (in M. H. S. M., Vol. vii).
Henry Stone, *The Battle of Shiloh* (in M. H. S. M., Vol. vii).
E. C. Dawes, *The Battle of Shiloh* (in M. H. S. M., Vol. vii).
E. A. Otis, *The Second Day at Shiloh* (in M. H. S. M., Vol. vii).
U. S. Grant, *Memoirs*, 168-228.
J. R. Young, *Round the World with General Grant*, ii, 469.
Henry Villard, *Memoirs*, i, 235-281.
U. S. Grant, *The Battle of Shiloh* (in B. & L. i).
D. C. Buell, *Shiloh Reviewed* (in B. & L. i).
R. W. Medkirk, *Skirmishing in Sherman's Front* (in B. & L. i).
W. P. Johnston, *Albert Sidney Johnston at Shiloh* (in B. & L. i).
G. T. Beauregard, *The Campaign of Shiloh* (in B. & L. i).
T. J. Jordan, *Notes of a Confederate Staff Officer at Shiloh* (in B. & L. i).
S. H. Lockett, *Surprise and Withdrawal at Shiloh* (in B. & L. i).
A. R. Chisholm, *The Shiloh Battle Order* (in B. & L. i).
The March of Lew Wallace's Division to Shiloh (in B. & L. i).
T. L. Snead, *With Price East of the Mississippi* (in B. & L. i).

V. Summer and Autumn of 1862 (Chapter 10)

The Sherman Letters, 159-166.
Home Letters, 229-233.
Official Records:
> Vol. *24,* 8-9, 23; Vol. *25,* 3-106 [After Corinth].
> Vol. *24,* 144-145; Vol. *25,* 109-352, 853-875; Vol. *109,* 275 [Memphis].

U. S. Grant, *Memoirs,* 228-249.

VI. The Vicksburg Campaign (Chapters 11-13)

The Sherman Letters, 168-209.
Home Letters, 235-279.
Official Records:
> Vol. *24,* 601-697; Vol. *25,* 244-536, 752-827, 849-853, 862-868, 874-877 [First Attempt].
> Vol. *24,* 699-796; Vol. *25,* 536-590, 675-897 [Arkansas Post].
> Vol. *36,* 4-331, 371-421, 430-467, 489-497, 501-553, 571-683, 704-787; Vol. *38,* 3-326, 591-892; Vol. *109,* 337, 346, 406; Vol. *110,* 392-472 [Manœuvres].
> Vol. *37,* 7-143, 148-424, 520-661, 689-699; Vol. *38,* 326-556, 842-1066; Vol. *110,* 472-515 [Siege and Jackson].

Richard Taylor, *Destruction and Reconstruction,* 178-194.
W. R. Livermore, *The Vicksburg Campaign* (in M. H. S. M., Vol. ix).
J. E. Johnston, *Narrative,* 147-252, 490-568.
U. S. Grant, *Memoirs,* 250-341.
C. A. Dana, *Recollections,* 29-102.
J. H. Wilson, *Under the Old Flag,* i, 141-236.
T. L. Snead, *The Conquest of Arkansas* (in B. & L. iii).
G. W. Morgan, *The Assault on Chickasaw Bluffs* (in B. & L. iii).
J. E. Johnston, *Jefferson Davis and the Mississippi Campaign* (in B. & L. iii).
S. H. Lockett, *The Defence of Vicksburg* (in B. & L. iii).
U. S. Grant, *The Vicksburg Campaign* (in B. & L. iii).
J. R. Soley, *Naval Operations in the Vicksburg Campaign* (in B. & L. iii).

VII. Chattanooga & Meridian Campaigns (Chapters 14-15)

The Sherman Letters, 209-233.
Home Letters, 278-287.
Official Records:
> Vol. *54,* 16-31, 278, 674-848; Vol. *55,* 3-782; Vol. *56,* 54-511, 527-528, 685-838; Vol. *109,* 91-99 [Chattanooga].
> Vol. *57,* 168-391; Vol. *58,* 13-492, 644-800; Vol. *109,* 517, 519 [Meridian].

W. F. Smith, *Historical Sketch of the Military Operations around Chattanooga, Tennessee, September 22 to November 27, 1863* (in M. H. S. M., Vol. viii).

T. L. Livermore, *The Siege and Relief of Chattanooga* (in M. H. S. M., Vol. viii).

T. L. Livermore, *General Thomas in the Record* (in M. H. S. M., Vol. x).

H. V. Boynton, *The Battles about Chattanooga, etc.* (in M. H. S. M., Vol. vii).

J. E. Johnston, *Narrative*, 253-261.

U. S. Grant, *Memoirs*, 341-401.

G. E. Waring, *The Sooy Smith Expedition* (in B. & L. iv).

C. A. Dana, *Recollections*, 132-155.

J. H. Wilson, *Under the Old Flag*, i, 263-315.

Henry Villard, *Memoirs*, ii, 229-263.

J. D. Cox, *Reminiscences*, ii, 36-38 (Knoxville).

O. O. Howard, *Autobiography*, i, 471-492.

U. S. Grant, *Chattanooga* (in B. & L. iii).

S. M. Byers, *Sherman's Attack at the Tunnel* (in B. & L. iii).

J. S. Fullerton, *The Army of the Cumberland at Chattanooga* (in B. & L. iii).

VIII. ATLANTA CAMPAIGN (Chapters 16-18)

The Sherman Letters, 235-241.

Home Letters, 288-308.

Official Records:
>
> Vol. *59*, 87-573, 582-873; Vol. *110*, 642-664 [Preliminaries].
>
> Vol. *72* (Reports of Grant, Sherman, chief technical advisers, Army of the Cumberland less 20th Corps); Vol. *73* (Reports of 20th Corps, Army of the Ohio, Cavalry); Vol. *74* (Reports of Army of the Tennessee, Confederate).
>
> Vol. *75*, 3-216, 654-720 [Resaca].
>
> Vol. *75*, 216-653, 720-807; Vol. *76*, 3-114, 858-887; Vol. *109*, 554-567; Vol. *110*, 680-707 [Oostenaula-Chattahoochee].
>
> Vol. *76*, 114-809, 877-1018; Vol. *110*, 707-731 [Atlanta].
>
> Vol. *78*, 3-354, 565-310 [Lines of Communication].
>
> Vol. *109*, 569-573, 594, 611-623, 630-638, 680-716; Vol. *111*, 44-60 [Supplies in Atlanta, Georgia, Carolinas campaigns].

J. D. Cox, *Atlanta*.

Henry Stone, *The Atlanta Campaign* (in M. H. S. M., Vol. viii).

J. B. Hood, *Advance and Retreat*, 69-242.

J. E. Johnston, *Narrative*, 261-370, 569-580, 584-586.

Jefferson Davis, *Rise and Fall*, 547-563.

U. S. Grant, *Memoirs*, 401-439.

J. E. Johnston, *Opposing Sherman's Advance to Atlanta* (in B. & L. iv).

W. P. C. Breckinridge, *The Opening of the Atlanta Campaign* (in B. & L. iv).

E. C. Dawes, *The Confederate Strength in the Atlanta Campaign* (in B. & L. iv).

O. O. Howard, *The Struggle for Atlanta* (in B. & L. iv).

W. H. Chamberlin, *Hood's Second Sortie at Atlanta* (in B. & L. iv).

G. W. Smith, *The Georgia Militia about Atlanta* (in B. & L. iv).

J. B. Hood, *The Defense of Atlanta* (in B. & L. iv).

J. M. Schofield, *Forty-six Years in the Army*, 117-161, 340-342.

O. O. Howard, *Autobiography*, i, 499-620; ii, 3-44.

J. D. Cox, *Reminiscences*, ii, 156-291.

J. B. McMaster, *A History of the People of the U. S.*, etc., 478-529 (Political reactions of Atlanta Campaign).

IX. Georgia and the Carolinas (Chapters 19-22)

The Sherman Letters, 241-251.

Home Letters, 309-354.

Official Records:

    Vol. *76*, 794-857, 1018-1031; Vol. *77*, 580-827 (Reports); Vol. *78*, 355-564, 811-889; Vol. *79*, 3-918 [Growth of Plan].

    Vol. *92*, 6-418, 420-451; Vol. *111*, 26-44 (Reports); Vol. *92*, 451-1013; Vol. *111*, 375-385 [March through Georgia].

    Vol. *92*, 611, 636, 701, 726-729, 740-743, 754, 797-800, 809-810, 820, 841-842; Vol. *98*, 17-1134; Vol. *111*, 44-60 (Reports).

    Vol. *99*, 3-1462; Vol. *111*, 386-414, 1049-1053 [March through Carolinas].

    Vol. *100*, 3-874; Vol. *111*, 415-420 [Final operations and Peace Negotiations].

Marching with Sherman, Letters and Diaries of Henry Hitchcock.

G. W. Nichols, *The Great March.*

J. C. Palfrey, *General Sherman's Plans after the Fall of Atlanta* (in M. H. S. M., Vol. viii).

J. E. Johnston, *Narrative*, 371-420, 587.

Jefferson Davis, *Rise and Fall*, 564-580, 625-699.

C. P. Spencer, *The Last Ninety Days of the War in North Carolina.*

Richard Taylor, *Destruction and Reconstruction*, 260-307.

H. S. Nourse, *The Burning of Columbia, S. C.* (in M. H. S. M., Vol. ix).

E. P. Alexander, *Military Memoirs of a Confederate*, 575-590.

Henry Stone, *The Battle of Franklin* and *The Battle of Nashville* (in M. H. S. M., Vol. vii).

O. O. Howard, *Sherman's Advance from Atlanta* (in B. & L. iv).

G. W. Smith, *The Georgia Militia during Sherman's March to the Sea* (in B. & L. iv).

D. Oakey, *Marching through Georgia and the Carolinas* (in B. & L. iv).

A. R. Chisholm, *The Failure to Capture Hardee* (in B. & L. iv).

H. W. Slocum, *Sherman's March from Savannah to Bentonville* (in B. & L. iv).

Wade Hampton, *The Battle of Bentonville* (in B. & L. iv).

H. W. Slocum, *Final Operations of Sherman's Army* (in B. & L. iv).

J. M. Schofield, *Forty-six Years in the Army*, 299-357.

J. D. Cox, *Reminiscences*, ii, 310-538.

U. S. Grant, *Memoirs*, 543-596, 612-613, 635-655.

C. A. Dana, *Recollections*, 288-290.

J. H. Wilson, *Under the Old Flag*, ii, 1-159, 276-307.

O. O. Howard, *Autobiography*, ii, 47-159, 210-212.

Horace Porter, *Campaigning with Grant*, 287-296, 313-320, 417-424.

C. C. Jones, *The Siege of Savannah in December 1864 and the Confederate Operations in Georgia* (1874).

J. B. Hood, *Advance and Retreat*, 243-311.

X. Post-war Career (Chapter 23)

The Sherman Letters, 252-382.

Home Letters, 354-402.

S. H. M. Byers, *Twenty Years in Europe*, 52-302.

G. M. Dodge, *Personal Recollections* (printed for private circulation, 1914) [Sherman's help to the trans-continental railroads, 184-206].

J. F. Rusling, *The Great West and Pacific Coast* (1877) [a few sidelights on Sherman's relations with the Indians].

John Sherman, *Recollections* (1895).

Reports of Inspection made in 1877 by Generals Sheridan and Sherman (1878).

W. A. Ganoe, *The History of the United States Army* (1924).

C. W. Moulton, *The Review of General Sherman's Memoirs Examined* (1875).

Richard Taylor, *Destruction and Reconstruction*, 321-363.

J. R. Young, *Round the World with General Grant*, ii, 290-295.

Ellis P. Oberholtzer, *History of the United States since the Civil War*, Vol. i, 1865-68; Vol. ii, 1868-72; Vol. iii, 1872-78.

J. M. Schofield, *Forty-six Years*, 406-423, 439-451.

(In addition, I have been able to tap several sources of personal evidence. They include, on the one hand, some who knew Sherman and his associates, and, on the other, some who have lived in the districts through which he marched. To the help of these friends I would here render grateful acknowledgment.)

INDEX

Other titles of interest

ADVANCE AND RETREAT
General John Bell Hood
New introduction by
Richard M. McMurry
376 pp., 6 illus.
80534-0 $14.95

**NARRATIVE OF MILITARY
OPERATIONS DURING
THE CIVIL WAR**
General Joseph E. Johnston
644 pp., 21 illus.
80393-3 $17.95

**SHERMAN'S BATTLE FOR
ATLANTA**
General Jacob D. Cox
New introd. by Brooks D. Simpson
294 pp., 7 maps
80588-X $12.95

**SHERMAN'S MARCH TO THE SEA,
Hood's Tennessee Campaign & the
Carolina Campaigns of 1865**
General Jacob D. Cox
New introd. by Brooks D. Simpson
289 pp., 10 maps
80587-1 $12.95

GENERAL LEE
A Biography of Robert E. Lee
Fitzhugh Lee
Introduction by Gary W. Gallagher
478 pp., 2 illus., 3 maps
80589-8 $15.95

**THE ANNALS OF THE
CIVIL WAR**
**Written by Leading Participants
North and South**
New introduction by
Gary W. Gallagher
808 pp., 56 illus.
80606-1 $19.95

**THE GENERALSHIP OF
ULYSSES S. GRANT**
J.F.C. Fuller
446 pp., 17 maps & plans
80450-6 $14.95

**MEMOIRS OF GENERAL
WILLIAM T. SHERMAN**
New introd. by William S. McFeely
820 pp.   80213-9 $17.95

**MILITARY MEMOIRS
OF A CONFEDERATE**
A Critical Narrative
Edward Porter Alexander
New introd. by Gary W. Gallagher
658 pp., 13 maps
80509-X $16.95

**PERSONAL MEMOIRS OF
P. H. SHERIDAN**
New introd. by Jeffry D. Wert
560 pp., 16 illus., 16 maps
80487-5 $15.95

**PERSONAL MEMOIRS OF
U.S. GRANT**
New introd. by William S. McFeely
Critical Notes by E. B. Long
xxxi + 608 pp.
80172-8 $15.95

**STONEWALL JACKSON AND
THE AMERICAN CIVIL WAR**
G.F.R. Henderson
New introd. by Thomas L. Connelly
740 pp.   80318-6 $16.95

**THE WARTIME PAPERS OF
ROBERT E. LEE**
Edited by Clifford Dowdey and
Louis H. Manarin
1,012 pp.   80282-1 $19.95

Available at your bookstore

OR ORDER DIRECTLY FROM 1-800-386-5656

VISIT OUR WEBSITE AT WWW.PERSEUSBOOKSGROUP.COM